D1270707

RHETORIC,
MATERIALITY,
& POLITICS

POLITICAL COMMUNICATION

FRONTIERS IN

Lynda Lee Kaid and Bruce Gronbeck
General Editors

Vol. 13

PETER LANG
New York • Washington, D.C./Baltimore • Bern
Frankfurt am Main • Berlin • Brussels • Vienna • Oxford

RHETORIC, MATERIALITY, & POLITICS

EDITED BY
BARBARA A. BIESECKER
& JOHN LOUIS LUCAITES

PETER LANG
New York • Washington, D.C./Baltimore • Bern
Frankfurt am Main • Berlin • Brussels • Vienna • Oxford

Library of Congress Cataloging-in-Publication Data

Rhetoric, materiality, and politics / edited by Barbara A. Biesecker,
John Louis Lucaites.
p. cm. — (Frontiers in political communication; v. 13)
Includes bibliographical references and index.
1. Communication in politics. 2. Rhetoric—Political aspects.
3. Materialism. I. Biesecker, Barbara A. II. Lucaites, John Louis.
JA85.R495 320.01'4—dc22 2009007198
ISBN 978-0-8204-9740-2
ISSN 1525-9730

Bibliographic information published by **Die Deutsche Bibliothek**.
Die Deutsche Bibliothek lists this publication in the "Deutsche
Nationalbibliografie"; detailed bibliographic data is available
on the Internet at http://dnb.ddb.de/.

© 2009 Peter Lang Publishing, Inc., New York
29 Broadway, 18th floor, New York, NY 10006
www.peterlang.com

Printed in Germany

Dedicated to Michael Calvin McGee
(1943–2002)

CONTENTS

ACKNOWLEDGMENTS

This volume has been a very long time in coming. It began in 1997 when a chance meeting between the two of us led us to recognize that we each had an interest in the relationship between rhetoric and visual culture. We thought it would be fun and productive to have a small forum on the topic at a professional conference, and we expected fifteen to twenty of our closest friends to show up. The forum took place at the annual National Communication Association conference, and when more than 150 people packed the room, we concluded that something was afoot. We then organized a small workshop at the University of Iowa's Obermann Center for Advanced Studies on visual rhetoric in the summer of 1999 and, subsequently, a national conference on visual rhetoric at Indiana University in the fall of 2001. We decided to produce a volume of essays from the two conferences, but along the way, we discovered that the relationship between rhetoric and visuality was really just one aspect of a much larger intellectual problem concerning the relationship between rhetoric and materiality. We thus adjusted our sights and asked contributors to do the same. As ideas were sharpened and focused, and as essays were expanded and condensed, we realized once again that there was more at stake than we had originally considered as the relationship between rhetoric and materiality was implicated by a third term—"politics"—which bore both intellectual and culture significance. Once again, we asked our contributors to adjust their sights, and much to our delight, they complied. The volume before you is the result of this tortured process, but then, such is the nature of the development of knowledge and the advancement of understanding. Rarely do scholarly projects end with the same questions and problems with which they began; or, at least in our experience, rarely do they do so productively.

It is, of course, a cliché to say that such volumes could not have been completed without the efforts of many people, but it is not less true for the saying. And so it is here. Those who participated in the Workshop on Visual Rhetoric at the University of Iowa and those who either delivered plenary presentations or organized seminars at the Visual Rhetorics Conference at Indiana University provided advice, criticism, and general support. We are deeply appreciative of their contributions to this project and want to acknowledge their role: Carole Blair, Ron Burnett, Kenneth Cmiel, Kevin DeLuca, Anne Demo, Peter Ehrenhaus, Joan Faber McAlister, Oscar Giner, Bruce E. Gronbeck, Hanno Hardt, Robert Hariman, Henry Krips, Steven Mailloux, James P. McDaniel, W.J.T. Mitchell, Thomas Nakayama, A. Susan Owen, Ramona Liera Schwichtenberg, Daniel Schowalter, Raka Shome, Brian Taylor, William Trapani, and Barbie Zelizer.

The work that led to this volume was also supported by numerous offices at three universities. At the University of Iowa, we offer thanks and gratitude to Jay Semel, Director of the Obermann Center for Advanced Studies, and Karla Tonella, the center's Academic Technologies Specialist, the former for providing a delightful place for the original Visual Rhetorics Workshop to convene, the latter for coming to our aid when it came to all matters technical, including a wonderful Web site. For providing the financial support necessary to our co-hosting the Visual Rhetorics Summer Workshop at the Obermann Center, as well the national conference at Indiana University, we also extend our thanks to the University of Iowa's Vice President of Research, David J. Skorton, the Department of Communication Studies, and, more specifically, the A. Craig Baird Fund and the Rhetoric Department. At Indiana University, we want to thank Robert Ivie and Gregory Waller, two men who served as the Chair of the Department of Communication and Culture at different stages in the development of the project and provided both continuing financial and intellectual support. We also appreciate the financial support of Indiana University Chancellor Kenneth Gross and then Dean of the College of Arts and Sciences, Kumble Ramaro Subbaswamy. At the University of Georgia, we thank the Department of Speech Communication.

For her help in preparing the final manuscript, we want to acknowledge the outstanding work of Melanie Loehwing at Indiana University. The index was prepared with the assistance of Aaron Preiss-Martin, Emily J. Porter, and Jane Munksgaard at the University of Georgia. And, finally, to Bruce E. Gronbeck we owe an extraordinary debt that can only be repaid by our extending to others the generosity of intellectual spirit he extended to us. Without his unwavering enthusiasm for a project that would never settle on the last word but always aimed to speak what's next, this collection of essays would not have made its way into print—in this book series or any other. We also want to thank Eugenia T. Crosheck (formerly Eugenia McGee) for her enthusiastic support for the project.

For permissions to reprint copyrighted material, we acknowledge the following:

Michael Calvin McGee, "A Materialist's Conception of Rhetoric," in *Explorations in Rhetoric: Studies in Honor of Douglas Ehninger*, ed. Ray E. McKerrow. Published by Allyn and Bacon/Merrill Education, Boston, MA. Copyright © 1982 by Pearson education. Reprinted by permission of the publisher. All rights reserved.

Rosamond Kent Sprague, ed., *The Older Sophists: A Complete Translation by Several Hands of the Fragments in* Die Fragmente der Vorsokratiker, *Edited by Diels-Kranz, with a New Edition of Antiphon and of Euthydemus.* Published by University of South Carolina Press, Columbia, South Carolina. Copyright © 1972 by University of South Carolina Press. Reprinted by permission of the publisher. All rights reserved.

American Indian Magazine, Cover, photo by Kathryn Gaitens. With permission of the Smithsonian National Museum of the American Indian.

"East Entrance of the Smithsonian National Museum of the American Indian," photo by Leonada Levchuk. With permission of the photographer.

"Geronimo, Rifle Photograph." With permission of the National Archives.

"Geronimo, Hat Photograph." With permission of the National Archives.

Barbara A. Biesecker
Athens, Georgia

John Louis Lucaites
Bloomington, Indiana

Rhetoric, Materiality, and Politics

Introduction

Barbara A. Biesecker, University of Georgia
John Louis Lucaites, Indiana University

The history of rhetoric is a history of change and adaptation. Whether understood as a theoretical concept, a cultural practice, or a sociopolitical phenomenon, rhetoric's meaning has been consistently situated and evaluated in terms of the social, political, and economic needs for and demands on discourse. What rhetoric was in fifth-century BCE Athens differed from what it was to become in medieval Paris or Renaissance Florence or early-modern London and Edinburgh, and so on. And so, too, for conceptions of rhetoric in the United States during the early part of the twentieth century when the progressive movement and an emergent democratic pragmatism prompted a fundamentally instrumentalist approach to the problems and promises of public speaking.[1] By the middle of the century, the focus on rhetoric as an instrument of democratic life had been inflected by growing concerns about the threat of fascism and its use of mass-mediated propaganda, and was thus increasingly subjected to the disciplines of communication ethics and a new social science dubbed "communication research."[2] Under this regime, rhetoric became a quasi-literary study driven largely by an interest in form and genre.

The generation of scholars to emerge out of the 1960s was heavily influenced by changing political currents as well as the "new rhetorics" of Kenneth Burke, and Chaïm Perelman and L. Olbrechts-Tyteca.[3] Increasingly interested in questions of ideology and power, and led by the likes of Michael Calvin McGee, Thomas Farrell, and Karlyn Kohrs Campbell, such scholars emphasized an understanding of rhetoric as a political and theoretical praxis—driven by critique rather than criticism—in more or less direct dialogue with contemporary European social and political theory.[4] And at the very heart of this project was an implicit historical-materialist sensibility driven by a Marxian understanding of the tension between idealism and materialism, and its implications for the relationship between theory and praxis.[5]

The problem this generation faced was that rhetoric had been located in the 1950s in departments of speech communication and theater, situated between the growing interest in speech communication science on the one hand and the performing arts on the other. As Michael Leff later put it, rhetoric was caught between "the rock" (of positivism) and the "soft place" (of romanticism).[6] Rhetoric thus labored to find a place between the *discovery* of truth and knowledge and the *interpretation* and *performance* of meaning and value. This struggle was exacerbated by the field's ideological commitment to a pedagogy rooted in Progressive Era democratic politics and a weak form of Deweyan pragmatism. Evidence of the problem was most pronounced in the graduate curriculum that, throughout the 1950s and 1960s, featured the history of rhetorical theory and a relatively formalist study of American and British public address. In short, rhetoric had become either the history of an idea or little more than a literary genre (at first neo-Aristotelian, but later driven by an interest in "metaphor," "fantasy themes," etc.), neither of which (alone or together) were fully up to the task of addressing the needs for the production of knowledge and understanding required to negotiate the emerging crises of late-modern society.

The predicament, thus, was to find a way to unshackle "rhetoric" from its neo-Aristotelian heritage—rooted as it was in a cookie-cutter formalism and an anemic sense of rhetorical effect—without losing its connection to the very basic sense in which it operates as a faculty or capacity (*dunamis*) for the discovery of the available means of persuasion in negotiating the problem of social and political judgment, i.e., the sense in which rhetoric is fundamentally an inventional and productive site for addressing situations of radical contingency in public and civic contexts.[7]

Although the turn to a rhetorical materialism was implicit in some of the currents of thought floating about in the early 1970s, it was Michael Calvin McGee who took the first crack at a formal statement in that direction.[8] His "Materialist's Conception of Rhetoric," reprinted as this collection's lead essay, was part of a *festschrift* in honor of Douglas Ehninger, whose earlier work on "Systems of Rhetoric" was an initial response to those who relegated rhetoric's disciplinary role to that of modern day handmaiden for communication science, characterized by John Bowers as its "prescientific function."[9] Ehninger's taxonomy sought to shift attention away from rhetoric as the history of an idea to its sociological and epistemological functions, which, he noted, alter and adapt to changing cultural problems across time. Such a shift, according to McGee, was essential to a materialist's conception of rhetoric, but only as an underlying assumption of rhetoric's critical theoretical possibilities. The problem, he implied, was that such work in the past had not gone far enough in recasting the muddied "connection between theory and practice" that enabled a too easy reduction of rhetoric as an idealized process of composition to discourse as a residual artifact of a symbolic interaction.[10]

McGee's goal was to reconnect theory and practice by focusing on the "description, explanation, and perhaps even prediction of the formation of consciousness." The key to his conceptualization of rhetoric as material was neither to understand rhetoric as a "peculiar" and idealized art form rooted in a "body of principles" necessary to achieve proficiency (i.e., the rules of composition or canons of knowledge necessary for effective discourse), nor to grasp its force as the result of a simple cause-effect relationship. Instead, McGee insisted on our appreciating rhetoric as a mode of consciousness operating within an economy of phenomenological experience, quite literally the *gestalt* created by the complex interaction of speaker, speech, audience, occasion, and change at a particular moment in time. The key term here was "experience," and with it, McGee was advancing, with Kenneth Burke, a notion of subjectivity inflected toward the practical or material force of living within the social and political orbits of symbolicity. Thus he underscored the continuum of rhetorical influence that extended from the most concrete incidence of microrhetorical experience to increasingly abstract socio- and macro-rhetorical experiences. Rhetoric, in other words, was not material in the sense of a "thing" like a rock or tree, but rather as a palpable and undeniable social and political force.

In no other essay over the course of his career would McGee so boldly decry the aestheticization of rhetoric and so clearly define the study of real speech as the analysis of the functional meaning of communicative acts. On his view, "real speech" does not merely *represent* the world but *mediates* the relations of human beings that together constitute it and, therefore, the material, as Michael McGuire noted, was for McGee "neither the antecedent conditions for rhetoric nor the discourse itself; it is the effect of discourse that is materially real."[11] Hence in stark contrast to an idealism that appreciated individual rhetorical acts for their aesthetically satisfying features and forms, McGee insisted on our taking measure of every persuasive act's role in the ongoing process of collective conversion or, better yet, coercion.[12] That said, his rhetorical materialism was not to be confused with a dialectical materialism that attributed to the underlying modes of production that animated the vicissitudes of collective being or human thought and speech. To the contrary, this approach took consciousness and social relations themselves to be two of the most significant material effects of speech. McGee's rhetorical materialism, then, boiled down to grasping rhetoric as social labor, as the mediating substance of the (re)formation of collective life: "[F]rom a materialist's perspective, ordinary discourse is a social function which permits interactivity among people. It is a medium, a bridge among human beings, the social equivalent of a verb in a sentence."[13]

McGee's rhetorical materialism obviously was not the only way to think about the relationship between rhetoric and the so-called "objective" or "real," but it did become the prevailing statement on such matters for the community of rhetoricians increasingly troubled by the challenges of post-structuralism and interested in addressing the problems and possibilities presented by our postmodern condition.[14] Indeed in the mid-1980s and early 1990s, as rhetorical studies continued to change with the world, McGee's rhetorical materialism, like the theories of language, subjectivity, and experience that subtended it, became subject to radical critique. In clear contrast to McGee and despite some significant differences between their projects, about which we and a number of the other contributors to this volume will have more to say, Michel Foucault, Jacques Lacan, and Jacques Derrida would together inspire a shift of theoretical and critical interest in the field from *rhetorical materialism* to *rhetoric's materiality*. And such a shift would require nothing less than traversing the fantasy of the sign, albeit in three very different ways, thereby attending as never before to the signifier and its constitutive effects. To be sure, when taken individually and, especially, of a piece, theirs is a post-foundationalist enterprise that refuses a "transcendental signified," and thus obliged theorists and critics in rhetorical studies to question vigorously the psychologistic usage of the concept of the "sign" that had informed McGee's and so many others' theories of communication and collective life.[15] As Derrida noted,

> Psychologism is not the poor usage of a good concept, but is inscribed and pre-scribed within the concept of the sign itself. . . . This equivocality, which weighs upon the model of the sign, marks the "semiological" project itself and the organic totality of its concepts, in particular that of *communication*, which in effect implies a *transmission charged with making pass, from one subject to another, the identity of a signified* object, of a *meaning* or of a *concept* rightfully separable from the process of passage and from the signifying operation. Communication presupposes subjects (whose identity and presence are constituted before the signifying operation) and objects (signified concepts, a thought meaning that the passage of communication will have neither to constitute, nor, by all rights, to transform). A communicates B to C. Through the sign the emitter communicates something to a receptor, etc.[16]

From ideas to discourse, from the science of the sign to that of the letter, from the sign to the gram or trace: together Foucault, Lacan, and Derrida would help transform dramatically the way we think about rhetoric.

By cultivating a new appreciation of the signifier's capacity to constitute a domain of reference rather than communicate meaning, Foucault would persuade some scholars in the field to stop reading "for the enigmatic treasure of 'things' anterior to discourse" and begin mapping "the regular formation of objects" that emerge only in it. According to Foucault, the aim of the archaeological project, and what sets it apart from all others that had come before, is to determine the discursive conditions of existence of a domain of reference and the effects of its functioning: When and how does something function as referent? What does it make possible? When does it stop functioning as referent, why, and with what consequences? What are the conditions under which a word has reference? What conditions make reference and truth possible? The answer to these questions cannot—as had been the case in the field for so long—be speakers or rhetors or even authors since those, too, are consequences of articulated statements. As Foucault put it in this regularly cited but less often understood passage in the *Archaeology of Knowledge*,

> If a proposition, a sentence, a group of signs can be called a statement, it is not therefore because, one day, someone happened to speak them or put them into some concrete form of writing; it is because the position of the subject can be assigned. To describe a formulation *qua* statement does not consist in analyzing the relations between the author and what he says . . . but in determining what position can and must be occupied by an individual if he is to be the subject of it.[17]

So it is that Ron Greene brings Foucault's insights into the condition of possibility for appearance and for making sense to bear directly on the art of rhetoric today. In his contribution to this volume, "Rhetorical Materialism: The Rhetorical Subject and the General Intellect," Greene begins by assessing the theoretical legacy of McGee's materialist turn, not the least of which has been a heightened appreciation of rhetoric's constitutive effects. Greene argues, however, that the general enthusiasm for the world-making power of rhetoric, especially as it is manifest in communication studies, must be tempered by a sober understanding of the material constraints on invention. Greene therefore insists on the need to rein in an ever-expanding notion of rhetorical subjectivity by attending vigilantly to the techniques and technologies by which individuals are transformed into rhetorical subjects whose characteristics and dispositions, value orientations, relations to other forms of subjectivity, and communicative labor are as determined as they are determining.

It is along similar analytical lines that John Sloop, Joan Faber McAlister, and Bruce Gronbeck explore the discursive transmutation of early-to-late-twentieth- and early-twenty-first-century U.S. citizen-subjects. In "People Shopping," Sloop explores the discursive rearticulation of the consumer in a case study of the cultural logics enacted by General Motors' campaign of the mid-1980s, which articulated their innovative "Saturn" automobile with the revived "America" animated by the Reagan administration's "Morning in America" campaign. Sloop's primary concern is to track the ways in which the car becomes a prosthetic for American citizenship and to consider how the materiality of this particular body medium contributes to the reshaping of the body politic from agents (as *people* shopping") to objects of corporate consumption (General Motors shopping for consumers).

With keen attention to the design of late-twentieth-century Midwest suburban housing developments and the discourses that are used to market them, Faber McAlister explores the salient signifiers of the "new subdivisions" that were part and parcel of U.S. middle class life as it approached the twenty-first century. Indeed, over the course of an analysis that draws on the political philosophy of Simone Weil so as to think class as social location in the most literal sense, Faber McAlister argues that the subdivision as "pantopic community" at once responds to and provokes the failing sense of community or rootlessness that Robert Putnam argued in *Bowling Alone* was endemic to late-twentieth-century U.S. public culture. The essay concludes with a cautionary note that seeks to identify the attendant dangers for civil society of these near seamless utopias that position their inhabitants to always already "feel at home."

Liberally taking his theoretical cues from Greene and Foucault, Bruce Gronbeck tracks the long career of Jacob Riis's social documentary photography, from its original publication in the early part of the twentieth century as documentary evidence of social injustice to its appropriation as a model of a unique photographic aesthetic in later years. The analytical aim of "Jacob Riis and the Doubly Material Rhetorics of His Politics" is to identify the interanimation of rhetoric and mediation as codependent technologies for the construction of particular modes of political consciousness. Thus, Gronbeck seeks to make a strong case for grasping both the manner in which the interpretation and usage of photographic images are shaped decisively by changes in media technology, as well as the manner in which they are mediated by an evolving rhetoric of technology. To that end, he argues, it is crucial not only to grasp how "images themselves become different images when materialized in different ways, in different communication processes, in different times and places" but also to understand how such images function differently as technologies that mediate the "perception of sight, sound, and duration-of-experience . . . such that one's relationship to self, other, and the external world" are changed in significant ways.

Like Foucault, Lacan would reject the presumption that the signifier's *raison d'etre* is to provide access to a signified, his now infamous algorithmic characterization of Ferdinand de Saussure's sign functioning as one of the more conspicuous formulations of what Yannis Stavrakakis aptly termed "the disappearance of the signified (not as a structural position but as the real point of reference of signification)."[18] By marking the irreducible asymmetry of the signifier (S) and the signified (s) (thereby granting priority and prestige to the former rather than the latter), eliminating the Saussurian ellipse (thereby refusing the presumed structural unity of the sign), and introducing the bar (thereby indicating that where Saussure would see a relation of reciprocity, Lacan would locate a separation and resistance), he would invite other rhetorical scholars to acknowledge that what we take to be the signified in any given case is the retroactive effect of the situated circulation of signifiers themselves.[19] As François Raffoul and David Pettigrew explain,

> For Saussure, the line between the signifier and signified suggests two different registers. The value of each signifier is determined by its differential negativity with respect to the totality of the other signifiers, yet for Saussure, each *signifier* ultimately refers to its particular *signified* in an arbitrary coupling according to linguistic convention. However, for Lacan the line between the two registers is a *bar* individuating that the signifier has *no* access to its signified. The signifier is left to slide in a field of signifiers, seeking its signified, yet encountering nothing but other signifiers.[20]

From one signifier, to another, to another, indefinitely or until—by a certain violence or force—the sliding is brought to a provisional halt that produces the "reality" (the Symbolic) to which an assemblage of signifiers is typically understood only to refer. Lacan would describe it this way in *Seminar III*:

> Day and night, man and woman, peace and war—I could enumerate more oppositions that don't emerge out of the real world but give it its framework, its axes, its structure, that organize it, that bring it about that there is in effect a reality for man [*sic*], and that he can find his bearings therein. The notion of reality that we bring to bear in analysis presupposes this web, this mesh of signifiers.[21]

For Lacan, then, to traverse the fantasy of the sign is to cede any and all assurances that "when I am presented with a representation . . . I know that it is only representation, and that there is, beyond, the thing, the thing itself. Behind the phenomenon, there is the noumenon, for example."[22] Notably, however, to pass through to the other side of the fantasy of the sign does not mean that we divest from our phantasmagorical productions; to the contrary, the traversal entails our "identify[ing] with the work of our 'imagination' even more radically, in all its inconsistency."[23]

It is this manner of thinking about signification that informs Chris Lundberg's "On the Materiality of Interpretation," wherein he urges us to reconceptualize rhetoric's materiality through a Lacanian perspective. First and foremost, Lundberg argues, rhetoric's materiality can be understood fully only if we acknowledge the irreducible impossibility of reference and communication. Because representations and "the real" can never be brought into perfect correspondence, and further, because pure communicative exchange is always an already failed process, all signification is necessarily rhetorical or tropological. Following Lacan's comic attitude, however, Lundberg regards the failed unicity of signifying practices as materially productive, simultaneously producing a rhetorical subject who is corporatized through tropological labor and who prompts the acts of signification that inevitably flow from it. One of the important consequences of theorizing rhetoric's materiality in this way is that it encourages us to read individual rhetorical texts as symptomatic and contextually variable expressions of an ineradicable desire to displace the fundamental antagonism of the social. Lundberg closes the essay with a brief psycho-rhetorical analysis of the rhetoric of contemporary evangelicalism.

It is precisely the thorny matter of reference and its relation to desire that Charles Morris queries in "Hard Evidence: The Vexations of Lincoln's Queer Corpus." Although rhetorical evidence is always, in some measure and to some degree, circumstantial and inferential, scholars traditionally have been relatively comfortable in talking about "hard evidence" and assuming objective standards of facticity that lead to conclusions judged to be beyond "all reasonable doubt." Morris takes such practices to task through an analysis of the contemporary historiographical dispute concerning Abraham Lincoln's alleged homosexuality and the ways in which the selective status attributed to evidence in this controversy locates all usage of evidence within an economy of desire that complicates our understanding of the rhetorical force of "history" as an interpretive discourse writ large. Morris's point is not to reject the use of evidence *qua* evidence in the making of historical judgments, but to recognize how the use of any such evidence is dispositive proof in the service of particular claims to belief or knowledge and to recognize how the use of evidence always already stands as material embodiment of cultural desires.

"Encomium of Helen's Body: A Will to Matter" is Nathan Stormer's experimental meditation on the relationship between words and things, will and matter. Artfully cast as an allegory, Stormer demonstrates how one might treat Helen's body as a singular signifier out of which a new theorization of rhetoric and materiality may emerge. He then develops his allegorical reading in an analytic that critically engages Judith Butler's discussion of the relationship among signification, desire, and matter and, more particularly, her appropriation of Baruch Spinoza's notion of *conatus*—namely, that "the mind is the idea of the body." According to Stormer, Butler's dependence on Spinoza (and in a different register, Hegel) leads her to an ethics of subjectivity that emphasizes the "rhetorical nature of being human." If, however, one is concerned with the "persistence of being," then the key question shifts to a thoroughgoing consideration of *what* matter rhetoric or the materiality of the signifier makes. One significant consequence of his rewriting and reading of the allegory is to urge readers to rethink the "essential 'humanity' of rhetorical action" by having exposed "the immanence of rhetoric to material vulnerability" and, thereby, having also questioned the conventional assumption that our capacity to act rhetorically is a function of our status as humans rather than our status as bodies that signify.

Finally, Derrida's interrogation of Saussure's theory of the sign and his subsequent argument that meaning is a consequence of language use and not its source would prompt still others in the field to refuse "the effacement of signifier . . . [that] is the condition of the very idea of truth" and, therefore, take as their primary task a description and account of the effects of the itinerary of the sensible inscription or trace.[24] In other words, Derrida's insistence on the sign's non-identity to itself and, likewise, his deconstruction of the metaphysics of presence on which structural linguistics and semiotics both depend would encourage us to engage rather than disavow the structurality of structure (or, put otherwise, to rethink the center not as "a fixed locus but a function"[25]), thereby obliging keen attentiveness to the movement of "difference-itself."[26] Indeed, as he explained in his first lecture delivered in the United States, the Derridean traversal of the fantasy of the sign entails nothing less than letting go of the reassuring certitude of a center, essence, existence, substance, subject, idea, or force that "governs [a] structure, while escaping structurality":

Thus it has always been thought that the center, which is by definition unique, constituted that very thing within a structure which governs the structure, while escaping structurality. This is why classical thought concerning structure could say that the center is, paradoxically, *within* the structure and *outside* it. The center is at the center of the totality, and yet, since the center does not belong to the totality (is not part of the totality), the totality *has its center elsewhere*. The center is not the center. The concept of centered structure—although it represents coherence itself, the condition of the *episteme* as philosophy or science—is contradictorily coherent. And, as always, coherence in contradiction expresses the force of a desire.[27]

So instead of treating the signifier as "a transcendental key that will unlock the way to truth," we put it to use as a *bricoleur* or tinker would, using it as a "positive lever" by which we may begin to take measure of dissemination's effects.[28]

It is precisely the sense that language use is not reducible to a meaning that proceeds it or a truth that obtains apart from it but, rather, that its structures and signifiers play an irreducible role in the production of discursive effects that informs "Shades of Derrida: Materiality as the Mediation of *Différance*." There, Kenneth Rufo argues for a shift away from a theoretical and critical preoccupation with the rhetorical subject or rhetorical subjectivity and to what he boldly identifies as "the most fundamental scene of materiality: the medium itself." According to him, the mistaken understanding of the material as the world "out there" to which language more or less successfully points has sent rhetorical theory and criticism awry, most notably effecting misguided notions of invention. What is needed, according to Rufo, is a robust conception of the materiality of mediation itself and a corresponding strategy of reading that cedes a doubled caution: on one hand, it attends to a text's incarnation without letting that reading be over-determined by the "technologies of circulation"; on the other hand, it refuses to reduce any text's effectivity to an extracted and idealistic "content." Rufo turns to Derrida's theoretical corpus to guide the development of a renovated conception of *mimesis,* focusing on the shift in Derrida's key concept metaphors from "trace" to "ashes" and "cinders" to "specters" and indicating how this transformation doubles as a representation of the material history of mediation as well.

Daniel Schowalter underscores the importance of rhetoric's materiality for understanding the politics of identity, as well as for theorizing resistance to the reigning hegemony. In "Disarticulating American Indianness in the National Museum of the American Indian," Schowalter turns our attention to how rhetorical practices are implicated in processes of technological remediation. He accomplishes this by taking his reader on a brief but meticulous tour of the recently opened National Museum of the American Indian on the Washington, D.C., mall, demonstrating how its singularly styled construction and sophisticated usage of new media/interactive technologies functions to disarticulate the conventional and received history of the "American Indian." It achieves this goal, he argues, by using the patron's experience of the museum to deconstruct the relationship between the material and the rhetorical and, in the process, to remediate the patron's relationship to "American Indianness" itself.

The political stakes—in the strictest sense of the term—of rhetoric's materiality are also made to come to the fore in Oscar Giner's "Portraits of Rebellion: Geronimo's Photograph of 1884" and in Dana Cloud's "The Materialist Dialectic as a Site of *Kairos*: Theorizing Rhetorical Intervention in Material Social Relations." The question that underwrites Giner's essay concerns the possibilities of rhetorical agency among oppressed and defeated peoples, especially when they are subject to the optical and ocular technologies of a dominant and domineering culture. In this essay, Giner focuses on a series of photographic portraits of the Apache warrior and shaman Geronimo following his capture and confinement to a reservation in Florida in 1884. Resisting the conventional modernist notion of the object or subject of a photograph as a passive agent, Giner compares two separate portraits of Geronimo with portraits of other captured Chiricahua Apaches to demonstrate how one performs rebellion by exploiting the signifying conventions of the dominant culture, or perhaps more to the point, Giner helps us to understand how rebellion itself is a mode of rhetorical performance enacted in the presence of an audience.

Also preoccupied with the possibilities of resistance and social change, Cloud's essay brings rhetoric into conversation with a Marxist dialectical materialism by engaging anew the problem of the conditions of possibility for revolutionary class consciousness. Agreeing with Ernesto Laclau and Chantal Mouffe (whose articulation theory is informed deeply by the Derridean deconstruction of the subject) that economic conflict alone cannot inspire systemic change, Cloud finds in the classical rhetorical concept of *kairos* the means to rhetoricize the materialist dialectic. Timely rhetorical interventions "not only mediate the tension between economic contradictions and ideological mystifications," but, more importantly, animate the performance of a localized and situated intelligence that "opens up space for a potentially revolutionary class agency." Drawing on the Boeing workers' strike of 2005, she illustrates how such a materialist conception of *kairos* is vitally important to the performance of a class consciousness that moves from an understanding of "class itself" to one that enables the capacity to act as "a class for itself."

Last but not least, William Trapani's "Materiality's Time: Rethinking the Event from the Derridean *esprit d'à-propos*" ponders the conditions of possibility not merely of resistance but of radical change, boldly challenging the approach to rhetoric's materiality advanced by a host of rhetorical scholars, including those as different as Greene and Cloud. Indeed, in the essay that brings the volume to a close, Trapani questions the wisdom of understanding the material or constitutive effects of rhetoric for political life primarily in terms of the rhetorical subject (however embedded or contextualized) on the one hand, or in terms of mediation and circulation on the other. By resorting to familiar categories of analysis and falling into the trap of the visible and seemingly verifiable, he argues, we risk too easy explanations of rhetoricity that either domesticate or altogether elide rhetoric's materiality, i.e., its eventfulness. Drawing on Derrida's explorations of "the event-machine" and the deconstructive logic of dissemination that foregrounds the interruption of temporality, Trapani theorizes rhetoric's materiality as its "disseminating and prosaic resistance to reappropriation" within an ordered and seemingly fixed economy of signification.

Rhetoric, Materiality, and Politics presents a spectrum of different, even competing, post-foundational approaches to grasping the relation of communication practices and contemporary collective life—and deliberately so. Indeed, from the start, the aim of this volume has been to prompt political hope not by occulting but, quite the contrary, openly staging a lively theoretical and critical conversation that has yet to come to a close, has yet to congeal into a consensus, has yet to have the force of habit. For that, we issue no apology as we can imagine no better manner of honoring the life's work of Michael Calvin McGee than by fostering the spirit of dispute.

Notes

1.   The comprehensive intellectual and social history of rhetoric and speech communication in the twentieth century has yet to be written, but one can get a sense for the connections by taking account of the role that speech pedagogy was to play in the development of rhetorical theory throughout much of the first half of the century. Traces of this relationship can be found in Herman Cohen, *The History of Speech Communication: The Emergence of a Discipline, 1914–1945* (Annandale, VA: Speech Communication Association, 1994), esp. 137–274; Michael C. Leff and Margaret Organ Procario, "Rhetorical Theory in Speech Communication," in *Speech Communication in the 20th Century*, ed. Thomas W. Benson (Carbondale: Southern Illinois University Press, 1985), 3–27; and J. Michael Hogan, introduction to *Rhetoric and Reform in the Progressive Era: Rhetorical History of the United States*, Vol. VI, ed. J. Michael Hogan (East Lansing: Michigan State University Press, 2003), ix–xxiv. See also William Keith, *Democracy as Discussion: Civic Education and the American Forum Movement* (Lanham, MD: Lexington Books, 2007).

2.   See J. Michael Sproule, *Propaganda and Democracy: The American Experience of Media and Mass Persuasion* (New York: Cambridge University Press, 1996); John Durham Peters and Peter Simonson, "The World in Turmoil: Communication Research, 1933–1949," in *Mass Communication and American Social Thought: Key Texts, 1919–1968*, ed. John Durham Peters and Peter Simonson (Boulder, CO: Rowman and Littlefield, 2004), 79–90; and Todd Gitlin, "Media Sociology: The Dominant Paradigm," *Theory and Society* 6 (1978): 205–53.

3.   These trends and tendencies are most apparent in *The Prospects of Rhetoric*, the report of two conferences held in the 1970s and designed to "outline and amplify a theory of rhetoric suitable to twentieth-century concepts and needs" (v). Conference participants in-

cluded forty of the leading rhetorical theorists of the time, though notably there were no women at the conference. *The Prospects of Rhetoric: The Report of the National Developmental Project*, ed. Lloyd F. Bitzer and Edwin Black (Englewood Cliffs, NJ: Prentice Hall, 1971). For a more complete history of the conference and subsequent volume, see Theresa Enos and Richard McNabb, eds., *Making and Unmaking Prospects of Rhetoric* (Mahwah, NJ: Lawrence Erlbaum, 1997).

4. The turn to "critique" as a politically engaged form of rhetorical analysis versus a modernist "criticism" that presumed a degree of analytical neutrality emerged initially in the pages of the *Quarterly Journal of Speech* as part of a forum over Forbes Hill's "Conventional Wisdom-Traditional Form: The President's Message of November 3, 1969," *Quarterly Journal of Speech* 58 (1972): 373–86. The charge was led by Karlyn Kohrs Campbell. See Karlyn Kohrs Campbell, "'Conventional Wisdom-Traditional Form': A Rejoinder" and Forbes Hill, "A Response to Professor Campbell," *Quarterly Journal of Speech* 58 (1972): 452–60. The issue was taken up again ten years later in Philip Wander's "The Ideological Turn in Criticism," *Central States Speech Journal* 34 (1983): 1–19, and in a forum that was to follow the following year that included a number of responses from, among others, Michael Calvin McGee, Lawrence Rosenfeld, and Alan McGill in *Central States Speech Journal* 34 (1984). The turn to a dialogue with European social and political theory was most pronounced in work by Michael Calvin McGee and Thomas Farrell. See, e.g., Michael Calvin McGee, "In Search of 'the People': A Rhetorical Alternative," *Quarterly Journal of Speech* 61 (1975): 235–49; Thomas Farrell, "Knowledge, Consensus, and Rhetorical Theory," *Quarterly Journal of Speech* 62 (1976): 1–14. The two trends came together in the late 1980s and early 1990s in what Raymie E. McKerrow was to name "critical rhetoric." See Raymie E. McKerrow, "Critical Rhetoric: Theory and Praxis," *Communication Monographs* 56 (1989): 91–111.

5. See Karl Marx and Frederick Engels, *The German Ideology*, ed. C. J. Arthur (New York: International Pub., 1970), esp. "Feuerbach. Opposition of the Materialist and Idealist Outlook," 39–56, and "Theses on Feuerbach," 121–23.

6. John Louis Lucaites, "Notes on Classical Rhetorical Theory, Professor Michael Leff at the University of Wisconsin, Fall 1977." In more recent correspondence, Professor Leff suggested that the phrase might be attributable to J. Walter Ong, though we have been unable to locate the reference in any published works. Michael Leff to John Louis Lucaites, e-mail, September 13, 2007.

7. The crushing blow against neo-Aristotelian formalism in rhetorical studies appeared in 1965 in Edwin Black's *Rhetorical Criticism: A Study of Method* (New York: Macmillan, 1965). Black's critique focused on the narrow conception of "immediate effects" that animated such work, and one of the less salutary—albeit in all likelihood unintended—effects of his work was to discourage more complex and nuanced considerations of rhetorical effect or effectivity. Thus, ironically, attention was directed away from the possible "material" influences of rhetoric broadly considered, and focused instead on formal questions of genre. See, for example, the papers from a special conference on "'Significant Form' in Rhetorical Criticism" held at the University of Kansas in 1976 and collected and published by Karlyn Kohrs Campbell and Kathleen Hall Jamieson, *Form and Genre: Reshaping Rhetorical Action* (Falls Church, VA: Speech Communication Association, 1978). The emphasis on genre as a site of invention proved to be a useful heuristic for rhetorical studies, but what it failed to acknowledge was the more radical sense of invention we find in Aristotle's *Rhetoric*. Put differently, Black's critique of "intended effects" in neo-Aristotelian criticism and the subsequent focus on form and genre under-

scored a conception of Aristotle's *Rhetoric* as a *simple* handbook for making individual orators effective in the most narrow sense. A more productive alternative is to read the *Rhetoric* over and against, say, Louis Althusser's conception of interpellation as a basic rhetorical social theory concerned with the faculty of constituting (i.e., "calling out") collectives/publics. From this perspective, the emphasis on enthymemes and topoi underscores the sense in which Aristotle's *Rhetoric* functions as a socio-psychology of Athenian society, and thus serves as a theoretical model for a more complex sense of rhetoric's effectivities (even as we might resist the characterizations of particular topoi as no longer applicable in subsequent or contemporary times). In this sense, it anticipates McGee's characterization of rhetoric's functionality in the context of coordinated micro-, socio-, and macro-rhetorical registers. See Aristotle, *On Rhetoric: A Theory of Civic Discourse*, trans. George A. Kennedy (New York: Oxford University Press, 1991); Louis Althusser, "Ideology and Ideological State Apparatuses," in *Lenin and Philosophy*, trans. Ben Brewster (New York: Monthly Press, 1971), 127–88.

8. One can see some of the early and very implicit gestures to the turn to rhetorical materialism in the proposals recommended in the chapter on criticism in *The Prospects of Rhetoric*, as well as in the growing emphasis on social movement theory and especially the taking-it-to-the-streets-level epistemology that was emerging. See *Prospects of Rhetoric*, 220–27; Franklin Haiman, "The Rhetoric of the Streets: Legal and Ethical Considerations," *Quarterly Journal of Speech* 53 (1967): 99–114; Robert L. Scott and Donald K. Smith, "The Rhetoric of Confrontation," *Quarterly Journal of Speech* 50 (1970): 120–30.

9. See Douglas Ehninger, "On Systems of Rhetoric," *Philosophy and Rhetoric* 1 (1968): 131–44; John Waite Bowers, "The Pre-Scientific Function of Rhetorical Criticism," in Thomas R. Nilsen, ed., *Essays on Rhetorical Criticism* (New York: Random House, 1968): 126–46.

10. Michael Calvin McGee, "A Materialist's Conception of Rhetoric," in *Explorations in Rhetoric: Studies in Honor of Douglas Ehninger*, ed. Ray E. McKerrow (Glenview, IL: Scott, Foresman, 1982), 23–25, 39.

11. Michael McGuire, "Materialism: Reductionist Dogma or Critical Rhetoric?" in Richard Cherwitz, ed., *Rhetoric and Philosophy* (New York: Routledge, 1990), 202.

12. McGee's conception of materiality responded in some measure to the popularity of genre studies that prospered in the 1970s and was marked most specifically by the work presented at the Kansas conference on "Significant Form" and subsequently published in the volume edited by Campbell and Jamieson on *Form and Genre*. McGee would return to the relationship between the materiality of rhetoric and formal/generic considerations at the "follow-up conference" held at Temple University in Philadelphia in 1983. See Michael Calvin McGee, "Against Transcendentalism: Prologue to Functional Theory of Communicative Praxis," in *Form, Genre, and the Study of Political Discourse*, ed. Herbert W. Simons and Aram A. Aghazarian (Columbia: University of South Carolina Press, 1986), 108–58. For a detailed bibliography of the work on form and genre that dominated much of rhetorical studies in the 1970s, see the selected bibliography in Simons and Aghazarian, *Form, Genre, and the Study*, 355–75.

13. It is important to note here that McGee distinguishes between "rhetoric," by which he means the embodied and performed phenomenon of speaker/speech/audience/occasion/change, and "discourse," by which he means the "residue" or "archaeological remnant" of a rhetorical act. As he puts it, "We can reconstruct the nature, scope, and consequence of a nuclear explosion by analyzing its residue when the raw matter and even the energy

inherent in its occurrence have dissipated. Thus it is possible to reconstruct the nature, scope, and consequence of rhetoric by analyzing 'speech' even when 'speaker,' 'audience,' 'occasion,' and 'change' dissipate into half-remembered history." See McGee, "Materialist's Conception of Rhetoric," 38–39.

14. McGee's sense of the materiality of rhetoric was implicit in his theory of the ideograph published two years earlier and was central to the rhetorical material history of the ideograph "equality" advanced by Celeste Michelle Condit and John Louis Lucaites in *Crafting Equality: America's Anglo-African Word.* McGee's material conception of rhetoric was not without its early critics, however—most specifically Dana Cloud, who took exception to it in a number of provocative critical essays. See Michael Calvin McGee, "The 'Ideograph': A Link Between Rhetoric and Ideology," *Quarterly Journal of Speech* 6 (1980): 1–16; and "The Origins of 'Liberty': A Feminization of Power," *Communication Monographs* 47 (1980): 23–44; Celeste Michelle Condit and John Louis Lucaites, *Crafting Equality: America's Anglo-African Word* (Chicago: University of Chicago Press, 1993); and Dana Cloud, "Materiality of Discourse as Oxymoron: A Challenge to Critical Rhetoric," *Western Journal of Communication* 58 (1994): 141–63; and "The Rhetoric of Family Values: Scapegoating, Utopia, and the Privatization of Social Responsibility," *Western Journal of Communication* 62 (1998): 387–419.

15. Jacques Derrida, *Positions*, trans. Alan Bass (Chicago: University of Chicago Press, 1981), 20.

16. Derrida, *Positions*, 23–4.

17. Michel Foucault, *The Archaeology of Knowledge*, trans. A. M. Sheridan Smith (New York: Pantheon Books, 1971), 95–96.

18. Yannis Stavrakakis, *Lacan and the Political* (New York: Routledge, 1999), 26.

19. For a more thorough explication of Lacan's overhaul of the Saussurian conceptualization of the sign on which the discussion here depends, see Jean-Luc Nancy and Philippe Lacoue-Labarthe's *The Title of the Letter: A Reading of Lacan,* trans. François Raffoul and David Pettigrew (New York: State University of New York Press, 1992), especially 27–59.

20. François Raffoul and David Pettigrew, "Translators' Preface" in *The Title of the Letter: A Reading of Lacan,* by Jean-Luc Nancy and Philippe Lacoue-Labarthe, trans. François Raffoul and David Pettigrew (New York: State University of New York Press, 1992), xi.

21. Jacques Lacan, *The Seminar of Jacques Lacan: Book III, The Psychoses, 1955–1956,* ed. Jacques-Alain Miller, trans. Russell Grigg (New York: W. W. Norton, 1993), 199.

22. Jacques Lacan, *The Four Fundamental Concepts of Psychoanalysis,* ed. Jacques-Alain Miller, trans. Alan Sheridan (New York: W. W. Norton, 1998), 106.

23. Slavoj Žižek, *The Ticklish Subject: The Absent Center of Political Ontology* (New York: Verso, 1999), 51.

24. Jacques Derrida, *Of Grammatology*, trans. Gayatri Chakravorty Spivak (Baltimore, MD: Johns Hopkins University Press, 1974), 20.

25. Jacques Derrida, "Structure, Sign, and Play in the Discourse of the Human Sciences," in *The Structuralist Controversy: The Languages of Criticism and the Sciences of Man,* ed. Richard Macksey and Eugenio Donato (Baltimore, MD: Johns Hopkins University Press, 1972), 249.

26. Gayatri Chakravorty Spivak, "Translator's Preface," in *Of Grammatology*, by Jacques Derrida, trans. Gayatri Chakravorty Spivak (Baltimore, MD: Johns Hopkins University Press, 1974), lxx.

27. Derrida, "Structure, Sign, and Play," 248.

28. Spivak, "Translator's Preface," lxxv. For an argument with regard to the significant difference between Derrida's and Lacan's rethinking of the sign—namely, that the latter appeals, ultimately, to "a reference point that is the *primary truth*" (lxvii), while the former does not—see pages lxii–lxvii of Spivak's "Translator's Preface."

CHAPTER 1

A Materialist's Conception
of Rhetoric

Michael Calvin McGee, University of Iowa

The contemporary history of rhetoric is the opposite of the typical history of other social sciences. In sociology, for example, early thinkers were overwhelmed by phenomena, so awed by the gargantuan presence of "society" that they forgot the first task of theory, to name and describe phenomena. There were so few *concepts* of "society" that, as late as 1940, Ortega could bemoan his reading of all sociological theory to that date, claiming not to have found a single definition even of "society," let alone the more telling phenomena which comprise "society."[1] Rhetoricians battle an opposite problem: we are overwhelmed with a history which goes back through two millennia of conceptualizing to pre-Socratic Greece. Supposedly, each writer who creates or modifies a concept does so on the warrant of experience with real phenomena, actual cases of "rhetoric." Over time, however, the connection between theory and practice is muddied. A proliferation of concepts forces us to pay more attention to what has been said about rhetorical practice than to actual public address.[2]

Today, the typical course in rhetorical theory is a *history* of rhetoric, and the "cutting edge" of scholarship in rhetorical theory seems to be the *philosophy of* (if not more specifically the epistemology of) rhetoric. The terms "history of" and "philosophy of" presume common knowledge of "rhetoric." The knowledge which is presumed, I believe, is of a "rhetoric" which is on its face uninformed by historical or immediate contact with actual practice.[3] The problem is not a new one, though in the past it has been regarded as primarily or essentially terministic. So when Donald Bryant listed the several meanings "rhetoric" has had through the centuries, he proposed that we distinguish between the theory and the practice of "rhetoric" by coining the term "rhetory" to refer to actual discourse.[4] It is not enough, however, merely to *distinguish* theory and practice at a definitional level. One must also decide what *relationship* exists between theory and practice—which "comes first" in a common desire to understand human communicative behavior. When the content of a *history of* rhetoric includes a treatise by Juan de Vives on figures and tropes, and when the content of a *philosophy of* rhetoric purports speculatively to account for the psychology of knowing, the implicit claim is that the theory and technique of rhetoric come less from human experience than from the metaphysical creativity and inspiration of particular writers. So, as Natanson observed, what has been called "rhetorical theory" through much of our tradition is not theory at all, but a set of technical, prescriptive principles which inform the practitioner while, paradoxically, remaining largely innocent of practice.[5]

The obvious alternative is to believe that practice "comes first," that the essential mission of rhetorical theory is not to *prescribe* technique but formally to account for what seems to be an essential part of the human social condition. The problem posed by such an alternative is the classic confrontation between idealism and materialism. Karl Marx's initial response to Feuerbach's *Das Wesen des Christentums* puts the question vividly:

> The production of ideas, of conceptions, of consciousness, is at first directly inter-woven with the material activity of men—the language of real life. Conceiving, thinking, the mental intercourse of men at this stage still appear as the direct efflux of their material behavior. . . . Men are the producers of their conceptions, ideas, etc., that is, real, active men. . . . In direct contrast to German philosophy [idealism] which descends from heaven to earth, here it is a matter of ascending from earth to heaven. That is to say, not of setting out from what men say, imagine, conceive, nor from men as narrated, thought of, imagined, conceived, in order to arrive at men in the flesh; but setting out from real, active men, and on the basis of their real-life-process demonstrating the development of the ideological reflexes and echoes of this life-process. . . . It is not consciousness that determines life, but life that determines consciousness. For the first manner of approach [idealism] the starting-point is con-sciousness taken as the living individual; for the second manner of approach [mate-rialism], which conforms to real life, it is the real living individuals themselves, and consciousness is considered solely as their consciousness.[6]

If we begin the construction of rhetorical theories as we would begin a textbook on public speaking, with an imagined picture of a human being assigned to compose a piece of persuasive discourse, and if we then make rules to help this fictional person succeed in the imagined task, we lose contact with the brute reality of persuasion as a daily social phenomenon— and even our rules for good speaking thereby lose force. A material theory of rhetoric, in contrast, begins with real speeches which are demonstrably useful to an end or are failures. Such an approach to theory would not aim at making rules of composition, but rather at the description, explanation, perhaps even prediction of the formation of consciousness itself.

With the possible exception of Kenneth Burke, no one I know of has attempted formally to advance a material theory of rhetoric. The task is imposing, for in many ways the world of traditional rhetorical theory would have to be turned upside-down to resolve a host of complicated philosophical issues. The "epistemic function" of rhetoric will become a cornerstone of theory-building rather than an interesting alternative approach to criticism.[7] Discourse, even language itself, will have to be characterized as material rather than merely representational of mental and empirical phenomena.[8] Such difficult and controversial concepts as "consciousness" and "ideology," "myth" and "phenomenon" will have to be explored.[9] Various methods of data-based historical research and theory building will have to be examined, and the mystifications of "semiotics" and "hermeneutics" resolved and eliminated.[10] Since none of this could occur in a vacuum, it also will be necessary at every point to justify distinctions between a material rhetorical theory and both rhetorical criticism and empirical communication research. Finally, since no materialists have been essentially concerned with rhetoric, apparently heretical rhetorical adaptations of such concepts as "phenomenology" and "dialectics" will have to be justified against methodological purists on both sides of the Atlantic.

Because it is the most direct strategy, I do not blush to advertise this essay as an exercise in fundamental conceptualization: I want to define the term "rhetoric" from a material perspective. My concern is with the creation and application of rhetorical theories. I do not ask the question *What is rhetoric?* so much as the question *What legitimizes the theory of rhetoric?* The alternative to *idealism*, I will suggest, is to think of rhetoric as an *object*, as material and as omnipresent as air and water. Just as oceanographic theory is controlled by the existence of water in nature, just as meteorological theory is warranted by the behavior of air, so a theory of rhetoric can be legitimate only when measured, directly and explicitly, against the objects it purportedly describes and explains.

Idealism in Rhetoric Defined

By the late eighteenth-century, the Renaissance-inspired "scientific revolution" had produced so many discoveries in physics, chemistry, and mathematics that such lights of the *Academie Francaise* as Destutt de Tracy sought to apply the same naive empiricism to the study of philosophies of the past. There was to be a "science of ideas," *ideology*, invented in the belief that the future was determined by the ideas of the past and that we can therefore predict the future by counting ideas. The difficulty, of course, is that a philosopher's idea of the world is neither empirical nor very influential. As Marx suggested in the passage quoted earlier, effective ideas are thoughts of *actors*, not of cloistered academics, and they are produced in the context of material necessity, not abstractly, naked of human passion. Marx did agree that the future could be predicted, but by the twentieth century, the pace of technological, economic, and political change was too rapid for even philosophers to understand and synthesize the principles involved. Materialists and idealists alike gave up any but the mythical vision of predicting broad swaths of the future. Such social scientists as Neil Smelser continue to treat human attitudes and opinions as defined and determined by situation, and the old "science of ideas" notion has been translated into a "history of ideas" dreamed by academics and only purportedly influential.[11]

Departments of "speech," concerned primarily with rhetoric, were birthed and brought to maturity in the climate of controversy I have just described. Early rhetoricians seemed to share Marx's anti-idealist impulses, for they were dissatisfied by the failure of literary scholars to account for *practical* discourse, communication designed to act upon and to be useful in the work-a-day world. In the end, however, two interests in practical discourse resulted more in the appreciation of bad literature than in the study of material functions of discourse. First, there was concern for ordinary discourse as a genre of literature, "public address," unique because it was meant more to be effective than to be timeless or beautiful. A valiant effort was made to use ancient pedagogical principles to deal with this literature on its own terms; but since most early rhetoricians were accustomed to think of all writing as literature, and since ancient treatises were meant to be textbooks, public address was treated as a specialized "art" form. Early writers were distinct from critics of poetry or the novel only in their appreciation of a particular author's intention to persuade or inform an audience more than entertain them.

This interest in the aesthetics of oratory carried over into a second concern, the teaching of composition skills. Because a public speaker can choose better or worse strategies of communication, and because there is an ancient literature consisting of specific advice on the making of such choices, rhetoric was thought of as a "body of principles" useful in practical classroom instruction. Ancient treatises on rhetoric were studied almost bibliographically at first, and then as themselves a kind of literature. Early writers were historians, distinct from literary and cultural historians only in the titles of books they read. Through the 1950s there was a heated debate among those who sought to test ancient advice experimentally and those who tried historically to understand the ancient advice and discover whatever was missed in our original search for books about rhetoric. With few exceptions, however, everyone seemed agreed that persuasive oratory was a peculiar "art" form, and that rhetoric was a "body of principles" giving advice on how to become proficient in that art.

It is possible to think of a public speech as "art." To do so, however, is to distort both material and ideal conceptions of theory and practice: from a materialist's perspective, ordinary discourse is a social function which permits interactivity among people. It is a medium, a bridge among human beings, the social equivalent of a verb in a sentence. To treat such a thing as if it were "art" is to see it as a product instead of a function, as goal, the equivalent of a noun in a sentence. If one tricks the mind to make process into product, the end result can be unhealthy preoccupation with the performance itself, a "sophistic consciousness" wherein the saying is more important than the doing. From an idealist's point of view, the "art/body of principles" notion of public address and rhetoric establishes a contradictory relationship between theory and practice. Theory in such a conception is said to be related to practice as instruction is related to performance. So Plato admits that there may be an "art" in rhetoric as there is an "art" in cooking. But it is a strange conception of both theory and art to believe that a football game is "art" because the coach teaches technique, or to believe that recipes are "theories" because chefs serve better and worse meals.

Perhaps because we have been teachers of composition and public speaking, we have been incredibly sensitive to idealists' reservations about the "artistic" status of oratory and about the ethics of teaching students the techniques of persuasion. When we first hear that rhetoric is a knack and not an art, we set out intently either to prove that Plato is wrong or to find a perspective on rhetoric which meets Plato's moral criteria. When we hear a journalist using Webster's definition of rhetoric as bombast and eristic, we cringe either in formulary apology or angry indignation.

Each such apology, retreat, or equivocation perpetuates a systemic contradiction in rhetorical theory: ours is a practical art, presumably in contact with the work-a-day world; but at the same time, we are much more involved in condemning unethical or ineffective speeches (with the warrant of *a priori* prescriptions) than with creating precise descriptions and explanations of prevailing persuasive practices. The typical rhetorician, theorist or critic, seems to emulate Plato: we judge a piece of discourse to be deformed, imperfect, or perverted. We then imagine it possible to reform, perfect, or recreate it. Using our prescriptive rhetorical "theories," we dream a more effective or more moral speech than the one we have heard. Finally, we turn the world upside-down by thinking that our imaginings are "real." From the idealist's perspective, rhetoric is concerned with practical discourse not as a process requiring description and explanation, but as the product of an imperfect world which has dictated the production of bad literature, prose too clear and intentional to be beautiful. Instruction begins with general knowledge of the subject matter of a discourse and ends with a finished speech or essay. The steps in between constitute a naive psychological model of the creative process: an advocate first "invents" instrumental arguments, "disposes" the arguments like soldiers on the battlefield, "styles" them in attractive language as one arms a warrior, "memorizes" specific passages to conceal the labor of artifice, and finally "delivers" the whole discourse. In the typical book on rhetoric, "principles" are taught in their proper order under the individual headings of a product-conception and product-model of rhetoric: rhetoric is the "invention/disposition/style/memory/delivery" of discourse.

The Material Model of Rhetoric

If we pay more attention to *how* rhetoricians arrived at their advice than to *what* that advice was, however, there is a process-model inherent in all textbooks on rhetorical technique. Aristotle, for example, did not pretend to have the experience of an effective orator, nor did he psychoanalyze the outstanding advocates of his day. Rather, he arrived at descriptions of internal motivations and mental processes by inference from observing the function of communication in Greek societies. He observed individual advocates ("speaker") delivering a finished discourse ("speech") to a group of human beings ("audience") in a particular social context ("occasion") with the intention of using the collective power of the group to control some problematic element of the shared environment ("change"). The conventional rules designed to improve students' language skills all consisted of his interpretation and description of particular communication events. The product-conception and product-model of rhetoric superseded the original material conception and model because of Aristotle's primitive attitude toward elements of the phenomenon he witnessed. "Audience," for example, was nothing but a lump of clay to be molded, important only in having properties resistant to the creative touch of "speaker." Like Carlyle's heroic shapers-of-destiny, Aristotle's "speaker" stood above and apart from the society of which she/he was a part, an autonomous individual who acted in an egocentric world of trickery and manipulation. "Occasion" was merely an excuse for "speaker" to work magic, and "change" was the glory of the advocate, the working of his/her will on a faceless, soul-less (if not mindless) mass of human flesh. Aristotle's primeval elitism is reminiscent of his teacher's *Republic* and consistent with his office as adviser to the despot Philip of Macedon. But if we ignore the *product* of his attitudes, there is in Aristotle's *method* a process-conception and process-model of rhetoric: Rhetoric is "speaker/speech/audience/occasion/change" operating in society through time.

Everyone who observes persuasion functioning in a society, and is impressed enough to write a treatise on technique, consciously uses a material conception of rhetoric, if only in formulary recognition of situational constraints on a would-be advocate's choice of strategy and technique. Not only idealism confuses the conception, however, for it is easy to let equivocations of the terms "object" and "material" cloud thinking. Though it is the only residue of rhetoric one can hold like a rock, it is wrong to think that this sheaf of papers, this recording of "speech," *is* rhetoric in and of itself. It is surely "object," and the paper and ink scratches are "material." But the whole of rhetoric is "material" by measure of human *experiencing* of it, not by virtue of our ability to continue touching it after it is gone. Rhetoric is "object" because of its pragmatic *presence*, our inability safely to ignore it at the moment of its impact. "Speech" bears exactly the same categorical relationship to rhetoric whether one conceives "rhetoric" as a body of prescriptive principles or as an objective social interaction. From the idealist's viewpoint, "speech" is the surviving evidence of an "invention/disposition/style/memory/delivery" mental process. From the material perspective, "speech" is an integral part of a "speaker/speech/audience/occasion/change" phenomenon, peculiar as an element of rhetoric because it survives and records the moment of experience.

The distinction between objective experience and objective sensation is important in dealing with all elements of rhetoric. Though one can hardly sense something without experiencing it, and though it seems impossible to experience what has not at one time or another been sensed, there is both a conceptual and procedural difference between specific cognitions and the overall impression one comes away with upon experiencing a set of particular cognitions. So, for example, I can study rattlesnakes by watching a peculiar caged beast perform in my laboratory—I can sense its every move, even kill and dissect it until I have perfect empirical knowledge of the creature. But this set of facts pales before my accidental confrontation with a rattlesnake coiled in my path, ready to strike. I pay attention to different facts in the forest, and it is the *relationship* those facts bear to each other and to me which I regard as salient, not the facts in and of themselves. In like fashion, I can study the empirical characteristics of "audience," the biography of "speaker," the content of "speech" in my laboratory—I can collect a set of facts, in other words, a set of sensations. But in the social world, such knowledge matters less than the specific *relationships* which "speaker/speech/audience/occasion/change" bear to one another in actual human experience.

Conceptually, only two of rhetoric's elements *could* be studied as a kind of sensation rather than as part of an experience. I can conceive a potentially rhetorical "occasion" which appears to invite "speaker/speech/audience/change" where none materialized, and the element "change" can be conceived and studied as the product of another process or even as a naked product, conceptually stripped of its rationale. But it is impossible to think of "speaker/speech/audience" existing in a vacuum, discrete and apart from one another. These elements each suppose one another. The terms themselves have meaning only in relation to one another—"speaker" puts one human being in a role *vis-à-vis* other human beings cast as "audience" in a social drama mediated by "speech."

Rhetoric is thus an almost mathematical paradigm of terms, for the "speaker" (2) can be linked through "speech" (+) to an "audience" (2), and because of the configuration of restraints and potentials present in an "occasion" (=), predictable "changes" (4) can occur. Of course rhetoric is like mathematics only in its structuring, in the fact that it is a form of relationships and not a set of facts. The necessity which characterizes a mathematical sequence does not adhere to predictions of "change" from observing a rhetoric because the human beings who play the roles of "speaker" and "audience" are not so obedient as arabic numerals. Procedurally, the distinction between experience and sensation establishes a relationship between rhetoric and communication research: the study of rhetoric is to the study of communicative behaviors as mathematics is to mechanics, as form is to content, as phenomenon is to cognition.

A principle begins to emerge in consequence of relocating rhetoric in the material world of objects: because rhetorics are forms, I can perceive them in any arena of experience where I am able to see the paradigm of relationships. "Speakers" do not have to be single individuals; "speeches" do not have to be words uttered in one place and at one time; "audiences" need not be present immediately; "occasion" is not restricted by time or space; and "change" may occur gradually over centuries as well as immediately in the presence of a single "speaker." Rhetoric, in other words, exists on a continuum from the absolutely specific experience of being persuaded to the absolutely general experience of having been conditioned to a pattern of social and political opinions. There are as many nuances of rhetorical experience as there are points on a line; but to make the argument clear, I will briefly describe the ends and middle of the continuum.

Microrhetorical Experience

An absolutely specific rhetoric could occur only when a single speaker sought to influence a single auditor—as the number of auditors increases to make the term "audience" appropriate, the experience is inherently abstracted by the listener's sense of being part of an entity larger than self, "audience." As a category of experience, however, it seems useful to conceive the most specific rhetoric occurring when a single "speaker" confronts a specific "audience" in one place, at one time, with a recommended belief or behavior which may not have been contemplated by "audience" without the agency of "speech." Thus "speaker" is absolutely specific when we refer to a human being making symbolic claims through any medium of communication. "Speech" is specific if we refer to the words of a single individual. "Audience" is specific *in relation to* a particular "speaker/speech"; that is, we may not always be able to pinpoint each individual auditor, but we can nonetheless give a name to an otherwise faceless "audience" by referring to "speaker" and/or "speech," as in the sentence "Oral Roberts' sermon of November 5, 1974 convinced his television audience to contribute five million dollars."

Like "audience," the "occasion" is made specific with reference to "speaker/speech." In theory, "occasion" is "speaker's" reason for being in a particular material setting (replete with altars, books, lamps, chairs, whatever) coupled with "audience's" reason for sharing the same time and space. My reason for addressing the Rotary Club may be as immediate as last week's invitation or as remote as my grandfather's charter-membership in the organization. The only thing preventing my "speech" from being the focal point for a history of civilization is Occam's Razor, for a skillful analyst could broaden the concept of "occasion" so much as to include the ontology of every person and thing present. But "occasion" is usually *made* specific by "speaker/audience" themselves—the various reasons-for-being-there are truncated by "speaker's" stated intentions ("I want to discuss Soviet policy in Afghanistan") and "audience" expectation ("We'd like you to speak on the subject of a free press"). Finally, "change," when specified, means *effect*, the sort of attitude and behavior modification rhetorical critics and communication researchers look for among auditors as a consequence of hearing "speech." I call this category of "speaker/speech/audience/occasion/change" experience *microrhetorical* because it is quantitatively concrete: specific human beings play the important roles—people with names which could in theory be called out, people with opinions to be counted engaging in behaviors empirically evident.

Sociorhetorical Experience

Human beings constantly fantasize roles larger than themselves, "playing like" they are "grocers," "unionists," "judges," "Christians," "Democrats," etc. Of course the term "fantasy" may be too strong, for our conditions of life force us to play social and economic roles simply to earn a living. But there is a clear distinction between the behaviors and beliefs of a grocer in his store, a judge in her chambers, and the behaviors and beliefs of the same persons at home, at a football game, or at the beach. It is a chicken-and-egg problem, often too difficult for even an experienced psychotherapist, to decide which is the "real" person, the private, flesh-and-blood human being, or the economic and political *persona* that human being portrays. Indeed, sorting out the various *personae* of the people around us is a chronic interpersonal and social problem: is Sue "playing like" my neighbor when she tells glowing stories of her trip to Florida, or is she a "real estate agent" bent upon selling me a plot of land in Aqua Acres?

The human role-playing capacity creates for everyone a more abstract and more sophisticated "speaker/speech/audience/occasion/change" experience. "Speaker" is identified by his/her membership in a social group, and it is the *public persona* we pay attention to. We are not conscious of "speaker's" individuality—he/she takes little personal risk in the interaction, knowing that it is a *role* speaking, not a private person. So even though a used car salesman identifies himself in a television commercial, it is "salesman" who speaks and "salesman" we hear, not "John Honicutt." "Speech," too, is role-defined, for having learned to survive in a particular political economy, we are accustomed to hearing set arguments in set order. "Audience" is also impersonal and abstract, for their interest is defined by the drama being enacted. Individuals in the audience matter only because they have a few dollars to spend, a vote to cast, a soul to save, a law to abide by, etc. Hence, "audience" is identified as "consumers," "constituency," "congregation," "citizenry," etc., to denote that they are playing one particular role in a social ritual, one of the many roles they assume willingly and unconsciously in day-to-day business. "Occasions" are as formulary as the roles being played—we resent being sold used cars in church, being converted to Christianity in the local supermarket, etc. There are thus fewer difficulties in limiting "occasion" conceptually here than in more specific rhetorics, for we learn to recognize particular "occasions" as we learn to manoeuvre in society. Finally, "change" in sociorhetorical experience means *success*. Groups are formed in societies, political and economic rituals are followed, to increase the individual's comfort, to parcel out the wealth and power of the society, to provide for some measure of collective security and stability. "Change" is an alteration of circumstance, moving from having less money to having more money, from having less influence to having more influence, from being lonely or forgotten to being part of a group and accounted for.

Macrorhetorical Experience

In addition to playing group-defined roles ourselves, human beings also create institutions, artificial entities animated and endowed with human characteristics. "Labor," "Government," "the Law" all are spoken of as having human abilities, including the ability to persuade. Individual "speakers" in a public *persona* literally announce a policy or make legal decisions; but there is a distinction between officers or agents speaking in an official capacity and those same people *speaking for* the institutional entity they represent. So, for example, there is a difference between union leader Lane Kirkland saying, "I demand higher wages for American workers" on one occasion, and saying on another, "The voice of Labor cries out for higher wages." In the first instance, Kirkland's demand is warranted by the power inherent in his office; but in the second sentence, he exercises collective power remanded to him by a mute giant, "Labor," for whom Kirkland must speak. In radically positivistic moods, we recognize that the personification of "Labor" is only a figure of speech. But we *make* such animations as "Constitution," "People," and "Destiny" real by emphasizing the coercive power of large groups of human beings: "Congress" never literally "speaks," but if we treat a new law as if it were conversation from an ordinary citizen, or even as if it were a policy statement issued in an election campaign by our local representative, we run the risk of being punished for defying "the will of Congress."

In our most general "speaker/speech/audience/occasion/change" experiences, institutions are cast in all the human roles, "occasion" is the totality of human experience, and "change" is the Utopian fantasy of "Society's" direction and goal. Unlike more specific rhetorics, however, *the same institution can be cast in nearly every role.* So from time to time "the People" are said to "speak." Nearly every officer of state has at one time or another characterized a particular "speech" as being "the will of the People." In all Anglo-American political systems, "the People" choose leaders and thus constitute the "audience" for all political discourse. "Occasion" is defined by the historical and circumstantial development of "the People's" interests and identity. Finally, "changes" of any sort are defined by "the People's" ideal vision of themselves living in a more perfect world. In macrorhetorical experiences, even the most concrete elements are normative and attitudinal, the creation of human dreaming, so that in this arena "peoples" can speak to "peoples" when China and the United States send representatives to negotiations in Geneva. Even the dead can participate, as in the sentence "Our founding fathers did not intend to allow the Nazis freedom of speech in Skokie."

In describing three categories of rhetorical experience, I have discussed "speaker/speech/audience/occasion/change" element by element, perhaps giving the impression that rhetoric is discretely analyzable by parts. That is, my procedure in treating rhetorical elements could imply that because "speaker" is listed first and "change" last, "speaker" naturally "comes first" when one describes rhetoric, just as "invention" naturally "comes first" when one creates a public speech. If this were so, we might create an *orthogonal* model of rhetoric: on the horizontal axis, we could represent the five discrete categories, picturing "speaker" confronting "occasion" by producing a "speech" which moves an "audience" to "change" belief and/or behavior. On the vertical axis, we might account for abstractions of rhetorical experience by labelling each element as it generalizes from individual to group to whole collectivity. Such a model would miss the point that rhetoric is a *gestalt* of relationships, because one could believe in error, for example, that the sociorhetorical experience of "audience" can become the subject of specialized research, that theorists can consider human membership in groups in isolation from "speaker/speech/occasion/change" elements. More importantly, the orthogonal model would be in one way too simple a description of rhetoric, and in another way much too complex.

Orthogonal conceptions of rhetorical experience are too simple because they encourage the mind to think in terms of categories. If we think that "speaker" actually "comes first," for example, we might be inclined to underestimate the coercive power of other elements on the "speaker." "Audience," we know, can so thoroughly intimidate "speaker" with its expectations that "speaker" is literally forced to say what the "audience" wants to hear, nothing more and nothing less. We have no trouble finding a situation in which "occasion" coerces "speaker" as well as "audience" into "speech," nor are we pressed to see "speech" trapping both "speaker" and "audience" in a web of argument which nobody likes, but from which no one can escape. Further, the elements do not constantly maintain the dominance-configuration they first assume: "speaker" could begin as the dominating element, coercing all others; but with the passage of time, "audience" can assert itself, coercing "speaker" into unpredicted and unwanted lines of argument. In time, "speaker" can regain dominance, or "occasion" could come back to dominate both "speaker" and "audience" with the press of events. Rhetoric, in other words, seems too dynamic a process to be represented by relatively static orthogonal models.

In another sense, orthogonal models of rhetoric are overly complex, for we could read each horizontal line of the grid as an independent model, judging that there are structured differences among rhetorical, sociorhetorical, and macrorhetorical experiences. One even could come to believe that it is necessary to look for macrorhetorical experience in every document if complete theoretical explanation is to be provided. In this mood, for example, we might see Lane Kirkland give a speech of encouragement to his grandson's football team. Is Kirkland simply encouraging athletes to perform well in an important game? Is he using his official power to endorse high school athletics? Must we search and strain for the sense in which Kirkland is acting as "the voice of Labor," showing how support for adolescent games is part of the American social and economic order? These mistakes, seeing three independent models and forcing abstractions unnaturally on wholly specific rhetorical experiences, derive from failing to recall that rhetoric exhibits a common structure of relationships. The differences among microrhetorical, sociorhetorical, and macrorhetorical experiences are differences in degree of abstraction. The "speaker/speech/audience/occasion/change" paradigm exists in a wide range of human experience, from the barely-social to the wholly-social. The relationships are a constant; hence, when a rhetoric exists at one level of abstraction, we are not obliged to make it seem larger or smaller than it appears to be, nor are we making our description more elegant and sophisticated by hypostatizing evidence.

A model of rhetoric, I suggest, should be *molecular* (see figure 1). Nothing here necessarily "comes first" to the eye or to the mind. We can focus on one element, but we see as we attempt to make it discrete that separating it from other elements is a complex manoeuvre involving the conceptual severance of four sets of relationships. It is not difficult to imagine the effect of such surgery on the integrity of the whole structure. Further, we can see that no element is necessarily dominant. It is perspective or orientation which creates the impression of "occasion/speaker/speech" elements existing in the foreground, the same perspective which made "speaker" John F. Kennedy seem to dominate the politics of the early sixties and made the "occasion" of the Vietnam War seem to dominate the politics of the late sixties. Because the model is three dimensional it can be rotated to make any element appear larger or smaller (see figure 2). This forces us to check theoretical claims that one element dominates a particular rhetoric by conceptually putting all the other elements momentarily in the foreground of contemplation. Finally, the molecular model does not refer to the levels of abstraction at which one might experience rhetoric. This encourages the mind to think of the common structure exhibited by all rhetorics rather than to sense differences in kind resulting from nothing more than degree of abstraction. It also inclines us to see that when abstract rhetorics *are* experienced, there seems to be a *unity of abstraction*; that is, with this model before us, it would be hard to conceive an abstraction of "speaker/speech" which was not accompanied by a corresponding, almost a mathematically proportional, abstraction of "audience/occasion/change."

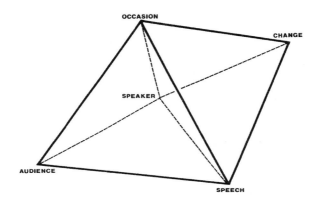

Figure 1: A molecular model of rhetoric

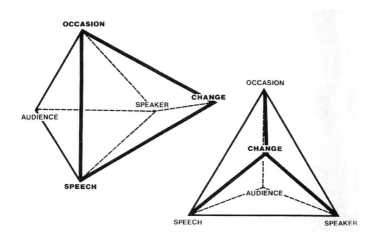

Figure 2: Different orientations to the molecular model

A Materialist's Definition of Rhetoric

Idealists could hope to isolate the ultimate formal definition of rhetoric, for though the strains of usage are often inconsistent and always complex, the question *What is rhetoric?* is conceivably answerable if we translate it to mean *How has the word "rhetoric" been used by persons claiming to instruct would-be advocates?* Conceiving rhetoric materially, however, makes it necessary to define it with regard to the solution of problems posed by the persistent recurrence of "speaker/speech/audience/occasion/change" at every level of social experience. Formal definitions must thus be truly theoretical, grounded in objective data rather than in the practice and opinions of cloistered academics using the word "rhetoric" in treatises on composition.

Since material theory in rhetorical studies is rare, any definition offered must be regarded as purely operational, designed to guide the mind toward solution of a special question which must be answered in the process of creating descriptions, explanations, and predictions. This essay is focused on the fundamental problem of linking theory with practice, hence the question *What warrants and legitimizes the theory of rhetoric?* My definition of "rhetoric," therefore, is intended to expose the questions which arise from an attempt to determine the material criteria of theory. I am not positing essence so much as continuing to define the issues which occur in the clash between idealism and materialism in rhetorical studies.

I will hazard one of those infamous italicized sentences which begin "rhetoric is . . ." and then call specific attention to the issues I want to raise with the chosen wording. *Rhetoric is a natural social phenomenon in the context of which symbolic claims are made on the behavior and/or belief of one or more persons, allegedly in the interest of such individuals, and with the strong presumption that such claims will cause meaningful change.*

The phrase "natural social phenomenon" is meant to suggest that rhetoric is a paradigm of relationships as described in the previous section. The material model of rhetoric is a portrayal of social process, a naturally recurring phenomenon with which we must cope, and in which we must participate. It is the *naturalness* of the phenomenon that creates the necessity to account for it. Bitzer speaks of "exigencies" created by material factors "inviting" a particular "discourse."[12] But his conception of "exigence" is serendipitous, for he holds between the lines a possibility that we might ignore or transcend the phenomenon which invites persuasion. We cannot. The "exigence" of rhetoric is that the phenomenon itself seems inescapable; indeed, as Augustine suggested, the phenomenon persists so much that skill in participating in it seems to come with raw and untutored socialization as

well as with particular education.[13] The first requirement of a material theory
of rhetoric which purports to account for practice would seem to be actual
description of "exigence," not the supposition of it. Without resort to
paradox, traditional vocabularies simply do not give us the resources to
describe the experience of rhetoric as it impinges on us, as it exists "naturally."

The phrase "in the context of which" is intended to suggest the relationship between "discourse" and "rhetoric" which makes usage of the two terms
theoretically problematic. In Foucault's terms, human discourse is an
"archaeological" remnant of a larger phenomenon. It stands out from other
elements of the phenomenon because it persists as the track, the spoor, the
evidence of a social process.[14] As I suggested earlier, to say that we study
rhetoric in a material way is not to claim that rhetoric is material because it is
a sensible discourse I may handle and manipulate like rock. Rather, discourse
is *part* of a material phenomenon particularly useful because it is residual
and persistent. We can reconstruct the nature, scope, and consequence of a
nuclear explosion by analyzing its residue when the raw matter and even the
energy inherent in its occurrence have dissipated. Thus it is possible to
reconstruct the nature, scope, and consequence of rhetoric by analyzing
"speech" even when "speaker," "audience," "occasion," and "change"
dissipate into half-remembered history. Reconstruction *of the whole phenomenon*, it seems to me, is a *prius* to an accounting of the rhetorical, for it is
the *whole* of "speaker/speech/audience/occasion/change" which impinges on
us: to confuse rhetoric with a discourse is the same error as confounding
fallout with nuclear explosion. Traditional ideal conceptions of rhetoric not
only make it possible to equate the terms "rhetoric" and "discourse," they can
encourage such confusion by falsely suggesting an inverse relationship
between the two terms. Thus, for example, it is often said that rhetoric is a
type or genre of discourse distinct from philosophy, poetry, or scientific
discourse. As we busy ourselves trying to locate an exclusionary principle
with which generically to mark out rhetorical discourses, we too often forget
that *there is no type of discourse which cannot function as "speech" in a
material rhetoric*. If we can say that all distinguishable forms of discourse
may function rhetorically, we are thereby suggesting that rhetoric is greater
than a discourse; "rhetorical" is a quality of discourse derived from the
discourse's presence and function within the larger phenomenon "rhetoric."

The phrase "symbolic claims" is meant to be more than a synonym for
"discourse" and/or "persuasion." *Every* interactivity of society contains or
comprises a claim on some human being's belief and/or behavior. Nothing in
the environment bespeaks our free-agency; indeed, we most often mark out

our own free-will as Nietzsche described in *The Will to Power*, by listing the ways in which we may in fact constrict the free-will of others.[15] In the paradox that the proof of freedom for one is simultaneously the proof of the necessity which restrains another, there is the truth that society itself is nothing but formal interaction, a process of mutual claims upon and controls of each individual's belief and/or behavior. Rhetoric is one of the phenomena in the context of which claim and control are possible: whenever an "audience" exists, it puts claims upon and to some extent determines the belief/behavior of "speaker," and nearly simultaneously "speaker" puts claims upon and to an extent controls the belief/behavior of an "audience." "War," "police power," and "economy" are other phenomena (perhaps not entirely distinct from "rhetoric") in the context of which claim and control are possible. Rhetoric would appear to be the most common context of claim and control because it is the most comfortable context: the claims and controls are *symbolic*, the representation and consequent sublimation of painful physical claims and controls. There is in rhetoric a sense of seduction, of control which, if it is not voluntary, is at least an acquiescence wherein a human being feels accounted for in some more personal way than a gun shoved into the rib. Rhetoric, I mean to say, Parke Burgess notwithstanding, is a species of coercion.[16] And it seems important in any material theory of rhetoric to describe the phenomenon *as* a coercive agency: traditionally, we pay more attention to the *degree* of force in claiming and controlling than to the *fact* of coercion. So we see a so-called "ethical argument" differing in kind from purely physical threats associated with fascist stormtroopers. Certainly it is more comfortable and preferable; but neither the motive of the advocate, nor the means of seducing agreement, nor the resulting degree of pain change the form of using symbols, whether called "argument" or "threat," to restrict the freedom of a human being to do and to believe as he/she alone thinks fit. That which is preferable in "rhetoric" as opposed to "war" is precisely the symbolic sublimation of pain, not the lack or absence of coercion in the act of controlling behavior/belief.[17]

The wording "behavior and/or belief" is meant to recognize that there is usually a congruity of thought and action when human beings interact socially, but at the same time to suggest that symbolic control is sometimes accomplished with great indirection through manipulation of belief structures alone. Traditional conceptions of ideal "rhetoric" have been able to cope well with the connection between a specific rhetorical phenomenon and the subsequent behavior of people who played the role of "audience." Thus, for example, those critics Black calls "neo-Aristotelian" have been able to build the arguments which plausibly suggest a link between a behavior recommended in the "speech" and subsequent actualization of that behavior in reality by "audience," as when a politician asking for the votes of certain constituencies receives them. Of course, as Black suggests, one cannot be certain that there is a cause-effect relationship between requesting and getting votes: dozens of variables intervene to make such a conclusion logically dubious. Still, when "audience" ratifies their "speaker's" claim upon them by acting out recommendations in reality, there is such a strong presumption of causal effect that challenging the link on logical grounds alone seems nitpicking.[18] Black's point is more profound, however, for in his stunning critique of Chapman's "Coatesville Address" the question turns not on the behavioral power of "speech" so much as on the attitudinal power of material rhetoric exhibited over long periods of time. As I already have argued, rhetoric need not always be particular. When "speaker/audience/ occasion/change" elements are abstract, particularly in the realm of morality, the "effect" is not on any human agent particularly, but on everyone indirectly, as each of us participates in a public, shared agreement as to the normative conditions of belonging to society. Behavior is often recalcitrant, "variable in every direction" as Ortega suggests, but it is always tugged by belief, coerced into new patterns by pure doubt as to its justifiability.[19] Since behavior and belief must be perceived as congruent, the attitudinal power of rhetoric must be described—and as Black argued, traditional ideal conceptions simply cannot cope with describing fabrications of normative structures, of "public morality" and "ideology."[20]

By the phrase "allegedly in the interest of such individuals" I mean to say that every "speaker" claims to be motivated by "audience's" interest. This calls to attention the relationship between "speaker" and "audience" as "leader" to "follower." Though idealists pay lip-service to the need to adapt to audiences, and though a great deal of technical effort has been directed at formulating check-lists to use in analyzing audiences, almost no attention has been given in traditional rhetorical studies to the leader/follower relationship obvious in nearly every material rhetoric.

Idealists merely *suppose* that "speaker" is active and a leader while "audience" is reactive and the constituency of followers. Even a tiny survey of material rhetorics quickly shows that the relationship between "speakers" and "audiences" is not so clear: like a spider crawling on the polished surface of a mirror, the interpenetration of "speaker" and "audience" is so complete that only rarely can one distinguish the reality from the image. Every "audience" comes together with an interest and the expectation that "speaker" will aid in procuring that interest. And every "speaker" comes to "audience" with the desire to accomplish an otherwise impossible task by mobilizing a collective mobilizing a collective force. What we see is almost a negotiation wherein "speaker" articulates the wishes and needs of "audience," and "audience" agrees to "speaker's" leadership as a means of securing their interest. Do "speakers" lead when they, in Plato's words, "do only what they think best," not "what they will"?[21] Will "speaker" be accorded the right of leadership if "audience" does not hear an articulation of their interest? Is "speaker" merely the "voice" of "audience"? Or is "audience" like clay and so pliable that they will sacrifice even their most heart-felt interest for the sake of "speaker," their leader?

When practice is the guide, the answer to each of these questions is at one time or another "yes." And at one time or another each leader/follower relationship appears to have been productive and disastrous, whether measured by an ideal Platonic "good" or by more pragmatic "general welfare" criteria. The nature of "leadership," in other words, is so equivocal that one must think in terms of "styles of leadership" fit for "audiences" in particular circumstances. The task of a material theory of rhetoric, it seems to me, is to account for leader/follower relationships. To achieve this goal, it would seem advisable to catalogue and to study what "speakers" allege to be the interest of "audiences" in "speeches," the documentary residue or rhetoric.

The "alleged interest" of "audience" also focuses attention on one of the central concerns of ideal rhetoric, the problem of discovering and describing "motive." One need not dwell long on the topic, for Kenneth Burke has described a material alternative to both the normative and behavioral conceptions of "motive."[22] The molecular model presented in the previous section, however, invites more general attention to "motive" than Burke or his predecessors intended: with the exception of a few arguments taken up tangentially by Burke, "motive" has been characterized less as a discrete category of experience than as a property of "speakers." Thus, for example, the interest and intention which "speaker" brings to "audience" is conceived as a motive which is more or less reprehensible as it approaches or ignores the general welfare allegedly present in the "speaker/audience" relationship. In arguing that the concept "motive" is in fact a short-hand term for "situation," Burke called attention to the error of confusing an agent's "purpose" with his/her "motive," the latter being a product not just of intent, but also of interactivity with other agents. Burke seems correct that a complete description of "motive" would be an elaboration of "occasion." But as "motive" is an abbreviation for "occasion," so one might claim that "speech" is an abbreviation of "motive" ("speech," of course, understood as part of material rhetoric and not as a synonym for "discourse"): as Wallace suggested, the interest of both "speaker/audience" exists in "speech" as the "good reasons" which warrant accepting "speaker's" recommendations.[23] Such "good reasons" are not identical to "speaker's" intentions and purposes because they must be persuasive, adapted to "audience" and made to appear interested only in the general welfare. Insofar as "speaker" frames "good reasons" to *move* "audience" toward a position consistent with but not wholly the same as their interest, such "good reasons" are also apart from "audience."

The interest of "audience" as portrayed in "speech," therefore, is a record of *interactive motive*, of "speaker/audience" interests mutually skewed for the purpose of accommodating each other. Interactive motives are a property of neither "speaker/audience" but rather a discrete category of experience. Significantly, as Wallace suggested, such motives are empirically accessible in the "speech" which survives rhetoric as residue of the phenomenon. Though the *intent* of "speaker" remains hidden in his/her psyche, to be guessed at with the help of *a priori* paradigms, *interactive motives* are available and warrantable by the evidence of "speech." Further, because *public* behaviors and beliefs can be guided *only* by interactive motives, the private interest of any "speaker" seems all but irrelevant to rhetoric—interactive motives govern *collective* beliefs whether "speaker" be Pope John Paul or the Ayatollah Khomeini.

The potential of a material theory of rhetoric is exposed in the suggestion that rhetoric implies "the strong presumption that such claims will result in meaningful change." As foreshadowed in the previous discussion of levels of rhetorical experience, this phrase is not intended to say that "speech" has "effects." The whole problem of "effect" seems picayune when one realizes that what actually happens as a result of "speech" is less important than the fact that every "speech" is a miniature predictive model of the "changes" which it recommends. Every "speaker," in other words, creates a picture of the world in the suggestion that "audience" perceives reality through the terms and with the resources of "speech." That world is a distorted structure of facts and inferences selected not for their reliable representation of the objective world, but rather for their salience to the satisfaction of intersubjective desires.

Insofar as "speaker/audience" have the power collectively to affect their world, "speech," regardless of its ultimate effects, is always a contingent model of (1) the existing environment essentialized into sets of salient facts; (2) estimates of activity sufficient to change essential facts; and (3) a predicted environment altered by intersubjective activity. Any who have worked with models of social change understand the difficulty of finding even an explanatory instrument, never mind the dream of prediction.[24] Yet in the work-a-day world we conduct a continual deliberation based on our ability to model the environment and to predict the consequences of changing it. How are such models constructed? What does "change" mean in the context of these models? How in actual material rhetorics do "speaker/audience/occasion" seem related to "change"? These questions arise regardless of the actual effects of "speech." But the possibility that "speech" is indeed an effective agency of "change" makes the model of "change" sketched in "speech" *theoretically* powerful, for, as I have argued elsewhere, an "audience" (or in its most reified sense a "People") has the capacity to create "change" by fiat of collective belief and behavior.[25]

The "speech" as theory, in other words, is distinct from ordinary theory in that those who react to it have the power to *make* it "true" if it happens to be technically (that is, logically or empirically) "wrong." We see, for example, the long line of political theorists who argued the impossibility of "democracy," on sound and reasonable principles, literally made "wrong" in their predictions by the collective belief and behavior of Anglo-Americans. Reading "speech" as if it were the favored theory of "change" at the moment of its utterance, I believe, could yield powerful descriptions and explanations of social process. Even predictions are possible in either or both of two circumstances: (1) if analysis of several rhetorics over long periods of time seems to reveal a high degree of redundance in the models of "change" they contain, and if it seems that events did alter the world in the same direction recommended by "speech," we would have some reason to characterize the redundant model as potentially predictive of "change" in the future; (2) further, if we can find evidence to prove claims of a contemporary "speech's" effectiveness, it is not improbable that a gambler's prediction of the shape of "change" might be verified. Of course such predictions could be reliable only by the standards of critical social science, not by the more rigid criteria of academic positivism.[26]

The definition just elaborated cuts across so many issues, real and imagined, and there are therefore so many lines of refutation to be adduced against it, that I am obliged to leave it as a caveat for those who might see less heresy than I intend: conceiving "rhetoric" as a material phenomenon alters the meaning of all rhetorical theory, for it puts upon a theorist the requirement that he/she begin with a body of data and not with a corpus of philosophical speculations and prescriptions.

Conclusion

Today, the typical course in rhetorical theory consists of the analysis, not of public address texts, but of philosophical manuals of instruction. Most of those manuals at least purport to be constructed from observations of "speaker/speech/audience/occasion/change" interactions—so if one wished to recover theoretical descriptions, explanations, and postdictions of the function of communication in historical societies, ancient treatises about rhetoric would be useful documents. The problem is not in traditional books about rhetoric, therefore, but in our reading and use of the classics. Instead of communicative interactions, most rhetoricians have seen a creative process, "invention/disposition/style/memory/delivery." Rather than ask what Aristotle *saw* in ancient Greece, we have concerned ourselves with what Aristotle *said* in Greek. It is good to use Aristotle in the same spirit and for the same reasons one would use Copernicus' *Heavenly Spheres* or Redi's theory of spontaneous generation. To say upon reading Aristotle's *Rhetoric* that one is "studying rhetoric," however, is to commit the most egregious of errors, for one is studying an honorable and ancient treatise *about* rhetoric, not *the thing itself.* A study of rhetoric, I have suggested, is predominantly a study of practice, and a "rhetorical theory" should be related to practice as generalization to data, not as prescription to performance. In this view, rhetoric is not an "art," nor it is a "body of principles"—it is a thing, a material artifact of human interaction.

I have approached my thesis conceptually, first constructing a molecular model of material rhetorics, then offering a formal definition of rhetoric-as-object, because I believe that a fundamental alteration of perspective is necessary to counterbalance the overwhelming influence of idealism in rhetorical theory. The problem Black exposed in his critique of the methods popular among rhetorical critics still bothers rhetorical theorists, biasing and inhibiting the development of grounded theories of rhetoric. To survey practice while counting enthymemes, acknowledging that people arrive at conclusions through thought, feeling, and intimidation, all in the context of writing formulary biographical prose—this is an exercise in futility which glorifies the obvious. Exactly the same mind-set is involved in studying Juan de Vives or Hugh Blair with the intention of understanding "rhetoric" when we know of material rhetorics in the context of which a set of "speakers" such as Burke, Franklin, Jefferson, Chatham, Adams, Fox, Madison, and Erskine acted in and on the real world.

If history matters at all to rhetorical theory, and I am convinced that it does, it is material history, not the history of ideas. For centuries those enamored of links in the great chain of being have read each other: bureaucratic thinkers from Aristotle to Bacon to Howell have thought it reasonable, usually on purely normative grounds, to restrict the "office" of rhetoric. If we were dealing with an Idea, reassignment of topics and thoughts might make as much sense as the shuffling of secretaries and clerks in business offices.

But we are not. Human thought cannot be bureaucratized unless there are "offices" corresponding to material realities. The sun does not go away by assigning or reassigning thought about it to the "office" of chemistry rather than physics—and wherever topics relating to "sun" are pursued, thought must be controlled *by the sun* rather than by administrative procedures in the "office" of thinking. Similarly, if we think to purify argument of non-rational passions by reassigning it from the "office" of rhetoric to that of ethics or logic, the real rhetorics which inspired us to investigate argumentation in the first place do not go away. Should we define rhetoric as an art or as a genre of literature or as a body of principles, we distort our own sociality, for we divert attention from the coercive power of the symbols which unite society and focus instead on the tricks of pretty language or on the gamesmanship of forensic and deliberative competition. These narrow notions of "rhetoric" permit no more than a debunking of practice—saying what it is *not*; and they almost preclude real understanding of practice—saying and appreciating what it *is*.

Notes

This essay, still imperfect after ten years' revision, began in Douglas Ehninger's passing curiosity as to what a "material" pre-Socratic or neo-Marxian theory of rhetoric might look like. Perhaps this adumbration gives some notion short of caricature.

1.   José Ortega y Gasset, *Man and People*, trans. Willard R. Trask (New York: W. W. Norton, 1957), 11–16.

2.   See, e.g., Lloyd F. Bitzer, "The Rhetorical Situation," *Philosophy & Rhetoric* 1 (1968): 1–14.

3.   Howell's "history of" eighteenth-century British logic and rhetoric, for example, is so committed to the primacy of textbooks on composition that he takes Boulton to task for failing to consider that the fashionable recipes for speech-making actually established criteria for public debate over the French Revolution: "James T. Boulton discusses Priestley's contribution to the debate in Britain between 1790 and 1793 over the French Revolution. . . . But Mr. Boulton does not recognize that the rhetorical theories of that era, and particularly Priestley's *Lectures on Oratory*, are important to the modern critic in defining the standards which the participants in that debate themselves observed." In my reading, there is not a single British politician or orator between 1761 and 1845 who appears to have adhered to or explicitly recognized a "standard for participation in debate" even remotely resembling the "rhetorical theories of that era." If one wished to correlate Priestley's theory and practice of rhetoric, the useful theoretical treatise is his *Lectures on History and General Policy* (1764), not his *Lectures on Oratory*. See Wilbur Samuel Howell, *Eighteenth-Century British Logic and Rhetoric* (Princeton, NJ: Princeton University Press, 1971), 647n536; and Joseph Priestley, *Lectures on History and General Policy*, 3rd. ed. (1764; Dublin: Luke White and P. Byrne, 1791), esp. 23–87, 228–80; Priestley, *A Course of Lectures on Oratory and Criticism*, ed. Vincent M. Bevilacqua and Richard Murphy (1777; repr., Carbondale: Southern Illinois University Press, 1965).
     Among those committed to a *philosophy of rhetoric*, Perelman is perhaps the most

sensitive to actual practice—he consistently, impressively illustrates principles of "the new rhetoric" by citing examples from the literature of public address. But they appear to be *nothing more* than examples, bits and pieces carefully ornamenting metaethical speculation, snippets from "great speeches"—emphatically *not* from ordinary persuasive discourse—which illustrate the mechanics of practical reason. So, for example, Perelman examines a relationship between social inertia and social change, noting that an advocate of change has the more imposing task. He makes the point by an analogy between physics and human consciousness, by referring to a quip by Jean Paulhan, by persuasively defining "change," by asserting the commonality of appeals to inertia, and finally, at long last, by quoting two sentences from a speech by William Pitt. Perelman's new rhetoric has no closer contact with actual rhetoric than metaphysics with social science, for he has not so much rediscovered rhetoric as he has redefined philosophy along more reasonable lines. As Eco suggests, "the so-called 'new rhetoric' (Perelman, 1958) has definitely reduced apodictic discourses to axiomatical systems alone, and has listed all other types of discourse (from philosophy to politics or theology) under the rhetorical heading." See Chaïm Perelman and L. Olbrechts-Tyteca, *The New Rhetoric*, trans. John Wilkinson and Purcell Weaver (South Bend, IN: University of Notre Dame Press, 1969), esp. 104–6; and Umberto Eco, *A Theory of Semiotics* (Bloomington: Indiana University Press, 1976), 277.

4. Donald C. Bryant, *Rhetorical Dimensions in Criticism* (Baton Rouge: Louisiana State University Press, 1973), 3–4.

5. Maurice Natanson, "The Limits of Rhetoric," *Quarterly Journal of Speech* 41 (1955): 133–39.

6. Karl Marx and Frederick Engels, *The German Ideology* (1845–46), in Karl Marx and Frederick Engels, *Collected Works*, 9 + vols. (Moscow: Progress Publishers, 1976), V, 36–7.

7. See, e.g., Walter M. Carleton, "What Is Rhetorical Knowledge? A Response to Farrell—and More," *Quarterly Journal of Speech* 64 (1978): 313–28.

8. Though it is a feeble effort at difficult synthesis, see, e.g., Rosalind Coward and John Ellis, *Language and Materialism* (London: Routledge & Kegan Paul, 1977).

9. For an excellent synthesis of the current state of thinking on such subjects and others, see Anthony Giddens, *Central Problems in Social Theory: Action, Structure and Contradiction in Social Analysis* (Berkeley: University of California Press, 1979).

10. See Fredric Jameson, *The Prison-House of Language* (Princeton, NJ: Princeton University Press, 1972); John R. Lyne, "C. S. Peirce on Rhetoric and Communication" (PhD diss., University of Wisconsin-Madison, 1978); and Michael J. Hyde and Craig R. Smith, "Hermeneutics and Rhetoric: A Seen but Unobserved Relationship," *Quarterly Journal of Speech* 65 (1979): 347–63.

11. Cf. Neil J. Smelser, *Theory of Collective Behavior* (New York: Free Press, 1962), esp. 2–21; and Michael Calvin McGee, "Social Movement: Phenomenon or Meaning?" *Central States Speech Journal* 31 (1980): 233–44. Also, cf. A. O. Lovejoy, *The Great Chain of Being* (Cambridge, MA: Harvard University Press, 1936); A. O. Lovejoy, "Reflections on the History of Ideas," *Journal of the History of Ideas* 1 (1940): 3–23; and Michel Foucault, *The Archaeology of Knowledge*, trans. Alan M. Sheridan-Smith (1969; Eng. trans., New York: Harper Colophon, 1972).

12. Bitzer, "Rhetorical Situation," 7–8.

13. Augustine, *On Christian Doctrine*, trans. J. F. Shaw, in *Great Books of the Western World*, ed. Robert M. Hutchins (Chicago: Encyclopedia Britannica, 1952), XVIII: 4.7.5–

9; 4.7.14; and 4.7.21.

14. Foucault, *Archaeology of Knowledge*, 215–37.

15. Friedrich Nietzsche, *The Will to Power*, trans. Walter Kaufmann and R. J. Hollingdale (New York: Vintage Books, 1968), 382–418.

16. Parke G. Burgess, "Crisis Rhetoric: Coercion vs. Force," *Quarterly Journal of Speech* 59 (1973): 61–73.

17. I recognize that I use the terms "freedom" and "constraint" eccentrically. Most Anglo-Americans who take up the topic of coercion see it as a direct opposite of freedom, much as Arendt acts as an ideologue in arguing for a communications concept of "power" antithetical to totalitarian employment of force and sheer terror. I have little quarrel with the conclusions of such arguments, though for me it is impossible to know reflexively whether or not my assent is ideologically conditioned by participation in Anglo-American culture. It seems to me that ideological conceptions of freedom as the opposite of force are clearly derivative from a dialectical opposition between unconstrained action and constrained action. Freedom, for most of us, is usually and erroneously associated with lack of constraint. In fact, I believe, to live in society is to experience a complex of constraints. "Pure freedom" as unconstrained action is a phantom, a vision made real only by intersubjective agreement or by ideological conditioning. The huge majority of us, from the time we are toilet trained if not before, develop a habit of acquiescence inconsistent with the idea of rational assent. We are pulled fighting and screaming into the world of civilized social animals, resenting and resisting laws and rules of all sorts. More and less preferable methods are used to overcome our resistance and resentment: we are paddled, bullied, caged, tied, persuaded, and threatened until we agree to behave "like a grown-up." Historically and presently, governments treat the general citizenry as adolescents, using all the tools of manipulation and indoctrination. If television commercials are an indication, even business corporations increasingly treat the people as willful children. Adults, however, are strong enough, particularly in groups, to offer more effective resistance than can toddlers to parents. So those with economic, political, or military power paddle with reluctance, preferring instead to persuade. Rhetoric in their hands is an instrument of coercion or constraint, a symbolic placebo replacing bayonets and the company store as a matter of pragmatic efficiency. Rhetoric, I conclude, is clearly *preferable* to more violent and ruthless means of social control; but it is, in its function, *distinct* from that which it sublimates only by measure of the degree of its force. See Hannah Arendt, "Lying in Politics," in *Crises of the Republic* (New York: Viking, 1972), 1–47; and Jürgen Habermas, "Hannah Arendt's Communications Concept of Power," *Social Research* 44 (1977): 3–24.

18. Edwin Black, *Rhetorical Criticism: A Study in Method* (1965; repr., Madison: University of Wisconsin Press, 1978), 27–90.

19. José Ortega y Gasset, *History as a System*, trans. Helene Weyl (New York: W. W. Norton, 1961), 199–216.

20. Black, *Rhetorical Criticism*, 132–47.

21. Plato, *Gorgias*, in *The Dialogues of Plato*, ed. and trans. Benjamin Jowett (New York: Random House, 1937), I:466B.

22. Kenneth Burke, *Permanence and Change: An Anatomy of Purpose*, 2nd ed. rev. (1954; repr., Indianapolis, IN: Bobbs-Merrill, 1965); Kenneth Burke, *A Grammar of Motives* (New York: Prentice-Hall, 1945); Kenneth Burke, *A Rhetoric of Motives* (New York: Prentice-Hall, 1950).

23. Karl R. Wallace, "The Substance of Rhetoric: Good Reasons," *Quarterly Journal of*

Speech 49 (1963): 239–49.

24. See Herbert W. Simons, Elizabeth Mechling, and Howard N. Schreier, "Mobilizing for Collective Action from the Bottom Up: The Rhetoric of Social Movements" (unpublished manuscript, Temple University, n.d.), 48–106, forthcoming in Carroll C. Arnold and John Waite Bowers, eds., *Handbook of Rhetorical and Communication Theory.*

25. Michael Calvin McGee, "In Search of 'The People': A Rhetorical Alternative," *Quarterly Journal of Speech* 61 (1975): 235–49.

26. See Giddens, *Central Problems*, 234–59.

CHAPTER 2

Rhetorical Materialism: The Rhetorical Subject and the General Intellect

Ronald Walter Greene, University of Minnesota

> Materialism is the affirmation of life, without either theoretical mystification or political authority. Materialism is always revolutionary.
> Antonio Negri, *Negri on Negri: Conversations with Anne Durourmentelle*

The revolutionary character of materialism did not impress the editors of the *Encyclopedia of Rhetoric*.[1] There is no entry for materialism, nor its many permutations: dialectical, structural, cultural, social, and/or physical materialism. The *Encyclopedia of Rhetoric* is silent as to whether a rhetorical materialism or a material rhetoric exists and, if it exists, whether it might be or should be old or new, one or another, classical or modern, postmodern or poststructuralist. However, one does find many flowers with materialist roots: the critical tradition of communication (Robert Craig), constitutive rhetoric (Maurice Charland), critical rhetoric (Raymie McKerrow), rhetoric and power (Andrew King), and the ideograph (Michael Calvin McGee).[2] As this associational list suggests, any materialist rhetoric would seem to manifest itself as a politically engaged rhetorical criticism of the strong and a commitment to empower the weak. While the proliferation of such a politically engaged rhetorical stance would support Carole Blair's contention that "to write rhetorical criticism from within a perspective of materialism is no longer unique," the *Encyclopedia of Rhetoric* would seem to relegate materialism to the family tree of modern and critical influences on contemporary rhetorical criticism.[3] As such, the concept of materialism is all too often submerged by the interpretive function of criticism that risks displacing and erasing materialism's revolutionary affirmation of life.

Due to "the critical disturbances of the late 1980s and 1990s," disturbances the *Encyclopedia of Rhetoric* duly notes, at least three materialist stances emerged in rhetorical studies: "a traditional one that insists upon considering the material conditions of discourse, another that focuses upon the lived-in body as a condition and consequence of rhetoric, and still another that understands rhetoric as itself material."[4] As Blair notes, a critic might embrace all three stances, but, on the theoretical level, each of the three stances might just as likely challenge one another as find common ground.[5] Moreover, the default perspective of many rhetorical critics remains the view that the material dimensions of rhetoric are locatable in some more primordial context or condition (capitalism, patriarchy, racism) that serves to explain the ideological motive lurking behind public address. However, a more significant disciplinary trend is the multiplication of the forms by which to account for rhetoric's materiality. As such, a materialist heterodoxy has taken flight: genetic models, everyday life, judgment, institutions, pedagogy, technologies, apparatuses, urban space, bodies, media, labor, and physical objects have all been authorized as different sites for exploring the material character of rhetoric.[6] Let a thousand flowers bloom!

I will resist the temptation to argue that with flowers come weeds. Instead, this chapter will affirm the value of materialism by advocating the importance of the general intellect (social knowledge) for imagining the revolutionary politics and critical practice of rhetorical materialism. If, as James Jasinski argues, the best rhetorical criticism is conceptually oriented criticism, perhaps a conceptually oriented materialist theory is also in order.[7] This chapter argues that a rhetorical materialism should be more committed to revising "central terms within the rhetorical tradition."[8] Perhaps more unsettling, a rhetorical materialism should move beyond the taken-for-granted terms of the rhetorical tradition and commit itself to the invention of new concepts that perform untimely interventions into the marrow of the rhetorical tradition. Unfortunately, what we might rightfully call the material turn in rhetorical studies, a turn I find invaluable, often seems satisfied with expanding the object domain available to rhetorical criticism. In contrast, this chapter argues that it will be necessary to place limits on an ever-expanding notion of rhetorical subjectivity authorized by the globalization of the object domain. Thus, a materialist rhetoric should avoid rediscovering a generalized rhetoricality inherent in cultural forms and objects. Instead, we should pay closer attention to the emergence of a more concrete rhetorical subject, a subject that speaks and is spoken to, and the different techniques and technologies organized to transform individuals into a communicating subject.[9] As such, I argue that the rhetorical subject should be approached less as an effect of a constitutive process of a generalized rhetoricality and more from within a specific apparatus of production.

Moreover, the history of the rhetorical subject's production draws our attention to how its problematization partakes in regimes of cultural, economic, and political value. In other words, the invention of the rhetorical subject gestures toward its production while its problematization gestures toward its governance. By understanding the rhetorical subject as immanent to the articulation of regimes of production and government, I will conclude by discussing how the rhetorical subject generates value through the immaterial labor of producing and appropriating the general intellect. As such, the revolutionary potential of the rhetorical subject is materialized in the antagonism and struggle over the value of the general intellect. Consequently, at the conceptual level, this essay argues that a materialist rhetoric should, first and foremost, be concerned with locating rhetorical practice and subjectivity within a material ontology of production. Moreover, at the level of critical practice, this essay will argue for an articulation model for assessing the productivity of rhetorical practices in opposition to the interpretive function of rhetorical criticism.

The Limits of Rhetorical Subjectivity

This chapter is interested in unpacking the claim that rhetoric is material by beginning with the production of subjectivity. To do so requires an investigation into the ideological. One of the central contributions of Louis Althusser was his insistence that ideology be conceptualized as a mode of production that constitutes "concrete individuals as subjects."[10] Althusser describes the material process of this subjectification in the following way: "[T]he subject acts insofar as he [or she] is acted by the following system (set out in order of its real determination): ideology existing in a material ideological apparatus, prescribing material practices governed by a material ritual, which practices exist in the material actions of a subject acting in all consciousness according to his belief."[11] Ideology is not so much an idea or set of ideas that make up a worldview, nor is ideology merely a "superstructural" effect of an economic mode of production. Ideology is a mode of production with its own (relatively) autonomous social practices. From such a perspective, ideology is not the interest lurking behind the back of the speaker or the critic, but a terrain and practice of turning individuals into subjects of a particular kind. Famously, Althusser leaves unanswered the differences between the varied modalities of materiality (actions, practices, rituals, and apparatuses) involved in the making of a subject. Nonetheless, we are left with the provocative possibility that a social formation is not so much the dialectical interaction between an economic base and a cultural superstructure (or a context and text, to use a rhetorical idiom) but the uneven configuration of different levels of production—levels of production that are themselves internally different across space and time. With an eye toward the accounting for the character of a social totality, the critical task according to Stuart Hall is to reveal how a social formation comes together as a "structure of dominance" by accounting for the articulation of different levels of production (ideological, political, economic).[12] However, Althusser's description of ideology as a practice that reproduces the conditions of production left in its wake a functionalist language; that is, in the last instance, ideology reproduces the relations of domination that remake and refresh the capitalist mode of production. In other words, the fear that the ideological prevents the production of an oppositional subject, a fear Joshua Gunn and Shaun Treat call "the zombie complex," has made it difficult to appreciate the material consequences of Althusser's intervention.[13]

Where might we find the rhetorical in such a material theory of ideology? Here Althusser's definition of ideology as a "'representation' of the imaginary relationship of individuals to their real conditions of existence" takes center stage.[14] The use of the imaginary, in this definition, gestures toward Althusser's encounter with Lacan and the importance of the unconscious as the ground of ideological production. In kind, the Lacanian formulation that the unconscious is structured like a language authorized the reconceptualization of the productive capacity of ideology in terms of signifying processes and discursive practices.[15] Thus, ideology describes how the "means of representation" partake in a general process of subjectivity, a process understood in terms of the structural logic of language. Increasingly, this emphasis on language came to be understood in terms of how a subject comes into being through its identification with an "other." In this process of identification, the psychic life of the individual and the social formation are linked together by the recognition of the symbolic order.

The concept that links the general process of ideological subjectification to particular discursive practices is interpellation. Interpellation describes the moment an individual recognizes him- or herself as the one addressed by a discursive practice. For example, Maurice Charland argues that in the *White Paper* of the *Parti Québécois*, the "rhetoric of interpellation" embeds a mode of address that hails an audience as (1) a collective subject, (2) a transhistorical subject, and (3) one free to choose.[16] From this perspective, interpellation describes a speech act, but does so with the presumption of successfully "turning" a reader/audience. Yet, as Judith Butler argues, interpellations do fail; one does not always recognize oneself as the one addressed by the speech act. Moreover, for Butler, the constitutive rhetoric of interpellation should not be associated with a subject recognizing itself in response to the creative power of a sovereign voice.[17] Interpellation cannot be reduced to a particular moment of enunciation, a particular speech act situated in time and place. Interpellation is better conceptualized as the cumulative effect of a process of (re)iteration and citationality.

Unfortunately, the tendency of the case-study approach in rhetorical criticism to "textualize" the case as a situated practice is likely to limit the understanding of interpellation to a moment of enunciation. While the concept of interpellation reveals how the rhetorical, both as a situated practice of persuasion and as a general process inherent to all discourses, takes on its material status by addressing subjects, it becomes too easy to confuse a materialist theory of subjectivity with an uncritical social constructionism. More specifically, we tend to replace a theoretical tradition that might be useful in formulating a rhetorical materialism with an emphasis on constitutive rhetoric, a substitution that highlights the text as a "sovereign voice."

To embed the material dimension of rhetoric into a generalized constitutive process is to displace the Althusserian configuration of the social as an articulation of different levels or structures of production. In other words, a "constitutive rhetoric" has the potential to materialize rhetoric at the expense of "dematerializing" textuality from any process of production. Moreover, the modalities of ideological materiality (actions, practices, apparatuses, and rituals) are increasingly forced to appear as texts for rhetorical studies to perform its critical interpretation. Thus, to speak of rhetorical materialism as the constitutive power of a speech act or to translate the material modalities of ideological subjectification into a generalized process of textuality is to harness rhetorical materialism to an interpretive project that unpacks a cultural form for what it constitutes, hides, and/or cannot contain about the nature of ideological power. Even when rhetorical scholars are armored with the poststructuralist lessons provided by Butler's insistence on interpellation as repetitive citationality immanent within an embodied praxis, our critical hermeneutics risks being limited to a general appreciation of how language and communication partake in the constitution of meaning. At its best, a constitutive rhetoric provides the foundation for approaching a text as an active intervention that reorganizes and/or reiterates a discursive field. However, reconfiguring the text/context relationship as one between a text and a discursive field still holds a person hostage to the text as a site of utterance and a critical act that demands the text speak about power. Moreover, the critical move toward a rhetorical understanding of subjectivity (a process more often understood as the cultural turn) tends to direct the interpretive gaze toward the internal working of a text, for example, the stylistic tokens that bring forth an ideal audience (or persona). Yet, how social agents are taught, formally or informally, to interpret texts is made invisible to a rhetorical theory of subjectivity that imagines the subject as an effect of a speech act.

From an Althusserian starting point, one might approach the representational character of public address as one material modality in the ideological
production of subjectivity. From a less Marxist but more semi-
otic/psychoanalytic theory of subjectivity, a critic might attend to how a subject comes into being through his or her insertion into the symbolic order of
language. From a semiotic starting point, the rhetorical is no longer one cultural practice among others, but a more general process that describes how all
practices form subjects of a particular kind. Yet, what began as a Marxist
concern about ideological subjectification and the articulation of different
levels of production has been increasingly hijacked to an investigation into a
more general process of rhetoricality.[18] What this means for the material dimensions of rhetoric is that materiality begins to appear as a common topic
for a critical hermeneutics that either explains the limit on the constitutive
force of a speech act (more often than not the body and/or structural forms of
power) and/or expands the cultural forms that a generalized rhetoricality infuses with meaning and power (for example, sculpture and quilts). If the
former, we have simply returned to a stasis point we thought we left behind:
a dual ontology that places materiality outside the rhetorical. If the latter, the
material character of rhetoric is captured by a forty-year disciplinary drive to
expand the object domain by which a critic can uncover a general process of
rhetoricality.[19] While the disciplinary drive to expand the object domain offers a way to bypass the limitations associated with traditional notions of rhetorical agency associated with white, masculine, and elite forms of public
address, the refiguration of the material and the rhetorical as two different
ontological planes dooms a materialist approach to a never-ending dialectical
criticism moving between one plane and another. Such a dialectical criticism
remains open to the charge of being neither rhetorical nor material enough
and leaves unexamined how that interpretive gap between ontological planes
emerged in the first place. In other words, "minding the gap" between the
rhetorical and the material becomes a technology for producing "well-
tempered" subjects."[20] To advance a material rhetoric to expand the object
domain risks the repetition of discovering a general process of rhetoricality
as the transcendental *telos* of our rhetorical criticism while ignoring how the
teaching and learning of such a cultural hermeneutics functions as a material
practice of subjectification. What I find troubling is how the substitution of a
general constitutive process (constitutive rhetoric) becomes a substitute for a
material theory of rhetoric, a situation that often gets bogged down into a
debate over the "limits" of the discursive plane while hiding the material history of rhetorical criticism from investigation.

Following the trajectory outlined in this section, I would contend that a material rhetoric has increasingly been deployed to describe how a general process of rhetoricality appears in different material forms (media, bodies, places, buildings, discourse) and how those material forms offer themselves for (critical) interrogation. The recognition of a plurality of material forms rescues a material rhetoric from a dual ontology. However, all too often, what begins as a material rhetoric (a study of the rhetoricity of material modalities) reproduces a dialectical criticism in which the discursive dynamic is evaluated in terms of its success to overcome a pre-existent context.[21] In contrast, I want to suggest that a materialist rhetoric (or rhetorical materialism) might more fruitfully describe how the persuasive, deliberative, educational, technological, and/or aesthetic dimensions of communication are integral to the articulation of regimes of value. As such, a rhetorical materialism should partake in a materialist ontology that configures the rhetorical subject as a particular kind of being invented by and for specific apparatuses of production.

Like a material rhetoric, rhetorical materialism understands the rhetorical as material; that is, it rejects a dualist ontology that separates speech from materiality. A materialist rhetoric does so by positing materiality as an immanent process of production in which rhetoric and communication are integral elements of any mode of production. However, we will need to abandon an understanding of rhetorical subjectivity as a generalized ideological effect of discursive and signifying processes. In other words, we need to place limits on rhetorical subjectivity as a general consequence of how language constitutes subjectivity. In turn, we need a more specific and concrete concept of the rhetorical subject. As a beginning, I suggest that a rhetorical subject refers to a subject that speaks and is spoken to. The history of being able to claim the "right" to speak and be spoken to is a story of cultural value and political struggle. The question that should guide rhetorical scholars concerning the production of subjectivity is how concrete individuals come to understand themselves as subjects who communicate rhetorically. As such, the rhetorical subject has a specific history, whose value has been subject to intense problematization, beginning with Plato, and one that requires a set of institutions, techniques, rituals, and knowledge to inculcate in the subject the requisite "rhetorical sensitivity."[22] Rhetorical subjectivity, therefore, should not be approached as any form of subjectivity that appears as a "meaning effect" and/or psychological effect of discursive processes inherent to "texts," but a specific kind of subjectivity ethically, politically, economically, and culturally produced and valued for the work it can and cannot accomplish. Thus, a rhetorical materialism first and foremost should be committed to addressing how the production and value of the rhetorical subject informs the articulation of political, cultural, and economic modes of production.

Governing the Rhetorical Subject

As I am writing this chapter, eight years removed from the publication of "Another Materialist Rhetoric," I find myself struggling with the problem of where this chapter sits in relationship to that first essay. One temptation is to view "Another Materialist Rhetoric" as the beginning of an argument and this chapter as something approaching a middle (optimistically) that will, in the future, be brought to a conclusion. The "rhetoric of continuity" would seem to demand that I do the impossible: to avoid those discontinuities in style and argument that appear between texts and within texts.[23] Of course, a rhetoric of continuity betrays my own desire to keep the first essay alive, to maintain its fleeting value. My contribution to the material problematic began with the latter Foucault's emphasis on the art of governance.[24] Specifically, my argument was to rethink the materiality of rhetoric as a "technology of deliberation" that informed governmental judgments to remake reality. Four key points are worth returning to: (1) a move from the semiotic to the technological, (2) the importance of institutions, (3) a critical interest in the organization of a governing apparatus, and (4) the importance of articulation as a methodological commitment. To explore each of these points, this section will turn to the production and articulation of the rhetorical subject.

If we begin with Althusser and emphasize the materiality of subjectification as the historical transformation of a concrete individual into a subject, then a Foucauldian approach to this process would emphasize the governmental dynamics of subjectification. As Nikolas Rose puts it, "[s]ubjectification is not to be understood by locating it in a universe of meaning or an interactional context of narratives, but in a complex of apparatuses, practices, machinations, and assemblages within which human being has been fabricated, and which presuppose and enjoin particular relations with ourselves."[25] From such a perspective, the ontological privilege given to language, and by implication, the rhetorical, must be given up for a more modest understanding of how the rhetorical subject might exist as one particular mode of subjectification. To be sure, there are many different ways the rhetorical subject might appear (deliberative citizen, orator-statesman, salesperson, audience, voter, consumer), but each of these forms requires a particular articulation of the rhetorical subject in specific political, cultural, or economic directions. It is the historical articulation of the rhetorical subject to different ontological forms that generates disagreement about its value. However, to focus our attention on what the specific character of a

rhetorical subject might be, Richard Lanham's ontological distinction between *homo serious* and *homo rhetoricus* provides a useful point of departure. For Lanham,

> [r]hetorical man is an actor; his reality public, dramatic. His sense of identity, his
> self, depends on the reassurance of daily histrionic reenactment. He is thus centered
> in time and concrete local event. The lowest common denominator of his life is a so-
> cial situation. And his motivations must be characteristically ludic, agonistic. He
> thinks first of winning, of mastering the rules the current game enforces. He assumes
> a natural agility in changing orientations. He hits the street already street-wise. From
> birth, almost, he has dwelt not in a single value-structure but in several. He is thus
> committed to no single construction of the world; much rather, to prevailing in the
> game at hand. He makes an unlikely zealot. Nor is conceptual creativity, invention
> of a fresh paradigm, demanded of him. He accepts the present paradigm and ex-
> plores its resources. Rhetorical man is trained not to discover reality but to manipu-
> late it. Reality is what is accepted as reality, what is useful.[26]

Lanham discovers *homo rhetoricus* to be an active figure underwriting any
understanding of the European Renaissance and, if we are to take his pro-
nouns literally, a gendered subject, i.e., a man. *Homo rhetoricus* has origins
in the Sophists of Athenian antiquity, and one might find its contemporary
manifestation today in the advertising executive or the political campaign
manager, even if he is often a she. To be sure, Lanham's rhetorical subject
would not satisfy many serious scholars, but what Lanham demonstrates is
the way an empty figure (the rhetorical subject) begins to take on a set of
characteristics and dispositions (content). Any disagreement over the character or proper disposition of the rhetorical subject, and how the rhetorical subject works to abstract or particularize the bodies that might occupy the
subject position, points to the history of its problematization, a history that
betrays any ontological priority to the rhetorical by pointing to the need to
fabricate, mold, and transform the rhetorical subject in particular directions.
It is the desire to fabricate the rhetorical subject that points to the technological dimensions of rhetoric—that is, how the rhetorical techniques and technologies manufacture a rhetorical subject.

   The first point to emphasize about a Foucauldian approach to subjectification is a shift from the semiotic to the technological dimensions of rhetoric.
From such a perspective, the semiotic does not go away as much as it is refigured as one of rhetoric's technological products. Thus, if we begin with
Foucault's distinction between four types of technologies (technologies of
production, technologies of sign systems, technologies of power, and technologies of the self), the rhetorical subject, offered by Lanham, has a particular relationship to sign systems: it is fluid, playful, antagonistic, and

flexible.[27] Yet, the rhetorical subject is not a naturally occurring being in the world; it must be cultivated. In other words, a rhetorical subject may live his or her life utilizing sign systems, but this requires training or pedagogy. Thus, rhetoric can move from its "typical" location within the terrain of meaning to appear as a technology of the self, using communication and other techniques, to help individuals develop relationships with themselves, as rhetorical subjects. For better or worse, the existence of the public speaking class is a rather shaky technology that produces different techniques (persuasive speeches, after dinner speeches, etc.) to instill in a student a sense of being a rhetorical subject. So, too, would a rhetorical criticism class or a class in the history of public address. Moreover, rhetoric becomes a technology of power when its techniques and technologies are used to create objects for persuasion, a target population, to be transformed through the act of persuasion. This was the primary way I imagined rhetoric working as a technology of deliberation: through a host of multiple discursive genres, particular populations, behaviors, and situations would become visible for the purpose of intervention and calibration. From this perspective, controversy is to be expected, and the rhetorical character of that controversy is a crucial element of any governmental intervention. However, if we were to stay closer to the rhetorical as a specific subject, then technologies of power would focus on how ways of speaking become objects of concern and how certain ways of communicating become active in submitting individuals to certain ends. For example, recent attempts to use "entertainment-education" to persuade women and men, mostly in the Southern Hemisphere, to use birth control is an example of rhetoric as a technology of power.[28] Finally, in a world in which our ability to manipulate things, to produce and transform things, are increasingly associated with communication technologies, rhetoric can appear as a technology of production, a way to manipulate things. For example, design dynamics and marketing, two modern-day rhetorical forms, are increasingly built into the production process associated with the exchange of commodities.

Thus, the rhetorical subject, as a particular subject, may exist as primarily a "symbol-using animal," but its fabrication requires a host of technologies to encourage the subject to imagine him- or herself as a rhetorical subject. For example, Darrin Hicks and I have argued that "debating both sides" of a proposition, with its roots in the sophistic practice of *dissoi logoi,* should be approached as a rhetorical technology of the self, one assigned the power to transform the ethical relationship between a subject and his or her convictions. Working through a particular moment when debating both sides was made an object of intense scrutiny (1954–1966), we have demonstrated

how the technique was valued for its ability to adjust one's convictions toward the norm of free and full expression and away from a substantive conviction associated with a particular policy option. At this point, the rhetorical
subject fashions itself as a liberal citizen committed to a proceduralist notion
of democracy.[29]

The debating-both-sides controversy also demonstrates how technologies
of the self are closely attached to specific institutions. It should not be a surprise that many of the technologies of the self advocated by rhetorical scholars to produce rhetorical subjects are likely to be found in specific
institutional forms, for example, educational institutions providing courses in
composition and communication in the United States. Thus, the second reason for a more governmental approach to the material history of rhetoric is to
highlight the relationship between technologies and institutional histories. A
central lesson I have taken away from the Althusserian approach to subjectification is how subjects emerge due to their contact with the type of specific
institutions he calls ideological state apparatuses. While the Althusserian
emphasis on ideology as representation has authorized a careful investigation
of the role media texts play in forming subjects, we have often lost track of
the internal workings of media institutions and how they contribute to particular visions of subjectivity. To appreciate the specific history and forms by
which the rhetorical subject might appear, it would be important to pay attention not only to media institutions, but to the whole cultural terrain associated
with educational institutions, state institutions, transnational networks, and
the institutional forms associated with advertising and public relations. For
example, the debating-both-sides controversy pulled together the close relationship between speech education and the extracurricular activity of competitive intercollegiate debate. This institutional interface was made visible,
in part, due to the importance of pedagogy to the mission of speech departments and rhetorical theory. It is the growing invisibility of pedagogy to rhetorical theory that makes it difficult to recognize how the discipline partakes
in the construction of a rhetorical subject. One of the most unfortunate effects
of Michael Calvin McGee's initial call for a materialist theory of rhetoric
was his insistence that we look beyond the institutional history of rhetoric to
the practices of persuasion in everyday life.[30] In so doing, the investments of
rhetorical studies, as an institution, in the fabrication and regulation of the
rhetorical subject is often dispersed into the act of criticism. To be sure, it is
important to pay attention to the practices of persuasion, but, even here, one
should pay close attention to their institutional histories. One might find important similarities and differences about the process of persuasion from the
standpoint of institutions involved with direct mail campaigns as opposed to

institutions attempting to persuade by the use of interactive blogs. Moreover, how well "technologies of public persuasion" circulate as cultural forms might be due to how institutional forms take care to produce and reproduce these rhetorical technologies.[31]

The third Foucauldian-inspired move required for a rhetorical materialism is the role of a governing apparatus in both contextualizing and localizing rhetorical practices. A governing apparatus exists to formulate and solve public problems. It is, therefore, an ensemble of different elements including, but not limited to, political appointments, think tanks, social movements, state and non-state institutions, discourses, technologies, and populations. For a governing apparatus to produce and reproduce itself requires the rhetorical work associated with representation, persuasion, and deliberation. A governing apparatus may have a specific national or local history, but it may also exist as a transnational and global space. In fact, as public problems take on more global dimensions, for example, climate change, we are likely to experience even more global forms of a governing apparatus. A governing apparatus exists, therefore, as a material space by which to investigate the effectivity of rhetorical practices by analyzing how they answer questions concerning such classic policy dynamics as the nature of the problem, the causes of the problem, what solutions are advocated, and which solutions are discounted. While I have done work on the existence of a population apparatus, a governing apparatus organized to deal with the problems associated with population growth, a governing apparatus may exist in less visible ways.[32]

For example, returning to the history of the rhetorical subject, one might speak to how the rhetorical subject traverses a citizenship apparatus—that is, an apparatus dedicated to solving problems associated with citizenship. At a minimum, we might include in such a governing apparatus institutions (state and non-state actors) that promote civic engagement among high school kids, discourses drawn from progressive education that encourage communication as a means of citizenship participation, rhetorical technologies like learning how to debate, and the measurement tools for evaluating the norms and behaviors of good citizenship. The rhetorical subject would seem to be an integral element of any citizenship apparatus built on a progressive foundation of communication, but one might also imagine a citizenship apparatus less committed to communication as a means for manufacturing good citizenship. In other words, some might prefer a citizenship apparatus distinct from such a heavy investment in participatory models of communication and prefer simply enlarging the number of voters who vote. Of course, perhaps the history of rhetorical theory is nothing other than the problematization and enticements in favor of a particular ideal of the rhetorical subject. In other words, the dominant form the rhetorical subject takes is the result of a balance of forces that occupy a rhetorical apparatus—that is, a governing apparatus dedicated to the problems associated with the speaking subject.

The different roles played by communication in a governing apparatus points to the need for a theory and method of articulation to guide the empirical work of a rhetorical materialism. As developed in cultural studies, articulation refers to connecting diverse elements into a working ensemble, what Hall calls "a unity in difference."[33] Following the suggestion of Ernesto Laclau and Chantal Mouffe, articulation is often associated with a discursive process of linking concepts to practices to orient the production of meaning.[34] This approach views articulation as primarily a discursive process and taking place as part of an ideological struggle for hegemony. From the standpoint of Stuart Hall, however, articulation requires a second move from discourse to the conjuncture: "A theory of articulation is both a way of understanding how ideological elements come, under certain conditions, to cohere together within a discourse, and a way of asking how they do or do not become articulated, at conjunctures, to certain political subjects."[35] Hall, then, envisions a more "structured" totality than Laclau and Mouffe, one that calls for more sensitivity to how "free" a signifier might be for re-articulation. Thus, an approach to articulation that does not reduce the social totality to a discursive field has, according to Jennifer Daryl Slack, "[o]pened the way for cultural theorists to consider the role of other social forces both in their specificity and in discourse, interrogating the ways in which they are complexly articulated in structures of domination and subordination and considering the ways they might be re-articulated."[36]

A double articulation requires that a critic explain how the significance of a cultural form depends on its links to a discursive field, as well as how this plane of signification is attached to a conjunctural history made up of different modes of production. It is a view toward how the plane of signification and ideology crisscrosses other planes of effectivity (affective, economic) that underwrites Lawrence Grossberg's claim that articulation provides the conceptual possibility for a theory and practice of contexts. Therefore, to inform rhetorical materialism with a theory and practice of articulation requires a critical stance that is less hermeneutic and more diagrammatic, one made possible by mapping the temporal and spatial disjunctures and conjunctures provided by different articulations.[37] From the materialist perspective I have laid out, a conjuncture might best be thought of as a spatio-temporal articulation of different apparatuses forming a diagram of power.

In my earlier work, I posited a governing apparatus as a peculiar site for the articulation of different social forces. If we were to begin with the rhetorical subject as a concrete, but empty, form, the articulation of a rhetorical subject requires (1) an appreciation of the discourses that give flesh to the concrete rhetorical subject as a subject with particular characteristics and dispositions, (2) the specific techniques and technologies deployed to bring about the valued disposition of a rhetorical subject, (3) the articulation of the rhetorical subject to other forms of subjectivity, and (4) other social forces and planes of effectivity that allow a rhetorical subject to formulate a new context. In discussing how to approach a history of subjectivity, therefore, Foucault argues, "Whoever wishes to study the history of subjectivity will have to uncover the very long and slow transformation of an apparatus of subjectivity, defined by spirituality of knowledge and the subject's practice of truth, into this other apparatus of subjectivity, governed by the question of a subject's knowledge of himself and the subject's obedience to the law."[38] The ways in which the subject interacts with and within different apparatuses speaks to the need for a methodological commitment to articulation. Thus, a double articulation about rhetorical subjectivity includes how one is invited to partake in a hermeneutics of the self that orients a concrete individual toward an ideal of the rhetorical subject, and how this rhetorical subject finds itself linked to other productive apparatuses.

The Rhetorical Subject and the General Intellect

In the last couple of years, I have become increasingly committed to making explicit how this Foucauldian starting point should participate in a rhetorical materialism that envisions itself as contributing to the creation of a Marxism "beyond Marx."[39] As such, I have argued that the production of the rhetorical subject requires its contextualization as a mode of communicative labor and as an element in the articulation of a class struggle.[40] But doing so requires a more materialist understanding of the rhetorical subject than the one provided by rhetorical appropriations of Marxism that advance a political/economic identity speaking in the interest of the working class. We need to be more sensitive to how communication and, more specifically, the rhetorical subject operate alongside an apparatus of subjectivity associated with changes in capitalism that understands that commodity production is not the only site for generating class antagonisms. An important element in the rearticulation of the rhetorical subject, I argue, concerns how it emerges as immaterial labor. Thus, this section will disperse the rhetorical subject into the historical changes in the modes of labor to make visible how the rhetorical subject operates to produce and extract value from the general intellect.

What is immaterial labor? In its broadest sense, immaterial labor is "labor that produces an immaterial product, such as ideas, images, forms of communication, affects, or social relationships."[41] In discussing the changes in the production process of commodities, Maurizio Lazzarato highlights how the commodity form increasingly gains value through the harnessing of immaterial labor. Two key changes are noted. First, the "informational content" of the commodity relies on a labor process increasingly required to handle information, make decisions, work in teams, and use communication technologies. Second, immaterial labor refers to the "cultural content" of the commodity. Lazzarato defines the cultural content as "[t]he kinds of activities involved in defining and fixing cultural and artistic standards, fashion, tastes, consumer norms, and more strategically, public opinion."[42] Immaterial labor does not mean that commodity production or manual labor has disappeared, but that at the qualitative end of capitalist social relations, labor produces the most value when, as Lazzarato puts it, "one has to express oneself, one has to speak, communicate, cooperate."[43] When we disperse the rhetorical subject into a capitalist apparatus of subjectivity, we discover a particular laboring subject that communicates to produce value. From this perspective, we can begin to understand why communication skills have such a high cultural value for firms when we keep in mind how communication skills partake in the harnessing of immaterial labor.

The capitalist mode of production increasingly breaks down the distinction between forces of production and relations of production when faced with the articulation of the rhetorical subject. Since communication finds itself as both a force and relation of production, the rhetorical subject would seem to have lost any critical function. The capture of the rhetorical subject by capitalism would seem to warrant Gilles Deleuze's maxim that "speech and communication have been corrupted . . . not by accident but by their very nature."[44] In other words, while rhetorical scholars might lament or celebrate the marginalization of rhetorical studies, a process Robert Hariman believes has something to do with the inability of rhetoric to professionalize itself in the early twentieth century, the rhetorical subject did find many new professions: in public relations, advertising, journalism, and propaganda.[45] From Deleuze's perspective, communication makes possible a "control society" where no one is "left alone for long" and everything is subjected to the force of a "modulation, like a self-transmuting molding, continually changing from one moment to the next."[46] A control society would seem to ensure the commodification of *homo rhetoricus* and command that everyone cultivate the required rhetorical sensitivity.

One solution to this state of affairs is to posit a subject outside of capitalism (the deliberative or radical citizen) as an antidote to the control society. However, such a view removes the rhetorical subject from its history of production and may only feed the state's demand for the immaterial labor of civic engagement, a kind of labor that contributes to governing public problems and produces the value of legitimacy for its rule. Not only does this political hope for the rhetorical subject ignore how political communication has been colonized by money, but it assumes that the critical function of the rhetorical subject needs to be located outside the mode of production. A more materialist place to start would be to begin with the real subsumption of communication by capitalism in order to trace how the rhetorical subject might disrupt capitalism's regime of value.

In other words, an affirmative criticism is necessary that begins with a premise, posited by Antonio Negri, that "the actuality of communism, then, is the actuality of community. Thereby, the desire for community is formed in a mature, visible and immediate way during the process of re-appropriating the means of communication."[47] To begin to understand the antagonism that is produced due to the contradictions of immaterial labor for capitalism, it is useful to return to Karl Marx's concept of the "general intellect," one of the few English words he uses in the *Grundrisse*:

> Nature builds no machines, no locomotives, railways, electric telegraphs, self-acting mules etc. These are products of human industry: natural material transformed by organs of the human will over nature, or of human participation in nature. They are organs of the human brain, created by the human hand; the power of knowledge, objectified. The development of fixed capital indicates to what degree general social knowledge has become a direct force of production, and to what degree hence, the conditions of the process of social life itself have come under the control of the general intellect and been transformed in accordance with it. To what degree the powers of social production have been produced, not only in the form of knowledge, but also as immediate organs of social practice, of the real life process.[48]

This passage appears at the end of what is known as the "Fragment on Machines" and highlights both the replacement of workers by machines (fixed capital) and how production becomes increasingly reliant on the social practices of real life. In today's language, the general intellect would not only describe machines that produce commodities and services, but all the "research and development" investments to invent new products, services, and concepts. The general intellect makes it possible to investigate how invention (rhetorical and otherwise) "becomes a business, and the application of science to direct production itself becomes a prospect which determines and solicits it."[49] For Marx, the absorption of the general intellect into the forces of production creates the potential of a crisis for capitalism because "automation and socialization create the possibility of—the necessity for—dispensing with wage labor and private ownership."[50] From where Marx stood, capital required the production of surplus value, a process that could only be extracted from appropriating the labor-time of wage labor. Thus, to the extent that wage-labor became less necessary due to machines, capitalism's existence as a mode of production was threatened.

In writing about the "Fragment on Machines," Nick Dyer-Witheford represents Marx's view as both "astoundingly prescient and sadly anachronistic."[51] It is prescient for how it predicts the coming of the "knowledge economy." The concept of the general intellect offers a way into why questions about the funding of research and development from industrial and state sources remains such an important, if often unreported, topic of public debate. However, the "Fragment on Machines" is anachronistic in its prediction that capitalism might fall due to the contradiction of making wage-labor less important to the production of capital. One problem with the "Fragment on Machines" is a conceptual assumption that as capital appropriates the general intellect, the general intellect becomes, like machines, fixed capital or "dead labor." Based on Marx's labor theory of value, the forces of production, like machinery, represent dead labor, while the labor power brought into relations of production to animate the forces of production is called living labor. Without the social relationship of wage-labor, surplus value cannot be generated. Yet, one of the important revisions of the "Fragment on Machines" is the dispersion of the general intellect back into the relations of production, i.e., into living labor. As Paulo Virno puts it,

> Marx [neglects] the instance when [the] general intellect manifests itself . . . as living labor. This is precisely the decisive aspect today. Today it is not difficult to enlarge the notion of the general intellect far beyond the kind of knowledge which is materialized in fixed capital, to include all those forms of knowledge which structure social communications and which impel the activity of mass intellectual labor. The general intellect understands artificial languages, system and information theories, the whole gamut of qualification in the way of communication, local knowledges, informal linguistic play, as well as certain ethical preoccupations.[52]

What Virno calls "mass intellectuality [. . .]: living labor in its function as the determining articulation of the general intellect" draws our attention back to the immaterial labor of the rhetorical subject and what Dyer-Witheford calls "the contest for general intellect."[53]

From the standpoint of rhetorical materialism, then, the general intellect is a useful concept for describing the articulation between the means of communication (computers, televisions, telegraphs, bodies, airplanes); the social dimensions of communication (cooperation, decision making, persuasion, affects); the "technologies of public persuasion," i.e., the cultural forms/commodities of communication (movies, speeches); the types of knowledge (natural, social, and human sciences) that promote better communication; and, finally, the kinds of subjectivity made possible by communication (consumer, citizen, soldier). From this standpoint, we can move rhetorical materialism "beyond Marx" because the subsumption of "the life process" breaks apart any remaining residue of a base-superstructure configuration of the social totality and the dual ontology separating out the rhetorical from the material. Moreover, the very distinction between production and reproduction becomes less tenable as new antagonisms emerge over the immaterial labor of care.[54] To put it differently, as mass intellectuality and immaterial labor emerge as a driving force for capitalism, the very idea of commodity production takes on a dimension that stretches out beyond the factory walls that tether Marxism to its past. As feminist-inspired materialists have been arguing for over three decades, commodity production is just one vector in a material ontology concerned with the social (re)production of the life process.[55] The collapse of the distinction between the forces and relations of production as well as economic production from social reproduction inaugurates a bio-political stage of capitalism that extracts value from the life process.[56]

A rhetorical materialism, then, should attend to how the rhetorical does some of the communicative work of immaterial labor and how the rhetorical subject becomes dispersed into a host of productive apparatuses articulated together by how the general intellect activates and regulates the life process ("bio-power" in Foucault's language). Thus, the cultural, political, and economic value of the rhetorical subject is increasingly brought to bear on a common antagonism between a "bio-power from above against a bio-power from below."[57] The revolutionary potential of rhetorical materialism is made manifest, therefore, in the class struggle over the general intellect. Put another way, the rhetorical subject finds a materialist grounding in the struggle of living labor to value the general intellect in ways that escape and resist the command logics of capital and the state. More ontologically, as living labor, the rhetorical subject partakes in a constructive process that potentially subtracts itself from a production process committed to its death (fixed capital or dead labor) by articulating an alternative regime of value: one more likely to orient the general intellect toward the collective needs and desires of the community.

If a rhetorical materialism is to activate the revolutionary potential of its philosophical legacy, it must do more than authorize a critical hermeneutics of cultural forms. We can no longer be content expanding the object domain under the sign of a material rhetoric. The discovery of a generalized process of rhetoricality requires a second articulation, an articulation of rhetoricality into the modes of production and diagrams of power. This chapter has argued that articulating the rhetorical subject to the shifting character of capitalist forms of labor explains how efforts to govern this generalized rhetoricality partake in the production, regulation, and appropriation of value. In other words, "the rhetorical subject" is a subject formed to generate the cultural, political, and economic value through ways and means of communicating. The need to govern the rhetorical subject is due to how a generalized rhetoricality infuses capitalism with its dynamic energy to produce and appropriate the social wealth of communicative labor. The revolutionary future of the rhetorical subject finds its constitutive power in its articulation to the contest for the general intellect and a bio-politics of living labor against the commands of empire.

Notes

1. Thomas Sloane, ed., *Encyclopedia of Rhetoric* (Oxford: Oxford University Press, 2001).
2. In the *Encyclopedia of Rhetoric*, see Robert T. Craig, "Communication Theory," 128–29; Maurice Charland, "Constitutive Rhetoric," 616–19; Raymie E. McKerrow, "Critical Rhetoric," 619–22; Andrew King, "Rhetoric and Power," 624–27; and Michael Calvin McGee, "Ideograph," 378–81.
3. Carole Blair, "Reflections on Criticism and Bodies: Parables from Public Places," *Western Journal of Communication* 65 (2001): 287.
4. Blair, "Reflections on Criticism and Bodies," 287–88.
5. For an example of the controversy generated by the encounter between different materialist traditions, see Dana Cloud, "The Materiality of Discourse as an Oxymoron: A Challenge to Critical Rhetoric," *Western Journal of Communication* 58 (1994): 141–63; and Ronald Walter Greene, "Another Materialist Rhetoric," *Critical Studies in Mass Communication* 15 (1998): 21–41.
6. For essays negotiating different varieties of material rhetoric, see the essays in Jack Selzer and Sharon Crowley, eds., *Rhetorical Bodies* (Madison: University of Wisconsin Press, 1999). Other examples include Cheryl Forbes, "Writing the Body: Experiments in Material Rhetoric," *Rhetoric Review* 19 (2000): 60–72; Ronald Walter Greene, *Malthusian Worlds: U.S. Leadership and the Governing of the Population Crisis* (Boulder, CO: Westview Press, 1999); Ronald Walter Greene, "John Dewey's Eloquent Citizen: Communication, Judgment, and Postmodern Capitalism," *Argumentation and Advocacy* 39 (2003): 189–200; Ronald Walter Greene, "Rhetoric and Capitalism: Rhetorical Agency as Communicative Labor," *Philosophy and Rhetoric* 37 (2004): 188–206; Ronald Walter Greene and Darrin Hicks, "Lost Convictions: Debating Both Sides and the Ethical Self-Fashioning of Liberal Citizens," *Cultural Studies* 19 (2005): 100–26; Wendy S. Hesford, "Rape Stories: Material Rhetoric and the Trauma of Representation," in *Haunting Violations: Feminist Criticism and the Crisis of the Real*, ed. Wendy Hesford and Wendy Kozel (Urbana: University of Illinois Press, 2001), 3–23; Karlyn Hollis, *Liberating Voices: Writing at the Bryn Mawr Summer School for Women Workers* (Carbondale: Southern Illinois Press, 2004); Mary Lay, Billie J. Wahlstrom, and Carol Brown, "The

Rhetoric of Midwifery: Conflicts and Conversations in a Minnesota Home Birth Community in the 1990s," *Quarterly Journal of Speech* 82 (1996): 383–401; Richard Marback, "Detroit and the Closed Fist: Toward a Theory of Material Rhetoric," *Rhetoric Review* 17 (1998): 74–92; Kent Ono and John Sloop, *Shifting Borders: Rhetoric, Immigration and California's Proposition 187* (Philadelphia: Temple University Press, 2002); John Sloop and Kent Ono, "Out-Law Discourse: The Critical Politics of Material Judgment," *Philosophy and Rhetoric* 30 (1997): 50–69; Liz Rohan, "I Remember Mama: Material Rhetoric, Mnemonic Activity, and One Woman's Turn-of-the-Century Quilt," *Rhetoric Review* 23 (2004): 368–87.

7.   James Jasinski, "The Status of Theory and Method in Rhetorical Criticism," *Western Journal of Communication* 65 (2001): 249–71.

8.   Jasinski, "Status of Theory," 255.

9.   The definition of the rhetorical subject as one that speaks and is spoken to should not be read as a defense of orality. In contrast, I am referring to the speaking subject; one can "speak" in many different media and in many different genres. More importantly, what counts as a rhetorical subject at any given time is an effect of privileged discourses that take the production of the rhetorical subject as its object domain.

10. Louis Althusser, "Ideology and Ideological State Apparatuses," in *Lenin and Philosophy and Other Essays*, trans. Ben Brewster (New York: Monthly Review Press, 1971): 171.

11. Althusser, "Ideology and Ideological State," 170.

12. Stuart Hall, "Signification, Representation, Ideology: Althusser and the Post-Structuralist Debates," *Critical Studies in Mass Communication* 2 (1996): 91–113. The cultural turn in the humanities tends to replace the ideological with the cultural as a terrain of representation. As this section will demonstrate, such a substitution brought with it a reduction of the cultural to the discursive (understood as the articulation of linguistic and nonlinguistic elements) but primarily concerned with signification and ideology. For a critique of the translation of the cultural for the discursive plane of signification, see Lawrence Grossberg, *We Gotta Get Out of This Place: Popular Conservatism and Postmodern Culture* (New York: Routledge, 1992).

13. Joshua Gunn and Shaun Treat, "Zombie Trouble: A Propaedeutic on Ideological Subjectification and the Unconscious," *Quarterly Journal of Speech* 91 (2005): 144–74.

14. Althusser, "Ideology and Ideological State," 162.

15. Rosalind Coward, "Class, Culture, and the Social Formation," *Screen* 18 (1977): 75–105.

16. Maurice Charland, "Constitutive Rhetoric: The Case of the *Peuple Québécois*," *Quarterly Journal of Speech* 73 (1987): 133–50.

17. For Butler's critique of interpellation modeled on the sovereign voice, see *Excitable Speech: A Politics of the Performative* (New York: Routledge, 1997).

18. On the relationship between rhetoric and rhetoricality, see John Bender and David E. Wellbery, "Rhetoricality: On the Modernist Return of Rhetoric," in *The Ends of Rhetoric: History, Theory, Practice*, ed. John Bender and David E. Wellbery (Stanford, CA: Stanford University Press, 1990), 3–42. In rhetorical studies, the idea of rhetoricality authorizes the "globalization" of the rhetorical object domain. For an introduction to the promise and perils of the globalization thesis, see the essays in William Keith and Alan Gross, eds., *Rhetorical Hermeneutics: Invention and Interpretation in the Age of Science* (Albany: State University of New York Press, 1996).

19. On this process of expanding the object domain, see Dilip Parameshar Gaonkar, "The Idea of Rhetoric in the Rhetoric of Science," *Rhetorical Hermeneutics*, 3–40.

20. I am glossing an important argument from within the terrain of cultural studies that cri-

tiques the primacy of the text as an object of cultural criticism. See Ian Hunter, *Culture and Government: The Emergence of Literary Criticism* (Houndmills: Macmillan Press, 1988); Tony Bennett, *Outside Literature* (New York: Routledge, 1990); and Toby Miller, *Well Tempered Self: Citizenship, Culture and the Postmodern Subject* (Baltimore, MD: Johns Hopkins University Press, 1993).

21. For example, while I find Lisa A. Flores and Dreama G. Moon's critique of the discursive logic of *Race Traitor* to be extremely persuasive, their concept of the "racial paradox" smuggles in the need for dialectical criticism to assess the limits and effects of rhetorical influence. See "Rethinking Race, Revealing Dilemmas; Imaging a New Racial Subject in *Race Traitor*," *Western Journal of Communication* 66 (2002): 181–207.

22. Apologies for my promiscuous use of rhetorical sensitivity. See Roderick P. Hart and Don M. Burks, "Rhetorical Sensitivity and Social Interaction," *Speech Monographs* 39 (1972): 75–94.

23. I am glossing a point about the "rhetoric of continuity" made by Gayatri Chakravorty Spivak, "Scattered Speculations on the Question of Value," *Diacritics* 15 (1985): 73–93.

24. A good place to begin is Michel Foucault, "Governmentality," in *The Foucault Effect: Studies in Governmentality with Two Lectures by and an Interview with Michel Foucault*, ed. Colin Gordon, Graham Burchell, and Peter Miller (Chicago: University of Chicago Press, 1991), 87–104.

25. Nikolas Rose, *Inventing Ourselves: Psychology, Power and Personhood* (Cambridge, UK: Cambridge University Press, 1998): 10.

26. Richard Lanham, *The Motives of Eloquence: Literary Rhetoric in the Renaissance* (New Haven, CT: Yale University Press, 1976): 4–5.

27. Michel Foucault, "Technologies of the Self," in *Technologies of the Self: A Seminar with Michel Foucault*, ed. Luther Martin, Huck Gutman, and Patrick Hutton (Amherst: University of Massachusetts Press, 1998), 16–49.

28. For example, see Ronald Walter Greene and David Brashears, "Bio-Political Media: Population Communications International and the Governing of Reproductive Health," in *Governing the Female Body: Gender, Health, and Networks of Power*, ed. Lori Reed and Paula Saukko (Albany: State University of New York, in press).

29. Ronald Walter Greene and Darrin Hicks, "Debating Both Sides," 100–26.

30. Michael Calvin McGee, "A Materialist's Conception of Rhetoric," in *Explorations in Rhetoric: Essays in Honor of Douglas Ehninger*, ed. Ray E. McKerrow (Glenview, IL: Scott, Foresman, 1982), 23–48.

31. The phrase "technologies of public persuasion" belongs to Dilip Parameshwar Gaonkar and Elizabeth Povinelli, "Technologies of Public Forms: Circulation, Transfiguration, Recognition," *Public Culture* 15 (2003): 385–97. It is my argument that the circulation of such technologies requires institutional uptake and support.

32. Greene, *Malthusian World*.

33. Stuart Hall, "Signification, Representation, Ideology," 111.

34. Key essays on articulation include Ernesto Laclau, *Politics and Ideology in Marxist Thought* (London: New Left Books, 1977); and Ernesto Laclau and Chantal Mouffe, *Hegemony and Socialist Strategy: Towards a Radical Democratic Politics* (London: Verso Press, 1985). Two essays in rhetorical studies deserve special attention: Barbara Biesecker, "Rethinking the Rhetorical Situation from within the Thematic of Difference," *Philosophy and Rhetoric* 22 (1989): 110–30; and Kevin Deluca, "Articulation Theory: A Discursive Grounding for Rhetorical Practice," *Philosophy and Rhetoric* 32 (1999): 334–48.

35. Stuart Hall, "On Postmodernism and Articulation: An Interview with Stuart Hall by Lawrence Grossberg," in *Stuart Hall: Critical Dialogues in Cultural Studies*, ed. David Morley and Kuan-Hsing Chen (New York: Routledge, 1996), 141–42.

36. Jennifer Daryl Slack, "The Theory and Method of Articulation in Cultural Studies," in *Stuart Hall*, 123.

37. Such a spatial turn has been underappreciated by rhetorical critics harnessed to the textual case study. Key theoretical texts for exploring this more spatial dynamic include Grossberg, *We Gotta Get Out*; Greene, *Malthusian Worlds*; Raka Shome and Radha S. Hegde, "Culture, Communication, and the Challenge of Globalization," *Critical Studies in Media Communication* 19 (2002): 72–89; and Gaonkar and Povinelli, "Technologies of Public Forms."

38. Michel Foucault, *Hermeneutics of the Subject: Lectures at the College de France, 1981–1982* (New York: Picador, 2005), 319.

39. Antonio Negri, *Time for Revolution*, trans. Matteo Mandarini (New York: Continuum, 2003), 252; and Antonio Negri, *Marx Beyond Marx: Lessons from the Grundrisse*, trans. Harry Cleaver, Alan Ryan, and Maurizio Viano (New York: Autonomedia, 1989).

40. For my initial attempts to bring my Foucauldian starting points more directly in contact with the history of capitalism, see Greene, *Malthusian Worlds*; "John Dewey's Eloquent Citizen"; and "Rhetoric and Capitalism."

41. Michael Hardt, "Immaterial Labor and Artistic Production," *Rethinking Marxism* 17 (2005): 176.

42. Maurizio Lazzarato, "Immaterial Labor," in *Radical Thought in Italy: A Potential Politics*, ed. by Michael Hardt and Paulo Virno (Minneapolis: University of Minnesota Press, 1996), 136.

43. Lazzarato, "Immaterial Labor," 135.

44. Gilles Deleuze, "Post-Script on Control Societies," in *Negotiations*, trans. Martin Joughin (New York: Columbia University Press, 1997), 175.

45. Robert Hariman, "The Rhetoric of Inquiry and the Professional Scholar," in *Rhetoric in the Human Sciences*, ed. Herbert W. Simons (Newbury Park, CA: Sage, 1989). For a discussion of the transformation of writing into forms of professional labor, see Christopher Wilson, *The Labor of Words: Literary Professionalism in the Progressive Era* (Athens: University of Georgia, 1985). One might more directly challenge Hariman's assumption of the failure of rhetoric to professionalize itself by turning to the founding of speech departments during this period.

46. Deleuze, "Post-Script on Control Societies," 179.

47. Antonio Negri, *Politics of Subversion: A Manifesto for the Twenty-First Century* (Malden, MA: Polity Press, 2005): 57.

48. Karl Marx, *Grundrisse*, trans. with a foreward by Martin Nicolaus (New York: Vintage, 1973), 706.

49. Marx, *Grundrisse*, 704.

50. Nick Dyer-Witheford, *Cyber-Marx: Cycles and Circuits of the Struggle in High-Technology Capitalism* (Urbana: University of Illinois Press, 1999), 220–21.

51. Dyer-Witheford, *Cyber-Marx*, 221.

52. Paulo Virno, "Notes on the 'General Intellect,'" in *Marxism Beyond Marxism*, ed. Saree Makdisi, Cesare Casarion, and Rebecca E. Karl (New York: Routledge, 1996), 270.

53. Virno, "Notes on the 'General Intellect,'" 270; Dyer-Witheford, *Cyber-Marx*, 14.

54. It should be noted that Michael Hardt and Antonio Negri's emphasis on immaterial dimensions of affective labor has been challenged for how it recognizes but displaces femi-

nist research and the labor of women in the area of "reproductive labor." See Susanne Schultz, "Dissolved Boundaries and 'Affective Labor': On the Disappearance of Reproductive Labor and Feminist Critique in *Empire*," *Capitalism, Nature, Socialism* 17 (2006): 77–83. One point of contact might be the shared work around the concept of biopolitics and social reproduction.

55. For example, see Lucy Bland, Charlotte Brundson, Dorothy Hobson, and Janice Winship, "Women 'Inside' and 'Outside' the Relations of Production," in *Women Take Issue*, ed. Women's Studies Group (London: Hutchinson, 1978), 35–59.

56. Michael Hardt and Antonio Negri, *Empire* (Cambridge: Harvard University Press, 2000).

57. Michael Hardt, "Affective Labor," *Boundary 2* 26 (1999): 176.

CHAPTER 3

People Shopping

John M. Sloop, Vanderbilt University

Where one automobile can go, all other automobiles do go, and wherever the automobile goes, the automobile version of civilization surely follows.
Marshall McLuhan, *Understanding Media: The Extensions of Man*

While the story is recounted less frequently now—more than fifteen years into production and after repeated failure to turn a profit—the narrative of the origins, representation, and organizational structure of the Saturn automobile remains both intriguing and instructive to cultural critics and management scholars alike. A fully owned subsidiary of General Motors, Saturn was conceived in 1985 as a company that would produce small cars to compete with the high sales volume Japanese automobiles produced by such companies as Honda, Nissan, and Toyota. As normally told, the story begins when a then anonymous, now celebrated, "Group of 99" laborers, managers, and engineers from a variety of GM plants were given several years, using a "clean sheet" approach, to design a company from top to bottom that would not only produce a high quality and competitive car, but would also alter most aspects of the production process, including relations between labor and management. Moreover, the group was told that General Motors planned to take lessons learned from the Saturn experiment and introduce these ideas to each of its other divisions.[1]

Indeed, regardless of one's critical perspective, Saturn—at least in its early years—was a rather uniquely structured corporation, especially when situated within the U.S. automobile industry. Located in Spring Hill, Tennessee (itself an interesting choice of location, far from the traditional Detroit standard), Saturn had a number of unique features, from management-labor relations to the physical plant to plans for Saturn retailers.[2] The most often-cited differences between Saturn and traditional automobile manufacturers included a labor contract in which workers could not be laid off and were paid bonuses based on production levels; a relatively high number of training hours as a portion of each work week; a system in which decisions of all types (from car design to marketing) were made jointly by teams composed of members drawn from both labor and management; lunch rooms and parking lots shared by labor and management; a system in which workers moved from job to job, rather than specializing in particular areas; a sales strategy that featured "retailers," rather than dealers; a system in which these "retailers" owned geographic areas, rather than single dealerships (to cut out competition); an exaggerated focus on customer service; and no-haggle, set prices on the cars, eliminating salespeople who would work on commission.

These structural changes were introduced to the United States' consumer public both through news reports about the company and through a series of folksy advertisements produced by Hal Riney and Partners (already well known, perhaps most immediately at the time, for their Ronald Reagan "Morning in America" advertisements, as well as their front porch ads for Bartles and Jaymes) articulating Saturn with traditional signifiers of "America" itself, including appeals to hard work, quality, fairness, and honest rural living.[3] Riney and Partner's penchant for the rural American imaginary would prove significant to Saturn in that, as Lauren Berlant observes in *The Queen of America Goes to Washington City*, the discourse of the Reagan "revolution" was one in which America's survival was depicted as "dependent upon personal acts and identities performed in the intimate domains of the quotidian,"[4] and in which citizenship is something scarce and sacred, "only for members of families."[5] Saturn's advertisements, paralleling the Reagan ideology, implied that Saturn was the type of company producing a product based in the "true" American tradition, a tradition that recently had been trodden on and had lost its edge.[6]

The combination of these early advertisements, Saturn's public relations, and customer service at the retail level fairly successfully constructed Saturn as, indeed, "A Different Kind of Company, A Different Kind of Car."[7] Nonetheless, despite early high demand for Saturns, the company was rarely (if ever) able to produce a profit in its early years and, over time, the situation worsened.[8] Its inability to turn a profit, coupled with a number of other competing interests (e.g., the Union of Automobile Workers [UAW] argued that the original Saturn labor agreement undermined the power of unions in general, other GM subsidiaries argued that too much financial support was provided to Saturn, other local UAWs pressured GM to manufacture Saturns outside Spring Hill at other GM plants that were being closed), ultimately led to a situation in which most of the unique features of Saturn—from labor-management relations to "sales persona"—were removed, with Saturn more or less becoming simply another division of General Motors.

For example, when Saturn finally did produce a mid-size car and an SUV, many of the new cars were produced at a plant in Delaware—a plant with a more traditional labor agreement and more traditional links to GM—rather than in Spring Hill. Further, and more recently, workers at Spring Hill approved a traditional labor agreement (e.g., workers can now be laid off during slow sales periods, worker-management relations are similar to those in other plants), and Saturn as a whole has become structurally/organizationally aligned with General Motors (e.g., they now share engineering and marketing with other GM subsidiaries rather than having engineers and marketing solely dedicated to Saturn). Moreover, Saturn's advertising moved from a focus on the values of the manufacturing and sales staff to a focus on consumers and the relationship between consumers and cars.

In this essay, I provide a critical narrative concerning the public story of Saturn (rather than Saturn as an institution or phenomenon), utilizing Saturn's story as it is represented through advertising, news stories, and trade books, in order to focus on a number of ancillary issues. First, and most overtly, I am interested in the ways in which the discourse surrounding Saturn specifically articulates and rearticulates the meaning of "America" and American citizenship within its historical moment.[9]

Second, and directly related to this volume, this reading of American citizenship, premised on an understanding of the automobile as a prosthetic, also invites a discussion about the relationship between materiality, culture (meanings and institutions), and rhetoric. That is, beginning with the assumption that a medium (such as the car) alters our understanding of our bodies, I am interested in providing a critique of the way in which this particular body-medium configuration is shaped by public articulations of the car. As my analysis unfolds, it will become clear that it is based on several assumptions—recently stated most clearly by Rosi Braidotti—about the relationship between the bodies, prosthetic technology, and cultural articulations about, as well as meanings of, bodies. Given that these assumptions will ultimately lead us toward the question of this volume's topic—the relationship between rhetoric and materiality—I want to briefly explain my reading of this relationship and how I will employ it before moving to the case study of this essay.

Embracing the ongoing discussion of the breakdown of distinctions between human and machine, Braidotti observes that "the body is caught in a network of power effects mostly induced by technology," effects producing a blurred meaning for bodies and technology that occurs on multiple levels.[10] For Braidotti, then, the subject does not emerge from a "natural, biological" materiality but instead through a "complex interplay of highly constructed social and symbolic forces."[11] The interplay between the material and the symbolic is complicated for Braidotti in that the subject is not simply embodied "in the flesh" but also in its relationship with a multiplicity of prosthetics (e.g., computers, automobiles, personal video systems). Hence, given her sources, in a move that reads as a meeting of Deleuze, Donna Haraway, and Marshall McLuhan,[12] Braidotti observes that subjectivity is a "process of becoming-subject that requires sets of cultural mediation; the subject has to deal with material and semiotic conditions, that is to say institutional sets of rules and regulations as well as the forms of cultural representation that sustain them."[13] In effect, then, it is not only that the subject emerges between the interplay of the material body and the multiple ways in which, to draw on Judith Butler, it "matters," but also that the possibilities of subjectivity are shaped by the materiality of its prosthetics and the ways in which they "matter." The body and its prosthetics are neither determinate of, nor autonomous from, existing meanings but are themselves shaped by the complex interplay of meanings, regulations, and institutions.

A quick look at the index of *Metamorphoses* would reveal that if "rhetoric" occurs as a term in the book, it is in such a minor sense that it goes unmarked. Again, rather than rhetoric, Braidotti claims interest in the "cultural mediation" between materiality and (always changing but ideologically disciplined) "semiotic conditions." While one could locate rhetoric solely in the realm of these "semiotic conditions" reproducing the dichotomy between the material and the rhetorical, I would like to offer that we position "rhetoric" *as* the energy of that cultural mediation. That is, I would like to assert that if we position "rhetoric" as the energy or flow mediating between bodies, body prosthetics, and "semiotic conditions," then we might productively shift the question away from the *difference between materiality and rhetoric* and away from questions about the *materiality of rhetoric* and toward a *rhetorical materialism* in which we understand that any time one attempts to talk about bodies and subjectivity, one is always already involved in the process of reshaping the flow of mediation, the flow of meaning. Hence, in this essay, as I work through a case study of cultural discourses about "bodies" and meaning, I want to position this very critical act as an illumination and alteration of the flow of meaning on contemporary "American" bodies in a particular way. Rather than a philosophical reflection on the relationship of materialism and rhetoric, this essay will be an example of criticism based on rhetorical materialism.

While I will make assertions about structural and economic factors that encourage an alteration of the marketing and sales of Saturn automobiles, my primary focus in this essay is on the relationship between the dominant cultural "meaning" (in Braidotti's words, one element of the "semiotic condition") of Saturn, the prosthetic body, and "American" subjectivity. If Marshall McLuhan was even partially correct when he noted that, because automobiles act as a prosthetic for the human body (and hence change the very meaning of humanity and the body), they "have become the real population of our cities," then we can look at representations (both marketing representations and news reports) of the automobile as also acting as representations of the contemporary "population."[14] Ultimately, then, this essay tells the story of Saturn's cultural logic as a way to trouble some general ways of understanding what it means to be a citizen and a consumer in contemporary culture. If the contemporary process of *becoming a subject* is mediated between the body, its prosthetics (materiality), and the meanings overlaid on them (the semiotic and cultural), the Saturn discourses offer an opportunity for critical intervention in the changing meanings of bodies and of human behavior. It provides an opportunity, in short, to reshape the flow of mediation—the realm of rhetoric.

As a final note before turning to the discourse about Saturn, I stress that I do not mean to overstate claims based on the readings of discourses concerning one particular automobile manufacturer. This essay is not, in other words, an attempt to make causal or overdetermined claims about the changing meanings of "America" or of "humanity" in general. Rather, I use the Saturn "text" as a route to probe thinking about—and discussions concerning—the relationships between and among criticism, discourse, materialism, media, citizenship, and our rhetorical understandings of self and others.[15] Because the story of Saturn has been told numerous times in numerous formats, including at least four books and hundreds of newspaper and magazine articles, the body of discourse from which I draw my claims is rather substantial. Relying on all four books, a random sample of newspaper and magazine articles, and Saturn's own advertisements, I will outline the broad parameters of the "meaning of Saturn" and the ways the emphasis of this meaning and its relationship to "America" and consumers change.[16] I will suggest that while the earlier discourse highlights individualism, the heteronormative family, and quality over structural constraints or identity categories (e.g., race, gender), the latter maintains this identity-free consumer space by transforming the consumer into commodity.

I develop my argument in three stages. First, I illustrate the overt articulation made between Saturn and "America" since Saturn's inception. Be-

cause Saturn is posited as a specifically American attempt to compete with
Japanese automakers and technologies, Saturn discourse allows both its pro-
ducers and consumers to be interpellated as uniquely American, to find purchase of a particular way of being an American consumer. Second, I
highlight the broad strokes of the "meaning" of Saturn in its early marketing
and early news coverage—this is a logic that articulates Saturn tightly with
hard work, quality, fairness, and individualism (ignoring structural constraints), a logic closely merging with U.S. culture as represented by the vision of the Reagan presidency and the "Morning in America" campaign.
Through the consumption of Saturns, we are invited to see ourselves as citizens free of identity markers or personal narratives that may have otherwise
acted as constraints on success. Third, after outlining the ways in which the
story of Saturn's decade-long financial failure is told, I discuss the ways that
Saturn—as a corporation and as an object of discourse—has changed. Given
Saturn's "American" articulation, I use these changes to think about changes
in "American" ideology. As I will illustrate, the discourse of Saturn moves
from equality to profitability, "humanity" to efficiency, and from unmarked
"individualism" to commodity/consumption. I will suggest that the discourse
concerning Saturn stands problematically as a metaphor for contemporary
logics of American citizenship, a move that takes us from a discourse similar
to Berlant's infantile citizenship (purchased through consumption) to a citizenship of commodification. Ultimately, I see this section as an occasion to
think about, to trouble, these articulations of humanity and of citizenship.
Finally, I will end this essay by returning to the topic of rhetorical materialism and how this essay hopefully helps us think about the act of criticism.

Saturn as America

From its public conception onward, Saturn was articulated, or identified, with
America itself. In advertisements, public relations statements, and news discourse, we find a repetitious melding of Saturn with the rebirth or renewal of
American industry and the "American tradition" of hard work and creative
industry. Conceived in an economic context in which American automobile
manufacturers were losing large market shares to Japanese automakers, Saturn was strongly identified as an attempt to renew and reassert "American
know-how."

        While Saturn was of course framed in more ways than one, the articula-
tion of Saturn and "America" is clearly one of the strongest in the early public discussions of Saturn, with the discourse articulating Saturn with America
appearing across advertising, public relations statements, and news stories.
For example, Vicki Lenz observes not only that General Motors' goal for

Saturn "was to design an American vehicle that could beat the Japanese in the small-car race," but she goes on to note—and I think importantly—that the name "Saturn" itself derived from the U.S.-U.S.S.R. space race: "In the end, NASA's Saturn booster rockets carried Americans to the moon, winning the race."[17] The very word, "Saturn," then, was chosen specifically to be united with "America," an America separate from, and in competition with, the rest of the globe.

Similarly, in his reflections of the meaning of "Saturn"—especially as articulated by GM—Joe Sherman waxes philosophical by observing that all U.S. citizens are "in the rings of Saturn . . . if Saturn couldn't retrain and give workers more self-esteem, if it couldn't make a good cheap car, then America was in tough shape."[18] This articulation, Sherman goes on to observe, was consistently reaffirmed by Saturn officials; for instance, he quotes Bruce McDonald, Saturn's vice president of communications, claiming that Saturn "is the rebirth of American technological might."[19] Similarly, Jack O'Toole begins his insider's look at Saturn (O'Toole was an original member of Saturn's founding committee of ninety-nine) with an epigram by Michael E. Bennett, then president of the UAW Local 1853 that served Spring Hill and Saturn, claiming that Saturn "would become America's hopes and dreams—hopes and dreams of leading the American auto industry back to helping Americans capture their American dream."[20] In short, Saturn insiders stressed repeatedly that Saturn was being initiated precisely in order to reassert the supremacy of American technology and know-how. The terms "Saturn" and "America" were tied together tightly by the Saturn corporation itself.

These grounds for envisioning Saturn were repeated and reiterated by writers in the popular press as well, years before the first car was built. Saturn becomes "America" in most of these articulations, and America is differentiated most often with "Japan" and/or Japanese automakers. For instance, when *Business Week*'s David Whiteside wrote about Saturn in 1985, fourteen months after GM had first introduced the idea, he began his essay by noting that "the idea was to beat the Japanese at their own game."[21] In 1986, *Newsweek*'s Jeff B. Copeland and David L. Gonzalez note, in warlike imagery, that Saturn emerged after GM's failed competitive attempts "when Japan first *invaded* the auto market."[22] Similarly, in the *St. Petersburg Times*, Alan Goldstein observes that Saturn is an attempt "to fight off the *Japanese assault* on [GM's] sagging share of the U.S. car market."[23] Later, after the first eighty Saturns had rolled off the assembly line, the *Washington Post* noted that Saturn had not only become one of the most ambitious events in the history of the automobile but that Saturn was gaining so much attention because it was loaded "with economic and symbolic significance" precisely because it was redefining how cars are made in the United States.[24] This theme emerges repeatedly in sources as different as *BusinessWeek*,[25] *Adweek*,[26] *Maclean's*,[27] the *New York Times*,[28] and *USA Today*.[29]

The articulation of Saturn as an "American" car also emerges when the first models are reviewed and purchased. For instance, in the *New York Times*, Doron Levin repeatedly observes that the new Saturns are unusual in that they are made by GM but feel and drive very much like a Japanese car.[30] *Car Talk*'s Ray Magliozzi responded to a query about Saturn by claiming that GM had successfully built an American car that could compete with its Japanese counterparts.[31] Further, when reporters covered the first Saturn ever to be purchased, *St. Petersburg Times* reporter Teresa Burney noted that when the Saturn retailer opened for business, numerous people in their cars unexpectedly "drove by, honking their horns and yelling 'Go America,'" providing anecdotal evidence of a general awareness that Saturn as a product and an industry was clearly identified with America itself, an "America" in direct competition with other nations' industries.[32]

While I will delineate the specific meanings that are articulated along with both "Saturn" and "America" later in this chapter, I want to underscore one early television advertisement that highlights and reifies the articulation made between Saturn and America, especially in relationship to economic competition with Japan. In the television advertisement "Monitors," the viewer sees what he or she is told by the male voiceover is a large group of workers and their families (with some children riding on what we assume to be their fathers' shoulders) walking to the Saturn plant in Spring Hill on a Sunday morning—their day off, the voice emphasizes—because they want to watch the first Saturns that are to be shipped to, and sold in, Japan. The voiceover reminds the viewer that Saturn was a corporate gamble taken at a time "when U.S. cars weren't selling particularly well." The viewer then watches as cars are unloaded in Japan with Japanese dock workers helping bring the cars ashore. This advertisement enacts a symbolic reversal of the Japanese invasion discourse discussed earlier. Working in the context of the general cultural discussions about the meaning of Saturn, this commercial views Saturn as not only America itself, but as an America enacting its own Japanese invasion.

While the reasons for the articulation of Saturn and America are, of course, overdetermined (e.g., GM's marketing of Saturn, cultural anxieties about Japanese products in general, news reporters' reifications of GM's public relations), the articulation is effective in the sense that it appears and reappears in news reports about the car. If we take the *St. Petersburg Times* story as evidence, we could suggest that those people driving in cars and shouting "Go America" at the Saturn dealership are evidence of the way in which Saturn and America became somewhat consubstantial in the popular imaginary.[33] When "Saturn" is imagined, it is imagined as thoroughly American, and it is the specific meanings of this version of America to which I turn my attention next.

The Saturn Nation, Part I: It's "Motoring in America"

While its identification with "America" continues to the present—at least through the force of its discursive history—the meaning of both Saturn and America are rearticulated in line with changes in economic conditions and cultural trends. In its early stages, I suggest that Saturn is articulated along two grounds, each stressing—overtly or implicitly—the notion of family, of equality, of a world in which identity markers are rendered meaningless, the individual rendered free of social barriers. In the first case, then, Saturn is represented as the product of a realigned (although thoroughly American) production process, one stressing a familial relationship between workers, employers, and their jobs. Second, Saturn/America is simultaneously articulated through a focus on consumers and their relationships within the marketplace—how are consumers treated, and how do they respond? Again, and as I will illustrate, these lines of articulation share similar themes. Reflecting Ronald Reagan's "Morning in America," Saturn represents an imagined return to "core" American values, a return necessary to once again make America a dominant world economic and manufacturing force. And, whether it is in the production process or in the act of consumption, these values suggest that to be American is to be an individual in a world free of structural constraints, a world in which hard work is rewarded along the lines of merit rather than along the lines of identity or identity markers (e.g., race, gender). Again, in Berlant's terms, we see in Saturn's "Motoring in America" these values emerging in a representational matrix focusing on individual quotidian acts within the context of traditional heteronormative family structures.

Saturn Teams: Communication, Caring, and Equity

In a 1991 essay in *Maclean's* discussing Saturn's unique relationship between labor and management, Richard "Skip" LeFauve—then president of Saturn—noted that "[t]he old system divides people into winners and losers . . . Here, we emphasize the need for partnership. . . . It sounds a little corny, but we want people to know that it's OK to care about each other."[34] LeFauve's claim underlines multiple comments made by workers, management, and observers of the early labor arrangement at Saturn. As constituted through discussions and explanations of Saturn's production process, Saturn provided a "family structure" for workers, one in which their hard work would be rewarded precisely because coworkers cared for one another, respected hard work, and were willing and able to ignore other social codings (e.g., race, gender, class) that traditionally would have encouraged moral valuations. In this representation, Saturn workers and management are not only content but are so dedicated to the Saturn concept that their work is at least partially an act of love. Both Saturn advertising and news reports stress that Saturn, in effect, was born in Reagan's America, a world in which a worker, provided with a strong family structure and free of structural constraints, will naturally work hard and succeed on the basis of the quality of his or her work.[35]

Perhaps the best place to begin such a discussion is with Saturn's early television advertisements—images that played a large role in how Saturn was understood culturally. In addition to the aforementioned "Monitors" advertisement featuring workers coming in on their day off to watch their cars being shipped to markets in Japan, two other television spots introduced Saturn not so much as a car as an ideology and work ethic. First, in "Launch," the viewer witnesses a traditional rural setting, the early morning signified by the sun rising over what one assumes is a farmhouse. The camera moves indoors, and the viewer sees an alarm clock and a variety of images of various family members sleeping. When the scene returns outside once again, we see the family patriarch feeding chickens and performing other chores while his family sleeps. When his chores are complete, he leaves home driving a late model domestic pickup, stopping to pick up a friend/coworker carrying a metal lunch box. While the sun begins to rise over their small town, the two pass a group of children playing on a dirt road, seemingly awaiting their school bus. Finally, as the pair drive onto the Saturn lot, the worker—in voiceover—observes that while working at other factories, he saw himself as someone who simply produced parts of cars. At Saturn, however, he has become one part of a team crafting quality automobiles from the bottom up. Herein we find featured the signifiers of Reagan's morning—the sunshine, the intact family, the workers arising early and working together, and the notion that hard work, industry, and pride naturally effect a return of traditional American values and products.

Similarly, an advertisement titled "8,000 Owners" focuses on those who build the cars rather than on the automobile itself. The viewer is at first presented with a montage of numerous and varied (in terms of style, gender, race, age) workers inside a factory while a voiceover—identified as one of those workers—explains the "Saturn difference." There are "no time clocks, no foremen" at Saturn, the worker explains, and, as a result, all eight thousand Saturn employees see themselves as owners rather than as workers. He goes on to observe, "Someone figured out there's something more important than machinery and equipment if you want to get a good product out the door. It's about people, their struggle to do something they always wanted to do but never had the chance." Again, viewers learn that Saturn has created a situation in which deregulation allows people to reach their fulfillment as human beings rather than leading to their exploitation.

This understanding of Saturn is fleshed out further in numerous television and monograph "biographies" of Saturn as it first begins producing cars. For example, after a long discussion of the great lengths to which Saturn went to create ergonomically safe working conditions, Vicki Lenz quotes one worker saying, "It's doing a job from the heart versus doing a job because you have to have a job."[36] Similarly, Jack O'Toole's history of the Group of 99 and the development of the "Saturn philosophy" consistently stresses the idea of happiness, pride, and family. O'Toole observes, "We believe that all people want to be involved in decisions that affect them, care about their jobs, take pride in their accomplishments, and want to share in the success of their efforts."[37] Rather than the "zombieism" that workers have traditionally faced in factories, O'Toole claims that Saturn humanizes workers, helping everyone to feel like brothers and sisters in an organization that can "really care about people."[38] Moreover, Saul Rubenstein and Thomas Kochan see in Saturn's "team concept" a way to help labor feel as if they are a "full partner in business."[39] Throughout their survey of Saturn, they stress repeatedly that the company is about "communication and coordination" and "trust" between workers and the company.[40]

News reports serve to strengthen such claims through repetition. For example, an essay in *Adweek* stresses that Saturn advertising reflects the "honest, hard-working and innovative Saturn employees, starting from scratch to build a new kind of car."[41] *Maclean's* observes that labor and management went to "trust camps" to learn the value of "consensus-building and teamwork," while the *New York Times* notes that the "most striking accomplishment of Saturn has been unusual harmony among managers, engineers and unionized productive workers."[42] Similarly, when *USA Today*'s Micheline Maynard visited Saturn, the reporter found that many workers prefer being at Saturn late in the day rather than going home, indicating that Saturn has become an alternate home, a space for freedom and creativity, with some of the workers willingly spending sixteen or seventeen hours a day at the plant. A "team leader" tells Maynard, "Sometimes it's hard to get people out . . . They want to stay and build another."[43] Of this attitude, *Business Week* notes that

Saturn's workplace changes are so exciting that Vice President of Human Resources James L. Lewandowski describes Saturn workers as almost "cult-like" in their attitude toward work.[44]

Irrespective of an alternative narrative in which workers are not as happy as represented by reporters, this dominant public representation found in the discursive mosaic of advertising, newspaper/magazine reports, and reflective industry accounts understands Saturn as an American workplace in which individuals reach fulfillment through the labor process.[45] Given the link between Saturn and America, this story of the happy laborer reifies the view of America and Americans as emerging most effectively when the laborer is domesticated, when we all become members of the same family, "unencumbered by any particular life narrative."[46]

Saturn "People": Erin, Roland, and the Irrelevance of Difference

Like the representation of the Saturn workforce, Saturn's consumers (who oftentimes become Saturn's sales force, narratives repeatedly stress) are again hailed as individuals who, through Saturn, are freed of the constraints imposed by social markings (e.g., race, gender) that would have encumbered them in the past. As Lauren Berlant notes of the discourse of the Reagan revolution, the consumer here is one who inhibits "a secure space liberated from identities and structures that seem to constrain what a person can do in history."[47] This narrative highlights the heroic individual and hides "the vulnerability of personal existence to the instability of capitalism and the concretely unequal forms and norms of national life."[48] While acknowledging a past in which structural constraints may have been the norm, Saturn's representation of the "consumer" exists in a culture in which, as Dana Cloud notes of the discourse about Oprah Winfrey, "difference" is no longer seen as relevant to economic or social success or failure.[49] That is, these representations implicitly suggest that Saturn offers a friction-free marketplace in which the only constraint to success is hard work, that constraints based on race, gender, sexuality, mobility, or age are not relevant.[50] Such an appeal equates Saturn with a domestic American consumer space, much like its labor space, in which constraints no longer exist, in which the consumer is "embraced independently of any particular life narrative."[51]

Before I discuss two of Saturn's most evocative television advertisements, I want to stress that part of the appeal of Saturn's ads emerged from the fact that they were often represented as "true stories." That is, Hal Riney and Associates, as well as spokespersons at Saturn, often claimed authenticity for the narratives told in each thirty- to sixty-second spot. As a result, each individual narrative could be read as potentially "true" because Saturn claimed that *most* of them were true. For example, Vicki Lenz claims that 97 percent of all Saturn ads are "real-life stories" despite seeming so far-fetched.[52] Further, Joe Sherman traced down one of the engineers featured in an ad because he wanted to follow up on the story told in the ad, and a *San Francisco Chronicle* discussion of the ads observed that many of them derived from actual customer and worker experiences.[53] Such discourse, coupled with the documentary-driven testimonial style of the ads, helped create a rhetorical field in which all the stories become believable and, as such, serve as evidence of the renewed "America" that Saturn was helping birth.

"Erin Walling," arguably one of Saturn's most memorable advertisements, opens with images of a professionally dressed woman entering a number of car dealerships and showrooms, finding herself confronted by stereotypically slick salesmen (all men). While we witness one salesman demonstrating the "vanity mirror" for Walling and another walking away when she announces twelve thousand dollars as the maximum she wants to spend on a car, we hear Walling saying in a voiceover, "I thought the days of women being treated differently than men were long gone. . . . Then I tried to buy a car." As she speaks, the camera captures her entering a Saturn retailer. While we see Walling speaking to a sales agent, she tells us that Saturn retailer Dave Peirce answered all her questions fairly and freely. Such treatment, she notes, encouraged her not only to buy a Saturn but to become a salesperson herself.[54] Saturn, like Reagan's economic and ideological world before it, stands as the route through which friction-free consumption might be reached. We can live in a space of freedom (much like the Saturn workers), the ad seems to offer, if only we choose to do so.

A second but perhaps more provocative commercial titled "Roland" opens with a middle-aged African-American Saturn salesman speaking directly to the viewer, and, like Erin Walling, explaining why he chose to sell Saturns. Visually, the commercial cuts between images of the speaker as a salesperson and supposed "home movie footage" reflecting his childhood. While he tells his story, the viewer sees the home footage of an African-American family together in a variety of activities—eating, playing catch, and posing with a new car. Roland reflects on his family: "We weren't rich; we were poor; I just didn't know it." As the image fades to one of his father alone with the car, Roland explains that his father was never quite happy with the purchase: "I don't think he felt he was treated fairly. Those were the times that we lived in." Like Erin Walling's discovery of freedom from sexism in a Saturn retailer, Roland finds a racist-free marketplace at the Saturn retailer. As he explains, "Saturn, to me, was really just an extension of my own personal values. We treat all of our customers the same. We don't call ourselves dealers because we really don't deal. People don't have to haggle and that's the way it should be." Roland then imagines aloud that if his father had been able to purchase a Saturn, "[h]e would have come home smiling." Again, the viewer is hailed to join this world free of constraints, a world in which structural impediments built on signifiers of difference no longer matter. In Saturn's America, in Saturn's (heteronormative) family, all are treated equally and have equal access to consumption.

The narrative of these advertisements is buttressed not only by the discourse of "authenticity" but also by narratives repeated in news stories that support the promise of friction-free and familial consumption. Hence, for example, Vicki Lenz repeatedly tells stories of Saturn customers who find Saturn to be free of the constraints of gender. One male customer observes that his "wife of twenty-five years feels comfortable taking the car in for service by herself. My younger sister doesn't have to get her brother to take the car in for service."[55] Customer Linda Bader claims that she loves Saturn because she wanted to buy a car "by myself, without my husband. I thought that if I can run a business, I should be able to buy a car ... My friend ... said, 'My mother just bought one; my sister just bought one; it's hassle-free.'"[56] Again, the stress lies on the way Saturn creates a universe without structural constraints (i.e., these women already run companies), albeit a universe in which the traditional heteronormative family is assumed (the women are wives, the customers vouch for other family members).

Saturn's public relations also emphasize the gender/racial equity promised by Saturn as a work and retail space. For example, Joe Sherman notes that Saturn engineer Beth Miakinin was featured in Saturn ads looking "assertive, attractive, brainy" in part to help the public understand that Saturn was a company that was free of old school prejudices.[57] Similarly, Jack O'Toole stressed that part of Saturn's success can be vouched for by the fact that the U.S. Labor Department praised Saturn for their exemplary voluntary efforts toward hiring women and minorities.[58] These claims, coupled with the advertisements, underline the picture of Saturn as the route through which a friction-free consumer and sales space might be achieved.

Returning to Berlant's analysis of post-Reagan citizenship, we find an interesting configuration being made by/through Saturn in the early 1990s. Berlant argues that the economic/racial climate of the early and mid-1990s had created a situation in which formerly "invisible" citizens (white males) began to feel exposed and vulnerable. While one reaction to this visibility was an ideological rage directed at those raced/gendered people who were stereotyped as the cause of the changing economic and political climate, another—the Reagan formula—denigrated the present and incited nostalgia for a past imagined as utopian horizon. As I have been suggesting, Saturn paralleled Reagan's "Morning in America" by promising the return to a space free of the friction of ideological differences that caused structural impediments: those who worked hard would succeed; those who wanted to consume could consume fairly. Moreover, as Berlant observes, this logic is coupled with the promise of renewed visibility of the heteronormative family. And, indeed, Saturn's promised structure-free world is one in which traditional families create hard workers and in which the consumption of Saturn itself provides purchase of the traditional domestic family.

Examples of Saturn as a familial space abound in the representations of Saturn. For example, Vicki Lenz's customer relations treatise is riddled with images of Saturn's semiotics of domesticity. After noting that she was driven by the desire to understand what made the "Saturn family" so special, she observes that Saturn is "perhaps not so different from the way we were taught to treat other people, and the way we treat our friends. Maybe we just tend to forget to apply that consideration to customers."[59] Lenz's evidence consists of not only numerous customers who tell us that "Saturn people are the nicest I have ever dealt with" or that they are treated "like a friend" and "like family," but she also looks for the specific behaviors that make the relationship of buyer with retailer to be something of a "marriage."[60]

Lenz cites customer Linda Bader observing that she was greeted the first time she went to Saturn, and she parallels this with "when you come to my house for dinner, and I'm waiting for you and greet you at the door."[61] Moreover, Bader observes, the greeter went on to introduce her to a salesperson just as if she was "introducing her brother! I already felt like, well, I'm in the Saturn family now."[62] Other customers explain that they felt as if they were at a friend's home when they were offered "one of those wonderful cookies," or were given "free drinks and fresh cookies."[63] Others indicate that the family feeling came to them because they received anniversary cards on the annual birth date of their cars or were given free T-shirts to match the colors of the cars they purchased.[64] In each case, consumers claim that Saturn reiterates already familiar signifiers of family caring and comfort—birthday cards, cookies, drinks, greetings.

Moreover, news articles also consistently point to Saturn's use of the "golden rule" as one route by which they maintain customer relations. Hence, *BusinessWeek* discusses a full money back recall Saturn instigated after a Texaco coolant began corroding engines. Saturn's full money back recall is cited as an example of "fair treatment" that would rarely be seen in the business world.[65] *USA Today* points to the Saturn sales philosophy as one that encourages a feeling of trust and familiarity between the company and its family of owners.[66]

Finally, Saturn's television advertisements also stress the traditional heteronormative family. "Small Favor," for example, opens with the image of a young white woman calling her Saturn retailer after purchasing a car with her husband. She asks the retailer to do her a "small favor" before she and her husband pick up the car that evening. In the next scene, we see the couple looking over their car, as a crowd of Saturn employees stands around them in a circle. As the husband looks in the backseat, he (and the viewer) notice(s) a baby seat. He then looks at his wife with questioning eyes and embraces her as she gives an affirmative nod, and we all understand that she is pregnant. The Saturn employees encircle the couple, applauding the new addition to the (Saturn) family.

Other Saturn television advertisements stress the heteronormative family theme simply by showing the viewer "traditional" families taking part in "traditional" behaviors such as picnics or baseball after the purchase of a Saturn (see, e.g., "Launch," "Baseball," "Magic Shop," "Playground," and "Roland"). One spot, "Nora Dunfee," indeed stresses that the heteronormative family—and its relationship with Saturn—will both stand the test of time. The spot opens with the image of a large statue on the lawn of an apparently upscale home. We are then shown an older white couple standing next to one another in the yard. The two begin to move slightly farther apart from one another as we hear the voiceover announce, "After years of marriage, Bedford, Pennsylvania, resident Nora Dunfee told her husband she needed some space." The commercial ends with the words "SATURN: 12 cubic feet of trunk space." At least metaphorically, then, Saturn assures us of the normalcy, the "invisibility" of traditional heteronormative domesticity and, in effect, stresses that such domesticity can be achieved through the purchase of a Saturn.

In both the worker's representation and the customer's representation, we see two overlapping views of the interpellation of what it might, and should, mean to be American. Represented as the quintessentially American company, producing the quintessentially American product, the discourse surrounding Saturn indicates that while "America" may have temporarily lost its way, a return to core domestic values, to the family, allows the rebirth of America—an America without constraints. In Saturn's hailing, we are promised a workspace and a consumer space free of constraint, in which one can find the recovery not only of lost values but of the family one needs to share in these values.

Articulated with America itself (via its contemporary economic struggles with Japan, its nominal roots in the cold war), Saturn enacted an articulation—and a particularly powerful one if we take early excitement over the car as an indication—that guaranteed a workspace and a marketplace that equated political agency with production and consumption. In essence, despite a few minor resistant readings, Saturn equated both family and "freedom to consume" with American agency[67]—an articulation that critic Lawrence Glickman argues is a long-standing theme in American ideology.[68] In consuming the *image* of equality and the *promise* of the intimacy of family, we find ourselves in the nostalgic past, a past that neither requires nor encourages political agency beyond consumption and domesticity.

The Saturn Nation, Part II: Consumer as Commodity

Despite the great initial enthusiasm for Saturn—both among those writing about the industry and among consumers—the corporation rarely found itself operating in the black. Moreover, a number of factors, many of them rooted in economic concerns as well as in tradition, conspired to constrain Saturn's development and growth—especially in Spring Hill. As I will discuss, these constraints were part of the material constraints that shaped the more recent portion of Saturn's narrative. In large part, as a rhetorical and cultural critic, I find this second portion of Saturn's history fascinating because of the way it is shaped and understood through the rhetorical roots laid down in the first portion of its history. That is, if Saturn is articulated with a nostalgic American vision of a friction-free market and workspace in which citizenship—understood through heteronormative frames—is purchased through the act of consumption, what does it mean when Saturn, at least this image of Saturn, fails? In this section, I outline the discourse describing the causes of Saturn's "failure," describe the shift in Saturn's image and representation from the rhetoric of family/equality to a rhetoric of commodification, and argue that, ultimately, Saturn's discourse represents a hyper-realization or radical intensification of the American-through-consumption model. However, rather than the intimate, familial citizen described by Berlant, we see a model of hyper-commodification, a discourse that not only posits consumption as an act of political freedom but that also turns back on the consumers, commodifying them.

I want to stress again that, as a critic, I do not mean to overstate my claims, to say that the discourse surrounding Saturn is the only discourse available through which to understand our roles as consumers or as "Americans." Rather, while I realize that I am making claims based on the transition in the fortunes, corporate structure, representation, and marketing of a single automobile, I take this essay as an opportunity to problematize what might be called a "people shopping" identity and to think through what we might want out of our relationship to each other and to a larger social whole.[69] In short, in this section, I hope to use the representations surrounding one product to ask some questions about the type of culture in which we wish to live, and the relationship we wish to have with our understandings of the material body. Following this, then, I suggest that the failure of Saturn and its subsequent transition in meaning/representation might serve to tell us something about one possibility in our current ideological field.

Representing Saturn's Corporate Failure

As early as 1994, industry observers noted that while Saturn consistently received high customer satisfaction ratings as measured by J. D. Power and Associates, their sales had fallen from a peak of 25,000 cars a month in 1993 to an average of 15,000 a month in 1994.[70] Further, in their 2001 investigation of management styles at Saturn, Rubinstein and Kochan observed that by the end of the 1990s, Saturn was failing in terms of both sales and management relations. That is, not only were retail sales down, but the local labor union was voting in ways that slowly moved the Saturn plant toward more traditional worker-management relations including, as Rubinstein and Kochan put it, the reestablishment of "us/them," rather than familial, ways of thinking about company relationships.[71]

Throughout 2002, local and national newspapers reported Saturn's financial failings with *BusinessWeek*'s David Welch claiming that Saturn had not only lost money every year of production but had also become an unglamorous purchase, especially compared to its representation in the early 1990s.[72] A year later, Welch observed that while Saturn's new SUV line, the Vue, was selling moderately well, the Ion and L-Series lines were disastrous: "Worse, the tiny Saturn unit continues to burn through money: Insiders tell *BusinessWeek* the long-suffering division—it has never made money in its 10-year existence—could lose $1 billion in 2003."[73] *USA Today* reported later in the same year that "[t]he 13-year-old brand has yet to earn a net profit. Inventories of unsold cars are piling up," and experts were suggesting that Saturn should be shut down completely, with GM putting its financial resources into its traditional divisions, like Chevrolet.[74] When the L-Series was cancelled in 2004, the *Chicago Sun-Times* reminisced that Saturn, which was supposed to be the great hope for GM earlier, "has been unprofitable in 12 of the 13 years since its founding in 1990 on the premise that better customer service and more employee input would produce a car good enough to halt market-share losses to Asian automakers."[75] In short, by the middle of the new decade, Saturn—once articulated as the American hope—had become an agreed-upon failure.

While the reasons for success or failure of any particular product are, of course, complex and overdetermined, those who wrote about Saturn primarily understood its failure as based dually in General Motors' general negligence and the failure of the local and international unions to support the new working relationships. For example, David Welch notes in *BusinessWeek* that "Saturn stands out as one of the great marketing failures in recent automotive history. After accomplishing the supremely challenging task of launching a hot new car brand ten years ago, GM proceeded to steadfastly ignore its new division as the Saturn product line got stale and the no-frills image grew stale."[76] Noting that the marketing budget for Saturn had been cut extensively, Welch observed that GM executives had cut Saturn at the request of other division heads who felt that Saturn was privileged to the detriment of their own divisions.[77] Similarly, Welch notes that Saturn's failure was also the result of GM's refusal to give it the resources to develop larger lines of cars, as well as SUVs.[78] Again, Welch underscores the idea that other division heads demanded that resources go to their more traditional automobile lines.[79] Similarly, the *Chicago Sun-Times* reported that Saturn's failure came as a result of GM's reluctance to allow Saturn to grow.[80]

In 2003, while still placing the blame directly on GM and the other division heads within GM, David Kiley blamed Saturn's failure on the fact that company heads had bowed to internal pressures and forced Saturn to share resources—which it formerly held on its own—with the rest of GM. Not only were Saturn models actually being produced in a Delaware plant geographically (and metaphorically) far away from Spring Hill, but GM was also forcing Saturn to share numerous car parts (e.g., shared vehicle platforms) and marketing plans (e.g., advertising budgets, rebate/finance offers, sales to rental fleets) with other GM divisions.[81] Similarly, after asking, "Is Beaten Up Saturn GM's Falling Star?" Earle Eldrige claimed that Saturn was failing (and was no longer "A Different Kind of Company") because its budget and distinctiveness had been chopped away by GM.[82] In each of these reports, spokespeople for General Motors claimed that they had to make the company more efficient and more adherent to the bottom line, and that the only way to do this was to erase Saturn's differences.[83] On the one hand, then, Saturn's failure as a corporation is represented as being caused by a stress on short-term economic incentives and jealousies within General Motors.

The arrangement between labor and management had also slowly changed, transitioning into something close to a "normal" or traditional set of management-labor relations. Again, as in the case of Saturn's relationship with GM, the cause for management-labor changes was based on labor's concerns with economic survival, rather than their early priorities, such as "family," "caring," and "sharing." Rather than the radical team-oriented approach in which labor and management worked together on all decisions and in which workers were paid partially on a bonus model and could not be laid off, the negotiated arrangement has become more traditional throughout Saturn's history to the point that the relationship is now almost standard. Indeed, an Associated Press story reported in 2003 that Saturn's local UAW had overwhelmingly approved a new labor agreement "that could eventually end the unique agreement the union has with GM," going on to note that the new pact allows GM to lay off Saturn employees for the first time in its history.[84] A month later, another AP story claimed that the new labor agreement was so standard that Saturn had become simply "another GM division."[85]

Given that Saturn's management-labor arrangement was perhaps the most visible aspect of its representation as "different," especially in its early years, the discussion of its failure is important because it is not only a change in workers' conditions but also a change in the public representation of workers' conditions and of their "family" commitment to building Saturn automobiles. Moreover, the representation of this transition, because of the articulation of Saturn with "America," is part of the struggle over the meaning of America and of Americans.

While the reasons for the return to a traditional labor arrangement, of course, are complicated, the representation of the reasons for this transition lay firmly at the foot of economic survival and efficiency. For example, when the new (but traditional) labor agreement was approved by a 2,953 to 317 margin by the Spring Hill UAW Local 1853, Mike Herron, the chairperson, noted, "We are in a position that either we adapt or die."[86] He went on to observe that GM had threatened to close the plant completely if workers did not return to traditional agreements that would allow the automaker to lay off workers during slow periods. Further, the new UAW contract was praised by auto industry analysts precisely because of its stress on competitiveness and profit. For example, Laurie Felax, vice president of automobile industry consulting/analyst firm Harbour and Associates, noted that the new contract was a smart idea from the workers' perspective because "Saturn's plant in Tennessee needs to be as competitive as any in the world—that's how you secure jobs."[87] In effect, these representations of Saturn significantly alter early "meanings" of the company. While workers and others could originally discuss the plant as focused on quality and equity (from which profits would derive), the mosaic of discourse in 2002–2004 concerning Saturn clearly highlights profitability/economic efficiency over all other concerns, including those of worker satisfaction and quality production. On this level, the meaning of Saturn as a corporation has shifted from the domestic and familial to one of profit and production.

Consuming Saturn, Saturn Consuming

While the representation of Saturn-as-corporation changes, so does the representation of Saturn-as-automobile. When, in 2002 and 2003, Saturn decided to alter their image in order to rearticulate their meaning in a different economic and manufacturing climate, they dropped Hal Riney and Partners (now Publicis and Riney) as their marketing firm (the only firm used to that point) and hired Goodby, Silverstein, and Partners. As we shall see, this move somewhat paralleled transitions in the company itself, as we see a shift from a representation of the car as the product of honest, hard-working individuals in a domestic corporate setting to a focus on the car as consumer and the consumer as commodity.

While Saturn's move away from images of heteronormative domesticity and individuality was partially performed simply through advertisements that no longer focused on individual narratives like the Erin Walling and Roland stories and less focus on the "familial" setting within dealerships, another part of this transition occurred as the result of an explicitly stated attempt by Saturn executives to defeminize the car. In a late 2002 *Chicago Sun-Times* article on the advertising change, Jill Lajdziak, Saturn's vice president for sales, service, and marketing, claimed that while Saturn, of course, was pleased with their large female market, they needed to appeal to men as well and would do so by featuring engine power rather than the people who manufacture Saturn.[88] Similarly, the next month, Lajdziak observed in *USA Today* that her goal was to make Saturn "less of a chick's car" by focusing on the car as a powerful commodity rather than emphasizing the overall family-centered atmosphere of some of the early advertising.[89] Combined with the overall alterations in change in the representation of Saturn labor, this transition in the gendering of the car was a part of the rearticulation from domesticity to commodification.

Further, and as intimated previously, these changes are most clearly seen in the changed television advertising strategy, with several of the commercials acting as representative anecdotes for the overall change in Saturn representation. Again, then, in 2003, after years of sluggish sales and corporate changes, Saturn's new advertising firm—Goodby, Silverstein, and Partners—produced commercials including one titled "Sheet Metal" that featured people behaving like cars. As one watches the advertisement, one sees a variety of individuals—with no car in sight—moving through the city as if they are cars. Hence, the viewer sees individuals backing up in driveways, stopping at stoplights, holding flashlights as they "drive" in the evening, and one being pulled over for speeding by a police officer who is also on foot. While the tag line of the commercial indicates that Saturn designers are attempting to build cars around individuals, the commercials visually provide a reversal in which humans themselves become the commodity. Rather than the car as individual, "Sheet Metal" envisions the individual as car. Rather than a "Morning in America" celebration of the heroic (and intimate) individual, we witness the celebration of commodification itself, a "sheet metal" logic in which the citizen is molded, shaped, and expected to act within the logic of consumption. Hence, the "Sheet Metal" advertisement focuses on individuals as cars, behaving and acting *as* cars, hence symbolically transforming the customer into the commodity itself, a transference in which the car and its manufacturer are highlighted over the quality of individual or manufacturing, and in which citizenship, via Saturn, is an act of consumption, an act of commodification.

In "Pac-Man," an advertisement for the Saturn Vue, Saturn's new automobile is seen driving through the suburbs, seemingly swallowing the small circles from the Pac-Man video game while the familiar sounds of Pac-Man accompany the visual texts. However, rather than swallowing the fruit and prizes on the Pac-Man video game, the automobile swallows people (presumably the family members of the driver). In effect, the advertisement visually transforms a stereotypical living space into the icons of a video game. Again, rather than individuals playing a video game, the automobile transforms those human bodies into icons in a virtual, video world.

Finally, and most significantly in my mind, is the advertisement "People Shopping." As provocatively suggested by alternately switching on which word of its title that one places emphasis, this third advertisement works on the premise that Saturn automobiles, anthropomorphized, are living, thinking beings who purchase human beings as drivers. The thirty-second version of the commercial begins with a game show setting in which three different Saturn automobiles compete to win a single white male who stands on stage, reversing our game show expectations. When the scene changes, the viewer sees what at first appears to be a car dealership but turns out to be a "People Dealership." As the plot unfolds, we see Saturns driving through the lot, looking at a variety of individuals on display with labels marking their names. Hence, for example, one Saturn drives by, perhaps considers purchasing "The Malcolm," a casually dressed white male. Throughout the lot are a variety of other individuals and groups of individuals, waiting to be purchased or chosen by the cars. In her discussion of our contemporary cultural condition, Braidotti observes that "one very widespread feature of the contemporary technological imaginary is the extent to which it promotes practices of prosthetic extension and proliferation of bodily parts, organs and cells."[90] In "People Shopping," there is a sense in which we have a meta-phorical reversal in which the common-sense understanding of the material-ity of the prosthetic overcomes or replaces a romantic notion of the human as romantic individual.

Ultimately, and in very significant ways, we see a movement here from people *shopping* to *people* shopping, a movement that ultimately intensifies Saturn's earlier articulation of the American consumer. If Saturn's "Motoring in America" represented a desire for a nostalgic return based on intimacy, the "heteronormative" family, and friction-free workspaces, the newer articula-tion is clearly little improvement. If Saturn stands as the idea of an American car, the very notion of becoming America is based on not only purchase through consumption, but through consumption *and* commodification. As Jean Baudrillard noted decades ago, the language of political involvement and language of consumption are merging: "'I buy, I consume, I take pleas-ure' today repeats in other forms, 'I vote, I participate, I am present, I am concerned.'"[91] While his concern is that we take consumption as an act of politics and politics to be an act of consumption (i.e., which prod-uct/candidate do we prefer), what does it mean when commercially, the act of consumption is not only an entryway to politics but also highlights the product over the human agent and the human agent as product? Indeed, this is an American subjectivity fully based not on intimacy but on a replacement of human agency with human commodity.

Conclusion

A number of conclusions can be drawn from this analysis of the meanings of Saturn, both in its origins and in its contemporary context. First, we can see the multiple ways in which the utopian ideologies of contemporary culture are reflected in contemporary advertising about commodities. From the do-mestic appeals of Reagan's "Morning in America" to the logic of corporation over individual, commodity over person, we can note the ways in which ad-vertising and public relations are a logical place for us to locate our critical concerns. Indeed, if advertising must, like all television and mass media (but maybe even more so), reflect the ideological assumptions of consumers and our republic, it becomes a frightfully important location for our reflections on contemporary culture and meaning. In her study of contemporary American citizenship, Berlant notes the importance of studying "the waste materials of everyday communication in the national public sphere as pivotal documents in the construction, experience and rhetoric of quotidian citizenship."[92] This study emphatically underlines the importance of Berlant's call. Moreover, given the remembrance of the Reagan ideology marking his death in 2004, we would do well to reflect now—in this context—on the limits and problems with the ideology of "Morning in America." This essay serves as one part of that reflection.

Also, this study urges us to think about the relationship between political ideology ("semiotic conditions"), mediation of that ideology ("rhetoric"), and the human body ("material"). Given my beginning assumption—drawn from Braidotti—and earlier discussion that we take the body as a "play of forces, a surface of intensities" and the human subject as a "process of becoming-subject" requiring sets of cultural mediation between "material and semiotic conditions," this study is one ideal place to explore a contemporary articulation of this relationship between bodies, body prosthetics (here, the automobile as prosthetic), and the semiotic layers through which we partially make sense of bodies and prosthetics.[93] In some sense, what we see here is the nightmare underside to Donna Haraway's cyborg dream. Rather than a world of endlessly shifting borders, an erasure of space between human-animal-machine, a move to permanently partial identities, we have a move toward an alteration of values in which "human" is valued as "commodity."

A number of parallels can be drawn: in his study of online shopping and virtual models, John Jordan's concerns are drawn from the fact that virtual model systems (those online models in which consumers attempt to clothe their "own" bodies) encourage the consumers to see their "selves" as less than perfect and only to be improved through the addition of commodities to be placed on the now always already commodified body. As he notes, such models are imagined by consumers but are given "rhetorical and ideological effectiveness" by the corporations' commodities and signifiers.[94] In short, individuals have access to inclusive, socially accepted meanings of their bodies only through purchase of proper commodities; the commodities in effect make the person. Such a transition or reversal occurs as well in the latter stages of Saturn advertising. Drawing on the media ecology approach employed by Jordan, we must ask if what it is to be human and to think as human is in large part a product of our media environment, should we problematize or celebrate current configurations of the "human" in this media environment? While Saturn advertising and online models are not the sole visions of citizenship available to us, and while Baudrillard's concerns about "Absolute Advertising" cannot be universalized, surely these ongoing reconfigurations of the representation of consumption should give us pause.[95]

A subpoint regarding the ethics of consumption can be drawn from this same conclusion. In his essay "Delectable Materialism," Michael Schudson asks us to begin to consider the ethics of acceptable consumption and bases part of his equation on the idea that there should be a "goal that people should have goods sufficient so that they will not be ashamed in society. Societies should be organized so that no one falls below a level that provides access to the consumer goods required for social credit and self-respect."[96] While laudable goals to be sure, we are called to prod such goals when commodities are represented as agents who choose human beings as commodities, when the "people shopping" equation is reversed in such a way that the global consumer ethic is determined by corporations rather than by "consumers."

Third, turning most directly to the purpose of this volume, I want to stress that this essay illustrates the role of rhetorical criticism as always already a part of the ongoing process of mediation between the material and the semiotic (again, in Braidotti's terms). In one sense, this conclusion hardly needs to be highlighted as it seems so commonsensical once uttered. However, this is a lesson that we often forget in practice. In his 1990 reading of the history of "object and method" in rhetorical criticism, Dilip Gaonkar noted that one route taken by critics (Michael Calvin McGee is his prime example) viewed rhetoric as a process that was ontologically prior to its products and hence led to a diminution of any "object" that might be called rhetoric, focusing instead on method or process alone.[97]

While my assumptions here certainly share a great deal with this route—a route that falls under the general rubric of "critical rhetoric"—I hope to have tweaked it to emphasize that criticism is not simply a process of intervening and changing the meaning of "texts" or of "bodies." Rather, in that subjectivity is always already in a process of emergence between the material and the semiotic, and given that I have reserved "rhetoric" as the energy of that mediation, the act of criticism itself is an alteration of that flow of energies and hence is always already a material and semiotic action. Rhetorical criticism flows between the material and the semiotic, reshaping the possibilities of mediation, in this case hopefully reshaping the history of "Saturn" in such a way that it reshapes the consumers that emerge as part of that history.

Notes

1.   Saturn's narrative has been told in print in numerous venues. While I will investigate a number of these narratives throughout this essay, two of the book-length narratives stand out as good starting points for the interested reader. First, Jack O'Toole's *Forming the Future: Lessons from the Saturn Corporation* (Cambridge, MA: Blackwell, 1996) provides an insider's view (from a member of the Group of 99) of the creation of Saturn and its growing pains. Second, Joe Sherman's *In the Rings of Saturn* (New York: Oxford University Press, 1995) is a charming and readable cultural history of Saturn that pro-

vides insight into those who worked at Saturn, as well as into the cultural clash that takes place when a large company and a number of its "northern" employees move into a small southern town.

2.   While numerous automakers have "moved" south in recent years (partially in order to work in non-union states), Saturn was one of the earlier companies to do so, and the only one that was based solely in the South. Some claim that this choice was made, at least in part, to provide symbolic distance from GM's headquarters in Detroit. O'Toole, *Forming the Future*, 47–56; Sherman, *In the Rings of Saturn*, 97–111.

3.   After mergers, they became Publicis & Hal Riney. They are no longer the advertising firm employed by Saturn.

4.   Lauren Berlant, *The Queen of America Goes to Washington City: Essays on Sex and Citizenship* (Durham: Duke University Press, 1997), 4.

5.   Berlant, *Queen of America*, 3.

6.   While I am careful in my own discourse to avoid using "America" to refer to the United States, I do so throughout this paper because this is the articulation made, assumed, and reified in the discourse surrounding Saturn automobiles.

7.   I will provide a number of examples of the ways that consumers discussed the company and the "family" atmosphere of the retailers later in the document. J. D. Power and Associates ratings of customer service can be found at http://www.jdpower.com/autos/articles/2008-Customer-Service-Index-Study. Ratings published by J. D. Power have become the benchmark used by many people to assess the overall performance of (especially) automobile manufacturers. Saturn's rankings the first several years placed them in the top echelon of customer satisfaction. Nina Padgett-Russin of the *Chicago Sun-Times* observed in 2002 that Saturn has received the Power Sales Satisfaction Award seven out of eight years and was the first non-luxury brand ever to receive the Top Customer Service Satisfaction Award since 1986. "Saturn Marks 20th Birthday," *Chicago Sun-Times*, December 23, 2002.

8.   The question of why the company failed to make a profit is certainly a complicated one. The various histories of the automaker would indicate that it was a combination of (1) the difficulties of working out the kinks of the new car-making process early in their history, which led to a deficit of cars in the first several years; (2) Saturn's high attention to customer service and recalls of faulty product that, while leading to high customer satisfaction, increased the cost of production; and (3) GM's slow pace in allowing Saturn to develop mid-size and luxury cars after first gaining customers at the small car level. The best two books dealing with these changes are Jack O'Toole's insider account (*Forming the Future*) and a "management studies" perspective, authored by Saul A. Rubinstein and Thomas A. Kochan, *Learning from Saturn: A Look at the Boldest Experiment in Corporate Governance and Employee Relations* (Ithaca, NY: Cornell University Press, 2001). The question of whether Saturn ever really turned a profit is an arguable one because the reports on this differ. While Jack O'Toole claims that Saturn turned a profit in their fourth year of production, reporters in the early 2000s claim that Saturn never made a profit in its history (see, e.g., David Welch, "Can Saturn Get Off the Ground Again?" *BusinessWeek*, October 14, 2002, 79; and David Welch, "Still Tiny, but Bleeding Like a Monster," *BusinessWeek*, June 2, 2003, 32). Nonetheless, even if Saturn did turn a profit one year, the overall notion that the company was unsuccessful financially is a sound one (O'Toole, *Forming the Future*, 175–76).

9.   Robert Asen recently described a "discourse theory" of citizenship. While I very much admire the type of work Asen describes in this essay, when I discuss "discourse" and

"citizenship" closely in this essay, I am not making use of Asen's theory. Rather, I am discussing the ways in which citizenship is being articulated discursively, the ways in which we are invited ideologically to understand our role as citizens. See Robert Asen, "A Discourse Theory of Citizenship," *Quarterly Journal of Speech* 90 (2004): 189–211.

10. Rosi Braidotti, *Metamorphoses: Towards a Materialist Theory of Becoming* (Malden, MA: Blackwell, 2002), 17.

11. Braidotti, *Metamorphoses*, 21.

12. Braidotti in fact never mentions McLuhan; I include his name here as this may be the most productive way for some media/communication theorists to think through the dynamic being discussed.

13. Braidotti, *Metamorphoses*, 21.

14. Marshall McLuhan, *Understanding Media: The Extensions of Man* (New York: McGraw-Hill, 1964), 218.

15. Marshall McLuhan is an important, but somewhat hidden, starting place for this essay in two ways. First, I use the term "probe" here specifically in order to invoke the sense in which it was used by Marshall McLuhan, in order to consider criticism as a way to help us as a community to think, to forward the conversation about, in this case, what it means to be a citizen and a consumer. For a discussion of "probes," see W. Terrence Gordon, *Marshall McLuhan: Escape into Understanding* (New York: Basic Books, 1997), 179–80. Second, while I do not want to stress this too strongly at the outset, I am interested in looking at representations of automobiles precisely because they are one of the dominant prosthetics employed by U.S. citizens. Public discussions of the automobile, then, act metaphorically as public discussions of the public itself. In effect, as McLuhan notes, there has become a "growing uneasiness about the degree to which cars have become the real population of our cities." McLuhan, *Understanding Media*, 221.

16. The four books are the three mentioned by Jack O'Toole (*Forming the Future*), Joe Sherman (*In the Rings of Saturn*), and Rubinstein and Kochan (*Learning from Saturn),* as well as *The Saturn Difference: Creating Customer Loyalty in Your Company* (New York: John Wiley and Sons, 1999) by Vicki Lenz, a how-to book for those interested in public relations and customer loyalty. Newspaper and magazine articles were drawn from LexisNexis. I attempted to choose essays randomly throughout the history of Saturn. Finally, television ads were drawn from FastChannel Network's archives. I am thankful to FastChannel for allowing me complimentary access to their archives early on in this project (http://www.fastchannel.com).

17. Lenz, *Saturn Difference*, 11.

18. Sherman, *In the Rings of Saturn*, 6.

19. Sherman, *In the Rings of Saturn*, 16.

20. O'Toole, *Forming the Future*, xi.

21. David Whiteside, "GM's Bold Bid to Reinvent the Wheel," *BusinessWeek*, January 21, 1985, 34.

22. Jeff B. Copeland and David L. Gonzalez, "Saturn Comes Down to Earth," *Newsweek*, November 10, 1986, 58 (emphasis added).

23. Alan Goldstein, "Residents Still Wait to Share in Saturn Riches," *St. Petersburg Times*, October 14, 1990 (emphasis added).

24. Warren Brown, "GM Paints Its High Hopes on Latest Model, Saturn," *Washington Post*, March 23, 1990.

25. "A Spark Plug Called Saturn," *BusinessWeek*, April 9, 1990, 94; James B. Treece, "Here Comes GM's Saturn," *BusinessWeek*, April 8, 1991, 32; David Woodruff, "At Saturn,

What Workers Want Is . . . Fewer Defects," *BusinessWeek*, December 2, 1991, 117; Troy Segal, "Finally Saturn Enters the Ring," *BusinessWeek*, October 29, 1990, 113.

26. Theodore P. Roth and Pat Hinsberg, "Saturn Ads: Facts and Folksy Figures," *Adweek*, October 1, 1990, 32.
27. Ross Laver, "Joining Hands," *Maclean's*, April 15, 1991, 46.
28. Doron Levin, "G.M. Saturn Plants Makes Friends," *New York Times*, January 23, 1990; Doron Levin, "A GM Car with a Japanese Feel," *New York Times*, December 11, 1990.
29. Micheline Maynard, "Enthusiasm Drives Saturn Workers," *USA Today*, August 31, 1990.
30. Levin, "GM Car with a Japanese Feel"; Treece, "Here Comes GM's Saturn," 56.
31. Ray Magliozzi and Tom Magliozzi, "Car Talk," *Atlanta Journal-Constitution*, October 18, 1991.
32. Teresa Burney, "Teacher Is Area's First Saturn Owner," *St. Petersburg Times*, October 26, 1990; Micheline Maynard, "Buyers Become Fast Fans," *USA Today*, April 29, 1991.
33. Burney, "Teacher Is Area's First."
34. Laver, "Joining Hands," 46.
35. While my focus as a rhetorical and cultural critic is on the discursive and visual representation of Saturn's production process, I should stress that Saturn's labor-management relations were indeed materially different than those normally established in the automobile industry. While the development of Saturn's labor-management structure and the ways in which these differences function from an organizational perspective have been discussed in detail in works such as O'Toole, *Forming the Future*—O'Toole was a union member who worked at Saturn and a member of the Group of 99 who created/formed Saturn—and Rubinstein and Kochan, *Learning from Saturn*, perhaps the best summary of Saturn's organizational structure is found, ironically, in cultural critic Brishen Rogers, "The Myth of the Happy Worker," *The Baffler*, December 1999, 41–50. In this essay, largely critical of Saturn, Rogers observes a number of material differences in the union-management arrangements. First, he notes, because management and labor were using a "team concept," labor had input of some sort on all decisions, including model design, work space design, break times, and advertising/marketing. Second, Saturn workers accepted a lower base pay with bonuses to compensate for their overall productivity and performance. Third, shop-floor rules designating job-specific assignments were replaced with promises "to work together on all problems" (Rogers, "Myth of the Happy," 45). Additionally, Saturn workers operated with few job titles, no reserved parking spaces, a shared labor-management lunchroom, and few differences in clothing (for more discussion of this, see Maynard, "Enthusiasm Drives Saturn Workers"; and Doron Levin, "Saturn: An Outpost of Change in GM's Steadfast Universe," *New York Times*, March 17, 1991). While Rogers goes on to provide a material critique of the "actual condition" of workers at Saturn, I am more interested in the contours of the narrative of the team worker and the articulation of the workers' relationship to the corporation. In short, as I will illustrate, a picture emerges of a laborer who is consistently caring and cared for, working with others (laborers and management alike) with a sense of individual responsibility within a team atmosphere.
36. Lenz, *Saturn Difference*, 57.
37. O'Toole, *Forming the Future*, 6.
38. O'Toole, *Forming the Future*, 30, 70.
39. Rubinstein and Kochan, *Learning from Saturn*, 2.
40. Rubinstein and Kochan, *Learning from Saturn*, 62, 67.
41. Roth and Hinsberg, "Saturn Ads," 32.

42. Laver, "Joining Hands," 46; Levin, "GM Car with a Japanese Feel."

43. Maynard, "Enthusiasm Drives Saturn Workers."

44. Treece, "Here Comes GM's Saturn," 56.

45. While it is not my job to get to the "truth" of how workers felt at the time, there is evidence that a counterhistory of Saturn could have been told and would have been far more dystopian than the dominant story. For example, Rogers argues that many workers felt that the "team" concept led workers to work so many hours because, in that they were given bonuses for production, team peer pressure was hoisted on "members who either miss work or can't make quota" (Rogers, "Myth of the Happy," 48). He goes on to note that management didn't need to police workers because workers policed each other as their own little "group of piranhas" (Rogers, "Myth of the Happy," 49). Similarly, early on, *U.S. News and World Report* quoted union leader Peter Kelly saying that the arrangement threatened unions in general and rolled back most worker gains (Micheline Maynard, "A Labor Deal that Clears Way for GM's Saturn," *U.S. News and World Report*, August 5, 1985, 22). In such cases, we see that a counterstory, one that could have been argued more forcefully, especially given that workers ultimately voted to return to traditional labor arrangements, was stifled as a utopian image of the "Morning in America" worker created a vision in which workers and management could operate jointly, as family, to release human potential.

46. Berlant, *Queen of America*, 1–54; Eric O. Clarke, *Virtuous Vice: Homoeroticism and the Public Sphere* (Durham, NC: Duke University Press, 2000), 39–40.

47. Berlant, *Queen of America*, 4.

48. Berlant, *Queen of America*, 4.

49. Dana L. Cloud, "Hegemony or Concordance? The Rhetoric of Tokenism in Oprah Winfrey's Rags-to-Riches Biography," *Critical Studies in Media Communication* 13 (1996): 132–34. Cloud illustrates that biographies of Oprah Winfrey go so far as to suggest that even acknowledging and fighting against structural impediments, such as built-in racism, leads one to economic ruin. Ignoring the civil rights movement, Winfrey is able to meet success on her own merits, such histories claim. The Saturn advertisements, as I will illustrate, acknowledge the impediments of the past but hold out Saturn as a space in which equality—and traditional American work values—might be achieved.

50. In our analysis of early advertising about "cyberspace" by different Internet carriers, Andrew Herman and I point to a similar phenomenon. The Internet was consistently advertised and discussed as a utopian space in which neither physical nor representational constraints could hinder the individual. Indeed, in such advertisements, one could "be whatever one wanted to be" and "go wherever one wanted to go" with no limits. Andrew Herman and John M. Sloop, "The Politics of Authenticity in Postmodern Rock Culture: The Case of Negativeland and the Letter 'U' and the Numeral '2,'" *Critical Studies in Mass Communication* 15 (1998): 1–20.

51. Clarke, *Virtuous Vice*, 40. Berlant notes that Reagan's discourse constantly discussed the citizen as emerging only in "families"; the discourse of Saturn—riddled with metaphor and literal discussions of family—bears this out. Berlant, *Queen of America*.

52. Lenz, *Saturn Difference*, 88.

53. Sherman, *In the Rings of Saturn*, 234; Jamie Beckett, "Saturn's Ringing Endorsement of American Life," *San Francisco Chronicle*, November 19, 1990.

54. This advertisement is especially interesting in a cultural and product context in which there are so few female salespeople. Helene Lawson provides a nice critique of the gender problematics of the automobile salesroom and the reasons why so few women meet

with success in automobile retailing. Helen Lawson, *Ladies on the Lot: Women, Car Sales, and the Pursuit of the American Dream* (Lanham, MD: Rowman and Littlefield, 2000).

55. Lenz, *Saturn Difference*, 26.
56. Lenz, *Saturn Difference*, 67.
57. Sherman, *In the Rings of Saturn*, 90.
58. O'Toole, *Forming the Future*, 175–76.
59. Lenz, *Saturn Difference*, xii, 24.
60. Lenz, *Saturn Difference*, 41.
61. Lenz, *Saturn Difference*, 103.
62. Lenz, *Saturn Difference*, 103 (see also 184, 186, 213).
63. Lenz, *Saturn Difference*, 115.
64. Lenz, *Saturn Difference*, 155, 163, 184.
65. James B. Treece, "Getting Mileage from a Recall," *BusinessWeek*, May 27, 1991, 38; Woodruff, "At Saturn, What Workers," 117; Paul A. Eisenstein, "Saturn May Rewrite Auto Marketing Book," *Journal of Commerce*, April 20, 1989; Magiliozzi, "Car Talk."
66. James Healey, "Saturn Spins Off New Sales Pitch," *USA Today*, October 29, 1990.
67. There are a number of subthemes about problems with Saturn that emerge simultaneously with the discourse analyzed. However, these discourses are clearly minority discourses. While one critic's role might be to help bring these to the front, I am much more interested in taking what I clearly see to be the dominant story being told (I doubt anyone who read these articles, books, and commercials would disagree much with the story I have told) and reread them in a way that helps encourage an undermining of the dominant story. However, for those readers interested in nondominant readings of the discourse, I would suggest the following. First, Joe Sherman's *In the Rings of Saturn* does an excellent job of pointing out the strained relations between the northern workers who move to Spring Hill to work at Saturn and the locals, who don't see themselves as benefiting from the plant. Moreover, Sherman is interested in the ways in which the Saturn plant worked to dislocate or eradicate part of the local flavor and culture Spring Hill had before the arrival of the plant. The southern–northern divide and the disruptions the city experienced are also covered in a number of interesting newspaper articles, including Goldstein, "Residents Still Wait"; Beckett, "Saturn's Ringing Endorsement"; and Darryl Fears, "GM Plant Ignites Civil War in Tennessee Town," *Atlanta Journal-Constitution*, December 18, 1991. There are also a few discussions of the way in which the "happy worker" of Saturn was something of a myth, as I noted in a previous endnote. One could look first at Rogers's now classic *Baffler* sidebar, "The Myth of the Happy Worker," as well as comments by Sherman about continuing gender problems/harassment in the plant (Rogers, "Myth of the Happy," 267–68). Moreover, in O'Toole's highly celebratory insider's take on Saturn, he consistently makes comments that essentialize women as different than men. For example, he notes of one of his team's female members, "Women see the world differently from men . . . Women intuit, or sense and feel, that which men try to solve with logic, data, and fact." He also notes that they chose CBS's Kathleen Sullivan to emcee a Saturn retailer announcement activity because they wanted to emphasize difference by not choosing men to represent them (O'Toole, *Forming the Future*, 62).
68. Lawrence B. Glickman, "Born to Shop? Consumer History and American History," introduction to *Consumer Society in American History: A Reader*, ed. Lawrence B. Glickman (Ithaca, NY: Cornell University Press, 1999), 1–16.
69. In short, I understand that I may be overstating some of my claims, but I do so because I

am using this analysis as a springboard to think through our roles as citizens and the role that consumption plays in our cultural lives.

70. David A. Aaker, "Building a Brand: The Saturn Story," *California Management Review* 12 (1994): 132. For a take on Saturn's economic downturn, see the Auto Editors of Consumer Guide, "How Saturn Cars Work: Saturn Car Company's Economic Downturn," *How Stuff Works*, http://auto.howstuffworks.com/saturn-cars6.htm.

71. Rubinstein and Kochan, *Learning from Saturn*, 123.

72. Earle Eldridge, "Is Beaten-Up Saturn GM's Falling Star?" *USA Today*, December 5, 2003; "Saturn 'Adapt or Die' Deal Adopted by UAW," *Gazette*, December 26, 2003; Scott Reeves, "Saturn to Become Just Another GM Division," *Toronto Star*, January 30, 2004; Matt Nauman, "Saturn Increasing Galaxy of Models," *Milwaukee Journal Sentinel*, February 24, 2004; Welch, "Can Saturn Get," 79.

73. Welch, "Still Tiny, But Bleeding," 32.

74. Eldridge, "Is Beaten-Up Saturn."

75. Joe Miller, "GM to End Saturn L-Series Sooner than Planned," *Chicago Sun-Times*, March 3, 2004.

76. Welch, "Can Saturn Get," 79.

77. Welch, "Can Saturn Get," 79.

78. During a tour of the Saturn plant in Spring Hill, I was surprised when the tour director bluntly blamed GM for failing to support Spring Hill by refusing to give it an okay to produce new models of cars.

79. Welch, "Still Tiny, But Bleeding," 32.

80. Padgett-Russin, "Saturn Marks 20th Birthday."

81. David Kiley, "Saturn Aims to Ring Up Younger, Male Buyers," *USA Today*, January 21, 2003.

82. Eldridge, "Is Beaten-Up Saturn."

83. Rubinstein and Kochan, in their managerial explanation of the collapse of Saturn, note that innovation is almost impossible in large businesses precisely because economic incentives overdetermine all decisions. While GM may have initially attempted to create a new workplace and a different type of company, material constraints created a situation in which stockholders encouraged a return to the norm. As Rubinstein and Kochan observe, the current paradigm holds that "the primary, if not the sole, purpose of American corporations should be to maximize shareholder wealth. Perhaps it is time to confront this issue and challenge this prevailing view by encouraging organizational forms that provide other stakeholders a voice" (Rubinstein and Kochan, *Learning from Saturn*, 144).

84. "Saturn 'Adapt or Die.'"

85. Reeves, "Saturn to Become"; Bush Bernard, "No-Layoff Policy May End at Spring Hill Plant," *Tennessean*, June 18, 2004.

86. "Saturn 'Adapt or Die.'"

87. Reeves, "Saturn to Become."

88. Padgett-Russin, "Saturn Marks 20th Birthday"; Stuart Elliott, "Saturn Campaign Tries Using Alternate Worlds to Change Its Image," *New York Times*, January 8, 2003.

89. Kiley, "Saturn Aims to Ring," B8.

90. Braidotti, *Metamorphoses*, 238.

91. Jean Baudrillard, *Simulacra and Simulation* (Ann Arbor: University of Michigan Press, 1994), 91.

92. Berlant, *Queen of America*, 12.

93. Braidotti, *Metamorphoses*, 21.

94. John Jordan, "Dressing the Body in Online Shopping Sites (Ad)," *Critical Studies in Media Communication* 20 (2003): 248–68.

95. Indeed, even given her concerns, Lauren Berlant imagines the possibilities of other types of citizenship, including a "diva citizenship," in her argument (*Queen of America*, 221–46).

96. Michael Schudson, "Delectable Materialism: Second Thoughts on Consumer Culture," *Consumer Society in American History: A Reader*, ed. Lawrence B. Glickman (Ithaca, NY: Cornell University Press, 1999), 354.

97. Dilip Gaonkar, "Object and Method in Rhetorical Criticism: From Wichelns to Leff and McGee," *Western Journal of Communication* 54 (1990): 291, 295.

CHAPTER 4

Material Aesthetics in Middle America: Simone Weil, the Problem of Roots, and the Pantopic Suburb

Joan Faber McAlister, Drake University

> To be rooted is perhaps the most important and least recognized need of the human soul . . . a human being has roots by virtue of his real, active, and natural participation in the life of a community, which preserves in living shape certain particular treasures of the past and certain particular expectations for the future.
>
> Simone Weil, *The Need for Roots:*
> *Prelude to a Declaration of Duties toward Mankind*

In the opening chapter of the bestselling book *Bowling Alone: The Collapse and Revival of American Community*, Harvard professor of public policy Robert D. Putnam describes a menacing twentieth-century crisis of community:

> For the first two-thirds of the twentieth century a powerful tide bore Americans into ever deeper engagement in the life of their communities, but a few decades ago— silently, without warning—that tide reversed and we were overtaken by a treacherous rip current. Without at first noticing, we have been pulled apart from one another and from our communities over the last third of the century.[1]

Putnam's book explores the causes and consequences of this "treacherous rip current" that has left Americans adrift. In contrast to the vibrant social groups of the 1960s that were "cultivated by assiduous civic gardeners and watered by increasing affluence and education," Putnam finds that civic organizations at the end of the century have withered and died; the result, he suggests, is that Americans are no longer rooted in communal life.[2] Far from alone in his appraisal, Putnam is joined by a host of scholars and popular commentators who not only share his concern, but regard anxiety about rootlessness and the desire for community as central features of contemporary American life at the turn of the twenty-first century.

In the decade before Putnam began his study, communitarians such as Amitai Etzioni launched debates over how to restore a sense of community that "hegemonized" political theory during the 1980s, according to Mark Reinhardt.[3] For such communitarians, the most urgent problems facing American citizens included "unshackled greed, rootlessness, alienation from the political process, rises in the rate of divorce, and all other phenomena related to a centering on the self and away from community in contemporary societies."[4] *U.S. News and World Report* echoed these concerns in 1995 when it warned of "a deep sense of anxiety in the land, not only about street problems like crime and homelessness but about more shadowy, philosophical issues as well: emotional dislocation and disconnectedness from dependable moorings."[5] The author of this article cited a number of recent books by cultural critics (such as Jean Beth Elshtain, Christopher Lasch, and Myron Magnet) characterizing this dislocation or "societal trauma" as a function of "economic and emotional rootlessness, cultural tribalism, and a rampant, market-driven individualism that is corroding family and neighborhood."[6] The links that *USNWR* makes between "American community," "roots," "family," and "neighborhood" are not only discursive characteristics of the texts it cites, but also central premises of the "New Urbanist" critiques of postwar suburbia that emerged during the same period. Central to this literature was an expressed concern regarding where Americans, particularly members of the "middle class" suburban family, were attempting (and failing) to make themselves at home in the final decades of the twentieth century.

At the same time that scholars, cultural critics, and journalists evidenced this solicitude, there was a popular explosion of interest in the housing development commonly called the "subdivision." These ubiquitous residential areas incorporate early suburban elements, such as single-family homes and spacious lawns, with more recent characteristics, such as prominent entrance markers displaying thematic titles, curving streets terminating in cul-de-sacs, and houses surfaced in neutral colors with only slight architectural variations between models. While these developments lacked the amenities of the "master planned community" (shared security, golf courses, clubhouses, and parks), they evidenced an aesthetic unity resembling the master plan, creating an overall effect that proponents call "cohesive" and critics describe as "plodding artificiality."[7]

While there is some disagreement over how to characterize subdivision design, there can be no doubt that the form has become immensely popular with builders and homebuyers. While it is difficult to determine exactly how many housing subdivisions had been built by the close of the twentieth century, estimates indicate that between 1964 and 2000, the number of homeowner associations (organizations created to enforce deed restrictions in these developments) went from approximately 500 to more than 200,000.[8] The growth in popularity of the subdivision during the same period that the home and neighborhood were being linked to the American crisis of community is significant.

In what follows, I argue that the relationship between the proclaimed loss of a sense of communal roots and the material aesthetic characterizing the subdivision's version of the neighborhood illustrates how a cultural space can come to be positioned as a solution to a social problem.[9] The particular solution that subdivisions provide for the problem of roots is one that has significant political consequences, in that it aestheticizes community in ways that encourage tribalism and substitute artifacts of material culture for the social practices that produced them, all while reassuring members of the community that the problem of rootedness has been solved. Viewing subdivision design as a case study in how material aesthetics can work to solve social ills also brings the relations between style and politics into sharper focus.

Since Edwin Black observed, nearly forty years ago, the "strong and multifarious links between a style and an outlook," rhetoricians have been examining the connections between stylistics, ideology, and subjectivity.[10] A significant extension of the relationships Black posited between aesthetics and politics has taken place in the work of rhetorical scholars such as Robert Hariman, Bonnie Dow and Mari Boor Tonn, and James McDaniel, whose writings have explored the role of style in the practices of political culture.[11] Although these studies have made significant strides in investing matters of style with substance, they have yet to contend fully with the theoretical stance of materialism, which renders aesthetics as mere ornamentation (and also limits the rhetorical critic's task to demystifying discourse to expose the real determinants of social relations). The failure to confront this framework has limited our ability to consider the significance of the political effects of aesthetics in relation to conversations about rhetoric, materiality, and materialism. Writing in the early 1980s, Michael Calvin McGee and Dana Cloud took positions on the degree to which discourse can be read as material and/or productive of material effects, critical analyses of the functions of material culture dramatically expanded the definition of the rhetorical "text," and the political implications of competing materialist theories became the subject of a high-profile and animated debate involving Cloud, Ronald Greene, James Aune, and Steve Macek.[12] Joshua Gunn has already detailed the key moves in this exchange, and it is likely to continue to provoke commentary in the journals of the field.[13] However, the larger implications of the debate over material/materialist rhetoric have not been explicitly addressed, such as the way this exchange has reduced the conversation to two competing camps—both of which fail to provide a convincing account of the discursive and embodied aspects of materiality and which also share a preoccupation with Marxist conceptual categories.

Unfortunately, scholars may find it difficult to fully embrace either of the divergent positions taken up by participants in the materiality/materialism debate. This is the case because a dilemma emerges for critics who are unwilling either to subordinate rhetoric (defined as the study of the distortions of "ideological discourses") to economic analyses of the "objective social realities, interests, and lived experiences of contending classes in capitalist society," or to locate the ontology of classes squarely in discursive processes, insist on the primacy of "communicative labor," and place all hope for social transformation in the "joys" such labor can afford.[14] Furthermore, despite their differences, both sides have allowed Marxist formulations and aims to dictate the terms of the debate, have made analyses of rhetoric's relationship to capitalism central, and have worked to heighten the distinctions (rather than explore the relationships) between and among textual aesthetics, rhetorical functions, political agency, and material conditions.

This essay brings together the themes of style, politics, and materiality with a case study that examines the functions of a material aesthetic of place through the lens of the political philosophy of Simone Weil. The concept of the "material aesthetic" can be drawn from a passage in Immanuel Kant's *Critique of Judgement* (a primary influence on Weil's aesthetic and moral theories) in which it is defined in terms of the experiential properties appealing to sensation, "charm or emotion."[15] As Robert Chenavier notes, Weil applies Kantian aesthetics to the material conditions of daily life but alters his formula substantially by assigning to human action (specifically in the form of labor) the function of mediating sensation and experience.[16] Weil, who credits Kant with noting that only time can perform the vital function of bringing order to experiences, also sees the temporal as superior to the spatial in the creation of community-as-place, a site that ideally "preserves in living shape certain particular treasures of the past and certain particular expectations for the future."[17] The concept of the material aesthetic, as extrapolated from Weil's writings, provides an opportunity to reconnect the rhetorical functions and political import of style with an analysis of the roles that spatiality, temporality, and materiality play in shaping social practices and social relations.

Although Weil has attracted much attention in the fields of philosophy, literature, and theology, she has seldom been mentioned in rhetorical studies.[18] It is perhaps no surprise that she has received little attention from rhetorical scholars, given her admiration of Plato, her denigration of Aristotle (in her judgment, a clumsy methodologist whose "research" conducted "by means of human reason" could never produce true wisdom and whose "constructions" lacked the ability to inspire), and the overtly religious subject matter that dominates her writing.[19] And yet, however incompatible with the rhetorical tradition her work may appear at first glance, Weil has much to offer critics and theorists exploring the relations between and among discourse, aesthetics, materiality, and political subjectivity. Her writing is characterized by an interest in the powers and limits of language and symbols; a conceptualization of class that is grounded in an analysis of workplace design; a commitment to political action that might improve the conditions of laborers; and critiques of capitalism, colonialism, and nationalism.[20] These aspects of Weil's writing, as well as her extensive treatment of the problem of roots and the political consequences of rootlessness (which Françoise Meltzer credits for both predating and expanding on the concept later taken up by scholars such as Gilles Deleuze and Félix Guattari), make her work uniquely suited to the task of examining the American crisis of community and one of its most popular forms of redress: refigured residential space.[21]

Weil's work also provides another means of addressing issues of class that have, according to Aune, been "thoroughly ignored by rhetorical scholars," an assessment echoed by Cloud's labeling of the discipline as "notoriously class- and economics-blind."[22] While Aune and Cloud have provided only Marxist frameworks for orienting rhetorical considerations of class positions and politics, Weil may offer a productive corrective to what many have identified as the limits of such an approach. In Weil's view, Marx fails to define class, identify the specific mechanisms of oppression, and explain problems of power that extend beyond the "struggle for subsistence," or to provide a convincing account of political agency and social transformation—all errors that must be addressed by any serious attempt to apply Marxist theories in critical scholarship.[23] Weil's own work models an approach to class that moves beyond a Marxist typology of "revenue" and "labor" to a much broader conceptualization of class as social location in the most literal sense: firmly grounded in the material culture of the spaces where subjects are most at home in daily life.[24]

Drawing on Weil's work, I argue that subdivision design offers an American middle class a solution to the problem of roots through a material aesthetics of community as pantopia—the always and everywhere home. In aestheticizing community in this way, the subdivision's pantopia negotiates a troubling contradiction noted in discourses on community: the desire to be rooted in both space and time, on the one hand, and the need to transplant Americans, on the other. However, the potential costs of this solution are significant when viewed in light of Weil's critique of the role of rootedness in political life. Beyond the specific concerns Weil raises about the narrow scope of labor and social obligation in the subdivision's pantopic community, her treatment of the problem of roots suggests that quick solutions foreclose important struggles over the nature and status of the collectivity within which we may find a sense of belonging.

In what follows, I begin by sketching the general contours of the problem of roots, examining how the crisis of community came to focus on the suburban middle class family and contemporary residential design. I then provide a rhetorical analysis of brochures used to market new housing developments in the American Midwest, in order to illustrate how the narratives of home and community deployed in such texts instruct potential residents to view the subdivision as a middle class pantopia, an amendment to Andrew Wood's omnitopia thesis.[25] Turning to the material aesthetics of these pantopic spaces, I detail how temporal and spatial aspects of the communities that they construct become problematic when viewed through Weil's theory of the role of roots in social relations. Following this analysis, I consider the consequences of the pantopic solution to the problem of rootlessness and end with a brief discussion of the more general contributions Weil's approach can make to understanding the rhetorical implications of material aesthetics.

America Uprooted

Albert Camus called Simone Weil's manuscript *The Need for Roots: Prelude to a Declaration of Duties Toward Mankind* one of the most important books to emerge after the French Revolution.[26] In a mixed appraisal of the work's potential to find an audience, T. S. Eliot classified *The Need for Roots* as belonging to a "prolegomena to politics which politicians seldom read, and which most of them would be unlikely to understand or to know how to apply."[27] Although Weil's study of rootlessness addresses the situation of France near the end of the German occupation most directly, it speaks more generally to the conditions and forces that uproot a people, the political hazards facing a collectivity that has lost its roots, and the possibilities for re-creating an environment in which subjects once again can become rooted.

According to Weil, key occurrences that can precipitate a loss of social roots include a substantial territorial migration, invasion by a conqueror, or revolution from within, each of which causes a radical break with history. In addition to these events, Weil identifies a preoccupation with money and a rapid modernization that dissolves traditional identities and practices as forces that can uproot particular subjects or (eventually) entire social bodies.[28] Centralization of public life in ways that replace diverse local and regional identities with rituals marked by a "dull uniformity" (as in the Mediterranean after Roman conquest) and an "atmosphere of moral decay" (as in the suburbs of Paris under the Third Republic) are additional factors in uprooting a people, as the state consumes all national geography as its own.[29]

A more insidious cause of uprooting is an unrestrained and misplaced patriotism that fails to distinguish between the nation (the country from which subjects derive their identities and to which they owe the highest order of obligations) and the state (the administrative body that oversees the county's resources). Such patriotism unites members behind the nation as an "absolute value," which denies the haphazard historical production of the given country, renders an honest account of the evils and failings of state policies and actions impossible, and exalts the nation above all other countries.[30] For Weil, any collectivity can be afflicted by rootlessness, but in America, insofar as it is constituted as a nation of immigrants and "a people deprived of the time dimension," the disease is endemic.[31]

In Weil's account, some potential consequences of rootlessness among a population are spiritual death and apathy; a vulnerability to the appeals of fascism, communism, and anarchy; and a tendency to favor imperialist actions that aim to uproot other collectivities.[32] Finding a way to re-root a population to prevent these outcomes is the aim of *The Need for Roots*. The task of re-creating an environment that nurtures social roots draws Weil's attention to processes for preserving and disseminating local, regional, and national histories, a reconsideration of the concept of social class, and a critical examination and reconstruction of the material "conditions of existence" in the literal structures that shape daily life.[33] These three themes are necessarily linked in Weil, for it is through schooling in histories that subjects come to identify with particular positions in a social body, and those positions cannot be considered apart from their literal social location in the places of work and residence in which their labors and lives are carried out. Weil finds a full analysis of these concepts and conditions lacking, even in Marx:

Few notions are so vague as that of social class. Marx, who built up the whole of his system upon it, never attempted to define it, nor even simply to investigate it. The only information to be extracted from his works on the subject of social classes is that they are things which engage in strife. That is not enough.[34]

Weil's critique of Marx rests on the way that class is a preexisting entity in his formulation, an abstract category detached from any specific time (history) and place (social space). Her own conception of social class proceeds from her firsthand study of the nature of the machines on the factory floor and the particular character of the places workers and peasants live, and extends to proposals for a cure for uprootedness that begin with detailed plans for redesigning these spaces.[35] The aesthetics of cultural spaces are thus linked to social practices and identities, helping to shape the ways in which subjects are related to one another and to the larger political collectivity. Overall, Weil hopes to discover a type of rootedness that engenders a "compassionate" love of one's nation as fallible and flawed and that stems from an awareness of its "precious, fragile, and perishable" character.[36] Such a love, Weil contends, can still be given, even in the full knowledge that it is entirely attributable to one's (arbitrarily occasioned) position as a member of one collectivity among (potentially equal) others.

Although the dangers described in *The Need for Roots*—insights primarily derived from her painful proximity to the rise of Hitler and the German occupation of France—seem more substantial than communitarians' complaints about stagnant public life at the turn of twenty-first-century America, there is a clear resemblance between them. Common themes include a lack of political and cultural vibrancy and the neglect of traditional social practices, as well as an interest in the role of social class in creating roots and a concern about the specific sites wherein daily life is lived and practiced. Far from being limited to the musings of a few social commentators, these themes run through a large body of discourse that scrutinized the nature and status of communal ties in America as the twentieth century drew to a close. This discourse includes the work of journalists, communitarian scholars, and New Urbanist planners, but the single text about America's crisis of community that has garnered the most popular attention is Putnam's *Bowling Alone*.

As a recent *Quarterly Journal of Speech* book review notes, *Bowling Alone* has become "a key text for scholars in communication who study public life."[37] Indeed, Putnam's book is a particularly important reference point for any critical analysis of popular commentary on the new American crisis of community. In the search for hard evidence to support his thesis that Americans have become increasingly disconnected from one another and have withdrawn from public life over the last three decades, Putnam compiles and analyzes thousands of individual studies and accounts, creating a compendium of sociological data concerning contemporary daily life. While not all the researchers that Putnam cites endorse his particular thesis, they do seem to share his concerns about the character of contemporary American daily life and politics, as evidenced by their careful studies of the numbers of card games played, letters mailed, church services attended, newspapers read, and stop signs observed, etc., over the past thirty years. This vast quantity of data, as well as the many scholarly and popular treatises that Putnam incorporates, indicate a social and political anxiety that extends well beyond the pages of *Bowling Alone*.

Although sociologists, political theorists, and journalists frequently diagnose urgent social ills, the discourse on lost community and rootlessness from the 1980s and 1990s is unique, not only because so many authors describe the same crisis, but also because of the unlikely victims they identify. Contrary to other high-profile issues during the same period (e.g., homelessness, AIDS, drug addiction), the described loss of community encompasses, even fetishizes, the average middle class American citizen, a sociopolitical subject often depicted as insulated from otherwise pervasive social ills. For Putnam, the decline in league bowling, a "solidly middle-American" sport, is a strong sign that the crisis has penetrated all levels of American society to reach affluent, educated, married homeowners. In other words, the problem has reached those whom he regards as traditionally the best members of communities.[38] This is particularly alarming to Putnam because his historical inspiration for a future revival of community is the movement launched by the group he calls the "middle class reformers" of the Progressive era, whose contemporary counterparts may be our best hope for re-creating communal bonds.[39] During the same period when the national press was reporting on the "disappearance" of the American middle class, the middle class subject was becoming highly visible as both casualty and potential hero of the crisis of community.[40]

According to some critics, the suburban middle class is particularly vulnerable to the feeling of rootlessness accompanying a loss of community. Former NPR *Talk of the Nation* host and author Ray Suarez argues that the new "rootlessness" and "loss of a sense of place" originates with suburbanites who fled from urban centers and now must "face the consequences of postwar America's choice: to run away from home."[41] New Urbanists join Suarez in blaming increasing suburbanization for tearing these Americans away from their roots, claiming that postwar suburban design isolates and fragments the middle class and destroys communal ties.[42] In advocating a return to traditional models of the house and neighborhood to re-create a sense of place, New Urbanists posit that particular features of domestic architecture and (sub)urban planning can cultivate or destroy rootedness, an argument consistent with a tendency to link roots and residential space in other texts.[43]

For Putnam, "residential stability is strongly associated with civic engagement" since "frequent re-potting disrupts root systems" and homeowners are the most "rooted" and active members of a community.[44] Similarly, from the communitarian perspective, Etzioni finds "residential communities" to be most "stable and deep-rooted."[45] From New Urbanist efforts to revive elements of traditional housing design (e.g., the front porch and white picket fence) to the sociological studies of residential practices cited by Etzioni and Putnam, widespread anxiety over rootlessness and loss of community directed attention to domestic space at the close of the twentieth century.[46] The proclaimed need for roots provided a rationale for the new crisis to focus on a particular place as the site for both the decline and potential rebirth of community: the suburban home and neighborhood.

The problem of roots is one of foundations, origins, and histories. Efforts to uncover the roots of a subject, institution, or practice are attempts to locate it diachronically in space and time, to pinpoint its origin (to identify the root of the word), find its essence (to get to the root of the matter), and situate it in a historical narrative (to trace its roots). In the biological metaphors so often operant in discourse on the crisis of community, establishing roots requires two things: undisturbed ground and sufficient time to grow. Roots require continuity in both space and time. This is why authors such as Putnam, Suarez, and Etzioni examine the relationships between community, suburbanization, and "residential stability," looking at both where Americans are living and how long they have lived there. Notably, however, the need for both stability and permanence to nourish the roots of community introduced an apparently irreducible contradiction into the discourse: If the American middle class is currently living in spaces that are not conducive to producing community, how can they be transplanted without uprooting? How can Americans stay rooted in undisturbed ground and still find a new place to call home? In other words, how can this economically and politically desirable social class be made to feel stable but remain mobile?

Proposals for simultaneously relocating Americans without disturbing existing roots offer different ways to dress up this paradox. Suarez characterizes urban revitalization as a return to "the old neighborhood" of the city and the suburb as a place middle class Americans were just visiting, rather than a true home. New Urbanists promise to replace suburbs with re-creations of the small towns and neighborhoods of American history, tracing roots to a shared history prior to urbanization. But while a handful of revitalization and New Urbanist projects have been launched in the last twenty-five years, subdivisions have been negotiating the problem of rootedness and the need for spatial and temporal continuity without requiring residents to return to urban space or invest in experimental ventures. In order to offer a solution to the problem of rootlessness, subdivisions simulate historical permanence, stability, and continuity. In other words, they create an instant sense of place by means of a particular aesthetic whose rhetorical effect is temporal.

New Familiar Places

The subdivisions I analyze are those marketed to "midrange" buyers in the Midwest (specifically, in Illinois, Iowa, and Minnesota) and built during the last decade of the twentieth century. The suburban housing developments that were pioneered near larger population centers on the coasts did not reach the Midwest until after they had become standardized and mass-produced commodities on a national scale. As such, recent Midwestern versions of the subdivision are particularly useful for examining how the contemporary suburban neighborhood and home are constructed as sites that build community by resolving the paradox of rootlessness. Before examining the material aesthetics of subdivision design itself, a rhetorical analysis of the promotional texts provides a means for considering how these spaces are positioned as the cure for rootlessness even prior to construction. Advertising brochures, billboards, and Web sites deploy cherished memories and fantasies of the old American neighborhood as ideal community and the childhood family home as the essence of both personal and national history, rootedness, place, and belonging. In effect, they serve a pedagogical function for potential buyers who are thereby instructed in how to view architecture as home and community.

Subdivision marketing frequently focuses on the housing development itself as product, rather than on individual properties. Developers invite housing consumers to buy into a particular neighborhood, a place to "put down roots," often before the individual houses are constructed. This is one reason that the signs, pamphlets, and entrance marker identifying the theme (which runs through the names and designs of the development, streets, and housing models) are created long before the houses are built. In the Midwest, subdivision themes invoke popular fantasies of small town and country life of American history to create narratives of place for new developments. For example, a Web site advertising South Pointe subdivision in Minnesota promises potential buyers the "comfort, luxury, and tranquility of small town charm" in a "friendly community and nice place to come home to."[47] Similarly, Kirk Homes of Illinois pronounces Bloomfield Village subdivision "a tightly knit community" and "friendly neighborhood" that will "make you feel good about coming home." The text also draws attention to the proximity of Wing Pointe development to a former small town (now a bedroom suburb for an expanding Chicago), which is characterized as a "charming historic downtown ... inviting a warm connection to the past."[48] Such appeals encourage consumers to experience a feeling of homecoming when they buy into a subdivision, which stems from the sense of shared history and belonging that the narratives offer residents.

Entrance markers, prominently displaying the newly invented "place names" (such as "Glen Oaks," "Briardale," and "Century Hills") and so often pictured in promotional materials, enhance the portrait of the subdivision as an eternal American small town. The use of such entrances references another practice of marking community boundaries: the signs placed along roadsides at the limits of small Midwestern towns. Like the signs that welcome or bid farewell to visitors and residents as they enter and exit the boundaries of municipalities, subdivision entrances mark the boundaries of a particular destination, identifying a tangible place to visit or to call home. Both subdivision markers and town signs are landscaped with trees, shrubs, rocks, and blooming plants, or emphasized with decorative walls and gates.[49] By re-creating the town sign, subdivision markers materially encode and perform community identity. Yet there are some important differences between the subdivision's entrance marker and the town sign.

Two common features of the town sign are a date recording the founding or establishment of the township and a numerical count of its population. Not coincidentally, subdivision markers exclude the year of "founding" or construction as well as the number of residents.[50] Omitting these elements obscures their recent construction and constantly shifting populations in order to create a sense of stable and timeless places—transhistorical communities—for their residents to call home. By encouraging residents to return symbolically to the hometown of American history, subdivisions both cater to and arouse desires for the old-fashioned "sense of community" that predates the popularly proclaimed crisis of rootlessness at the end of the twentieth century.

Another common theme in subdivision advertising is the representation of rural life as a kind of shared pastoral paradise before America's fall into a fragmentary urban and industrial age. Suburbs have long been perceived as a "refuge from modernity," a place where people can live a slow-paced, simple life in harmony with nature and one another, escaping the fears of urban crime, class conflict, and diversity that cities may represent.[51] The promise of a return to an untroubled American country life and communal relations of the past permeates the materials promoting Midwestern subdivisions. Christian Builders peddle Linbar Estates subdivision with the invitation to "[c]ome home to the country where acreage lots and a comfortable neighborhood provide room to spread your wings and an opportunity for you and your family to create new friendships!"[52] Dozens of other subdivisions throughout the Midwest use the phrase "country living" to market houses. In inviting potential buyers to "come home" to country settings, builders placate fears that one can "never go home again" and offer a site wherein all the desirable elements of an imagined rural past (a place and time when barn building, county fairs, and other shared events brought people closer together) can be instantly recovered by the suburban family. In some cases, subdivision marketing not only appeals to desires for safety and familiarity, but also exploits fears of the crime, racial politics, and the poverty of contemporary urban settings. For example, Regency Homes describes its Otter Ridge development in a suburb of Des Moines, Iowa, as "a quiet, family community where you'll feel at ease letting the kids or grandkids ride bikes or play in the backyard," marking a contrast between this setting and the nearby urban environment.[53] Promotional materials for Manchester Cove subdivision are more explicit in the type of fears that may be put to rest in this development near Chicago, described as "a superb blend of country atmosphere, historic charm and suburban amenities in one community" that "boasts a new police station" as well as "the lowest per capita crime rate in the southwestern suburbs."[54]

The repetition of the mythic narratives of small town and country life in hundreds of subdivisions in Iowa, Minnesota, and Illinois produces a Middletown, USA, effect.[55] When developers promote and construct subdivisions in similar ways and employ the same themes over and over again to give the subdivision character and charm, the settings they create become familiar scenes throughout the Midwest. This allows residents, despite frequent transplanting, to experience a feeling of "always coming home" because home becomes identified with subdivisions anywhere.

While they depict developments as established communities, subdivision materials also sell the suburban house as the home of childhood memories and a way to return to personal family roots. The companies that supply design schematics to Midwestern builders describe the special need of today's homebuyers to recover a sense of home as the concern that should animate marketing materials. Design Basics, Inc. instructs developers who want to appeal to "Generation X" and "Late Baby Boomer" buyers that these consumers' urgent need for a sense of home should be the focus of marketing materials:

> Far fewer of them have had the familiarity of a stay-at-home mother, or even a two-parent household. Influences throughout their lives such as the Gulf War, poverty, AIDS and gangs, have caused them to have an uncertain outlook on their future. Consequently, this generation embraces more conservative values and, in general, expresses more caution about their future than their optimistic Boomer-parents did at the same age . . . Xers will certainly place a greater emphasis than ever on home as a source of security in their life, a principle they value having been raised in times of uncertainty.[56]

This characterization echoes Putnam's description of "Gen Xers" as lacking a "sense of belonging" and as "less embedded in community life" than the previous generation.[57] In their periodical *Home Plans*, Design Basics, Inc. also includes several lengthy fictional accounts to illustrate the motives of these contemporary buyers-in-crisis, paired with plans for the houses that will make their dreams come true.[58] In these first-person testimonials, unnamed narrators articulate fond childhood memories to desires for particular features that the accompanying plans offer.

For example, one housing plan is placed next to a mother's reminisces about her childhood, which explain her desire to re-create these memories for her own daughter. She recounts all the familiar places of her memories, such as "down by the railroad tracks," "among the entanglements of weeds and mud down by the creek," "the sticker patch," and in "our garden."[59] This list of outdoor childhood haunts bears a resemblance to the thematic street names inside subdivisions, such as "Olde Mill Court" of Riverbend subdivision in Cedar Rapids, Iowa; "Ancient Oak Drive" of the Oakcrest subdivision in Peoria, Illinois; and "Stoney Creek Lane" of North Park subdivision in Rochester, Minnesota, all of which seem to simulate places of memory.

A second narrative describes the memories of a man who, as a child, "lived in a friendly neighborhood where the summer didn't begin until the first block party," where "games," "prizes," and "go cart races" were shared before "my family moved away from the old neighborhood."[60] Throughout this catalog of childhood stories, the narrator lists the features he desires in a new house, emphasizing his love for "craftsmanship design of the past."[61] In so doing, the text positions the re-creation of historic features of "home" (in the form of the accompanying architectural plans) as the means to recover the "old neighborhood" and a sense of rootedness that has been lost.

In yet another account, a man recalls incidents from a childhood spent in the country and a one-room schoolhouse: "It was almost Norman Rockwell–

like, with my youthful days passing quickly, whether I was fishing in our local pond or exploring the wildlife among the woodlands" in "a time that was more reflective of my grandparents' era."[62] The narrator proceeds to identify various features of the dream house, describing how each design element will "bring back the quiet time I spent . . . with childhood friends around the playground," and "signifies the quiet innocence of my country school," "replicate[s] the wonderful clatter of shoes in the low room of the old schoolhouse," or expresses "desires to bring the coziness of the past into the present."[63] This narrative offers the recovery of a Norman Rockwell childhood that predates the current crisis of rootlessness.[64] As Suarez points out in *The Old Neighborhood*, the period during which "the broad American masses all 'knew' the same things" by reading mainstream publications like *The Saturday Evening Post* is now viewed as a time of "consensus culture" and a "shared set of norms" in which all Americans were socially rooted and that has now been lost.[65]

A final narrative expresses the fictional buyer's desire to re-experience the "feelings of excitement I remember when we moved into the home I grew up in."[66] This portion of the brochure explains how particular rooms of the new housing plan will re-create the places remembered from childhood. The narrator attributes the capacity to "stir comforting memories" to design elements, such as the porch that will function as "the place where I will think of my father and his front porch that I spent many-a-day frolicking with his German Shepherd and Labrador mix," and the two-story floor plan that calls to mind her "Grandmother's stairway, where I was scolded time and time again for sliding down its steps and playing with the miniature ceramic tea set."[67] Materials such as this brochure symbolically fill the new house with the family members, pets, and toys of childhood places, invoking "comforting memories" that create an immediate sense of history and homecoming for the new resident of the subdivisions offering these housing models.

Salient functions of subdivision marketing texts include the creation of an instant sense of place throughout the Midwest, the mythologization of such spaces as the eternal American home, and their depiction as safe communities to put down roots. It is these functions that contribute to the constitution of the subdivision as a pantopia: the ideal always and every place. Drawing on Michel Foucault's concept of "heterotopia," Andrew Wood has argued that the "overlapping narratives of time" apparent in exhibits from the New York World's Fair of the early mid-twentieth century helped to "inspire the design and execution" of contemporary master planned communities that mix historic references, such as the Victorian and modern architecture found in Disney's (in)famous Celebration development.[68] More recently, Wood and Anne Marie Todd have proposed "omnitopia" as a concept describing the contemporary "mutable environment whose disparate locales convey their inhabitants to a ubiquitous, ever-present continuum."[69] While Midwestern housing developments employ transhistoric narratives and features, rely on ubiquity as part of their overall effect, and traffic in utopian promises of idealized space, they operate less as heterotopic or omnitopic places, and more as a "pantopia," an always and everywhere perfect place.

In the introduction to his early twentieth-century novel by the same name, Frank Harris explains that the term "pantopia" conveys a sense that the "ideal was everywhere . . . and always possible."[70] Similarly, Martin Buber describes the pantopia as like a utopia in that it presents such a "universally valid image of perfection" that allows for the "possibility of withdrawing into the attitude of a calm spectator" from the present time and topos, from "this place" and "this people."[71] In applying the concept of "pantopia" to changing receptions of Greek literature, Peter Murphy argues that pantopic appeals have a cosmopolitan character, evidenced by "the exploration of a topos that is universal" for the audience.[72] If there is a cosmopolitan quality to the subdivision's pantopic space, its universe encompasses (and is perhaps limited to) Americans who are consumers in a particular midrange housing market. However, as David Harvey notes, the recent American variant of cosmopolitanism has a very specific character:

> It . . . idealizes America as a beacon to humanity and exports Americanism as a "portable ethos" and as an object of universal desire . . . but the myth cannot be sustained without emphatic denunciations and demonizations of "evil empires" (one of Reagan's favorite phrases) and resistant spaces—Cuba, Iran, Libya, Serbia or, for respectable suburbanites, "the inner city" (with all its racial codings).[73]

Pantopic space is created through a fantasy that is not only an affirmation of the suburb as the site of the "good life" for the middle class, but also consistent with the way that the "American Dream" (popularly signified as home-ownership) is legitimated by projecting it onto the "foreigner" in ways that affirm its vitality while warranting a cosmopolitan approach to transnational relations.[74] In fact, realtors even use the term "cosmopolitan" to sell houses in developments in suburbs near Chicago.[75] It appears, then, that the pantopic subdivision is a space in which cosmopolitanism can quite comfortably make itself at home.

This Old/New House

The exterior features of subdivision houses also help to create the pantopic character of these cultural spaces. It is no accident that these homes appear at once to look old and new. The "instant aging" of these new developments is achieved by reproducing key features of historic homes in new, "maintenance-free" vinyl form. Architectural references to models of the family home from earlier periods of American history are typical, such as colonial pediments over paneled doors, double-hung sash widows common in Georgian architecture, and Victorian three-sided bay windows.[76] Perhaps the most intriguing means of creating a sense of historic charm for subdivision houses is the conversion of previously functional domestic technologies into decorative elements. Specifically, the windows, entrances, surfaces, and other elements of housing exteriors frequently exhibit stylized tributes to earlier methods of constructing, protecting, and heating and cooling houses. For example, subdivision houses often have windows with shutters, and although these devices are functionally obsolete, they lend old-fashioned charm to housing façades. The shutters on new suburban housing models in the Midwest are narrow, immobile, and only frame windows facing the street. Christian Builders, Inc. offers numerous models, such as the "Fairfield," the "Huntington," the "Lakeview," the "Regal," and the "Richmond" that feature shutters on street-side windows.[77] On each model, the shutters are less than half the width of the windows, a ratio that is emphasized when one pair of shutters borders two adjacent frames, reducing each shutter's contribution to less than one fourth of the window expanse. The shutters on the "South Hampton" (versions I and II), "Kensington," "Sterling," and "Mansfield" models available from Jerry's Homes, Inc. in subdivisions in and around Cedar Rapids, Iowa, as well as all the models by Construx Design Group, Inc. for Briardale subdivision in Peoria, Illinois, have shutters of this type, which are all patterned to simulate the louvers or panels of their wooden Georgian colonial ancestors.[78] At one time, the shutter was an important means of securing fragile glass against storms and thieves. But whether contemporary shutters have shrunk or the panes have merely outgrown them, they could not possibly close to protect their windows, even if they had hinges or latches (which they do not).

Most of the models offered by Midwestern builders also have muntins on the windows: small bars that create a grid effect over the surface of the glass.[79] Like shutters, muntins are an archaic domestic technology that held small panes of glass in a window frame before the use of large single-paned windows became widespread in the Victorian period. Unlike the wooden frames that once held single, individual panes, however, subdivision muntins are typically strips of vinyl applied to the interior surface of contemporary double-paned windows. They no longer serve any practical purpose, but add historic "charm" to the houses they grace.

Another residual feature of historic dwellings that is replicated in contemporary subdivisions is the chimney that (in addition to the fireplace itself) was formerly part of the heating system for houses. The presence of a chimney increases the price of a subdivision property, particularly those that are large or ornate. The more expensive models offer sizable brick or stone chimneys, sometimes wider at the base and then curving to a smaller top section ("cottage" style), or stepped (resembling Tudor brick). Although brick or stone was once necessary to create a fireproof chimney, contemporary subdivision versions are decorative casings for modern chimney pipes and are completely unnecessary for operating the fireplace. The brick or stone covers the plywood box through which the pipe runs; this area could easily be surfaced with the same siding as the rest of the house's exterior, as is done in less expensive models. Even in these cheaper models, the distinctive, rectangular shape of the chimney is retained (often exaggerated by having it visibly rise above the roof line), despite the fact that the pipes they now house are small and round. For that matter, the pipes would function as well if exposed.

Perhaps more than any other feature of historic domestic design, the porch has recently garnered increasing attention from architects and urban planners. Often celebrated as representing old-time small town or rural community life, the porch is also embraced for its capacity to reestablish traditional social ties. In fact, porches have become such a common sight in New Urbanist developments that they have been called the key signifier of this movement.[80] Midwestern subdivisions also retain the porch, although they have converted this once practical outdoor space into an ornamental entrance. Christian Builders, Inc. offer several housing models with porch-like façade details, such as the "Bayfield," the "Lakeview," the "Seville," and the "Springbrook," which all have enlarged cement stoops framed by a pair of columns that support shallow pediments.[81] Other models, such as the "Creekview," the "Excelsior," and the "Fairfield," extend the porch area along a narrow section at the front of the house behind short railings, although none are large enough to hold more than one or two chairs, unlike the Victorian outdoor dining rooms associated with large rural families, or the South's roomy verandas.[82] Regency Builders of Des Moines offers one model, the "Bradbury," that re-creates the double-tiered porch of the southern plantation, in miniature form, on the façade of a Georgian colonial-style dwelling.[83] Jerry's Homes, Inc. has similar porch detailing on several models, including the "Sterling" and the "Hawthorne," which manage to squeeze in four posts by doubling the standard two or placing them only a few feet apart, visually exaggerating the size of the small overhangs they support.[84]

In all cases, these "porches" are prominently labeled on the floor plans, even when the designated space is barely large enough to contain the word. It is as though a few elements of the grand old wrap-around farmhouse porch (as seen on television shows like *The Waltons*, and in countless "country decorating" magazines) have been borrowed to create a compressed version for subdivision houses, not large enough for residents to use, but highly visible and recognizable from the street.[85] Construx Design Group, Inc. offers several entrance options for the "Suitor II" model: the "Colonial" and "Traditional" entrances with two steps and narrow windows bordering the front door (the only difference is that the Traditional has a pediment, while the Colonial does not); the "covered porch," a narrow strip that runs along the front of the house behind a railing; and the "construx porch" (the builder's signature design), which merely adds a pair of columns to the Traditional in place of the windows.[86] This construx porch's function, like so many similar entrances, is to create the illusion of a porch with the outlines of posts and roof, much like a one-dimensional picture. From the front door, the columns or posts are so close to the façade as to make the entrance indistinguishable from other small concrete stoops. From the street, however, the columns appear to support a separate roof and the depth of the area is difficult to gauge. The result is the semblance of a porch that provides "curb appeal" at minimal structural expense.

To say that a style can have substance—that material aesthetics have constitutive rhetorical effects—is not to say that all styles have equivalent impact. The construx porch of the subdivision's pantopia is much like a picture of a porch: it functions as a visual rhetoric in important ways, but does not significantly reconfigure space. This simulated porch creates a key signifier of historic communal life, but it falls short of the other virtue New Urbanists attribute to porches: practical utility in creating an outdoor gathering space. While it hardly follows that building sizable porches is a sufficient condition to produce communal social practices, the shallow porch detailing described is even more problematic. What is most troubling about the illusion of a porch that the subdivision's pantopia creates is not that it fails to produce community, but that it reassures residents that the porch is not absent and that the traditional practices New Urbanists frequently associate with the porch (such as greeting pedestrians or visiting with neighbors over a glass of lemonade) have been recovered in the contemporary version of the suburban neighborhood.

Methods for surfacing subdivision houses also mimic outdated or even ancient materials for building dwellings. The most common means of covering new houses is vinyl siding. This usually comes in a variety of light, neutral tones; is shaped to mimic the overlapping clapboards of colonial New England; and has a wood-grained pattern to simulate the look of painted lumber, a traditional material for constructing American houses. In addition to siding, many builders offer other surfaces (at extra cost). A common option is to have sections of brick bordering the door or along the lower half of the house, Tudor style. Other choices, such as the Christian Builder's "Cascade" model, feature round stones.[87] One subdivision near Peoria, Illinois, uses these stones as a defining feature of the development, which is called "Fieldstone Estates," a reference to the rural practice of constructing foundations or dwellings from rocks removed from fields during plowing.[88] A nearby subdivision, "Cobblestone Estates," architecturally references a popular material of the Greek revival period.[89] In all of these houses, the effect is created by facing the front side with brick or stone, or creating a thin veneer that has aesthetic, but not structural, value. Converting former construction materials into façade decor gives contemporary subdivisions a visual link to the stone cottages and brick houses of the past, lending archaic appeal to these modern dwellings. In replicating Georgian shutters, pre-Victorian muntins, the Tudor chimney, and the Victorian-era rural porch, contemporary subdivisions aspire to "classic" or "timeless" design to create a generalized aesthetic of "pastness."

The timeless character that the pantopic community subdivision offers rootless residents is created not only through the conversion of archaic domestic technologies into aesthetic elements, but also by camouflaging modern amenities in ways that preserve the classic look of these homes. For example, electric lights are disguised as colonial lanterns at the entrances of subdivision houses. Bulbs, some shaped to resemble flames, are placed inside fixtures of glass and metal, and sometimes screwed into a plastic base molded into the shape of a dripping candle. These simulated lanterns, usually located on the garage and near the front door, reinforce the other historic details, such as shutters and muntins, that give subdivision houses an anti-quated look. Such stylized relics of earlier eras facilitate the distancing of subdivisions from contemporary life, an aspect of subdivision aesthetics marking a sharp contrast between these spaces and the suburbs of the 1950s and 1960s.

While early suburban housing design included some historic signifiers, such as shutters, these former models also celebrated signs of the modern, boasting large single-plate picture windows, prominent sliding glass doors, large television antennas, cement patios, and carports or street-side parking. In contemporary subdivisions, modern windows are disguised behind muntins, "French doors" open onto wooden balconies or decks, and recessed garages with paneled doors (that hide minivans, compact foreign cars, and SUVs) have replaced carports or street parking, where enormous Cadillacs and station wagons were once proudly displayed. The protective and restrictive covenants of late-century subdivisions also prevent the signs of the modern from interrupting this aesthetic by forbidding the installation of dishes and requiring vehicles to be parked inside garages.

The banishing of signs of recent technology from subdivisions points to a key aspect of their function: providing a haven from the contemporary crisis of dislocation and rootlessness. If suburban sprawl is responsible for the demise of American community, as many critics and scholars suggest, then the efforts of subdivisions to invoke diverse elements of earlier models of the home and neighborhood facilitate efforts to re-create the ideal settings of communal life prior to the moment it allegedly began to disappear. Subdivision design archives a variety of historic signifiers in eternally new condition to suspend the home and neighborhood in an atemporal space. In doing so, the pantopic subdivision's material aesthetic operates not only to effect the spatial characteristics of a utopia, a perfect nowhere, but also to create the temporal character of a perfect "nowhen": a place out of time. These temporal rhetorical effects go beyond the tendency to privilege space over time that Michel de Certeau noted (whereby the "proper place" is established through strategies that "reduce temporal relations to spatial ones") by actually simulating an escape from time.[90] This development is significant because, for de Certeau, it is only the temporal dimension of life in public places that makes the tactics rhetorical agents can use to interrupt spatial strategies of social control possible.[91] Turning to the writing of Weil on rootedness and social life provides a critical lens through which both the temporal and spatial dimensions of the pantopic material aesthetic take on an even more ominous cast than they do in de Certeau, in that they threaten to undermine the ethical character and spiritual life of an entire people.

The Politics of Material Aesthetics

Adapting Simone Weil's programmatic solution to the problem of roots to contemporary suburbia is an experiment fraught with difficulties, not the least being the problem of extracting her proposals from the very specific situation they address: the future of France after World War II. However,

aligning the more general themes treated in Weil's theory of rootedness and
social life with the places being marketed as the solution to America's crisis
of community does point the way to a particular critique of the suburban
answer to the problem of roots. In light of Weil's analysis, objectionable
characteristics of the new home being offered middle class Americans
include the way these places appear to supplant local and regional histories
for a nationalist myth, limit the nature of obligations and social ties in the
neighborhood-as-community, aesthetically encode unity and cohesion, and
remove all signs of the workplace from the favored site of social relations.
Overall, the rhetorical effects of the pantopic subdivision's material aesthetic
undermine the ordering function of temporality and rob community members
of that realm of action that best mediates human experience and forms the
basis of ethical social relations: labor.

Weil's observation that Kant had rightly discovered the vital role of time
as the "schema" that orders sensations gives greater weight to the common
complaint that subdivision aesthetics are disorienting for those who try to
navigate them.[92] For Weil, order is "the first of the soul's needs" and it
proceeds from a particular "texture of social relationships," a formulation
that renders what we might call the "social order" in explicitly aesthetic and
experiential terms.[93] Adopting this view prompts us to consider the dangers
that may enter through the door opened by the material aesthetics establishing a "timeless" character for subdivision architecture. To the extent that the
pantopic subdivision is created through an idealized image of the American
small town or rural community that displaces flaws, injustices, and failings, it
may facilitate what Weil characterizes as a dangerous, absolute, patriotic
devotion to the nation. Given her stringent opposition to colonialism, the
destruction of native cultures, and the associated exploitation, oppression,
and enslavement of nonwhite peoples, Weil might point to dramatically
different narratives of westward expansion and the horrific racial dimensions
of life in small town and rural America, as told from "other" perspectives.[94]
Her warning that such patriotism cultivates a willingness to uproot other
collectivities and warrants a fanatical imperialism seems prescient in light of
Murphy's observation that pantopic appeals engender cosmopolitanism and
the political and ethical critiques of the American variant of this ideology
that Harvey, Honig, and other scholars have offered.[95] Overall, pairing
Weil's predictions with an analysis of the suburban neighborhood indicates a
significant relationship between the reconfiguration of this social space and
ideologies and policies with far-ranging effects.

The nature of obligation in the pantopic community also seems problematic in relation to Weil's account of social relations, as in her view that the

sense of duty to one's neighbors is the very heart of communal justice. A community in which the only obligation to one's (literal) neighbor is upkeep of one's own property so as to maintain the uniformity of the space (and even this obligation cannot be presumed but must be written into a form of law called the "restrictive covenant") seems to fall considerably short of the rooted collectivity Weil envisioned.[96] In such a collectivity, social relations are grounded in a Kantian commitment to view each human member as an end rather than a means, thus upholding the commandment to "love your neighbor as yourself."[97] In addition, the unified and cohesive style that guides the subdivision's theming, façade design, and (strictly enforced) construction guidelines seems contrary to the aesthetic that Weil favored in her lectures on architecture. The detailed notes of one of Weil's students indicate that she ascribed a capacity to encourage or inhibit particular behaviors to architecture (the cathedral is given as an example) and that a measure of the "sufficiently unpredictable, so that we feel the need to bring some feeling of unity to it" marked the difference between an aesthetic that is merely pleasant to the senses and one that embodies true beauty.[98] This emphasizes the role of the subject in the aesthetic interaction, and the way that those who perceive, occupy, and navigate architecture create (or perform) it. In short, architecture that too readily prescribes unity displaces the agency of different subjects in the aesthetic encounter.

But viewing subdivision design through the perspective Weil provides raises more than general aesthetic objections. Fetishizing the architectural forms that accompanied earlier models of domestic space for their communal associations, long after the shared labor that helped to create these social bonds has disappeared, also appears as a poor solution to the problem of rootlessness. Shutters were once a means for neighbors to work together to prepare for a storm, and the porch provided a cool escape from the kitchen for preparing and eating meals. Retaining the vestiges of these practices elevates the cultural forms while displacing the vital labor that, for Weil, should be the center of a living community. Given her very specific proposals to redesign the spaces, machines, and décor of factories and residences to create an "atmosphere" that gives the proper meaning and value to labor, it seems possible that Weil might prescribe a similar renovation of American suburban space.[99] Weil was far from opposing private property and home ownership, as she found it "desirable that the majority of people should own their own house and a little piece of land round it," but she saw owning the "tools of their trade" and creating an environment that integrates the workplace and the home while celebrating the merit and social function of labor as paramount in re-rooting subjects.[100] To advance a version of community that is entirely residential would seem to risk depriving members of the roots that can stem from the shared sense of purpose fulfilled that revered labor can provide. The subdivision aesthetic that is not only a haven from visible signs of the workplace but also from modernity itself cannot provide the carefully integrated and historicized approach to daily work that Weil recommends.

On the whole, Weil's treatment of the problem of roots points the way to a critique of contemporary suburbia's solution that neither presumes its aesthetic is merely bourgeois ideology masking the positions of the residents within capitalism nor proposes that New Urbanist alterations to the aesthetic alone will produce good community. Indeed, if I am correct in seeing in Weil's account a useful perspective from which to view the role of material aesthetics of place in shaping communal relations, spatial styles and configurations become constitutive but not determinative elements of social life. For Weil, changing factory design is the *first* step in transforming the worker's labor from an experience of pointless suffering to one of joyful sacrifice, as workplace aesthetics are the material conditions of production (understood as the literal relation between the body and the machine) rather than class entities in an abstract social structure.[101] And yet, the reconfiguration of factory aesthetics must be born out of a larger commitment to re-create the workplace as an environment that gives greater meaning and value to the practices that take place there. In other words, the path to rootedness that Weil details in her writing necessitates a movement toward the site of labor, precisely the reverse of the retreat into residential enclaves that contemporary suburbia enacts. Such an embrace of sites of work would prompt a transformation, not only in the way the suburb has long facilitated a distancing of the home from the office, but also in the way it has disavowed the home *as* workplace, by privatizing and denigrating domestic labor.[102]

But beyond concerns with the particular instantiation of community that the pantopic subdivision offers, Weil's extensive study and detailed proposals should provoke a much deeper sense of discomfort with the promises these places seem to make. The complexities of this problem, the difficulty of discovering a means of nurturing a sense of belonging in some without displacing others and of locating subjects without permanently fixing them in inequitable relationship to one another in the social economy, are formidable. The apparent ease with which a pantopic home for Middle America solves the problem of roots should give us pause.

The application of Weil's study of the problem of roots to the recent American crisis of community also illustrates how her work can contribute to current conversations about the relationships between aesthetics, politics, and materiality. In place of Marxist historical materialism, Weil offers a theory of social location grounded in the material aesthetics of place, urging us to spend more time analyzing the factory floor and the family home than cleaving to historical narratives and hypothesized structures. Instead of understanding or interpretation, Weil provides the concept of "attention": an orientation of the body, mind, and vision that turns a critical gaze on the "texture of social relationships" shaped by the material culture of our daily lives.[103] It is perhaps with her guidance that we should more carefully consider the links between social spaces and social practices, for, as she notes, it would be the gravest of misfortunes "if the stones that will, maybe for several generations, determine the whole of our social life were allowed to be thrown together just anyhow."[104]

Notes

1. Robert D. Putnam, *Bowling Alone: The Collapse and Revival of American Community* (New York: Simon and Schuster, 2000), 27.
2. Putnam, *Bowling Alone*, 16.
3. Mark Reinhardt, "Look Who's Talking: Political Subjects, Political Objects, and Political Discourse in Contemporary Theory," *Political Theory* 23 (1995): 689–720.
4. Daniel Bell, *Communitarianism and Its Critics* (Oxford: Oxford University Press, 1993), 1.
5. Wray Herbert, "Our Identity Crisis: In Angry Times, Can We Rebuild a True Sense of Community?" *U.S. News and World Report* 118 (1995): 83–84.
6. Herbert, "Our Identity Crisis," 84.
7. The first quotation is from Craig Whitaker, *Architecture and the American Dream* (New York: Clarkson N. Potter, 1996), 9. The second is from James Howard Kunstler, *Home from Nowhere: Remaking Our Everyday World for the Twenty-First Century* (New York: Simon and Schuster, 1996), 84.
8. Evan McKenzie, *Privatopia: Homeowner Associations and the Rise of Residential Private Government* (New Haven, CT: Yale University Press, 1994), 176–77. Although some urban neighborhoods have formed such associations, most residential growth and development is still in new construction outside the large urban centers.
9. The phrase "material aesthetic" is drawn from Immanuel Kant's use of the concept to designate experiential properties appealing to sensation, "charm or emotion," as found in Immanuel Kant, *The Critique of Judgement*, trans. James Creed Meredith (Whitefish, MT: Kessinger Publishing, 2004), 47.
10. Edwin Black, "The Second Persona," *Quarterly Journal of Speech* 56 (1970): 119.
11. Bonnie Dow and Mari Boor Tonn, "'Feminine Style' and Political Judgment in the Rhetoric of Ann Richards," *Quarterly Journal of Speech* 79 (1993): 286–302; Robert Hariman, "Decorum, Power and the Courtly Style," *Quarterly Journal of Speech* 78 (1992): 149–73; Robert Hariman, *Political Style: The Artistry of Power* (Chicago: University of Chicago Press, 1995); James P. McDaniel, "Speaking Like a State: Listening to Benjamin Franklin in Times of Terror," *Communication and Critical/Cultural Studies* 2 (2005): 324–50.
12. James Arnt Aune, "An Historical Materialist Theory of Rhetoric," *American Communi-*

cation Journal 6 (2003), http://www.acjournal.org/holdings/vol6/iss4/mcmcgee/aune.pdf; Dana L. Cloud, "The Affirmative Masquerade," *American Communication Journal* 4 (2001), http://www.acjournal.org/holdings/vol4/iss3/special/cloud.htm; Dana L. Cloud, "The Materiality of Discourse as Oxymoron: A Challenge to Critical Rhetoric," *Western Journal of Communication* 58 (1994): 141–63; Dana L. Cloud, Steve Macek, and James Arnt Aune, "'The Limbo of Ethical Simulacra': A Reply to Ron Greene," *Philosophy and Rhetoric* 39 (2006): 72–84; Ronald W. Greene, "Another Materialist Rhetoric," *Critical Studies in Mass Communication* 15 (1998): 21–41; Ronald Greene, "Orator Communist," *Philosophy and Rhetoric* 39 (2006): 85–95; Ronald W. Greene, "Rhetoric and Capitalism: Rhetorical Agency as Communicative Labor," *Philosophy and Rhetoric* 37 (2004): 188–206; Michael Calvin McGee, "A Materialist's Conception of Rhetoric," in *Explorations in Rhetoric: Studies in Honor of Douglas Ehninger*, ed. Ray E. McKerrow (Glenview, IL: Scott, Foresman, 1982), 23–48; Michael Calvin McGee, "Text, Context, and the Fragmentation of Contemporary Culture," *Western Journal of Communication* 54 (1990): 274–89.

13. Joshua Gunn, "Rhetoric of Feet," *American Communication Journal* 7 (2004), http://acjournal.org/holdings/vol7/iss1/.

14. The first two quotations are taken from Cloud, Macek, and Aune, "'Limbo of Ethical Simulacra,'" 73; Greene, "Orator Communist," 90, 92.

15. Kant, *Critique of Judgement*, 47. The influence of Kant on Weil's philosophy is widely noted in the secondary literature on her work. However, one need look no further than the repeated references throughout the text of Simone Weil, *Lectures on Philosophy*, trans. Hugh Price (Cambridge: Cambridge University Press, 1978) for confirmation of the debt her aesthetic theory owes to Kant.

16. Robert Chenavier, "Simone Weil: Completing Platonism through a Consistent Materialism," in *The Christian Platonism of Simone Weil*, ed. E. Jane Doering and Eric O. Springstead (Notre Dame, IN: University of Notre Dame Press, 2004), 64–65.

17. Praise for Kant's recognition that only temporality orders experience and time is the wellspring of morality and truth can be found in Weil, *Lectures on Philosophy*, 113, 99. The quotation on community is taken from Simone Weil, *The Need for Roots: Prelude to a Declaration of Duties toward Mankind*, trans. Arthur Wills (New York: G. P. Putnam's Sons, 1952), 43.

18. Exceptions include brief quotations in Linda M. Park-Fuller, "Performing Absence: The Staged Personal Narrative as Testimony," *Text and Performance Quarterly* 20 (2000): 20–42; Quentin J. Schultze, "The 'God Problem' in Communication Studies," *Journal of Communication and Religion* 28 (2005): 1–22. Other scholars of communication who have mentioned Weil include Ronald C. Arnett, "Interpersonal Praxis: The Interplay of Religious Narrative, Historicality and Metaphor," *Journal of Communication and Religion* 21 (1998): 141–63; Douglas Birkhead, "An Ethics of Vision for Journalism," *Critical Studies in Mass Communication* 6 (1989): 283–95.

19. Platonic influences on Weil's work and her fascination with religious practices, sacred texts, and theological concepts are widely noted in the secondary literature on her writing, including John M. Dunaway, *Simone Weil*, ed. David O'Connell, Twayne's World Authors Series (Boston: Twayne Publishers, 1984); John Hellman, *Simone Weil: An Introduction to Her Thought* (Waterloo, Ont: Wilfrid Laurier University Press, 1982); Simone Pétrement, *Simone Weil: A Life*, trans. Raymond Rosenthal (New York: Pantheon Books, 1976); George Abbott White, ed., *Simone Weil: Interpretations of a Life*

(Amherst: University of Massachusetts Press, 1981). The first quotation on Aristotle is taken from the translation of "La Source Grecque" in John M. Dunaway, *Simone Weil*, ed. David O'Connell, Twayne's World Authors Series (Boston: Twayne Publishers, 1984), 31; the second reference is from Weil, *Need for Roots*, 148.

20. For a discussion of the treatment of language in Weil's work (particularly with regard to her relationship to Wittgenstein), see Thomas R. Nevin, *Simone Weil: Portrait of a Self-Exiled Jew* (Chapel Hill: University of North Carolina Press, 1991), and Peter Winch's introduction to Weil, *Lectures on Philosophy*. A key source for Weil's conceptualization of class, proposals for political action, and critique of capitalism and nationalism is Weil, *Need for Roots*.

21. Françoise Meltzer, "The Hands of Simone Weil," *Critical Inquiry* 27 (2001): 611–21.

22. James Arnt Aune, "Critique of Commodity Aesthetics," *Quarterly Journal of Speech* 73 (1987): 387–400; Dana L. Cloud, "Rhetoric and Economics: Or, How Rhetoricians Can Get a Little Class," *Quarterly Journal of Speech* 88 (2002): 342–58.

23. Hellman, *Simone Weil*, 17–36.

24. Karl Marx, *Capital: A Critique of Political Economy*, vol. 3 (New York: International Publishers, 1970), 885–86.

25. Andrew Wood, "A Rhetoric of Ubiquity: Terminal Space as Omnitopia," *Communication Theory* 13 (2003): 324–44.

26. The quotation paraphrased here is translated from the original French by Meltzer, "Hands of Simone Weil," 613.

27. Eliot's description is drawn from his introduction to Weil, *Need for Roots*, xii.

28. According to Weil, alienation from labor also erodes roots, as does the "outlandish doctrine" of popular Marxism (as perpetrated by "very ordinary middle class intellectuals"), which cannot be adopted by the working class and advocates legal reforms that would do nothing to redress its suffering. Weil, *Need for Roots*, 46–47.

29. Weil, *Need for Roots*, 163, 22.

30. Weil, *Need for Roots*, 131.

31. Weil, *Need for Roots*, 50, 231.

32. Weil finds Marxism guilty of proposing a kind of "working class imperialism" that is just as damaging as national imperialism. Weil, *Need for Roots*, 152–53.

33. Weil, *Need for Roots*, 73.

34. Weil, *Need for Roots*, 126.

35. The secondary literature on Weil consistently notes the extended (and painful, given her frailty and poor health) period of time she spent working in the factories and fields. Biographers more often describe this work as motivated by naïve idealism or view it as either political activism or ascetic ritual, rather than as an opportunity to conduct research. However, there is no doubt that Weil's labor experiences inform and shape her political philosophy. See, for example, Francine Du Plessix Gray, *Simone Weil: A Penguin Life* (New York: Penguin Putnam, 2001), 82–102; Hellman, *Simone Weil*, 33–36; Nevin, *Simone Weil*, 78–83; Pétrement, *Simone Weil*, 214–47.

36. Weil, *Need for Roots*, 171.

37. Diane Miller, "Better Together: Restoring the American Community," *Quarterly Journal of Speech* 91 (2005): 229–30.

38. Putnam, *Bowling Alone*, 94–112, 204.

39. Putnam, *Bowling Alone*, 399–400.

40. For articles on the decline of the middle class, see Jack Beatty, "The Vanishing Middle

Class," *St. Petersburg Times*, city ed., June 12, 1994; Bruce D. Butterfield, "When 'Middle Class' Is Merely a Memory: The Downsized American Dream," *Boston Globe*, city ed., January 19, 1992; Barbara Ehrenreich, "Is the Middle Class Doomed?" *New York Times*, late city final ed., September 7, 1986; James Hansen, "The Incredible Shrinking Middle Class," *Rocky Mountain News*, October 11, 1994; Gene Marlowe, "'Anxious Class' Seeks Answers, Solutions," *Tampa Tribune*, metro ed., April 16, 1995; Dave Saltonstall and Chrisena Coleman, "The Shrinking Middle Class: Many Falling Backward in Economy," *Daily News* (New York), December 17, 1997; and Lester C. Thurow, "The Disappearance of the Middle Class," *New York Times*, late city final ed., February 5, 1984.

41. Ray Suarez, *The Old Neighborhood: What We Lost in the Great Migration, 1966–1999* (New York: Free Press, 1999), 25.

42. Andres Duany, Elizabeth Plater-Zyberk, and Jeff Speck, *Suburban Nation: The Rise of Sprawl and the Decline of the American Dream* (New York: North Point Press, 2001).

43. This tendency to link community with specific places is common in both popular and scholarly discourse. In *The Social Production of Urban Space* (Austin: University of Texas Press, 1985), Mark Gottdeiner explains that communal social relations are often conceptually linked to particular configurations of social space (170–73). Similarly, David Harvey's *Spaces of Capital: Towards a Critical Geography* (Edinburgh: Edinburgh University Press, 2001) identifies a persistent strain in geographic scholarship that displays "an acute sensitivity to place and community, to the symbiotic relations between individuals, communities, and environments" (34). The common practice of using the term "community" to refer to a residential area makes the association between communal social relations and the places where we live particularly strong.

44. Putnam, *Bowling Alone*, 204.

45. Amitai Etzioni, *The Spirit of Community: The Reinvention of American Society* (New York: Simon and Schuster, 1994), 121.

46. Joongsub Kim, "Creating Community: Does the Kentlands Live Up to Its Goals?" *Places: A Forum of Environmental Design* 13 (2000): 48–55.

47. "Parade of Homes," *Christian Builders*, http://www.christianbuilders.com/content _parade.htm (cited content no longer available).

48. "Illinois New Home Builder," *Kirk Homes*, http://www.kirkhomes.com/home/ home_page.cfm (cited content no longer available).

49. Subdivision entrance markers have been so successful in re-creating the town sign as elaborate entrance marker that the original markers of city limits have begun to suffer by comparison. The referential relationship between the town sign and the subdivision entrance marker has become two-way, as the former are now being remodeled to resemble the latter, with more extensive landscaping and a carved stone (rather than a painted wood or metal) sign in areas that have experienced a lot of residential growth.

50. In all my visits to subdivisions in Iowa, Minnesota, and Illinois (nearly one hundred different developments), I have never seen an entry that included a year of construction or a population number.

51. J. R. Short, *Imagined Country: Society, Culture and Environment* (London: Routledge, 1991), 34, 45–46.

52. "Parade of Homes," *Christian Builders*, http://www.christianbuilders.com/content _parade.htm (cited content no longer available).

53. "Community Details: Otter Ridge," *Regency Homes,* http://www.regencyhomes.com/

(site now discontinued).

54. "Manchester Cove in Mokena," *Hartz Homes*, http://www.hartzhomes.com/community
.php?reg_id=1&com_id=42 (cited content no longer available).

55. My use of this term refers to the collection of socio-anthropological studies of residents
of a small Midwestern city that became a touchstone for twentieth-century characterizations of daily American life, published in Robert Staughton Lynd, *Middletown: A Study
in Contemporary American Culture* (New York: Harcourt, Brace and Company, 1929).
When first published, *Middletown* was hailed as an excellent source for assessing the
"interests and mood of the average American audience" in Mary E. Whiteford, untitled
review of *Middletown: A Study in Contemporary American Culture*, by Robert Staughton
Lynd, *Quarterly Journal of Speech* 16 (1930): 535.

56. Carol Shea and Bruce Arant, eds., *Home Plans*, vol. 1, *Seasons of Life: Designs for
Spring's New Beginnings* (Omaha, NE: Design Basics Publications, 2000), 2.

57. Putnam, *Bowling Alone*, 274–75.

58. Shea and Arant, *Home Plans*.

59. Shea and Arant, *Home Plans*, 4.

60. Shea and Arant, *Home Plans*, 24–25.

61. Shea and Arant, *Home Plans*, 26.

62. Shea and Arant, *Home Plans*, 48, 50.

63. Shea and Arant, *Home Plans*, 52.

64. Norman Rockwell was well known for his idyllic depictions of "everyday American life"
on the cover of *The Saturday Evening Post* from 1916 to 1963. Fred and Norman Rockwell Bauer, *Norman Rockwell's Faith of America*, new ed. (New York: Artabras Publishers, 1996). *The Saturday Evening Post* had stopped printing Norman Rockwell's
paintings by the time they began to depict civil rights struggles, as noted in Victoria Gal-
lagher and Kenneth S. Zagacki, "Visibility and Rhetoric: The Power of Visual Images in
Norman Rockwell's Depictions of Civil Rights," *Quarterly Journal of Speech* 91 (2005):
175–200.

65. Suarez, *Old Neighborhood*, 13.

66. Construx Design Group, Inc. "Floor Plans" (unpublished plans, Springfield, IL, 1999),
74.

67. Construx Design Group, "Floor Plans," 76–78.

68. Andrew Wood, "The Middletons, Futurama, and Progressland: Disciplinary Technology
and Temporal Heterotopia in Two New York World's Fairs," *New Jersey Journal of
Communication* 11 (2003): 63–75, 65.

69. Andrew Wood and Anne Marie Todd, "'Are We There Yet?' Searching for Springfield
and *The Simpsons'* Rhetoric of Omnitopia," *Critical Studies in Mass Communication* 22
(2005): 208.

70. Frank Harris, *Pantopia* (New York: Panurge Press, 1930), ix.

71. S. N. Eisenstadt, ed., *Martin Buber: On Intersubjectivity and Cultural Creativity*
(Chicago: University of Chicago Press, 1992), 228.

72. Peter Murphy, "The Roar of Whispers: Cosmopolitanism and Neohellenism," *Journal of
Modern Greek Studies* 15 (1997): 279.

73. David Harvey, "Cosmopolitanism and the Banality of Geographic Evils," *Public Culture*
12 (2000): 546. This Harvey passage quotes and paraphrases Timothy Brennan, *At Home
in the World: Cosmopolitanism Now* (Cambridge: Harvard University Press, 1997), 308.

74. Bonnie Honig, *Democracy and the Foreigner* (Princeton, NJ: Princeton University Press,

2003), 80.

75. "Shorewood, Illinois Relocation Guide," *RelocateAmerica*, http://www.relocateamerica .com/illinois/cities/shorewood; "Illinois Real Estate and Demographic Information," *Neighborhood Scout*, http://www.neighborhoodscout.com/real-estate/illinois/; "About Wheeling, Illinois," *Relo Home Search*, http://www.relohomesearch.com/MarketContent Detail.aspx?StateCD=IL&SAID=38626.

76. Some reference works identifying such historic features of American home exteriors include Rachel Carley, *The Visual Dictionary of American Domestic Architecture, A Henry Holt Reference Book* (New York: Henry Holt and Co., 1994); James C. and Shirley Maxwell Massey, *House Styles in America: The Old-House Journal Guide to the Architecture of American Homes* (New York: Penguin Putnam, 1996).

77. "Parade of Homes," *Christian Builders*, http://www.christianbuilders.com/content _parade.htm (cited content no longer available).

78. Construx Design Group, "Floor Plans"; Jerry and Ron Grubb, "Home Plans" (unpublished plans, Jerry's Homes Inc., 2000).

79. "Parade of Homes," *Christian Builders*, http://www.christianbuilders.com/content _parade.htm (cited content no longer available); Construx Design Group, "Floor Plans"; Grubb and Grubb, "Home Plans."

80. Dean MacCannell, "'New Urbanism' and Its Discontents," in *Giving Ground: The Politics of Propinquity*, ed. Joan Copjec and Michael Sorkin (London: Verso, 1999), 108.

81. "Parade of Homes," *Christian Builders*, http://www.christianbuilders.com/content _parade.htm (cited content no longer available).

82. "Parade of Homes," *Christian Builders*, http://www.christianbuilders.com/content _parade.htm (cited content no longer available).

83. "Bradbury," *Regency Homes,* http://www.regencyhomes.com/designs/bradbury (site now discontinued).

84. Grubb and Grubb, "Home Plans."

85. Walter Alzmann et al., *The Waltons* (CBS Television, Warner Brothers Television, 1972–1981).

86. Construx Design Group, "Floor Plans."

87. "Parade of Homes," *Christian Builders*, http://www.christianbuilders.com/content _parade.htm (cited content no longer available).

88. "Parade of Homes," *Christian Builders*, http://www.christianbuilders.com/content _parade.htm (cited content no longer available).

89. "Parade of Homes," *Christian Builders*, http://www.christianbuilders.com/content _parade.htm (cited content no longer available).

90. Michel de Certeau, *The Practice of Everyday Life*, trans. Steven Rendall (Berkeley: University of California Press, 1984), 38.

91. De Certeau, *Practice of Everyday Life*, 38–39.

92. Weil, *Lectures on Philosophy*, 113.

93. Weil, *Need for Roots*, 10.

94. It is safe to assume that the idea of "Eternal America" would be no less (perhaps considerably more, given her views on the extermination of Native Americans) blasphemous in its construction of a nation as an absolute value than "Eternal France" for Weil. Weil, *Need for Roots,* 131.

95. Harvey, "Cosmopolitanism and the Banality"; Honig, *Democracy and the Foreigner*; Murphy, "Roar of Whispers." For a more detailed discussion of the political and ethical

dimensions of cosmopolitanism, see Brennan, *At Home in the World*.

96. For a careful study of the rise of the restrictive covenant as a means to address fears of difference in suburbia, see Robert M. Fogelson, *Bourgeois Nightmares: Suburbia, 1870–1930* (New Haven, CT: Yale University Press, 2005).
97. Weil, *Lectures on Philosophy*, 213.
98. Weil, *Lectures on Philosophy*, 184–88.
99. Weil, *Need for Roots*, 73–74.
100. Weil, *Need for Roots*, 55.
101. Weil, *Need for Roots*, 73–74.
102. It is worth noting how changing technology has helped to increase the popularity and significance of the home office in ways that begin to allow nondomestic labor to infiltrate the space of the private home. However, the corresponding reconfiguration of housing design also preserves public/private distinctions and reinforces a gendered division of labor that devalues domestic work, as recounted in Lynn Spigel, "Designing the Smart House: Posthuman Domesticity and Conspicuous Production," *European Journal of Cultural Studies* 8 (2005): 403–26. Although the new economics of the home allow the workplace to penetrate domestic space, they have yet to elevate the status of traditional housework.
103. Weil, *Need for Roots*, 10.
104. Weil, *Need for Roots*, 73.

CHAPTER 5

Jacob Riis and the Doubly
Material Rhetorics of His Politics

Bruce E. Gronbeck, University of Iowa

No picture is pure image; all of them, still and moving, graphic and photographic, are "talking pictures," either literally, or in association with contextual speech, writing or discourse. Pictures are social, visual, spatial and sometimes communicative. As visual text and social communication they construct literal social space within and between the frames and fields of which they're made. . . .

    Pictures are political *as such*; it is not merely that some pictures, because of their subject matter, are more obviously public and political than others.

                John Hartley, *The Politics of Pictures: The Creation
                of the Public in the Age of Popular Media*

To conceive of pictures as talking is to value them as relational, as intermediary objects in communication processes, even as the sources of messages in and of themselves. And to conceive of pictures as political is to value them as instruments of power, as intermediary objects in rhetorical processes of identity construction, influence, and even domination. Hartley's *Politics of Pictures*, the opening of whose chapter on agoraphilia I just quoted, is devoted to both textual analyses of "public pictures" as well as institutional analyses of the media (print and electronic advertising and journalism) as they turn people into disciplined, responsive, and responsible publics.[1]

    Such arguments about communicative and political potentials of pictures, particularly (but not only) photographic images, usually rest on Shapiro's basic axiom: "There is an implicit epistemological code hovering around a photograph. Of all modes of representation, it is the one most easily assimilated into the discourses of knowledge and truth, for it is thought to be an unmediated simulacrum, a copy of what we consider the 'real.'"[2] That axiom will be probed and battered as this chapter progresses, but it will stand as foundational, at the least, to what Jacob Riis thought he was producing when he set out to take and then publicly exhibit some photographs within the *fin de siècle* reformist environment of late-nineteenth-century New York City. More than that, the "realisticness" of Riis's photographs—made all the more real seeming with improvements in photo-reproductive technologies after World War II—became subjected to ever-evolving discourses of knowledge and truth even well after his death.[3]

More particularly, this chapter will explore what I will construct as doubly material and discursively articulated rhetorics of the politics embodied in Jacob Riis's photographs of New York City tenements and their inhabitants, manipulated technologically by photographic and imagaic printing processes, and then articulated within oral, written, environmental, and even electronic communication matrices. That is, within evolving historical contexts, I will be probing (1) how the subjects of Riis's pictures were construed by him and others in different ways as the technologies of their presentation—and the social conventionalization of those technologies—changed from the late nineteenth, the early twentieth, and on into the late twentieth and early twenty-first centuries; (2) how the photographs themselves were remade over time into literally different *materia,* which in turn made them objects of variable rhetorical functions and consequences; and (3) how they function, not simply as pictures, but as aspects of multimediated communication processes, with varied relationships to speech, to written argument, to spaces and places (environments) whose functions as backgrounds affected their rhetoricity as foregrounds, and even to electronic inscription in discursive arenas far removed in time and space from Riis and the slums of New York City.

The Materiality of Photography and Communication Matrices

A picture may be worth a thousand words, but in and of itself, a picture cannot tell us what those words are. People cannot really isolate "a picture" and certainly cannot depend on it for symbolic expression on its own content. That is true because pictures have no actual existence until materialized—scratched on a cave dwelling wall, painted on a canvas, pixilated into patterned dots on a screen, etched on a storefront window, or chemically captured on photo-sensitive paper. Even the "pictures in your head" are materialized through cortical stimulation. And, too, that which is pictured is likewise material to the extent that a so-called subject can be captured more (photographed) or less (cartooned) realistically, aestheticized via stylizations, and recontextualized so as to position the subject as foreground against various meaningful backgrounds. Thus, pictures—especially the kind we are dealing with in this chapter, photographs—are doubly material: pictorial technologies must be used to bring them to life, and modes of presentation and contextualization offer us realms of meaningfulness within which to comprehend, evaluate, and even act in response to them. And third, not only are photographs doubly material, but they always are communicative and political because they are articulated as part of what I will call, after Catherine Caha Waite, a matrix.[4]

More specifically, I am interested, first, in the materiality of photography as a technology. To be sure, it is easy enough to argue that viewing photographs involves, as do most viewing experiences, fundamentally both a physiological and a cultural process,[5] or, to prefer Jonathan Crary's dialectic, a psychological and a historical process.[6] That is, insofar as photographs embed images, they present themselves to us as stimuli bombarding a human mind-body but yet also meaningful only within a social chronotope. Granted, but that is not all. Photographs additionally are material objects, printed on paper, glass, T-shirts, steel plates, pixilated circuits. They can be very, very small or as large as we're willing to pay for them to be. They can be opaque or visible only when light is passed through glass, celluloid, or some other transparent surface. They can be framed and mounted individually on a wall, melded with other material, visual, verbal, and acoustic media, sequenced as moving images, or deindividualized in collage. And most important for this chapter, changes in the materiality of photographs can alter in highly significant ways the physiological-cultural or psychological-historical processes of viewing them. The images themselves become different images when materialized in different ways, in different communication processes, in different times and places. Riis's pictures are changed radically in their journey from 1888 to today.

Second, I also argue that photographs as items of realist (or, better, realistic) mechanical chemical technologies are material in another sense: they seem to be a merely presentational medium, in Riis's case showing us the actual world of immigrants, poor New York citizens, abusive living conditions, commercial spaces, and street-smart children who increasingly dominated his thinking and his photography as he matured. Some of his most famous pictures were shot almost haphazardly in the middle of the night, with only a few actually posed. He saw them as epistemologically unproblematic, as direct records of human social-economic life from which he said "there is no appeal"—that is, as records whose status was the same as they would have been had other observers actually stood in the presence of the people, objects, and places themselves.[7] The photographs have been recognized as born in an attitude and act of realistic depiction, and, more than that, because they originally were projected as magic lantern slides likely at least ten feet across, they even were hyperrealistic in their communicative force.

But then, as their modes of public presentation changed, so did the status of their subjects—from documentary evidence of social life to illustration of verbal arguments, from illustration to art object living in not simply a social but also an aesthetic sphere, and finally back to documentary evidence, though of a very different class of human behaviors and motives than those that characterized them in the 1890s.

My understanding of the material rhetoric of photography, therefore, arises out of the naïve realism that picture-taking so often entails—the consequences of the idea that seeing is believing, that sight is the human being's most important sense for knowing (ocularcentrism).[8] As photographs are moved from context to context in time and space, perspectives on them change, their subjects therefore are seen in different ways, and so their very materiality is remade symbolically; and when features of photographic images are changed technologically—by rendering them in a different presentational technology (e.g., the engraving of Gilbert Stuart's portrait of George Washington on the one-dollar bill) or reproducing them via varied chemical processes and on diffuse surfaces—the images carry altered expressive, informational, and persuasive force.

This leaves us, third, with what I called communication matrices. Caha Waite's theorization of communication matrices was influenced by Marshall McLuhan's thinking about relationships between and among information taken in via different senses. Human thought depended to McLuhan on relationships or "ratios" between and among sense-data coming into the sensorium via sight, sound, touch, etc. His basic theorem in this regard was simple: "The transformations of technology have the character of organic evolution because all technologies are extensions of our physical being."[9] Further, each of the mechanical, chemical, electronic media extended parts of the body: film, photography, and television, the eye; radio, the ear; the railroad, one's feet; the computer, the central nervous system.[10]

So when Caha Waite suggested that "the lived body . . . mediates one's experience of the world," she was picking up thoughts where McLuhan left off.[11] Among other things, in exploring screen arts, she became interested in "multisensory perception" that facilitates "an awareness of time and space based on rhythms that are not necessarily part of one's ordinary experience."[12] As the body, particularly the eye and the ear, work to process sound and rhythms, space and spatialized images, and images or bodies in motion, it organizes perceptions as Gestaltists would have them: in figure-ground patterns at a micro-level, in zones of experience from those close to those far away at a macro-level of understanding. The multisensory mix of ear and eye perception produces the communication matrix within which phenomenological life is lived.

The great value of both McLuhan on ratios and Caha Waite on communication matrices within which we comprehend what she also calls "variable-flex experience"[13] is that they force us to deal with this chapter's subject matter, Riis's photographs, as what I have labeled "multimediated discourse."[14] Simply, we experience talk about photographs, photographs embedded in texts, written discourses read aloud, or a television program and a movie as multimediated. We must sort through the aural, literate, and visual or pictorial channels delivering sense-data to our ears and eyes and then, picking up various aural-literate-visual markers or significant symbols, construct Caha Waite's matrices. Meaning making in the face of multimediated discourse becomes a complex process of symbol recognition, pattern recognition, and interpretation based on individual skills, training, and experience in symbol and pattern recognition as well signification. And, as we will see, multimediated matrices provide perceptual complexes within which can be articulated, even sutured, meanings from varied spheres of human experience.

Riis's photographs, as we will see, always have been embedded in symbolically rich environments: public talk about the pictures, print media using them to argue for slum reform, print and even physical spaces employed to aestheticize them. In the language of Ron Greene and others, the photographs are articulated with other communication channels and with the environments within which they are presented to audiences so as to produce varied rhetorical effectivities.[15]

And so I am concerned with Jacob Riis's reform-minded photography as subjected to doubly material rhetorics: a rhetoric whose political force changes with modes of presentation and representation, but also as a rhetoric whose place in political realms changes with the recontextualization of those people, objects, and places that are the subjects being positioned within discourses. Those doubly materialist rhetorics are organized in communication matrices through articulations that produce figure-ground and variable-flex experiences, which in turn empower them politically. As Hartley intimated, pictures *as such* are political—and all the more so when we understand their relationships to other communication modalities.

This chapter, in summary, is illustrative of what is now termed a rhetoric of technology. "So what is a rhetoric of technology?" Charles Bazerman asks. He answers that "[i]t is the rhetoric that accompanies and makes technology possible in the world. It is the rhetoric that makes technology fit into the world and makes the world fit with technology."[16] And so, photography made possible a different kind of visual reproduction, thanks to chemistry and metallurgy, than had been available before the nineteenth century.

Its originary features were such that it could be used for only certain kinds of representations: the requirement of relatively long, daylight exposure of photo-sensitive plates meant that its objects had to be stationary and relatively close to the plates (if only because distant light was dynamic), and it was used for depiction of close-up or medium-shot objects and people. Those were the worlds that "fit" the early technology. As the photographic technologies evolved, so did the objects capable of being photographed, modes of printing and circulation of images, and the like. Material changes in the technologies impacted social and even psychological aspects of photographing and then viewing the world.

Central to rhetorical considerations of the photographic technology, therefore, is the impact of technological progress and flexibility in applications on qualities of human experiences with the medium. Likewise important is temporality: what happens with the re-presentation of images in varied times and places? In the words of Vivian Sobchack,

> [i]n the still photograph, time and space are abstractions. Although the image has a presence, it neither partakes of nor describes the present. Indeed, the photograph's fascination is that it is a figure of transcendental time made available against the ground of a lived and finite temporality. Although included in our experience of the present, the photograph transcends both our immediate present and our lived experience of temporality because it exists for us as ever engaged in the activity of *becoming*.[17]

Unless destroyed, the image endures out of time, capable of always being resituated, as Sobchack argues, "against the ground of a lived and finite temporality." Her use of the word "against" is particularly insightful, as the image comes as a visitor from another place and is subject to the treatments that human beings give to any stranger. Relationships must be negotiated with the people, locations, and objects inscribed on a picture—and hence my interests in articulation of communication matrices.

More broadly still, this chapter is framed within what is now termed "media ecology studies." Media ecology is generally defined as the study of media as environments.[18] Media ecologists are interested in ways in which, and the mechanisms as well as institutions by which, dominant media work in societies both to structure them institutionally and even to modify or remake individual and collective consciousness.[19] "Media, consciousness, and culture" becomes a shorthand phrase embodying those concerns: exploration of relationships between media and both collective organizations of societies and individual modes of consciousness when citizens use particular media.[20] This particular study, in its largest frame, pursues such concerns, examining the material and articulatory uses of media within shifting social circumstances and institutions.

And so, then, to execute this project, I begin with a brief background on Riis himself, then examine some of his photographs in four contexts: (1) the late 1880s through early 1900s, when he traveled around the East Coast and then into the rest of the country, giving magic lantern shows that urged slum reform; (2) the 1890s through 1910s, when his books, magazine articles, and newspaper pieces were published and accompanied by some of his photographs; (3) the 1970s, when new prints of his photographs provided grounds for celebrating him as America's first great nighttime documentary photographer; (4) and finally, the 1990s to the present, when scholars of cultural studies radically resituate his pictures as evidence for a politics of surveillance and class warfare—a startling yet not particularly surprising turn in judgment about his photographic and even social-political work. In moving across these contexts, the photographs themselves are remade materially and their subjects likewise are substantially altered.[21]

We will return to ruminations about a doubled sense of materiality and the matter of articulation in visual rhetoric at the end of this chapter.

Jacob A. Riis, Photographer and Citizen

When Alexander Alland Sr. published the first art book collection of Riis pictures, he called the work *Jacob A. Riis: Photographer and Citizen* because he wanted to "compact the long and versatile career of a remarkable man and show how his many roles converged in a crusade for human decency."[22] That compaction, abetted by Ansel Adams's preface to the book, aestheticized the photographs and telescoped his journalistic, public-intellectual, and political careers into a singular commitment—a commitment to civic duty. Coming sixty years after his death, Alland's book could reduce and essentialize Riis's lifework without objection. Those wishing an equally celebratory but more personalized peek at the man in 1974, however, could turn to another product of that year, Edith Patterson Meyer's biography, *"Not Charity, But Justice"*: *The Story of Jacob A. Riis*.[23] As much as Alland was committed to refurbishing Riis's photographs for new generations, so was Meyer intent on memorializing his grand social spirit and moral commitments.

The man who was the object of such attention was born in Ribe, Denmark, in 1849, immigrating to the United States at twenty-one, penniless on the streets of New York. He lived an all-American immigrant life, earning a living for a while with his carpentry skills, then getting a job as night police reporter on the Lower East Side once his language skills caught up with his ambition. His newspaper work for the *South Brooklyn News*, the *New York*

Tribune, and the *New York Evening Sun* exposed him to the worst of late-nineteenth-century slum life, and the more he saw of it, the more indignant he became in the face of poverty, urban decrepitude, immigrant victimage, and the roles of environmental conditions in degenerating the quality of lives—definitely a nurture advocate in the nature-nurture debate.[24] He worked out of an office near the police outpost in Mulberry Bend, and his autobiography brims with stories of late-night ventures where he followed the police, firefighters, or health officials into the worst of the Bend's environments to get his stories.[25]

As he grew more distraught with what he was covering, Riis was motivated to move his work in two directions: he starting taking pictures of the squalor in which he lived and worked in 1887, and began writing short pieces for other newspapers. This led to church lectures, illustrated with magic lantern slides. In one of those audiences, the editor of *Scribner's Magazine* was in attendance, and invited Riis to write a piece for the magazine, illuminated with engraved versions of some of his slides. In the December 1889 number of that organ, for $150,[26] Riis sketched out the basic themes of what would become his book *How the Other Half Lives*.[27]

The article became a book in less than year, and a bestseller at that—indeed, it is still in print. Riis's lecturing and writing career blossomed to the point that he could give up his newspaper work, earning his living as a reformer publishing books about the slums, in particular about the children who lived there.[28] With his friend and fellow Progressivist Theodore Roosevelt, who then was president of the New York City Board of Police Commissioners, Riis agitated for new city codes and destruction of the worst tenement districts. The first abuses were attacked in 1896–1897 and then more systematically in the 1901 Tenement Law, with more legislation and slum-clearing activities following in New York City and elsewhere. Schools with playgrounds, fresh air camps, publicly and privately funded settlement houses, and various kinds of health-oriented clinics for the poor were his passion until his 1914 death. He wrote and lectured until the end, still using his own and others' photographs as supplements to his discourse.

The Life and Times of Jacob A. Riis's Photographs

It is Riis's pictures, however, that provide our focus in this chapter. We now will follow their journey through the late nineteenth and twentieth centuries.

Jacob A. Riis, Lanternist

[P]erhaps I had better explain how I came to take up photographing as a—no, not exactly as a pastime. It was never that for me. I had use for it, and beyond that I never went. . . . To be precise, then, I began taking pictures by proxy. It was upon my midnight trips with the sanitary police that the wish kept cropping up in me that there were some way of putting before the people what I saw there.[29]

Riis continues writing in his autobiography of learning about a German product, *Blitzpulver,* a lye-and-magnesium powder, that he could burn to produce a bright flash; it made him the greatest nighttime photo-documentarist of his age.[30] He had no particular skills or interest in the aesthetics of photography, though he "had use for it." Invading tenements, alleys, and alcohol dives, sometimes with other photographers and almost always with police escorts, he took or had taken pictures of human misery. Occasionally he posed his subjects, but usually he shot what he found, as he found it. Today, the studies of his lantern slides and photography are legion, following Alland's 1974 book and its prefatory accolades by Ansel Adams.[31] The magic lantern slides started all the fuss.

Magic lanterns are projection boxes invented sometime in the seventeenth century and popular worldwide into the twentieth century. They were the first screen-based collective artistic medium,[32] using everything from candles and low-grade oils to limelight and electric bulbs as light sources to project round or rectangular images from the front or back of screens.[33] Multiple lanterns could be aimed at the same screen and equipped with mechanical switching devices that made dissolves possible, and two or more pieces of glass could be moved against each other to create a sense of motion. With the coming of photography by the mid-nineteenth century, pieces of glass—soon standardized as 3.25 by 4.00 inches—would have positive photographic images printed on them, and often were hand colorized to create more realistic images of the world. Magic lantern shows were offered for information and entertainment, and reports in *Frank Leslie's Illustrated Newspaper* (1855–1922)[34] show politicians campaigning with magic lanterns and news outlets reporting election results in cities via gigantic outdoor projectors.[35]

At first, Riis took his photographs to city authorities and to publishing outlets, but didn't get very far politically with those actions, so on February 28, 1888, he had some magic lantern slides made from his negatives and lectured on slum reform in the Broadway Tabernacle, generating $143.50 for social missionary causes.[36] Churches and missionary societies became common sites for magic lantern shows; indeed, he believed, they were the great sources of the public "awakening" to slum conditions.[37]

One of his lantern lectures, "The Other Half and How They Live" (1891), delivered to the Sixth Convention of Christian Workers in the United States and Canada, was transcribed and printed. The transcription contains specific references to the fifty-nine slides that he used. Key to our understanding of his lecturing procedure is this note, which he wrote on the transcription: "As I speak without notes, from memory and to the pictures, the result is according to how I feel."[38] A common practice among lanternists was to arrange a series of slides in a stack, letting one's sight of the next slide cue the lecture or commentary.

Believing that "there was no appeal" from the facts visible in pictures, Riis worked in a rhetorical setting in which the visual channel included the documenting objects, while the verbal and acoustic channels overlaid human reactions and interpretations on them. The slides he saw as realistically portraying lives as led among the other half, with his lectures inscribing them with social significance: moral judgments, political and even ideological implications. A sentimental style of discourse was at work.[39] A writer quoted in Meyer called "the short vignette" the essence of his style, "to begin with a quick, dramatic statement of a person's plight, then to reveal the tension between the relentless struggle for survival and the quick emotions of love, anger, greed, and friendship . . . closing with an appeal to the reader's sense of justice."[40]

Such a style was sentimental insofar as it described both a scene and how spectators should react to it. Consider this segment of the 1891 lecture, as Riis shows before-and-after pictures of a child who was rescued from the slum:

"Her hair was matted with blood and her whole body was covered with sores," says the official report. After she had been in the care of the Society for the Prevention of Cruelty to Children six months, that was the way [second picture of Antonia Candia] she looked. [Applause.] The Christian care she had made the difference. What would have been the future of that child? Can you read it in this face and tangled hair [pointing to the first picture]? I can, and no doubt you can see the future of that child there. My experience shows it every day in the week the future that would have been hers had she not found these friends.[41]

He finishes by pointing out that the society has rescued between 50,000 and 60,000 children in sixteen years. Soon thereafter, Riis describes a baby dying in the summer heat, which was 115 degrees in its bedroom, finishing his vignette with the conclusion that "[w]hen they hand around the hat for [the Fresh Air Fund] next year, don't let it pass. Your little mite may be just the one to save such a little miserable life as that."[42] The coupling here of two (and more, actually) stories about children whose lives and deaths were controlled by the better half's intervention into the world of the other half illustrates Maren Stange's understanding of Riis's lecturing habits: "As the lectures proceeded, slides were related to each other in pairs or groups for which Riis's remarks served as 'relay,' moving audiences along through story-telling sequences of images like those encountered in comic strips or films."[43] With the pictures preceding (usually) recollection and commentary, they were the foregrounds that drew on and yet also organized Riis's background experiences.

Those habits and approaches to persuasion were possible because of the doubly material rhetorics at work: (1) printing photographs in 1891 on glass allowed them to be projected as larger-than-life images, dominating one wall of a dark room and, in the dark, functioning as a close-up, real-seeming documentation of life; and (2) because the images indeed were understood to be realistic objects imprisoned in Riis's pictures, they were conceived as unproblematic stand-ins for life itself. The glass-based positives of the pictures gave them a materiality that allowed their enlarged presentation to collectivized people, and a discourse of realistic depiction put the objects in the pictures into a dialogic—what Hartley in the opening quotation describes as "social" and "communicative"—relationship with the viewers. If the pictures were "real," then the people looking out from them were directly confronting those peering in at them. Riis's words overlaid talk of feelings and emotional reactions on that dialogic relationship, as well as the personal experiences he related through those words; together, words and recalled experiences formed a phenomenologically rich discursive environment evoked by the photographs and then organized as a symbolic matrix by them.

In summary, the subjects of Riis's photographic magic lantern slides were "real" because of the presumed transparency of photography; as well, the lanternist's modes of show and tell were acutely presentational, making the slides seem like window panes onto the material world. The subjects were construed as irrefutable evidence—that very word in Latin (*evidere,* out of or from sight) inscribing that which is seen as real. And then, when we remember that lanternists used the slides themselves as *aides-mémoire,* triggering an assortment of past experiences that could be recalled and even performed by a speaker, we can see a communication matrix wherein foregrounded pictures interpellate and yet draw associations from the background narratives, facts, and individuated experiences in the life of that speaker.

Jacob A. Riis, Book Illustrator

The 1890 book *How the Other Half Lives* represented a significant shift in Riis's modes of slum reform rhetoric. In the magic lantern shows, he would use dozens of pictures and shape his descriptions, sentimental appeals, and argumentative commentary to those pictures. They verbally elaborated, decorated, interpreted, and channeled the central discourses of the visual, and his bodily performances served as personal testimony to the crises demanding reforms. The book, however, radically increased word count and discursive complexities even while reducing the pictures to but forty-three. Furthermore, less than half of those pictures—eighteen—were photographic; six were diagrams of housing units and nineteen were sketches and engravings made from his photographs.

Why deemphasize and replace the photographs? Answers to that question are mostly speculative: perhaps he thought of books as a different medium, perhaps he was more proud of his work as writer than his skill as photographer.[44] Maybe he was sensitive to the fact that sketch art in its various forms was still the medium of choice in newspapers and magazines. And he most certainly knew that the half-tone picture printing process was still in its infancy, with the resulting images of poor quality: lacking contrast, faded even with missing sections, blurry and small, usually taking up only a portion of the page.[45]

An excellent example of the dominance of verbal prose over pictorial representation can be found in the book's chapter on Chinatown. Riis inveighs against the pagan worshippers, the Chinese Americans, whom he believes adopt Christianity only for personal gain, who lure in the innocent through laundry service and gambling, and who seemingly keep a clean street only to cover up opium dens and their enslavement of white laborers, especially women. The only picture in this chapter is a Chinese-American male standing by a telephone pole, bearing the caption "The official organ of Chinatown" because communications are tacked on the post rather than sent through the wires. Presumably, the direct look of the man into the camera captures his attitude: "a blank, unmeaning stare, suggesting nothing, asking no questions, answering none." The description continues:

> Whatever is on foot goes on behind closed doors. Stealth and secretiveness are as much part of the Chinaman in New York as the cat-like tread of his felt shoes. His business, as his domestic life, shuns the light, less because there is anything to conceal than because that is the way of the man. Perhaps the attitude of American civilization toward the stranger, whom it invited in, has taught him that way. At any rate, the very doorways of his offices and shops are fenced off by queer, forbidding partitions suggestive of a continual state of siege. The stranger who enters through the

crooked approach is received with sudden silence, a sullen stare, and an angry "Vat you vant?" that breathes annoyance and distrust.[46]

Of interest is the nineteenth-century book version of the accompanying photograph.[47] The facial expression that Riis took to be "a blank, unmeaning stare" is washed out, as are the messages on the telegraph pole that he later describes as posts for gambling games and warnings about raids. The bottom half of another man bent over shows up in a distracting manner on the right edge of the picture. The whole photograph conveys a sense of daytime brightness, in contrast to what Riis said was an important quality of his pictures: a blackness that lent "a gloom to the [lantern] show more realistic than any the utmost art of professional skill might have attained."[48] Indeed, in the book the photograph seemed not to justify whatsoever the condemnation of Chinatown that was being preached. The engraving was incidental.

In *How the Other Half Lives*, Riis's florid literary style, developed as he moved from newspaper reporting to essay writing, dominated the work. Especially because most of the photographs were offered as engravings or minimalist watercolor renditions, the pictures were distinctly secondary to the verbal images and arguments for reform. As a writer, Riis's vision was to be found in verbal description. The writer-audience relationship in the communication matrix was constructed less dialogically than monologically. He was clearly the expert, the one who knew because he had experienced all the situations and places that he constructed and assessed discursively. The pictures, then, were but passing illustrations, not the sources of probity per se; they engaged the mind's eye, to be sure, but not the heart and will of social actors. They had been subordinated to the world of prose.

The readers' sense of materiality of both photographs as medium and the people, places, and objects within their frames had all but vanished, disembodied by technologies incapable of sustaining their direct address as "talking pictures." Rather, the literate conventions for producing persuasive words—the vehicles in the nineteenth century understood as primary for producing both conviction (the correctness of arguments) and persuasion (the feelings that drove people to action) in the rhetorical theories of modernist thought—held centerstage.[49] The Lockean belief that language was the tool for producing, organizing, evoking, and empowering ideas governed persuasive theories and practices in a century when print came to dominate the public sphere. Riis's photographs were incidental to the reformer-writer's political actions. The matrix tightly corseted the pictures that were so dominant in Riis's lectures.

We will examine particularly one of the engraved pictures later in this chapter.

Jacob A. Riis, Artistic Photographer

Riis died in 1914, and so did most of his influence; he was memorialized in the Jacob A. Riis Settlement House, a few annual memorials, and a fresh-air camp out on Long Island, yet the reform movement swept past his proposals. He was rediscovered, however, after World War II, thanks to the diligent searches of photographer Alexander Alland Sr. and the negotiating skills of Grace Mayer, curator of prints at the Museum of the City of New York.[50] Riis's family found glass negatives and positives as well as old prints, Alland made stunning exhibition prints from the negatives, and Mayer added captions from Riis's books in mounting a 1948 exhibit of the work. Over the next quarter century, Riis's pictures worked their way into the American history of photography, and finally, in 1974, Alland published a biographical and commentary art book of eighty-two high-quality prints. Both Alland and museum staff photographer John Harvey Heffren reworked Riis's negatives and positives, cropping some, adjusting exposure and contrast, straightening others, even improving focus. As well, glossy silvertone prints were made, further enhancing the viewers' experiences with Riis's work. He became viewed as a first-class artist, even though he always had protested that he was not.[51]

Right from Alland's collection, with Ansel Adams's preface, Riis was beatified as a photographer whose pictures "are magnificent achievements in the field of humanistic photography"—magnificent because of "the intense, *living* quality" in Riis's work.[52] Adams was particularly impressed with the intimate, empathetic gaze of the subjects at the camera: "They did not realize that they were looking at you and me and all humanity for ages of time. Their postures and groupings are not contrived; the moment of exposure was selected more for the intention of truth than for the intention of effect." The truth of their lives, to Adams, was only underscored by Riis's mastery of the technology: "[T]he quality of his flash illumination is extraordinary; the plastic shadow-edges, modulations and textures of flesh, the balance of interior flash and exterior daylight—what contemporary work really exceeds it in competence and integrity?"[53] Adams could not help himself. While trying to recognize those who became the objects of Riis's attention, he was drawn into the effects of the photographic technology on viewers.

Adams's relationship to Riis's photographs anticipated the engaging opening to Roland Barthes's *Camera Lucida*: "One day, quite some time ago, I happened on a photograph of Napoleon's youngest brother, Jerome, taken in 1852. And I realized then, with an amazement I have not been able to lessen since: 'I am looking at eyes that looked at the Emperor.'"[54] While Barthes at first seems transfixed by the space between the image and the photograph—and between Jerome's eyes and his own—he is more determinatively caught up in trying to articulate the technology's impact on his own subjectivity and its relationships to photography's subjects, events being photographed, indeed, the vision of the photographer. Adams, as did Barthes, aestheticized Riis and his pictures but yet materialized especially the people captured on the photographic plates. A doubly materialistic rhetoric was at work in full force.

Once the pictures are removed from Riis's lectures and printed words, as they very nearly are in Alland's collection—and as they so often are in online collections of American social-documentary photography—then they are just that, pictures. They are decontextualized, freed from their originary times and places; they can be recontextualized, becoming parts of alternative constructions in other times and places. Adams goes so far as to suggest they even can be freed from the exigencies of particular times and places: "Alland's beautiful prints, by exalting the physical qualities of Riis's work, intensify their expressive content. The factual and dated content of subject has definite historic importance, but the larger content lies in Riis's expression of people in misery, want and squalor." And the next sentences remark that

> [t]hese people live again for you in the print—as intensely as when their images were captured on the old dry plates of ninety years ago. . . . I think that I have an explanation for their compelling power. It is because in viewing these prints I find myself identified with the people photographed. I am walking in their alleys, standing in their rooms and sheds and workshops, looking in and out of their windows. And they in turn seem to be aware of me.[55]

Ansel Adams was making two moves in this paragraph, on the one hand distancing himself aesthetically by decontextualizing the photographs, referring to their "larger content," but on the other throwing himself into a communicative, yet rhetorical, relationship with the people photographed. He simultaneously asserted aesthetic distance—what Edward Bullough originally called "psychical distance" to distinguish artistic, contemplative mentalities from psychological engagements with life experiences—and empathetic involvement with 1890s New Yorkers.[56] What we have is a double articulation, where (artistic) expression carried Adams in one direction, and (social) content ferried him to another time and place. And so experientially, he likewise was doubled materially, with Alland's masterful prints turning Riis's photographs into art objects even as the now-enhanced contents of those enlarged, corrected, silvertone prints were portals into an unforgotten world. Adams was wrestling with his own subjectivity in the face of a doubly material pictorial discourse.

As Alland laid out his book, the photographs lay on the recto side when it was opened, short texts on the verso pages. Those texts included only minimal information about the subject matter, or, in some cases, a quoted sentence or two from *How the Other Half Lives*. The words were bare descriptions; the pictures were large and striking, meant to dominate the eye—and the mind. As well, the format of a coffee-table art book, with its long horizontal *vis-à-vis* its comparative short vertical dimensions, drew the reader's glance from the sparse print of the verso pages to the rich images of the recto pages.[57]

Print and picture stood in a frozen matrix within which the usual Western left-to-right reading practices hurried readers to the luscious silvertone prints. And then, the reader—Adams's perspectives and reactions are testimony—could contemplate and even dialogue with the prints, which seemed to him to live both in and out of time. Riis conceived of as artistic photographer transcended context in precisely the ways that Barthes thought Napoleon's brother Jerome's photograph did.

Jacob A. Riis, Spying Elitist

Once Riis's works were back in circulation, his pictures and verbal texts also could be taken up within the developing scholarly work in cultural studies. Interestingly, his photographs came once again to be read through his lectures and books, particularly through the seemingly stereotyped and essentializing descriptions of Germans, Jews, the Chinese, and African Americans of lower Manhattan.[58] Riis's words not only condemned him as an elitist, but partook of a linguistic code that was made to override whatever documenting of New York City life earlier generations had seen in the photographic codes.

The gaze of the subjects that Adams had found so affecting and powerful became, to later culturalists, a defiant glare offered by the underclass for their overlords.[59] Riis was charged with actually increasing the distance between viewers and subjects of his photographs.[60] He was accused even of practicing "photography as [political] surveillance,"[61] encasing his pictures in a "language of benevolent violence" that "waged a war on the poor."[62]

Here, then, were critiques of culturalists that turned Riis the performer/reformer into an object himself by reinterpreting his verbal discourse and separating it—except raced epithets—from the images. That is, Riis's ethnic and raced descriptions originally had engaged potentially sympathetic audiences with his subject matters and reinforced his position on the nature-nurture argument: that all of these immigrants were degraded human beings because of environmental characteristics, not their ethnicity per se. That argument was lost, however, even though it had been important in the era of the eugenics debates.[63] Furthermore, as Jackson argues, the sort of objectification that photographs viewed outside their original rhetorical contexts seemed to produce never occurred in Riis's lectures, articles, and books because of the dual, sentimentalized discourse in which he clothed his arguments: he used the languages of both secular (Progressive) slum reform and religious (social gospel) commitments to make reform happen, with images of human sadness and misery embedded in both of those languages.[64]

The other approach to defense of Riis's photographs and photographic practices in combination with his words comes from Bill Hug. After narrating Riis's own life as an immigrant, the frustration he felt in the face of nonresponses to slum life from both church and state, and Riis's actual abilities with both word and camera, Hug suggests that Riis had to engage in "purposeful ambiguities," posing as a typically elitist white American in his words in order to open cognitive and affective spaces in listeners' and readers' minds for the force of pictures and their depictions of the decayed environment.[65] As well, notes Hug, Riis's descriptions of most national ethnics, including even (and unusually) African Americans, were always mixed with both positive and negative stereotyping. Hug's is a creative rationalization and certainly attempts revisionist cultural history, though as yet it receives little attention.

No matter how much Riis has been defended by the likes of Jackson, Hug, and others, the critical cultural framings have produced new realms of critique. Photography, again, is a material technology allowing those of us with the eyes of the culturally sensitive to jump back more than a hundred years. As with Ansel Adams, so with contemporary cultural critics and historians.

Yet there are important differences between his gaze and theirs. Adams, a photographer, was doing everything in his power to free himself from his own situation and even, in some ways, from that within which the photographic subjects lived. He decontextualized the photographs so as to aestheticize them and the actions of the photographer. The culturalists, on the other hand, have sought to use the pictures as portals leading into the subjects themselves as well as the mindset—and maybe even the motives—of the photographer. The culturalists turn to conventions of both photography (especially the gaze and technical manipulations of contrast, composition, focus) and social life (coded environments, clothing, postures, poses) in order to radically contextualize the images and the image maker. By "radically," I mean that culturalists assume that cultural conventions of looking and seeing, of material conditions and human facial/bodily displays, can be read as comparatively unambiguous signifieds.

If visual codes operate within unambiguated processes of signification, then culturalists can argue that a presumed do-gooder like Riis in fact was living a lie that is materialized in the eyes of subjects who glare back at the photographer—and us. If Riis's pictures are precoded within social belief systems and ideologies—if he was what Anthony Woodiwiss terms a "cultural representationist"[66]—then Riis's subjects gain voice and talk a politics of voyeurism, class stratification, and, yes, Christian or "benevolent violence."[67] Central to the communication matrix in these sorts of cases are culturalist truisms and the *realpolitik* of an age. Culture tells individuals what is and is not, what is valuable and what is not, what is socially constructive and socially destructive.

The Italian Rag-Picker: A Case Study

So far, I've dealt mostly with general trends in the remanufacture of Riis's pictures across time and the contexts within which those pictures were read. Let me get more explicit by examining a particular photograph, "At the Home of the Italian Rag-Picker" (90.13.2.90).[68] I select it because a reproduction of the lantern slide is available; the picture was turned into an engraving for Riis's *Scribner's Magazine* article and *How the Other Half Lives*, and then was "adjusted" for later reproduction after World War II.[69]

It is, of course, difficult for a reader to experience what the slide would have looked like at a magic lantern show, its image blown up to (perhaps) ten feet across, illuminated by a gas- and lime-burning lamp.[70] Projecting lantern slides that I have reconstituted from the 35mm transparencies of the images available from the Museum of the City of New York, I can say that the image of the Italian rag-picker tends to wash out because the picture was overexposed by the flash of *Blitzpulver* that Riis was using in a dark basement, though I suspect that viewers could have made out clearly her Madonna-like pose with her baby in lap amid the bags of rags in her living area. They might even have sensed what Pascal sees: "The light from the flash powder created shadows that emphasize the filth on the walls and the tired lines on the woman's face, but it also gave her the radiant glow that often illuminates the face of the Virgin Mary."[71]

When Riis showed the Italian rag-picker in his 1891 lecture to the Christian workers, he seemed to treat her sympathetically, befitting her heavenward gaze:

> If you want to understand just what [the struggle to keep children alive] means, come with me at three o'clock some morning in July or August when these stony streets are like fiery furnaces, and see those mothers walking up and down the pavements with their little babes trying to stir some breath of God's air to cool the

brows of the sick child and hear the feeble wails of those little ones! Then tell me they have no cause of complaint, that they ought to be content. Here [shows picture of "Home of the Italian Rag-picker"—Italian woman with child in her arms] is one of them, an Italian baby in its swaddling clothes. You have seen how they wrap them around and around until you can almost stand them on either end and they won't bend, so tightly are they bound. It is only a year ago that the Italian missionary down there wrote to the city mission that he did not know what to do with these Italian children in the hot summer days, for "no one asked for them." They have been asked for since, thank God! Christian charity has found some of them out.[72]

Here, the Italian rag-picker was fit into the rhetorical flow of an object lesson of engaged ghetto motherhood. Her upward glance, together with the tone and narrative structure of this segment of the lecture, made her a gendered, transcendent figure who needed—and deserved—to be rescued by Christian charity. One senses Riis's impromptu style of speaking, with the digression about how tightly the baby is wrapped, yet his points about working mothers and the need for Christian charity to intervene in tenement children's lives were clear. That picture materialized the female saints of the slums.

By the 1890 book, however, the picture had been turned into an engraving by Kenyon Cox, who simplified the setting and flattened her clothing into plain white fabric, even though Riis was trying to capture the "vivid and picturesque costumes" that "lend a tinge of color to the otherwise dull monotony of the slums they [Italian mothers] inhabit."[73] The roll of her eyes became less stereotypically supplicating, and it was no longer possible to identify her as a basement dweller. Furthermore, while Riis explicitly recognized that "[t]he women are faithful wives and devoted mothers,"[74] yet the whole chapter was devoted to showing what happens when the Italians with their "Mediterranean exuberance" were thrown into the part of the lower Manhattan African-American area that became known as Little Italy: they lived lives of filth by picking through dumps to find whatever they could sell, never learning English and so forced to deal with middlemen (the infamous *padrones*) for contacts with others, and expressing their hot-headedness with the knife.[75] The engraving of the Italian rag-picker had much too little rhetorical power to stand as anything but a faint reflection of Riis's coarse description of what the New York environment had done to these "gay, lighthearted" people.[76] The remanufacture of a projectable photograph as a simplified sketch all but dematerialized both the image itself and the Italian rag-picker herself. The startling quality of the image as well as the romantic portrayal of its subject were overrun by a flood of harsh, descriptive, judgmental prose.

Once the negative of the Italian rag-picker was corrected and brought back as a beautiful positive print by Alland, however, it circulated as an aesthetic object. Adams's praise for Riis's techniques resounded. It became a standard piece in collections of American photographic masterpieces.[77] Its composition was attractive enough to make it the subject of digital play with three-dimensional computer imaging, even as both Hales and Hug sought to give it a deep history by arguing that it was evocative of Renaissance depictions of the Virgin and child.[78] It entered a zone of timeless art.

Alland managed to adjust the contrast, darkening the whole picture so as to bring out much that had been lost in Riis's flash: the textured cement (or mud) walls, the dirty plank floor, the ticking of her bags of rags, even the pattern of her shirt and work apron that Riis had characterized in his book. Cropping the negative let Alland turn the picture into a more obvious portrait, create more tension between what had been in Riis's original a balanced left- and right-hand side of the picture, and remove most of the distracting hat that was hanging on the wall of the original. The swarthiness of the woman was emphasized through a darkening of the complexion of both her and her baby; the stereotypically Italian features were more forcefully marked.

Overall, the dire straits in which such mothers had been depicted in Riis's books took on more iconic presence in the Alland print even as it justified Adams's paean to Riis's ability to make us feel the presence of the scene. Both the technological reconstitution of the photograph and the subjective construction of what Carrie Tirado Bramen calls the picturesque—"the aesthetic discourse of the urban picturesque [that] helped to equate ethnic variety and urbanism with modern Americanism"—made the photograph one of the most popular among all that Jacob Riis took.[79] It is that sense of Riis as a "tour-guide" that gives probity to the arguments for the picturesque.[80]

And yet, of course, the same features that made the Italian rag-picker a Madonna earned the Danish immigrant a sullied—at least highly controversial—reputation as a tour guide who also was an exploiter of the Other. The sheer power of the rematerialized photograph and its subject stirred cultural historians, in turn, to wrestle with the relationships between and among pictures, their subjects/objects, and, almost always, Riis's stereotyping prose. Keith Gandal is another of the cultural historians who seeks a position from which to view all three. While he does not mention the rag-picker photograph particularly, he does focus on Riis's treatment of Jews and Italians. What he sees at work is a kind of Christian voyeurism, spectacle for its own sake: "[T]he more shocking, the more extreme the diversities, the larger the gesture by which they could be reduced to nothing, the grander the spiritual fundament that could be laid bare."[81] Gandal regularly refers to the details always pointed out by Riis—the particular marks in clothing, expression, and behavior that denoted and connoted ethnic identity—as evidence for his voyeurism and the presumed titillation of looking by late-nineteenth-century Christian audiences.

And so the Italian rag-picker, her baby and her basement, Riis's talk and his prose, and his audiences and his personae tumble through a century and a quarter of reaction, commentary, celebration, and condemnation. Over time and across space, technological shortcomings and innovation, together with the multiple aesthetic, critical, and cultural perspectives on photographic technology and its employment by an early experimenter and social reformer, created discursive formations built on two different yet interacting material rhetorics. The communication matrices within which the Italian Madonna was positioned altered the materiality of both the photograph and its subject.

The Doubly Material Rhetorics of Photographic Images

In an attempt to bring this study to a close that reflects on its possible relevance to contemporary rhetorical studies, let me consider some implications of what I have called "the doubly material rhetorics" of Jacob Riis, his photographs, and the sociocultural articulations of his pictures into discursive contexts, as well as of his reputation and products into social-political-aesthetic American life. Rhetoricians over the last third-century, at least from Michael Calvin McGee's pioneering essay on material rhetoric through Ronald Walter Greene's aggregation of relevant studies in an effort to provide a new and improved conception of rhetoric's materiality, have struggled to posit a definitive understanding of the ways in which discursive activities such as talking and writing to others are related to the material world and to cultural life more generally.[82]

I certainly have no wish to return to various proposals for understanding relationships between words and things, people, places, and instruments of power. Suffice it to say initially that theorists and critics over that time have understood discursivity as having material effects (McGee) including profound effects on people whose lives are improved or (more likely) deteriorated by powerful rhetors (Cloud);[83] as representing bits and pieces of the (fragmented) material world long enough for us to process it rhetorically and thus symbolically or socially (McGee); as discursively masking agents' power over and knowledge of the nondiscursive (material) world (McKerrow);[84] as operating as a human technology that stabilizes "meaning by distributing populations, discourses and institutions onto the terrain of a governing apparatus so that a series of judgments might be made about the art of government" (Greene);[85] or even as a rhetoric or set of discursivities about the nature of and uses for material technologies themselves (Bazerman).[86]

Whatever position one assumes on the issues informing the relationship of discursivity to the material and social worlds, and in accordance with Greene's interesting move to evoke the notion of discourse itself as a technology, I have been suggesting that rhetorics of—and not just about—mechanical and electronic technologies themselves also must be examined with an eye toward materiality. The focus here must be on physical manipulations of *materia* that makes it an intermediary between human perception and the world outside the perceptual process. Here, a technology is to be understood not simply as a mechanism for the "display, exhibition, and consumption" of reproduced images or objects, but as means of altering humans' perception of sight, sound, and duration of experience, thus remaking our base understandings of and actions in individualized and social worlds (Caha Waite's argument).[87] Communication technologies such as photography, then, are not simply conduits for moving images from here to there, but remanufacturers of "semiotic codes, modes of address, and audience reception patterns" such that one's relationships to self, other, and the external world are changed in significant ways.[88] And this, in fact, *is* a material process. Technologies can remake our subjectivities and positionalities in the world as well as our relationships to it.

As Bazerman says, "[t]echnology constantly invites social, legal, personal and economic discussions that shape how that technology becomes incorporated into new ways of life."[89] Bazerman emphasizes the rhetoric *about* technologies, but as we have seen, there is as well rhetorics *of* technologies, that is, symbolic inscriptions, reconstructions, and recontextualizations of the technologies themselves such that, in their very re-inscription, remaking, and resituation, they are "incorporated into new ways of life"—at the least, new ways of understanding life; at the most, new ways of living it.

In the matter of this study, therefore, material rhetoric has been understood in two ways: as a plastic technology (picture-bearing vehicles) that can be remade, re-represented, and even reconstituted in various media, and as those aspects of brute reality that can be linked or mapped with various other aspects of symbolic life in a grid that I will call, after Greene, "a structure of signification."[90] Those structures of signification, forming what he terms "a logic of articulation," help us understand how Riis's magic lantern shows, articles, and books assembled (1) words, (2) varied visual representations, and (3) the material depictions of immigrants and their environments and then distributed (4) populations (the underclasses and the overclasses, the governed and the governors), (5) discourses (of reportage, reform, exhortation, aesthetic appreciation, and cultural condemnation), and (6) institutions (the newspaper business, slum lords, *padrones,* Christian charitable outlets, city and later national governments) onto "the terrain of a governing apparatus so that a series of judgments might be made."[91]

And thus, verbal namings and characterizations, photographic visualizations, and the human performances captured in those visualizations formed communication matrices that articulated relationships among segmented groups within a collectivity, types of discursive practices common to that collectivity, and various institutions operating within it. Multiple communication channels—verbal, visual, performative—sutured into human experiences at different times and in different places, peoples, modes of interrelating them, and institutional interests and mandates governed them in descriptive and normative ways.

Those normative judgments, as Greene suggests, of course were aimed at showing us "the art of government,"[92] but more than that, what John Tagg terms "the institutional nature of signifying practices, their patterns of circulation in social practice, [and] their dependence on specific modes of cultural production."[93] Such, as Hartley noted at the beginning of this essay, is the fate of important "public pictures." That is, even as the pictures were remade across time by and for different institutions, they were simultaneously subjected to varied logics of articulation conventionalized within those institutions—the depictive and judgmental language of social reform oratory, the reportive and hortatory language of reform writing, the aestheticized discourse of the coffee-table art book, the righteous indignation of cultural critiques of domination and assertions of civic empowerment following the critiques so typical of contemporary (C)ultural (S)tudies.[94] Even discursive forms, especially when warranted by such institutions as journalistic outlets, church programs, political parties, or governmental offices, come with the power of cultural legitimation, imposing sanctioned patterns of understanding and assessment on human life, thought, and action.

Neither the technological alterations of the pictures nor the varied institutional discursive practices and the places they circulated their discourses by themselves were sufficient to account for the regular revisions of Riis's reputation and accounts of his motives or effects on others. The technological remanufacturing of the pictures always was melded with the articulatory practices of evolving, culturally sanctioned institutions—reform movements, new journalism, art history and criticism, late-twentieth-century cultural critique of representational practices and race/class/gender. Riis's pictures could never "mean" independent of times and places or of discursive practices typical of and appropriate to those times and places.

And so, we have seen doubly material rhetorics of politics employed by and then on the Danish immigrant, who ended his autobiography with, among other reminiscences, this assessment of his life work in New York City:

> The work is bearing fruit. On the East Side the young rise in rebellion against the slum; on the West Side the League for Political Education runs a ball-ground. Omen of good sense and of victory! So the country is safe. When we fight no longer for the poor, but with the poor, the slum is taken in the rear and beaten already.[95]

Of course, it was not really beaten, but only re-formed as reform movements are wont to do, until the next sets of urban crises rocked New York City again and again through the century that Riis's autobiography opened into. His reputation and our understanding of the fruits of his work ebbed and flowed with each new crisis and each new discursive construction of that crisis by still another aesthetic or politico-cultural institution. And his precious pictures likewise were subjected to a rolling politics of rearticulation, sometimes integrated into his biography and often cut free from its particular features. As a result, doubly material rhetorics of politics keep him alive in public memory even to this day.

And, theoretically, studies of communication practitioners such as Riis, whose mediated discourses roll through varied social-political-aesthetic venues, shaping and yet being reshaped by them, illustrate the utility of employing as critical apparatuses analytical processes and conceptualizations that are grounded in the media ecology tradition. In that tradition, "at the multimedia society level of understanding 'media as environments,'" we also "may conceptualize 'environments as media.'"[96] The modes and places of his photographic exhibitions became "messages" as McLuhan would have understood that idea. Jacob Riis, his photographs, his use of them, and their fate in variously contextualized articulations evidences the usefulness of that theoretical tradition in rationalizing complex communication practices such as those that marked his life and its heritage.

Notes

1. John Hartley, *The Politics of Pictures: The Creation of the Public in the Age of Popular Media* (New York: Routledge, 1992).
2. Michael J. Shapiro, *The Politics of Representation: Writing Practices in Biography, Photography, and Policy Analysis* (Madison: University of Wisconsin Press, 1988), 124.
3. Fiske argues that students of the communication arts, especially, should be less concerned about the philosophical force of "realism" and more about what he terms "realisticness" or "real-seemingness," as that notion signals relationships between messages and both their makers and their consumers. I agree. See John Fiske, *Television Culture* (New York:

Methuen, 1987).

4. Catherine Caha Waite, *Mediation and the Communication Matrix* (New York: Peter Lang, 2003).

5. Teresa Brennan, "The Contexts of Vision," in *Vision in Context: Historical and Contemporary Perspectives on Sight*, ed. Teresa Brennan and Martin Jay (New York: Routledge, 1999), 219.

6. Jonathan Crary, *Suspensions of Perception: Attention, Spectacle, and Modern Culture* (Cambridge: MIT Press, 2001).

7. Jacob A. Riis, *The Making of an American* (1901; repr. New York: Macmillan, 1935), 177.

8. Martin Jay, *Downcast Eyes: The Denigration of Vision in Twentieth-Century French Thought* (Berkeley: University of California Press, 1994).

9. Marshall McLuhan, *Understanding Media: The Extensions of Man* (New York: McGraw-Hill, 1964), 164.

10. Cf. Barrington Nevitt, *The Communication Ecology: Re-Presentation versus Replica* (Toronto: Butterworths, 1982), chapter 7.

11. Caha Waite, *Mediation and the Communication*, 76.

12. Caha Waite, *Mediation and the Communication*, 79.

13. Caha Waite, *Mediation and the Communication*, 112.

14. I have written about meaning making as existing across aural, literate, and visual channels or codes specifically in "Unstated Propositions: Relationships among Verbal, Visual, and Acoustic Languages," in *Argumentation and Values*, ed. Sally Jackson (Washington, D.C.: National Communication Association, 1995), 539–42, and in "The Spoken and the Seen: The Phonocentric and Ocularcentric Dimensions of Rhetorical Discourse," in *Rhetorical Memory and Delivery: Classical Concepts for Contemporary Composition and Communication*, ed. J. Frederick Reynolds (Hillsdale, NJ: Lawrence Erlbaum Associates, 1993), 141–57. The underlying theories on what has come to be called media ecology studies I overview in "The Orality-Literacy Theorems and Media Ecology," in *Perspectives on Culture, Technology, and Communication: The Media Ecology Tradition*, ed. Casey M. K. Lum (Cresskill, NJ: Hampton Press, 2006), 335–65.

15. Ronald Walter Greene, "Another Materialist Rhetoric," *Critical Studies in Media Communication* 15 (1998): 21–41.

16. Charles Bazerman, "The Rhetoric of Technology," http://www.education.ucsb.edu/bazerman/articles/16.rhetoftech.html.

17. Vivian Sobchack, *The Address of the Eye: A Phenomenology of Film Experience* (Princeton, NJ: Princeton University Press, 1992), 59.

18. "What is Media Ecology?" *Media Ecology Association*, http://www.media-ecology.org/media_ecology/index.html.

19. Lance Strate and Edward Wachtel, eds., *The Legacy of McLuhan* (Cresskill, NJ: Hampton Press, 2005), introduction.

20. For example, Bruce E. Gronbeck, Thomas J. Farrell, and Paul A. Soukup, eds., *Media, Consciousness, and Culture: Explorations of Walter Ong's Thought* (Thousand Oaks, CA: Sage, 1991).

21. I understand the argument about "substance" in a Burkean sense as a rhetorical-symbolic, not metaphysical-ontological, discourse. That is, the empirical world is regularly marked symbolically so as to specify its defining features, relationships between and among selected aspects of that world, valuable and invaluable dimensions. Yes, rocks are rocks, period; yet, what human beings do to and with them are grounded in their symbolically

constructed substantiveness: as missiles in combat, the materials for sculpture or house building, a formation deemed worthy of being designated a national park. A material rhetoric in this sense, then, focuses on ways that materiality is shaped, displayed, or inscribed symbolically, in ways made publicly meaningful.

22. Alexander Alland Sr., *Jacob A. Riis: Photographer and Citizen*, pref. Ansel Adams (New York: Aperture, 1974), 5.

23. Edith Paterson Meyer, *"Not Charity, but Justice": The Story of Jacob A. Riis* (New York: Vanguard Press, 1974).

24. Even his scathing analysis of Chinatown opium dens and immoral denizens ended with a plea to bring into the United States more Chinese women/wives to entrench a kind of home life that could stop the behavior of Chinese men on the Lower East Side—an argument to change the environment in order to improve immigrant society. See Riis's most famous work, *How the Other Half Lives: Studies among the Tenements* (1890; repr. New York: Charles Scribner's Sons, 1904). This is a reissued version of the original, but with "restored" photographs. See also a more contemporary version, *How the Other Half Lives: Studies among the Tenements of New York, with 100 Photographs from the Jacob A. Riis Collection, the Museum of the City of New York*, pref. C. A. Madison (1890; repr. New York: Dover Publications, 1971), 83. This is a re-edited version with added pictures and with pictures, diagrams, and sketches sharpened. I generally used this edition, as I own it.

25. Mulberry Bend was, literally, a bend in Mulberry Street, which Riis (quoted in Meyer, *"Not Charity, but Justice,"* 35) described as "ordinary enough to look at from the street, but pierced by a maze of foul alleys, in the depths of which skulked the tramp and the outcast thief with loathsome wrecks that had once laid claim to the name of woman. Every foot of it reeked with incest and murder. Bandits' Roost, Bottle Alley, were names synonymous with robbery and redhanded outrage. . . . [It was] the wickedest, as it was the foulest, spot in the city." See similar recollections in Riis's autobiography, *Making of an American.*

26. James B. Lane, *Jacob A. Riis and the American City* (Port Washington, NY: Kennikat Press, 1974), 51.

27. Jacob A. Riis, "How the Other Half Lives: Studies among the Tenements," *Scribner's Magazine* 6 (1889): 643–62. The book (see note 24) came out the next year.

28. Jacob A. Riis, *The Children of the Poor* (New York: Charles Scribner's Sons, 1982); *Children of the Tenements* (1897; repr. New York: Macmillan, 1925); *A Ten Years' War* (1900; repr. New York: Books for Libraries Press, 1969); and even *The Battle with the Slum* (New York: Macmillan, 1902), though it was largely a tenement reform document.

29. Riis, *Making of an American*, 172, 173.

30. Even his altered formula for *Blitzpulver* was dangerous; he burned up two tenement areas and often his clothing during his nighttime escapades.

31. E.g., Edward T. O'Donnell, "Pictures vs. Words? Public History, Tolerance, and the Challenge of Jacob Riis," *Public Historian* 26 (2004): 7–26; Gregory S. Jackson, "Cultivating Spiritual Sight: Jacob Riis's Virtual-Tour Narrative and the Visual Modernization of Protestant Homiletics," *Representations* 83 (Summer 2003): 126–66; Bonnie Yochelson, *Jacob Riis 55* (New York: Phaidon Press, 2001); Bonnie Yochelson, "The Masked Image: Recapturing the Work of Reformer Jacob Riis," *Humanities* 19 (May-June 1998), 15–21 (available at http://www.neh.gov/news/humanities/1998-05/riis.html); Reginald Twigg, "The Performative Dimension of Surveillance: Jacob Riis's *How the Other Half Lives*," *Text and Performance Quarterly* 12 (1992): 305–28; Maren Stange, "Jacob Riis

and Urban Visual Culture: The Lantern Slide Exhibition as Entertainment and Ideology," *Journal of Urban History* 25 (May 1989): 274–303; Maren Stange, *Symbols of Ideal Life: Social Documentary Photography in America 1890–1950* (New York: Cambridge University Press, 1989); Peter Bacon Hales, *The Photography of American Urbanization, 1839–1915* (Philadelphia: Temple University Press, 1984); and Alan Trachtenberg, *The Incorporation of America: Culture and Society in the Gilded Age* (New York: Hill and Wang, 1982).

32. Lev Manovich, *The Language of New Media* (Cambridge: MIT Press, 2001), 282–83.

33. Riis likely used limelight—a phenomenally bright but dangerous illumination process wherein a piece of lime was lit, with a hydrogen and oxygen mixture blowing across it to create a startlingly white light that could project an image at greater distances than ever before seen. See William Welling, *Collectors' Guide to Nineteenth-Century Photographs* (New York: Collier Books, 1976).

34. *Frank Leslie's Illustrated Newspaper* (1855–1922), out of New York, is available in research libraries, sometimes in its original form and almost always on microfilm. It was a highly popular nineteenth-century collection of public interest news stories, accompanied by sketches, woodblock engravings, and (later) photography. It carried social commentary that often suggested the need for the kinds of reform that Riis advocated, though its artistic renderings did not have the persuasive power of Riis's photographs, nor did it pose as the serious, argumentative advocate that Riis was. See Joshua Brown, *Beyond the Lines: Pictorial Reporting, Everyday Life, and the Crisis in Guilded-Age America* (Berkeley: University of California Press, 2002). The book was written in 2002, then made into an e-book in 2003.

35. Thanks to Jack Judson and his tours of his private museum in San Antonio, TX—the best collection of magic lanterns and lantern accessories/documents in the United States (Jack Judson, "Magic Lantern Castle Museum," http://www.magiclanterns.org). Cf. David Robertson, Stephen Herbert, and Richard Crangle, eds., *Encyclopaedia of the Magic Lantern* (London: Magic Lantern Society, 2001).

36. Riis, *Making of an American*, 193.

37. Riis, *Making of an American*, 159. Riis generally is credited with being a Christian reformer, that is, an adherent to the social gospel rather than a Progressivist per se (see especially Jackson, "Cultivating Spiritual Sight"). That orientation certainly stands out in the pieces of his lectures that survive today.

38. This is a hand-penned note on the transcription of an 1891 magic lantern show he presented to a Christian convention—the only surviving full script of his work so far as I know. Jacob A. Riis, "The Other Half and How They Live," *Christians at Work. Proceedings of the Sixth Convention of Christian Workers in the United States and Canada. Washington D.C. First Congregational Church. Nov. 5th–11th, 1891.* [Microfilmed pamphlet.] Riis papers, Library of Congress, reel 5, container 10.

39. See Edwin Black, "The Sentimental Style as Escapism, or the Devil with Dan'l Webster," in *Form and Genre: Shaping Rhetorical Action*, ed. Karlyn Kohrs Campbell and Kathleen Hall Jamieson (Washington, D.C.: National Communication Association, 1978), 75–86.

40. Meyer, *"Not Charity, but Justice,"* 45–46.

41. Riis, "Other Half and How," 296.

42. Riis, "Other Half and How," 296.

43. Stange, *Symbols of Ideal Life*, 13.

44. One might expect Riis's autobiography to help with this question, but it does not. He

suggested that at the time he was writing the book, he still was giving magic lantern-based lectures, though feeling distanced from the pictures: "[The world of the pictures] seemed a long way off and in no way related to me. . . . I sat there for as much as five minutes perhaps, while the man with the lantern fidgeted and the audience wondered, I suppose, what was coming next. Then it was the pictures that did not change which fretted me; with a cold chill I knew I had been lost, and went back and finished the speech. No one way any the wiser, apparently. But I was glad when, the following week, I wrote the last page in my book" (*Making of an American*, 199). If we take this as an authentic recollection, then a point, inspired by Sobchack, made earlier in this chapter bears repeating: recontextualizing photographs can make them strangers. Maybe Riis found the words he then was writing more familiar friends.

45. Half-tone printing involves separating a picture into narrow stripes and then converting the image to a series of dots: larger and more numerous dots for blacks, small dots with more space between them for gray-tones, and no dots for white space. When Riis wrote his first book, the perfection of half-tone printing was still a decade off, which explains why his pictures in the 1890 book appear so faded and muted.

46. Riis, *How the Other Half* (1971 ed.), 78.

47. Riis, *How the Other Half* (1904 ed.).

48. Riis, *How the Other Half* (1971 ed.), 176.

49. The rhetorical theories dominating much of nineteenth-century instruction—grounded in George Campbell (*The Philosophy of Rhetoric*, ed. Lloyd Bitzer [1776; repr. Carbondale: Southern Illinois Press, 1963]), Hugh Blair (*Lectures on Rhetoric and Belles Lettres*, ed. Harold F. Harding [1783; repr. Carbondale: University of Southern Illinois Press, 1965]), and Richard Whately (*The Elements of Rhetoric*, ed. Douglas Ehninger [1828; repr. Carbondale: Southern Illinois University Press, 1963])—were conceptualized as traveling on what came to be called the persuasion-conviction dichotomy: the idea that one must either first move emotions persuasively and then channel them rationally in particular directions (Campbell's idea) or, vice versa, argue audiences into a set of beliefs rationally and then enflame their emotions to produce action (Whately's preferences). While visualization was talked about by all three of these rhetorical theorists and their nineteenth-century proponents, they all agreed that the oral and the printed word was a principal weapon capable of producing both conviction and persuasion.

50. See Yochelson, "Masked Image," for details.

51. Riis, *Making of an American*, 172.

52. Ansel Adams in Alland, *Jacob A. Riis*, 6.

53. Adams in Alland, *Jacob A. Riis*, 7.

54. Roland Barthes, *Camera Lucida*, trans. Richard Howard (New York: Noonday Press, 1981), 3.

55. Adams in Alland, *Jacob A. Riis*, 6.

56. Edward Bullough, "'Psychical Distance' as a Factor in Art and as an Aesthetic Principle," *British Journal of Psychology* 5 (1912): 87–117.

57. The pages in Alland's book were 8.75 inches wide by 10 inches tall—a set of dimensions certainly selected to show off the photographs.

58. For an overview of Riis's ethnic commentary, see O'Donnell, "Pictures vs. Words."

59. O'Donnell, "Pictures vs. Words," 15.

60. Twigg, "Performative Dimension of Surveillance."

61. Stange, "Jacob Riis and Urban," 296.

62. Susan Ryan, "'Rough Ways and Rough Work': Jacob Riis, Social Reform and the

Rhetoric of Benevolent Violence," *American Transcendental Quarterly* 11 (September 1997): 193.

63. See the story of Francis Galton in Jim Holt, "Measure for Measure: The Strange Science of Francis Galton," *New Yorker*, January 24/31, 2005, 84, 88–90.
64. Jackson, "Cultivating Spiritual Sight."
65. Bill Hug, "Walking the Ethnic Tightwire: Ethnicity and Dialectic in Jacob Riis' *How the Other Half Lives*," *Journal of American Culture* 20 (1997): 45.
66. Anthony Woodiwiss, *The Visual in Social Theory* (New York: Althone Press, 2001).
67. Ryan, "Rough Ways and Rough," 193.
68. Riis's negatives, slides, and positive prints were given accession numbers by the Museum of the City of New York in 1990. I will use those numbers to identify particular slides.
69. Yochelson, *Jacob Riis 55*, 41.
70. On the use of limelight versus electrified lanterns, see note 33. See also Riis, *Making of an American*; and Stange, *Symbols of Ideal life*, 2n5.
71. Janet B. Pascal, *Jacob Riis: Reporter and Reformer* (New York: Oxford University Press, 2005), 120.
72. Riis, "Other Half and How," 296.
73. Riis, *How the Other Half*, 90, quoted in Yochelson, *Jacob Riis 55*, 40.
74. Riis, *How the Other Half* (1971 ed.), 90.
75. Riis, *How the Other Half* (1971 ed.), 43–47.
76. Riis, *How the Other Half* (1971 ed.), 47.
77. "Masters of Photography: Jacob Riis," *Masters of Photography*, http://www.masters-of-photography.com/R/riis/riis_italian_ragpicker.html.
78. An online computer image of the rag-picker was available at D. Riley, *Rileystyle 2004*, http://www.rileystyle.com/project/depression (site now discontinued). The Madonna-and-the-child argument is found in Hug, "Walking the Ethnic Tightwire"; as well as Hales, *Photography of American Urbanization*.
79. Carrie Tirado Bramen, "The Urban Picturesque and the Spectacle of Americanization," *American Quarterly* 52 (September 2000): 446.
80. Lane, "Jacob A. Riis," 55.
81. Keith Gandal, *The Virtues of the Vicious: Jacob Riis, Stephen Crane, and the Spectacle of the Slum* (New York: Oxford University Press, 1997), 38.
82. Michael Calvin McGee, "A Materialist's Conception of Rhetoric," in *Explorations in Rhetoric: Essays in Honor of Douglas Ehninger*, ed. Ray E. McKerrow (Glenview, IL: Scott, Foresman, 1985), 23–48; Greene, "Another Materialist Rhetoric," 21–41.
83. Dana L. Cloud, "The Materiality of Discourse as Oxymoron: A Challenge to Critical Rhetoric," *Western Journal of Communication* 58 (1994): 141–63.
84. Raymie E. McKerrow, "Critical Rhetoric: Theory and Praxis," *Communication Monographs* 56 (1989): 91–111.
85. Greene, "Another Materialist Rhetoric," 30.
86. Bazerman, "Rhetoric of Technology."
87. Crary, *Suspensions of Perception*, 31.
88. Manovich, *Language of New Media*, 7.
89. Bazerman, "Rhetoric of Technology."
90. Greene, "Another Materialist Rhetoric," 35.
91. Greene, "Another Materialist Rhetoric," 30.
92. Greene, "Another Materialist Rhetoric," 30.
93. John Tagg, *The Burden of Representation: Essays on Photographies and Histories*

(London: Macmillan, 1988), 23.

94. Barbie Zelizer, "When Facts, Truth, and Reality are God-Terms: On Journalism's Uneasy Place in Cultural Studies," *Communication and Critical/Cultural Studies* 1 (2004): 100–19.

95. Riis, *Making of an American*, 282.

96. Lum, *Perspectives on Culture*, 31.

CHAPTER 6

On Missed Encounters: Lacan and the Materiality of Rhetoric

Christian O. Lundberg,
University of North Carolina, Chapel Hill

A deceptively simple question animates this: can an account of either the formal properties of discourse as a system or a description of communicative exchanges embedded in social contexts define rhetoric without remainder? This question implies another: how might either of these general accounts of rhetoric be reconciled to the irreducible plurality and specificity of rhetorical events, texts, and practices? The materiality of rhetoric thesis orbits around these two possibilities for defining rhetoric's function and, by implication, around the nagging question of rhetorical theory's relationship to the specific phenomena it addresses. At least two general trajectories or possible logics for detailing the materiality of rhetoric spin outward from this orbit—and though there are almost as many conceptions of rhetoric's materiality as there are rhetoricians, my concern here is to detail the logic underwriting a commitment to rhetoric's materiality. One possible logic holds that the formal qualities of discourse as a durable productive system embody the materiality of rhetoric.[1] The other possibility locates rhetoric's materiality primarily as a "natural social phenomenon" relying on processes of communicative exchange, and is also defined as "residual and persistent."[2] Neither of these logics necessarily excludes the other, and each may be present in admixture in any given framing of rhetoric's materiality, but the presence of one or both of these presuppositions is a hallmark of a materialist rhetoric.

The goal of this essay is to offer a Lacanian rereading of these presuppositions that avoids reducing rhetoric either to a system of discursive operations or to a contextually nested set of communicative habits without remainder. As an alternative, I propose a focus on rhetoric as inextricably tied to Lacan's conceptions of trope and enjoyment as material embodiments of a durable principle of non-mediation. To develop this reading, I briefly introduce a distinction between *taxis* as a model of rhetorical mediation and *metaxy* as a studied practice of non-mediation. Taking *metaxy* as inspiration, I provide a Lacanian interpretation of the materiality of rhetoric, making a case for its usefulness to the field of rhetoric by putting it to use in a reading of the discourse of Christian fundamentalism. Finally, I draw out a few conclusions regarding the problem of rhetorical interpretation suggested by this reading of rhetoric's materiality.

Rhetoric and *Metaxy*

Reading Plato's *Symposium*, Eric Voegelin discovered something remarkable about the term "*metaxy*," a preposition meaning "between." Voegelin's reading turns on Diotima's claim that Eros is a "great daimon . . . between (*metaxy*) god and mortal."[3] Though daimons do the difficult work of mediating the divine and the human, daimonic *metaxy* does not constitute a midpoint between gods and humans. *Metaxy* is the unmediated suspension between two opposites: daimons participate fully in both the divine and human, but are also more than a simple combination of the two. *Metaxy* is thus taken by Voegelin to mark an ontological condition noteworthy enough for him to render it in the nominal form: "the *metaxy*" or *metaxis*.[4]

Plato's *metaxy* is significant for my purposes because it works loosely in the registers of the affective (eros) and mediation. One might ask, where is the *metaxis* in rhetoric or, more precisely, where is rhetoric in need of an erotic/affective daimon? If rhetoric's disciplinary anxieties are any indicator, the answer lies in the lacunae between *theory* as a set of conceptual principles representing rhetorical processes and *practice* as an uncertainly coordinated application of theory to the production and interpretation of texts. Hence, rhetoric's perennial question: does the aggregation of specific practices create theory, or does theory prefigure a reading of practices? To crib a question of Michael Calvin McGee's that I will return to later, which comes first?

The various iterations of the materiality of rhetoric thesis answer the question of theory's relation to practice by divesting rhetoric of a number of hidden commitments—"ideals" in McGee's language—that hold the social and material worlds at arm's length. For McGee, ideal investments create the problem of theory and practice by overdetermining rhetorical readings of everyday discourses, producing a glaring disconnect between rhetoric and reality by importing presuppositions about the subject and the domain of rhetoric that reduce rhetoric to a classical oratorical model at the expense of attention to everyday rhetorical processes.

Despite the introduction of new terms as the materiality of rhetoric thesis becomes more nuanced over time, the materialist critique often repeats the binary between the ideal and the material laid out by McGee. In the hands of his inheritors, McGee's original binary ideal/material expands to include two basic constellations of terms. The "ideal" expands as a point of critique: including not only the claim that ideas are the driving force in history and an overly narrow conception of speech as "speeches," but also humanist conceptions of self and intention, the centrality of representation, and a self-conscious embrace of interpretation—collectively the "mystifications of hermeneutics" as McGee might have had it.[5] Alternatively, the "material" expands as a productive category to encompass new iterations of discourse and/or context as an alternative to hermeneutic interpretation: against the mystifications of hermeneutics, the materiality thesis advances a demystifying turn to articulation as the observation of everyday logic and function of discursive context. Thus the materialist alternative advances beyond an object-centered view of rhetoric as durable effect against an ideational bias, toward an ever more expansive view of discourse constituting the subject. Similarly, the materialist alternative advances beyond the critical categories of representation and interpretation toward attention to logics of power and articulation that produce reality.

I want to argue that the materialist "advances" displace the problem of theory and practice as well as the related problem of discourse and the social with a more specific *metaxical* problem: how might we *read* a logic of articulation? In a recent treatment of rhetoric and *taxis*—traditionally arrangement, but also a mode of textual articulation—Nathan Stormer has suggested that the core issue in the rhetorical tradition is the relationship between the "order of discourse and the order of things."[6] Stormer's formulation exemplifies the telos of rhetorical materialism as technology mediating not only discourse and reality at the level of their production, but simultaneously suturing a theory of discourse as a descriptive tool and the realities that discourse refers. Here Stormer exemplifies what I see as the ultimate goal of rhetorical materialism, arguing that articulation theory serves as a principle of *taxis*, mediating the divide between the order of discourse and the order of reality by reading them as simultaneous.

Though *taxis* is a productive metaphor, what does framing the relationship between discourse and reality as *taxis* prevent rhetoric from thinking? To be sure, current iterations of the materiality of rhetoric do not attend to the "betweenness" of theory and practice, deferring to a *taxical* mediation of the two. Against the seductive mediating tendencies of *taxis*, I believe we should assert the productivity of *metaxis* as studied (im)mediation, as a site of enjoyment that flows from the gap between discourse and the world it describes, providing the material support for the subject, rhetoric, and reality. Here one might embrace Augusto Boal's definition of *metaxis* as "the state of belonging completely and simultaneously to two different, autonomous worlds: the image of reality and the reality of the image."[7]

But if rhetoric is *metaxic*, it requires daimons. Here, Lacan's erotic daimons' "enjoyment" and "trope" open the way toward an account of rhetoric's materiality that cultivates "betweenness" between theory and practice, or more specifically, the ideal and the material. Lacan's work, I want to suggest, offers a technology of *metaxis*, pointing to the reasons why it is perhaps not words, discourses, or communicative contexts but processes of signification and representation that shape reality. These processes do not only describe, frame, represent, or explain reality; they also fail in this task. However, this failure is unequivocally productive because it necessitates a turn to strategies of trope and practices of enjoyment that collectively produce subjects and their worlds. The domain of trope and enjoyment is the site of *metaxy*, reducible neither to the logic of discursive system nor to the social as a spared space of meaning. Rhetoric, on this reading, requires attention to the remainder that escapes the *taxical* reduction or reality to systems of discourse or social context, and to the excesses produced in the failure of mediation.

Lacan and the Materiality of Rhetoric

Even after topology, graphs, and set theory became Lacan's preferred vocabularies for explaining psychoanalysis, he employed "rhetoric" as a concept uniting his work. Declaring in *Seminar XX* that "the universe is a flower of rhetoric," Lacan sutures his concerns with the production of the self, enjoyment, and language as a symbolic operation: "[T]his literary echo may help us understand that the ego (*moi*) can also be a flower of rhetoric, which grows in the pot of the pleasure principle. . . . That is what I am saying when I say that the unconscious is structured like a language."[8]

This version of rhetoric mirrors what critics identify as "anti-realism" in radical versions of the discursive turn, namely that "discourse not only influences reality, it *is* . . . reality."[9] Lacan's declaration that "it is the world of words that creates the world of things. . . . Man speaks, then, but it is because the symbol has made him man" seems to confirm the instinct that Lacan reduces reality to discourse.[10] Despite this nod to the radical discursive turn, there are other possibilities for a Lacanian framing of the relationship between the world of words and the world of things. As Ellie Ragland-Sullivan has put it, Lacan's conception of the relationship between discourse, reality, and subjects does not require a straightforward "'language equals reality' reduction."[11]

But is this right? How can "the world of words create the world of things" without reducing language to reality? The answer lies in the creative potential of signification's failure—words describe, enframe, and comport reality but simultaneously and productively fail to do so: this is the animating impulse of Ernesto Laclau's definition of psychoanalysis as "failed unicity," which marks the world-building capacity of failed signification.[12]

There are three sites of discontinuity that disrupt the seamless unicity of subjects within language relating to their world. For subjects, the failure of unity lies in a requirement for external principles to order and give sense to an already ongoing experience of existence. This is, according to Lacan, the point of the mirror stage: the principles that unify one's own subjectivity are not given internally but are received from an external reservoir of images of the self and practices of self-reference. For instance, there is no unique vocabulary for referring to one's self that does not require either a borrowed pronoun that all other subjects can lay claim to—for example, "I" or the third person: in my case, "Chris." Here subjectivity is a species of the more general category unicity. Subjectivity is a retroactive process of naming, and as a result, practices of subjectification are split between one's lived experience and external semantic referents that both identify and defer one's uniqueness as a subject.

This split subject implies a second split between a retroactively claimed subjectivity and this subject's employment of language. Unicity also fails in the gap between speech and the other's reception of it. Lacan frames this problem in two ways. The first framing notes that all speech is both addressed to specific others and a general ("big O") Other. For instance, this essay is aimed at a reader, but also implicitly aims at the Symbolic order in attempting to bring to bear a set of recognizable semantic moves and identifiable content. This is a problem in the order of discourse's reception: misreading is simple misunderstanding, but it is also a constitutive condition given that one can never be sure that there is a seamless overlap between a reader, audience, and the Symbolic order. This gap is related to a second one between the subject and the Symbolic: there is an irreducible gap between the speech of a specific subject and the order of discourse as an external set of logical relations. Thus, the split in discourse extends beyond the order of reception—inhering in the classical distinction between *langue* and *parole*, which I explore in greater depth later in this chapter. Gaps in the orders of production and reception produce a tragic failure of unicity between the subject and the Symbolic. The subject requires discourse as a medium for its articulation and action, but subjects are never quite fully at home in it. Martin

Heidegger has famously argued that "language is the house of being"; a Lacanian revision might hold that language is the hotel of being. Language provides an uncomfortable "not quite" habitus for a nomadic subject who does not own his or her abode.

Finally, unicity fails in the relationship between the Symbolic and the Real—a problem of ontology and reference. Lacan's argument about ontology relies on a distinction between reality and the "Real." The Lacanian Real is unassimilable excess; it is a constitutive outside whose terms can only be articulated in a tragic reduction to representation. Ontology presumes the possibility of grounding a thing in the Real, articulating the possibilities and modalities of its existence, but only succeeds in grounding beings in a representation of reality. If the Real is uncodable, ontology is impossible on its own terms: there is no adequation between the Real and the Symbolic processes that code the Real in the order of language and reality. Put in terms of reference and representation, the conventional doctrines of sign and representation hold that signs and representations refer to objectively existing entities. But it is equally plausible that acts of representing and acts of naming also produce the realities to which they refer. Framing the problem in this way does not require that words literally generate the substance of things; rather, it requires that in thinking the terms of the relationship between discourse and reality, we carefully mark the fact that the relationship is not automatic—representation requires artifice and labor to sustain itself. Put in terms of *metaxis*, since the relationship between words, the reality they generate, and the Real is not automatic, rhetoric is in need of enjoyment and trope as erotic daimons that hold together a constantly failing unicity.

Thus, despite this three-fold failed unicity, subjects act as if they are unitary, speak as if communication is possible, and represent reality all the time. What is it that sustains the subject and its discourses despite the condition of failed unicity? The answer to this question marks what is uniquely material about Lacan's conception of rhetoric, and explains how Lacan can assert that discourse creates reality without reducing reality to discourse. Rhetoric is signifying in a condition of failed unicity, and as a result, its *metaxical* materiality hinges on two functions: (1) rhetoric is material because signifying in a condition of failed unicity requires trope as a specific instantiation of the material durability of the sign despite its failings, and (2) rhetoric is also material because it finds its life in enjoyment as a practice embodying subjects and discourse in the tropological economy.

Rhetoric is material because it is tropological: if failed unicity implies that in the absence of a "One" signifier grounded in the Real to which all signifiers refer, all signification is rhetorical, doing the contingent labor of working through reference's failures by recourse to trope. That is to say, where a referential relationship to the Real fails, metaphor and metonymy fill in. Tropes supplement the failures that cumulatively constitute the condition of failed unicity: the failure to generate a stable subject, to found common identities, or to generate commensurable intersubjective symbolic exchanges.

But trope alone is insufficient. If a formal account of discourse or of communal mediation cannot overcome the condition of failed unicity, a principle is needed that accounts for persistent seeming unicity of subjects, signs, and communicative contexts. How can Lacan affirm a repetition, regularity, and logic in discourse that gives it the flavor of structurality while simultaneously asserting that discourse is constantly and constitutively failing as a structure? The answer is a special kind of labor done by the subject: enjoyment. Though one cannot account for discourse as a structure, the labor of subjects in speech produces regularities that may be more appropriately called an economy. A tropological economy produces the formal possibility of speakers, acts of speech, and communication, but an economy also requires labor and investments. Enjoyment is the name for the labor done by the subject's investments in the practices of signification and subjectivity that grant an economy of trope durability and regularity. Hence, as hinted from the near start, the solution to the paradox of words making the world without reducing the world to words requires erotic daimons. Enjoyment and trope are *metaxical* practices that mediate failed unicity, inhabiting an impossible suspension between the formal properties of discourse and subjectification and the concrete experience of being a subject in the banal order of experience.

The Lacanian term for enjoyment is "jouissance," intended to capture the tensions and pleasures of sex, something that is overwhelmingly powerful, something that generates satisfaction, but also something that is not necessarily pleasurable. How can enjoyment be all of these? First, jouissance is an agent. It is not a characteristic of a subject, deterministically responding to the subject's drives or intentions: enjoyment underwrites subjectivization through language, but it is also the material substrate within which the performance of subjectivity is situated.[13] Jouissance is, in one sense, prior to subjectivity. It is not ontologically or temporally prior, as in Aristotle's predicateless being, but it can be read as a prior material condition for the production of subjectivity.

Jouissance should also be theorized as excess. Consider a hypothetical hypochondriac who constantly complains about imagined symptoms: "pain in my neck, in my back, in my head." The hypochondriac's complaint does not aim at the palliation of the pains as much as it aims at alleviating the subject's anxieties; complaining generates surplus enjoyment not related to physical relief. "Jouissance is what serves no purpose."[14] While other systemic accounts of affect organize pleasure in terms of utility, jouissance is pleasure that does not intentionally aim at the production of anything, but paradoxically produces everything in the subject's world, including its subjectivity. Here jouissance is outside *taxis* paradoxically because it both entails excess not reducible to the register of mediation, and because it works against utilitarian accounts of discursive function that privilege the functions of discourse.

What does this have to do with the sign, trope, and materiality? Here, I will meditate at greater length on the rhetorical labor done to supplement the condition of failed unicity at the three sites identified earlier: at the site of the subject's constitutive split, at the site of the subject's split with the symbolic, and finally, at the site where language mediates the impossibilities of reference. These three moments define the materiality of speech, the materiality of the speaking subject, and finally, the materiality of discourse as a set of durable sedimented metonymic relations, which I will frame in terms of the unconscious.

First, the split between the subject and the symbolic: Lacan's critique of structural linguistics is that Saussure pays insufficient attention to speech as a paradigmatic representation of the subject's symbolic labor. Lacan argues for the distinctiveness of speech as the "key" to the analytic experience and by extension to discourse, arguing that psychoanalysis finds "in speech . . . its instrument . . . material, and even the background noise of its uncertainties."[15] Invoking the letter, or the "material support that concrete discourse borrows from language," Lacan distinguishes between *langue,* or the logic of symbolization, and *parole,* the specific speech acts of speakers.[16] At the level of *langue*, an economy precedes the speech acts of any given speaker, bounding speech with a set of logical semiotic operations—either metonymic combination or metaphoric substitution. Second, speech acts cannot be understood as solely produced within the bounds of language as an intersubjective exchange. The logical structure implied by signification exceeds any given context in generating speech acts.

There are two ways of reading the classical structural linguistic algorithm for the relationship between the signifier and the signified:

$$\frac{\underline{S}}{s}$$

The main point of contention between Lacan and Saussure is not the "S" representing the signifier, nor the "s" representing the signified, but the "—," the bar dividing the two. For Saussure, the "—" represents a conceptual distinction between the signifier and the signified, which enables differential signification, but the distinction is mediated by a relationship of reference, by a "bi-univocal correspondence between the word and thing, if only in the act of naming."[17] The psychoanalytic framing of the "—" reads it as a *bar,* as a prohibition or productive repression of the thing that is signified by the signifier. The bar provides an antidote to presuppositions of effortless reference: Lacan's bar marks the fact that "reference" is labor, a site of jouissance where the signified is constantly being slid under the signifier.

Framing the bar as labor requires that Lacan specify the mechanisms through which the labor is accomplished. Against Saussure, Lacan turns to an unlikely ally: Quintilian. "The properly signifying function thus depicted in language," argues Lacan, "has a name . . . on the last page, where in the shade of Quintilian, relegated to some phantom chapter concerning 'final considerations on style.'"[18] Lacan's critique of referential signification is that it is insufficiently attentive to the rhetorical labors of trope and enjoyment. While there is no referential relationship between signifier and signified, metonymy links a signifier with a unit of meaning by creating an accidental connection between the two. Metonymies are raised to the level of signs when they begin to function as metaphors: while there is no direct reference, reference is a metaphor for signs that act as if they refer to objective realities. But metaphor is also a practice of enjoyment, representing an intensifying affective investment (*cathexis*) in the power of a sign or, rather, a laborious crossing of the bar between signifier and signified.

The introduction of trope articulates the way that iterations of logical operations, "the letter," imperfectly materialize the symbolic, so that though they fail to constitute a structure, signification produces an economy of enjoyment whose substrate is the socially situated acts of speakers. Thus we may say that the "materiality of rhetoric" may be first understood as the labor of a desire that funds signification by "sliding" the signified under the signifier. In practical terms, this means that because signification is irreducibly rhetorical (relying on trope as support), it is also material, that acts of representation and meaning production are tied fundamentally to the material circulation of enjoyment and the subject's affective labor.

What is it that labors, enjoys, and desires? The split between *langue* and *parole* returns us to the second site of rhetoric's materiality: the materiality of the subject. But for many theorists of rhetoric's materiality, the subject is the problem. Ron Greene is correct in noting that the subject is a privileged site for rhetoric as a "politics of representation," rejecting the latter because it occludes the materiality of rhetoric.[19] The psychoanalytic strategy for thinking the materiality of the subject as a rhetorical practice takes the opposite approach: it presumes the constitutive ineradicability of the subject's obsession with making reference work as the critical question of rhetoric's materiality. Paradoxically, instead of abandoning a representational politics in the name of materiality, we should focus all the more intently on the representation, because it is precisely in representation's failure that the subject is produced and thrown into an economy of signs that materializes and exceeds it, making the subject "subject to" tropes and practices of enjoyment that produce, prefigure, and move beyond it.

Subjects are rhetorical artifice, nodes in a tropological economy produced by the split between speech and the Symbolic. The mirror stage is the most famous way of representing Lacan's split subject.[20] Infants encountering their images in mirrors do not recognize that they are the subjects in the mirrors. In figuring out that when they move, the children in the mirrors move, infants begin to identify with their external images. The point is not that the child figures out that she is the body in the mirror, but that the child requires mirrors to impose retroactive unity on her experience. Subjectivity is this experience of identifying with an image of one's self that is not natural, but mirrored by a specific location within the Symbolic order. As a result, there is a cleavage between the experience of subjectivity and the external image that codes it. Lacan inverts the classic logic of subjects using speech to represent themselves because signifiers are mirrors: "a signifier represents a subject for another signifier."[21] Here, the signified is primary, and the subject a secondary effect, and this experience squares uncomfortably with the lived experience of being a subject: the structure of mirrored subjectivity is a rhetorical tropological exchange—there is a metonymic connection between an unformed subject who is not integrated into the symbolic and an image of who the subject is supposed to be. Elevating metonymic connection to a metaphor that retroactively names subjectivity, the mirrored subject manages its gaps through a metaphorical misidentification with an image by *enjoying* its own subjectivity. Once again, this is a site of *metaxis*, where subjectivity is an erotic daimon bridging a divide between image and experience: more precisely (in Boal's terms) between the autonomous registers of the "reality of the image" of the subject and the "image of the reality" of the subject.

This moment refuses a binary between extra-rhetorical "ideal" representations of subjectivity and the materiality of discursive structures. This is a productively perverse incarnational move—an embodiment that might be rendered as a "corporizing" disembodiment. In *Seminar XX*, Lacan frames the problem this way:

> Consider "enjoying a body" . . . that symbolizes the Other—it perhaps can help us focus on another form of substance, enjoying substance . . . the substance of a body . . . defined only as what enjoys itself . . . we don't know what it means to be alive except for the fact that a body is something that enjoys itself. It enjoys itself only by "corporizing" the body in a signifying way.[22]

Hence, jouissance is neither structure nor free-floating sentiment, but economy and substance: a tropologically produced material cause of the signifying body's affects and labor. Enjoyment is intimately related to the tropological and rhetorical production of subjects, so much so that jouissance and the subsequent embodiment of all the subject's functions are inseparable from, if not identical with, the subject of trope. The signifier is the material cause of jouissance, and jouissance is the material substrate within which the (dis)embodied subject negotiates gaps in language through trope.[23] On this reading, the subject is produced as a secondary excess of more fundamental processes of figural exchange in an economy of enjoyment. The locus of agency in the formulation "the signifier represents a subject for another subject" inheres in the logic of signification, where the subject is caught up in a larger economy of tropological exchanges that serve as a "social support."[24]

The dual gaps between *langue* and *parole* and the subject's relation to the Other converge and extend outward in an economy of tropological exchange, where the subject makes and is made by speech. The letter, signification, and its concrete embodiment in speech are the "material support that concrete discourse borrows from language."[25]

Like McGee, Lacan's conception of materiality is defined by persistence and effect, though Lacan is not as concerned with the durability or effect of individual rhetorical fragments as he is with a more general persistence inhering in the idea that what is said cannot be taken back.[26] The persistence of rhetorical utterances as material entities that cannot be taken back goes by another name in the Lacanian corpus—the unconscious.

Thus, a third site of rhetoric's materiality: the unconscious solves the problem of reference by changing its locus. Signifiers only refer to reality indirectly—their primary referent is unconscious discourse, or the speech of others. Where Freud's unconscious represents the subject's interiority, Lacan revises Freud by framing the unconscious as the reservoir of all the possible metonymic associations potentially inhering in a signifier by way of past usage. The materiality of the unconscious lies in signification's implicit reference to a polysemous field of sedimented metonymic connections that might not be intended by or apparent to the speaker, but that structure the conditions for reception.

To say that the unconscious is structured like a language demonstrates that the unconscious does not presume easy reference between signifier and signified, referent and representation, or image and reality. The unconscious is the labor that has been done by other subjects in sliding their signifieds under their signifiers. The unconscious is structured *like* a language because it is a result of the structural possibilities for polysemous meaning in any act of signification, but it is *not* a language because it does not obey concrete rules of reference. The exchange of signs between subjects always says both too much and not enough—too much in that it is saturated with a virtual infinity of possible metonymic connections, and not enough in that the vertiginous possibilities for meaning cannot be disciplined by acts of specification. Hence, the exchange of signs between subjects must fail, or is suspended in *metaxical* immediation between the logic of signs and the concrete condition of exchange.

Consider Freud's famous example of the term "rat." Invoking more than a rodent, the signifier "rat" accesses a plurality of sedimented metonymic usages including dirtiness, a sense of immorality metonymically associated with dirtiness, and disease. Phonetic similarity between the word rat and monetary payments (*Ratten*) implies associations to money and greed. Each of these associations represents an unconscious connection held in the sign "rat." The unconscious is both outside the usage of a given sign by a specific subject, inhering in each of these connections, and is simultaneously present in the subject's speech in the repetition of metonymic associations that supplement a signifier's intended relationship to reality. Given this characterization of the unconscious, there is a constant tension in the gaps between *langue* and *parole*, the subject and the other, and within reference because the moment of speech necessarily contains unexpected and uncontrollable associations that belie the possibility of consummating a communicative exchange.

Toward Criticism as an Economy of Trope and Enjoyment

How might criticism attend to the materiality of speech, subject, and the unconscious? The core problem is that *taxis*-centered approaches read against the immediation and excess that inform Lacan's conception of material rhetoric. Excesses cannot be "too excessive" lest they lose the ability to be coded in the logic of a system or situation. The danger is that in relying on *taxis*, critical practices implicitly reproduce a reductive account of texts by reading exclusively through logics of form, articulation, or context at the expense of reading the ways that these logics fail. The danger of *taxis* is also its explanatory power: *taxis* presumes that every rhetorical phenomenon reproduces the logic of a theory of rhetorical function at the level of specific rhetorical practice, *without remainder*. As a result, it becomes easier to encounter texts without reading them as affectively invested, performing the erotic *metaxis* of trope and enjoyment.

A critical disposition that ignores enjoyment blinds rhetorical criticism to the warp and woof of the impossibilities inhering in the radical splits within the subject, between the subject and the social, and between language and its referents. *Taxical* mediation makes it especially difficult to read practices such as intense religious affiliation that are only sensible as acts of enjoyment. For example, Christian Fundamentalism relies on a rhetorical commitment to marginality—to framing identity oppositionally and under duress from the secular world. This fundamental fantasy retroactively reorders the plurality of conflicts in the social field through the metaphor of marginality. For instance, the metaphors of constitutive marginality and threatening non-fundamentalist others connects metonymically with subsidiary social antagonisms over reproductive rights, civil unions, prayer in schools, and the like. But each of these practices continues not only because of a commitment to a moral worldview, or even because of a commitment to repeating marginality. The durability and intensity of these practices are only sensible as part of a larger tropological economy that highlights the enjoyment in reasserting not only specific sites of antagonism, but also asserting antagonism generally. We might read backward through the economy of trope and enjoyment: put bluntly, metonymic antagonisms give content to the person in the Lacanian mirror. Antagonism provides a technology for mediating identity negatively by declaring simultaneously "I am not" but also by providing a set of enjoyable tropes through which a subject manages the fundamental gaps that it uncomfortably inhabits.

The tropological economy that metonymically connects such metaphors of marginalization in religious fundamentalism with a number of sites of antagonism only makes sense when understood as a practice of enjoyment. Fundamentalists may feel threatened or marginalized by culture, but the phenomenal experiences of rage, sadness, or tragedy conceal a deeper affective investment in framing oneself as one who has the truth and is persecuted for it. Antagonism is durable precisely because it entails surplus enjoyment: in the case of the fundamentalist, hating the other and their practices is as much about framing the self as it is imposing a moral agenda.

This affective investment must be figured into analyses of fundamentalism, if only for the political reason that rhetoric will continue to take skirmishes with specific fundamentalist discourses more seriously than the economy of surplus enjoyment that sustains them.

It is difficult from the perspective of a theory or articulation or context to account for the ubiquity of representations of violence in evangelical Christian discourses by doing anything more than declaring that they are unhappy historical accidents.[27] Christian fundamentalism is constituted by the consumption of texts that move beyond antagonism and moral regulation toward representing violence against non-fundamentalist others. *The Passion of the Christ* is instructive here. Fundamentalist identity grew out of a battle over modernity and the politics of knowing in the early twentieth century. The fundamentalist identity that emerged from this battle was organized around repeating tropes of victimhood: the modern-day inheritors of this legacy are evangelical discourses about losing the culture war and religion being pushed out of the public sphere. Yet fundamentalism has also been able to exert substantial social influence, as voting patterns in recent elections suggest. Practices of fundamentalist publicity are faced with the difficult challenge of maintaining a public subject position defined by constitutive marginality alongside increasing social influence. The solution lies in the rhetorical productivity of representations of violence that reaffirm fundamentalist marginality and the fallenness of secular society. Utilizing theological commitments to the concept of the "Body of Christ" and visual stagings inviting the viewer's misidentification with the person of Jesus, *The Passion of the Christ* provides the evangelical community a metaphor for reasserting its cultural marginality: the beaten Jesus is synecdoche for the fundamentalist community.

But the enjoyment in tropes of victimhood formally requires a villain: invoking metonymic connections between Jesus's Roman persecutors and the American empire, the victim position inhabited by Jesus also implies a metonymic connection with the contemporary secular sphere. This metonymic connection tropologically resolves the contradictions in fundamentalism's hegemony by fantasizing a society that desires fundamentalism's destruction. This explains the film's rampant gore: an intensely hyper-real staging of Jesus's torture is powerful affective reaffirmation of the fundamentalist public's constitutive marginality. A tropological economy operates here: the film text implies metonymic connections that work through the paradox of fundamentalist identity. Fundamentalist identity positions its subjects in a common social space with other fundamentalists and in an identity-affirming rhetorical antagonism against its non-fundamentalist others. This exchange of pleasurable identities and antagonisms sutures the more general anxieties of a symbolically made subject who is constitutively divorced from itself and other subjects in the order of discourse.

Evangelical viewers reported that the violence of the film made them intensely uncomfortable. But this discomfort masks a deeper affective commitment generated by the film to the fundamentalist community. This is enjoyment in its most precise form, a seemingly unbearable or repulsive investment that does the difficult work of giving substance to subjects. The apparent unpleasantness of *The Passion of the Christ* conceals the surplus enjoyment it generates as a technology for mediating the relationship between the self, other subjects, and the Symbolic. General vocabularies of affect as articulation are too imprecise to read this dynamic because articulation theory as *taxis* is constitutively prohibited from paying attention to the economic excesses of enjoyment.

Rhetorical criticism requires a theory of interpretation that is up to the task of reading fundamentalism specifically and the relationship between enjoyment and identity more broadly. Such a theory of interpretation necessitates refusing the seductions of *taxical* mediation because what is at stake in fundamentalist discourse is more than a set of specific articulations or insular contexts that produce it. Fundamentalism, as all belief, is lodged in an economy of enjoyment and trope that exceeds it, and reading it requires attention to the excesses of an economy beyond the individual context or set of articulations that produce it. All belief is more than itself; it is an exchange of tropes whose durability and persistence can only be read by pointing to the *metaxis* beyond it.

Rhetorical criticism should claim a domain beyond insular texts, slavish adherence to contexts, and *taxical* articulation by attending primarily to tropological economies and affective labor promiscuously crossing the orders of the Symbolic, Imaginary, and the Real. In this disposition, public affiliation is specifically a structure of fantasy, an enjoyable trope negotiating the gaps manifest beyond it at the level of the subject, communicative relationships with other subjects, and with the Symbolic order more generally. On this reading, the task of rhetoric is to read backwards through the economies of trope, excess, and enjoyment—paying attention to the specific economy of representations of violent antagonism that constitutes fundamentalism as an identity and therefore as a material technology that negotiates the anxieties of being a subject. For critical practice to attend to this excessive economy, it must avoid the seductions of *taxis*, consciously cultivating a studied practice of tragic (im)mediation—or a practice of interpretation that is explicitly owned.

Interpretation and the Return of the Repressed
Problem of Theory and Practice

Fundamentalist enjoyment implies questions about the status of interpretation. The first is the question of the automaticity of interpretive practices. In articulating a materiality of rhetoric as *taxis*, materialists such as McGee and Greene often flirt with the temptation to think that explicit reading protocols are either disfiguring ideal impositions on the material functions of rhetoric, or that they flow automatically from an observation of context or the logic of their articulation. Usually the attempt to resist the explicit development of interpretive protocols employs a disavowed observational hermeneutic, paradoxically feigning critical neutrality under the guise of simply observing the movements and processes of everyday discourse. The simple observation of a site of material production is not in itself sufficient for spontaneously generating interpretive protocols, unless one can identify a *taxical* relationship between the materiality of rhetoric and specific rhetorical phenomena that seamlessly authorize interpretive protocols. But in asserting a *taxical* mode of attending to the materiality of rhetoric, materialists bracket *metaxis*, paradoxically exempting the act of interpretation from the very symbolic failings and principles of (im)mediation that produce the drive toward the material in the first place.

This is a problem of reference. For instance, when McGee claims that rhetorical inquiry ought to focus on the symbolic constitution of everyday life in the persuasive and "coercive power of the symbols which unite society," he flirts with a call for a science of reading such connections.[28] Even though rhetoricians should eschew the "idealist" tendency to presume an ahistorical reality outside discourse, the essential goal of rhetorical criticism is to work through moments of coordinated symbolic action bounded by a context. In other words, there is a presumed referential relationship between a representation of rhetoric as a "natural social phenomenon" or object in everyday discourse and the messy reality of rhetorical practices.[29]

Can one articulate the terms of mediation between a critic interpreting the materiality of rhetoric and the empirical "reality" that is the discursive function of rhetoric's materiality? The difference turns on a disavowed doctrine of interpretation in rhetorical materialism that claims non-interpretive status: *taxis* is a hidden reading protocol that authorizes interpretation, while *metaxis* explicitly asserts interpretation as a tragic impossibility. Here I suggest returning to Lacan's meditation on love to distinguish between *taxis* as (non)interpretation and *metaxis* as a tragic mode of interpretation.

The opening gambit of *Seminar XX* is an exploration of the tension between the law, love, and sex: law and love stand for two principles of *taxis*, or modes of disciplining trope and enjoyment by reducing them either to formal rules for reference or to a communally produced conception of meaning. Lacan responds to a hypothetical lawyer who asks him about discourse that "I felt I could respond . . . that language is not the speaking being."[30] Lacan tells the imaginary lawyer that at the level of form, language is based on a system of rules, of codes that govern its proper operation, but that the speaking being is an altogether different thing that can only be understood by assuming that one is "in bed, a bed employed to the fullest, there being two of you in it."[31] The function of the law is to read out or limit excess, to discipline surplus enjoyment so that it is channeled toward a productive end. Law is an interpretive principle of *taxis*: law serves to "divide up, distribute, or reattribute everything that counts as jouissance."[32] When applied to language, the problem of the "law" is that it relies on rules, structures, and programs as a way of accounting for the social world, and in doing so, it ignores the central relationship between failure and enjoyment.

The alternative to the law is not love, or the sexual relation, since the presupposition of relationship and implicit unity suppresses the function of enjoyment, ignoring its own kind of failures. Love is a *taxical* interpretive strategy that assumes discourse is consensual shared intercourse or coordinated symbolic effect, a blessed union of act and meaning. While love is often figured as a desire for unity between two irreducibly unique subjects, Lacan figures love as a narcissistic demand on the other. Love's demand is narcissistic in that it reduces the other to an object for the sake of achieving a subjective "one-ness," of rendering subjects divided by lack and language as unified selves and able to be unified with others. In this instance, Lacan's argument about love is really a critique of *taxis*, which presumes meaning can be reduced to an account of symbolic unities without remainder.

The ideology of love as union with the beloved in their intrinsic uniqueness masks the status of love as a demand on the beloved, driven by enjoyment in figuring the beloved as an extension of one's imaginary apparatus. The ideologies of love, relationship, and reference forge an (un)natural connection between the ontology of rhetorical function and the act of interpretation, thereby occluding the question of disconnection and the enjoyment that sutures it: where love is *taxis*, enjoyment is *metaxis*. The ideology of love as attention to the other on its own terms highlights interpretation as a practice of intervention as opposed to a simple act of revelation or consensual meaning making.

There is an affinity here between the labors of the lover and the lawyer that mirrors *taxis* in rhetorical studies of materiality. The main options within the materiality of rhetoric thesis are either the rhetorical as context and social process (underwritten by identification and symbolic action) or as articulation, a doctrine of the formal properties of discourse. Both the lover's and the lawyer's theories of language miss the function of trope and surplus enjoyment in producing failed unicity. For example, the idea that a theory of articulation can exorcize the problem of interpretation is a lawyerly solution. There are affinities between Greene's turn to articulation and psychoanalysis: both harbor suspicions about the hermeneutic reliance on unities and moments of commensurability between subjects and texts. But a psychoanalytic theory of rhetoric's materiality breaks ranks with articulation theory on the question of representation. Articulation strives to break free of the subject and representation by offering "a materialism based on how rhetoric traverses a governing apparatus. Instead of focusing on how rhetoric represents, we should focus on how rhetoric distributes different elements on a terrain of a governing apparatus."[33] If articulation means abandoning the question of representation, it turns a blind eye to the tropological supplements and practices of enjoyment that representational failure engenders. Articulation theory displaces what is productively problematic about interpretation in the search for a solution to the problem of the subject: that the hermeneutic project is never fully consummated does not mean that we should adopt a "logic of articulation" that risks an implicit observational hermeneutic by framing the task of rhetoric as simply observing the operations of articulation. Instead of throwing rhetorical practice too quickly at the feet of articulation, one might theorize the materiality of interpretation by detailing the constitutive failures of hermeneutics, and the *metaxic* enjoyment that sustains them.[34]

Alternatively, reference to the context that generates a discourse, either through consensus, identification, or coordinated symbolic action in everyday speech, is a rhetoric of lovers. For those inheriting the tradition of McGee's "Materialist's Conception of Rhetoric," there is a natural affinity between the articulation of rhetoric's materiality and the practice of observing everyday discourse, which represents a context as a shared history. This framing of rhetoric's materiality ignores both enjoyment in structure and the gap that generates it. It ignores enjoyment by assuming that meaning is generated on the fly, bound up in historically specific moments of process-based consensus instead of sedimented structures of enjoyment that produce the subject. This is why Lacan is fundamentally suspicious of the reference to communal practices of meaning making as a basis for an account of signification—because such a reference tends to privilege moments of shared symbolic action at the expense of articulating failures and gaps. There is both a structure that dictates the possibilities for signification and a gap between the lived experiences of subjects and communities negotiating this gap:

> Reference to the experience of the community, or the substance of this discourse settles nothing. For this experience assumes its essential dimension in the tradition that discourse establishes . . . long before the drama of history is inscribed in it . . . these structures reveal an ordering of possible exchanges . . . is inconceivable outside of the permutations authorized by language.[35]

Doesn't it stand to reason that a sufficient account of the materiality of rhetoric would automatically generate critical protocols informing criticism? Alternately, wouldn't an account of criticism that foregrounded material modes of interpretation naturally imply an accompanying (if implicit) account of the ontology of language? The difficulty lies in the presupposition that either mode of inquiry "naturally" generates the other. One is only able to claim primacy for practice by naturalizing the ontological status of language under the rubric of simply observing "everyday language." Despite McGee's rejoinder that one does not have to discuss ontology to do rhetorical criticism, a *taxical* mode of rhetoric's materiality relies on an irreducibly ontological claim to situate the reality of discourse in the Real of context.[36] A description of rhetoric's social and material function implicitly drives the modes of criticism. This ontological and referential claim is naturalized by inartistic proof: the materialist critic is just "observing the everyday function" of discourses.[37]

Materialists attempt to cast out the problem of theory and practice by establishing the relative priority of each term: "It is not enough," argues McGee, "to *distinguish* theory and practice. . . . One must also decide what *relationship* exists between theory and practice—which 'comes first' in . . . communicative behavior."[38] McGee avers that the "obvious alternative" to ignoring practice by making a fetish of theory is to believe "that practice 'comes first,' that the essential mission of rhetorical theory is not to *prescribe* technique but formally to account for what seems to be an essential part of the human social condition."[39] A theory of articulation is methodologically cognate with McGee's solution, arguing one should abandon fictions of the subject and interpretation in favor of simply tracking the productivity of points of articulation and struggle in culture.

To return to sex, perhaps one might discern romanticism in McGee's presumption that an exhaustive description of the relationship between theory and practice might be sufficiently articulated to allow for a rational prioritization of both registers. Such a prioritization, one in which practice comes first, would discipline modes of theorizing and interpretation by centering them on the Real of everyday discursive practice. Thus, a prurient Lacanian question to the problem of whether theory or practice, interpretation or the material realities of rhetoric come first: What if in this "relationship" neither of them "comes" first, if at all?[40] What if the relation between theory and practice or between interpretation and the material rhetorical practices it interprets is bound up in an insufferable jouissance driven by a missed meeting or an impotent liaison? What if these relationships can never be consummated, but must remain suspended in *metaxis*, in a productively failed unmediated encounter of autonomous registers? In the light of this unbridgeable gap, perhaps the best response is to track the productivity of our failures in closing it, casting rhetorical sutures as an enjoying and enjoyable supplement, and materially situated interpretation as *metaxy*. What if there is no such thing as a rhetorical relationship? Even if this is the case, there is certainly rhetoric.

Notes

1. I include here concepts like the materiality of the sign, the microanalytics of power, and articulation theory. Exemplars of these positions include rhetoricians who draw theoretical inspiration from Foucault's conception of discourse—for example, Carole Blair, Raymond McKerrow, Maurice Charland, and, more recently, Ronald Greene.

2. Michael Calvin McGee, "A Materialist's Conception of Rhetoric," in *Explorations in Rhetoric: Essays in Honor of Douglas Ehninger*, ed. Ray E. McKerrow (Glenview, IL: Scott, Foresman, 1982), 38.

3. Plato, *Symposium*, in *Plato: Lysis, Symposium, Gorgias*, Loeb Classical Library v166, trans. W.R.M. Lamb (Cambridge, MA: Harvard University Press, 1925), 202d13–e1.

4. In the course of this essay, I refer to the concept of the "daimon" as an embodiment of Voegelin's interpretation of *metaxis*. In doing so, I do not intend to make a claim to historical understanding of the daimon, as much as I would like to extend Voegelin's suggestive reading of the daimon as representative of the unmediated suspension between two opposites, a disposition that I am arguing (as a provocation to rhetorical materialism) inheres in a Lacanian reading of the relationship between the Lacanian "Real" and the rhetorical understanding of the "Ideal," and, by extension, between rhetorical theory and practice. One way of presenting the work that the idea of the daimon does here is to frame it as analogical, reading a close parallelism between Voegelin's representation of daimonic *metaxy* and the relationship between theory and practice in the materiality of rhetoric. A second way to think about the figure of the daimon is that if it is not quite analogical, it is at least *anagogical*—while there are points where a perfect parallelism

between the daimon and rhetorical immediation may break down, the comparison holds as a kind of "in spirit" treatment of the problem of the "ideal" and the "material," and between theory and practice in rhetoric. For a treatment of the distinction between analogical and anagogical modes of interpretation that primarily arises in the context of medieval biblical interpretation, see Sallie McPhague's *Metaphorical Theology* (Chicago: Fortress Press, 1982). Thanks to editors Lucaites and Biesecker for the useful suggestion.

5.   McGee claims that a materialist rhetoric requires that the "various methods of data-based historical research and theory building will have to be examined, and the mystifications of 'semiotics' and 'hermeneutics' resolved and eliminated." McGee, "Materialist's Conception of Rhetoric," 25.

6.   Nathan Stormer, "Articulation: A Working Paper on Rhetoric and *Taxis*," *Quarterly Journal of Speech* 90 (2004): 261.

7.   Augusto Boal, *The Rainbow of Desire: The Boal Method of Theatre and Therapy* (New York: Routledge, 1995), 43.

8.   Jacques Lacan, *Seminar XX, On Feminine Sexuality; the Limits of Love and Knowledge, 1972–1973. Encore: The Seminar of Jacques Lacan, Book XX*, trans. Bruce Fink, ed. Jacques-Alain Miller (New York: W. W. Norton, 1999), 56.

9.   Dana L. Cloud, "The Materiality of Discourse as an Oxymoron: A Challenge to Critical Rhetoric," *Western Journal of Communication* 58 (1994): 142.

10. Jacques Lacan, "The Function and Field of Speech and Language in Psychoanalysis," in *Ecrits*, by Jacques Lacan, trans. Alan Sheridan (New York: W. W. Norton, 1977), 65.

11. Ellie Ragland-Sullivan, "Stealing Material: The Materiality of Language According to Freud and Lacan," in *Lacan and the Human Sciences*, ed. Alexandre Leupin (Omaha: University of Nebraska Press, 1991), 61.

12. Ernesto Laclau, "The Future of Radical Democracy," in *Radical Democracy: Politics between Abundance and Lack*, ed. Lasse Thomassen and Lars Tønder (Manchester: Manchester University Press, 2005), 256.

13. Lacan writes that there is a gap "between this One (of phallic jouissance) and something that is related to being, and behind being, to jouissance." Lacan, *Seminar XX*, 6.

14. Lacan, *Seminar XX*, 6.

15. Jacques Lacan, "The Agency of the Letter in the Unconscious or Reason Since Freud," in *Ecrits*, trans. Alan Sheridan (New York: W. W. Norton, 1977), 147.

16. Lacan, "Agency of the Letter," 147.

17. Lacan, "Agency of the Letter," 149.

18. Lacan, "Agency of the Letter," 157.

19. Ronald Walter Greene, "Another Materialist Rhetoric," *Critical Studies in Mass Communication* 15 (1998): 29.

20. Jacques Lacan, "The Mirror Stage," in *Ecrits*, trans. Alan Sheridan (New York: W. W. Norton, 1977), 1–11.

21. Lacan, *Seminar XX*, 142.

22. Lacan, *Seminar XX*, 23.

23. Lacan's affinity with the performatively flavored account of materiality as an embodied practice in the habitus of enjoyment is obvious from the following: "I will say that the signifier is situated at the level of enjoying substance (*substance jouissante*). . . . The signifier is the cause of jouissance. Without the signifier how could we even approach . . . the body? Without the signifier, how could we center something that is the material cause of jouissance? However fuzzy or confused it may be, it is a part of the body that is signified in this contribution." Lacan, *Seminar XX*, 224.

24. As Lacan argues in *Seminar XI*, "the kind of exchange involved here is the exchange . . . of those social supports, which in a different context, are known as subjects." Jacques Lacan, *Seminar XI, The Four Fundamental Concepts of Psychoanalysis, The Seminar of Jacques Lacan, Book XI*, trans. Alan Sheridan, ed. Jacques-Alain Miller (New York: W. W. Norton, 1998), 5.

25. Lacan, "Agency of the Letter," 147. The full quotation is instructive on this point: "[S]peech is the key to that truth, when his whole experience must find speech alone in its instrument, its context, its material, and even in the background noise of its uncertainties . . . psychoanalytic experience discovers in the unconscious is the whole structure of language . . . the notion that the unconscious is just the seat of the instincts will have to be rethought. But how are we to take this 'letter' here? Quite simply, literally. By letter I designate that material support that concrete discourse borrows from language."

26. In referring to this set of potential connections as the "material" of the unconscious, Lacan reasserts the stupidity of signification as an overdetermined and always saturated field of meaning: "For it is with those stupidities that we do analysis and that we enter into the new subject—that of the unconscious . . . we will draw certain consequences from [the analysand's] words—words that cannot be taken back, for that is the rule of the game. From that emerges a speaking that does not always go so far as to be able to 'ex-sist' with respect to the words spoken, that is because of what gets included in these words as a consequence thereof." Lacan, *Seminar XX*, 22.

27. For example, one might cite McGee's treatment of Christian fundamentalism, "Secular Humanism: A Radical Reading of 'Culture Industry' Productions," the inaugural essay of *Critical Studies in Mass Communication* 1 (1984): 1–33. Here, McGee defers to a *taxical* account of fundamentalist belief in at least two ways. First, McGee argues that belief is a product of experience, and here, experience refers to inherited narratives that frame everyday life. McGee's explanation frames the relationship to such narratives as both conscious and importantly "volitional" (2). By contrast, a *metaxical* alternative frames belief as a kind of excess that is not reducible to commitments at the level of group consciousness or narrative, as an affective response that is unconscious and outside of a simple vocabulary of intention. As a result, it is difficult on McGee's reading to situate fundamentalism in a broader public economy that overdetermines investments at the level of specific practices, or at the level of specific texts. Second, McGee explicitly argues that an analysis of fundamentalism should eschew theoretical frameworks that pay more attention to the apparatus of explanation than empirical phenomena (2–3, 7): here, I reemphasize that though attention to everyday practices is important, one cannot resolve the meaning and function of such practices simply at the level of texts—thus, even though McGee goes to great lengths to argue against rhetorical overdetermination of fundamentalism, in the end, his analysis focuses to a large extent on the textual narratives of scripture. Attention to the critical apparatus is important if one is to avoid the seduction that sees belief as autotelic, or not aiming at an excess beyond it.

28. McGee, "Materialist's Conception of Rhetoric," 45.

29. As McGee defines it, "[r]hetoric is a natural social phenomenon in the context of which symbolic claims are made on the action and/or belief of one or more persons, allegedly in the interest of such individuals, and with the strong presumption that such claims will cause meaningful change." McGee, "Materialist's Conception of Rhetoric," 59.

30. Lacan, *Seminar XX*, 2. This explanation foreshadows much of the later work of the seminar—for example, the distinction between language and *la langue* (the linguist's

representation of linguistic codes, and the stupid mother tongue of the speaking subject).

31. Lacan, *Seminar XX*, 12.

32. Lacan, *Seminar XX*, 3. This disciplining is not necessarily always through direct repression. In fact, the law serves the function of *reassigning* jouissance; its ultimate function is to cause the subject to misrecognize the subject's frustrated desire for access to the other, or for self-identity S (barred A) as the little *a* object.

33. Greene, "Another Materialist Rhetoric," 38.

34. Greene's treatment of interpellation is his most lawyerly moment—the efficiency of interpellation in his account is stunning. What of failed interpellation or impotence in the governing apparatus? Greene's presentation of the governing apparatus's power is stark: "As an alternative conceptualization for a materialist rhetoric I am suggesting that critics focus on how rhetorical practices create conditions of possibility of a governing apparatus to judge and *program* reality." Greene, "Another Materialist Rhetoric," 41. The idea that the apparatus "programs" implies an automaticity to the apparatus's acts of programming, that it manipulates social space in the same way that Microsoft writes code for software.

35. Lacan, "Agency of the Letter," 148.

36. Ekaterina Haskins, "Embracing the Superficial: Michael Calvin McGee, Rhetoric, and the Postmodern Condition," *American Journal of Communication*, 6 (2003): 3.

37. It is of course possible to argue that McGee's later works address this problem. For instance, in "Text, Context, and the Fragmentation of American Culture," *Western Journal of Speech Communication* 54 (1990): 274–89, he argues that criticism is a kind of intentional reconstruction of the rhetorical object by the critic. This move does, in some way, concede that interpretive protocols are not naturally derivable from the fragmented conditions of "post-modern" discourse. Yet, this version of the critical act does not vindicate McGee from the problems of reference, and may be an insufficient account of the relationship between interpretation and enjoyment. McGee is only able to sustain his claim, as Greene notes, by presuming that the material processes of rhetoric seamlessly match the changing social context of mediation, which is a kind of employment of the politics of reference that does not significantly revise the earlier claims to the materiality of rhetoric as much as it provides a caveat that creates a kind of interpretive humility.

38. McGee, "Materialist's Conception of Rhetoric," 23.

39. McGee, "Materialist's Conception of Rhetoric," 24.

40. The term "jouissance" is related to the French slang word for orgasm: "*jouir.*" Lacan intends the term, as opposed to a concept like pleasure, to capture a kind of enjoyment that is, in some ways, unbearable or insufferable, as if the moment before climax were extended forever without release.

CHAPTER 7

Hard Evidence: The Vexations of Lincoln's Queer Corpus

Charles E. Morris III, Boston College

Tripp's greatest casualty is hardly Lincoln, whose legend has survived so many spurious stories, nor the honest historians and eyewitnesses whose judgment he often impugns. In the end, his real victim is history itself, always hovering uneasily between a science and an art, balanced only by its ethic of seeking unbiased truth from all available evidence.

Scott Alarik, "Questionable Look at President's Intimate Life"

Every generation, it seems, gets the Lincoln it deserves.

Christopher Capozzola, "The Gay Lincoln Controversy"

For several years now, I have been cruising Abraham Lincoln. Only recently did I discover the significance in claiming this. My earnest scholarly effort to establish a shared attraction between us—analysis, say, of his bed, his intimate letters, testimony regarding his social intercourse, friendships, marriage—has gone unrequited, and has mostly served to invite others to speculate about, if not diminish, my motives. With Lincoln, it seems, hard evidence does not mean convincing proof, but rather a vexing corpus that proves only the historically contingent rhetorical embodiment of desire for Lincoln. And this, his many other suitors have failed to comprehend, constitutes the hard evidence, a persuasive case, that Lincoln is queer.

C. A. Tripp's posthumously published *The Intimate World of Abraham Lincoln* has sparked the latest battle in an ongoing cold war—cultural and academic entwined—over Lincoln's sexuality. This battle is more deeply pitched because, unlike the last confrontation precipitated by Larry Kramer in 1999,[1] Tripp's bold claim that Lincoln exhibited "a plentiful homosexual response and action" and was, according to the Kinsey scale he applied, "a classical 5: predominantly homosexual, but incidentally heterosexual," is advanced by means of an impressive, if ultimately inconclusive, arsenal of evidence spanning the whole of Lincoln's sexual life.[2] Kramer's "history" failed to sustain a national audience because his reputation as a provocateur fit readily into the homophobic assault that discredited him, and because the smoking gun of his case, Joshua Speed's diary, was never revealed and is widely believed to have been a fabrication of Kramer's imagination.[3] By contrast, Tripp emerged wearing a mantle of academic ethos (and with the imprimatur of Simon and Schuster), disavowed political motive, and made clear from the outset that a convincing historical case rests on compelling evidence. In a sense, Tripp made his last stand on enemy ground, which is to say the positivist ground of historiography—and therefore has been afforded at least a begrudging visibility proving difficult to dismiss. However, I will argue here that, as revealed in the copious response to Tripp's book, an evidentiary struggle over Lincoln's sexuality is illusory, one that masks the heteronormative presumption undergirding and protected by the rhetorically constructed material status of evidence itself.

But Tripp's "folly" offers a last laugh—Lincoln's laugh, and a bawdy one at that. The body of evidence about Lincoln's sexual body might well be impervious to outing, but in mounting it, we discover that Lincoln has outed us, historian and advocate, straight and gay alike—lured us out with our pants around our ankles. The vexations of Lincoln's corpus, I contend, provide the ground for a queer refiguring of our understanding of the past as "mirror" and/or "lamp," and in keeping with Gavin Butt's project of "queering the evidential," offer a displacement of "so-called verifiable truths from their positivistic frames of reference to render them instead . . . as projections of interpretive desire and curiosity."[4] What I seek to instantiate through this interrogation of evidentiary materiality is a queer critical politics of revelatory inducement, not historical adducement, and to consider desire as a material force in rhetorical productions of the past.

The timing of Tripp's volume would seem to have been propitious. Tripp lived just long enough to complete the draft (he died in May 2003), and its delayed publication date coincidentally launched a year replete with Lincoln commemoration: the Abraham Lincoln Bicentennial Commission and Library of Congress's joint program marking the anniversaries (140th and 150th, respectively) of Lincoln's death and Walt Whitman's publication of *Leaves of Grass*; the dedication and opening of the Abraham Lincoln Presidential Library and Museum (ALPLM) in Springfield, Illinois; Discovery Channel's "Greatest American" campaign in which millions voted during a four-week, seven-hour primetime event, ultimately ranking Lincoln second to Ronald Reagan; *Time*'s choice of Abraham Lincoln for its annual "Making of America" special issue.

Indeed, Tripp's justification for his study—"[T]he benefits of uncovering the facts in the case of Lincoln are especially great, owing in no small measure to his own supersecrecy, and the rest to an overlay of romantic fictions. Lincoln is much too important to deserve that, too central a figure in history to keep obscuring basic facts of his life"—appears perfectly orchestrated to accompany both George W. Bush's declaration at the ALPLM dedication that "Lincoln embodied the democratic ideal—that leadership and even genius are found among the people themselves, and sometimes in the most unlikely places. . . . Lincoln's career and contributions were founded on a single argument: That there are no exceptions to the ringing promises of the Declaration of Independence; that all of us who share in the human race are equal," and the observation of *Time* executive editor Priscilla Painton, who conceived of the issue titled "Uncovering the Real Abe Lincoln": "[T]his year, with a wealth of new research emerging, there's fresh passion to get past the icon and find the real character." As Jean Baker wrote in her introduction to Tripp's book, "Clearly the matter [of Lincoln's sexuality] has seized the public's attention, and it needs to be addressed."[5]

However, despite *kairos* and the sheer bulk of printed response to *The Intimate World of Abraham Lincoln*, there remains a serious question as to the broader will to find the "real" sexual character of Lincoln (even if it were possible), but more important, an obstinate invisibility of the *process* by which such historical discoveries are publicly constituted and legitimated as "real," as material, thus shaping their cultural and political meaning and value. Although I agree with Barry Schwartz's characterization of the relationship between history and commemoration as being "reciprocal" and "highly interdependent," his faith in the discipline of history does not seem to admit of the possibility that this relationship could also be mutually contaminating. I am deeply suspicious of the firm distinction Schwartz draws between their "techniques and achievements":

> History disenchants the past, commemoration and its sites sanctify it; history makes the past an object of analysis, commemoration makes it an object of commitment. History is a system of "referential symbols" representing known facts about past events and their sequence; commemoration is a system of "condensation symbols" expressing the moral sentiments those events inspire. History, like science, investigates the world by producing models of permanence and change. Commemoration, like ideology, promotes commitment to the world by symbolizing its values and aspirations.[6]

My suspicion here generally concerns "The 'bourgeois science' of history . . . as an aspect of the culture of heteronormativity against which queer subjects (ostensibly) align themselves."[7]

However, a more particular suspicion of the entailments in Schwartz's configuration is rooted in the long-recognized if often-obfuscated rhetorical nature of "referential symbols" and historians' fidelity to the "science" that exhibits them. As Joan Scott observes,

> [t]he status of evidence is, of course, ambiguous for historians. On the one hand, they acknowledge that "evidence only counts as evidence and is only recognized as such in relation to a potential narrative, so that the narrative can be said to determine the evidence as much as the evidence determines the narrative." On the other hand, historians' rhetorical treatment of evidence, and their use of it to falsify prevailing interpretations, depends on a referential notion of evidence which denies that it is anything but a reflection of the real.[8]

More troubling even than the sleight of hand that Scott identifies is the extent to which some historians—and this, I would argue, is largely true of the Lincoln establishment—render inconsistent judgments regarding the status of evidence.[9] They apply a strict methodological rule of law and question rhetorical and political investments when evidence is garnered and interpreted by those who counter prevailing narratives, while allowing themselves a more generous evidentiary standard warranted by their own unmarked commitments and the assumption that those commitments govern writ large, both inside and outside the academy. Tripp understood this as an inherent barrier to his project: "From the moment anything comes along with the possible power to destabilize large areas of Lincoln scholarship, it can be viewed as a major threat by historians who have invested much of their lives sifting and sorting conventional interpretations. Not that anything sexual is by itself that important, particularly not in the case of a larger-than-life figure like Lincoln, whose essential qualities are undimmable. But scholarship itself is damnably dimmable."[10]

As such, evidence in support of a hegemonic, which of course means straight, Lincoln is material, muscular, and malleable; evidence in support of a homosexual Lincoln is immaterial, insufficient, and ideological. Thus constructed, "evidence" itself can be understood as a condensation symbol not only for the "truth" it ostensibly speaks, but also the heteronormative presumption of cultural authority against which queer narratives of the past must struggle. The irony in Tripp's case, as for so many dedicated to establishing gay history or memory, is that the materiality sought through evidence turns out to be a hologram, and straights are at the switch. From my perspective, evidence within this scene also functions as metonymy for commemoration passing as history. Historian Michael Chesson, in more than one sense, was right when he averred, "I could build a Lincoln Log cabin of homophobic denial. . . . There's been a cover-up, a conspiracy of silence for experts to hide what they regard as dirty linen in Abe's faded carpetbag."[11]

The silence most interesting to me here is not that which governs any given piece of evidence enabling inferences regarding Lincoln's sexuality. Rather, I emphasize the silence that obfuscates, in Scott's terms, "the rhetorical treatment of evidence" itself, and the rhetoric of evidence that I understand as central to Lincoln's queerness, Lincoln's queer eloquence. However much one might admire Tripp's ambition and audacity, and the inevitable trouble he stirred, his objective to "prove" Lincoln's homosexuality was rather doomed from the start. This is not because, as so many of his detractors have asserted by way of misreading Foucault, homosexuality did not exist during Lincoln's era.[12] Nor because, as Jonathan Ned Katz accurately observed, "[i]f, in the nineteenth century, the sexual was, properly, the potential reproductive intercourse of penis and vagina, there existed many erotic desires and acts that were not recognized as such."[13] Rather, at this stage in the development of our understanding of nineteenth-century physical and emotional intercourse among men—whether we call it homosociality, homoeroticism, or homosexuality—potential evidence is inherently more minefield than gold mine in the epistemic dilemma of historical intimacy. Christopher Capozzola explains,

> Nor can we really "prove" Lincoln's sexuality at all. Evidence presents a thorny problem for every historian of the nineteenth-century boudoir, especially when it comes to same-sex desire. Here, the evidentiary standard is raised ever so slightly, almost anything can be explained away, and it gets hard to see the substance for the shadows of the doubts. The subjects themselves aren't even reliable. Lincoln's contemporary, the poet Walt Whitman—who really, *really* liked men—left nothing irrefutable in his archive. Oscar Wilde, to his grave, denied everything.[14]

Such a quagmire is deepened further when in this case one discovers that Lincoln's enormous corpus yields so little on which to base a cohesive and ultimately compelling account of his sexual persona; all that is really "there" are tantalizing fragments inviting rhetorical materializations of the conceits and vulnerabilities of recognition and desire; as William Herndon memorably put it, "Lincoln to the world is a profound mystery—an enigma—a sphinx— a riddle, and yet I think I knew the man."[15] However, to say only that "our empathy can lead us to confuse the past with the present"—noting historian Christine Stansell's conclusion that "Tripp was determined to rescue a hidden gay hero"—is but half of the story.[16] Tripp's "rescue" caused tremors in the bedrock of heteronormative presumption, unearthing queer antipathy that revealed itself in desirous conceits regarding the shifting evidence on which the often conflated history and commemoration of Lincoln is built.

In order to appreciate Tripp's disruption, one must resist the temptation to focus on how he wants to make his case, or even the case itself, but on the idiosyncrasies—or, more generally understood, the errors, distortions, or failures—through which he often brings us to his perspective on Lincoln's homosexuality. Because the game is rigged (or put differently, because our conventional embrace of evidence's materiality proceeds without vigilant consideration of its rhetoricity, the materiality of motive and power attending and embodied in it), the assemblage of proof of course dominates one's focus, all the more so because Tripp himself demands its fidelity:

> Thus, the rule here has been to seriously consider and possibly accept for analysis only particular homosexual examples in Lincoln's life that are supported by at least two separate facts or pieces of evidence. This guards against what is called in probability theory a "type one error." But there have also been surprises in the other direction, where what started out as a promising source of some new revelation has suddenly vanished into nothingness.[17]

And so one's anticipation or aversion is cast with Tripp's configuration of Lincoln's coupling with presidential bodyguard Captain David Derickson, his early puberty and youthful same-sex poetry, his New Salem bedmates, the absence of romance with Ann Rutledge, his crush on Colonel Elmer Ellsworth, his long-term relationship with Joshua Speed, and his bankrupt marriage.

In its exhibition of singular evidentiary fragments and cumulative tally, Tripp's case makes plain the simultaneous and striking force and fragility of any serious claim to Lincoln's homosexuality. Michael Chesson, speaking on behalf of the "pro" side of the ledger in the book's two-part afterword, put it well: "Tripp, for all his research, sophistication, and insight, has not proved his case conclusively. There is no smoking gun that we can link to Long Abe . . . Nor, perhaps, has Tripp proven his case beyond a reasonable doubt. But any open-minded reader who has reached this point may well have a reasonable doubt about the nature of Lincoln's sexuality."[18] Given what Stansell called the "dossier of ambiguities," one is tempted to take solace in the assessment of Richard Brookhiser, who despite observing that "Tripp alternates shrewd guesses and modest conclusions with bluster and fantasy . . . arguments [with] a (spurious) scientific sheen. And he has an ax to grind," ultimately concluded, "In any case, on the evidence before us, Lincoln loved men, at least some of whom loved him back."[19]

Lincoln himself always cast his eye beyond such small rewards and concessions, however, and in transgressing the orbit determined by historiographical and heteronormative pull, we might do the same. To proceed requires fixation on Tripp at his most vulnerable and innovative interpretive moments, summarized generously by Jean Baker: "Given his background,

Tripp saw things obscured to those untrained in sexuality. On the other hand, his notion of factual verification defied the canons of the discipline of history, and because of the nature of the subject, there is considerable circumstantial evidence in *The Intimate World*."[20] It is precisely the sexologist's defiance of disciplinary history—Tripp's inclination to "credit quieter evidence and to listen to nearby implications"—that cracks the blinders on our field of vision, not only regarding the indirect evidence regarding Lincoln's sexuality, but, more important, the indirect evidence of those "circumstances which afford a certain presumption" against such a reading.[21] In other words, Tripp's circumstantial case exposes the disciplinary process by which a threat to the normal is rendered as circumstantial, meaning insufficient, ideological, and immaterial. Here we might take Thoreau as our guide: "Some circumstantial evidence is very strong, as when you find a trout in the milk."[22]

Two types of circumstantial evidence marshaled by Tripp illuminate this double trajectory. The first concerns the currency of erotic investment. Whereas critics of Tripp's homo-Lincoln thesis like to isolate the passage in Thomas Chamberlain's *History* describing David Derickson's presidential bed-sharing (and "making use of his Excellency's night-shirt!") as insufficient proof of a sexual liaison, Tripp himself supplements this account with reference to Derickson's own memoir, taking as material the phatic conversation between these men:

> Derickson received the president's request to meet him, and went right over to do so; after a handshake Lincoln asked if he "would have any objection to riding with him to the city." It's clear that almost as soon as he entered Lincoln's carriage for their first ride to the city, their connection was immediate. There was a charged atmosphere of mutual esteem, one well-primed for moving toward some kind of culmination. As Derickson described it, their conversation proceeded through many small but rapid steps, with Lincoln's questions about his background. These are precisely the kinds of redundant questions in pursuit of small increments of intimacy that quickly become tiresome in ordinary conversation—but not here, perhaps because the interest was not on facts but rather on the chance they offered the partners to increase the quality and extent of their closeness within an almost classical seduction scene.[23]

As Tripp suggests here, the rhetoric of facts can bespeak in double-talk a complex art of desire.

Similarly, Tripp draws on the letters of Colonel John Cook, commander of the Springfield Greys, and those of Elmer Ellsworth himself to convey Lincoln's "special interest" in the young military man and those "inducements" to bring him to Springfield to study law with Lincoln. This was the *beginning* of an "intimate" but chaste friendship (Ellsworth was "definitely and explicitly heterosexual") that would last until Ellsworth was killed in 1861, devastating Lincoln. Tripp does not require an erotic confession to glean an erotic lure: "Most Lincoln scholars have gone out of their way to repeat or to re-invent the conventional notion that Lincoln's attention to Ellsworth was merely a surrogate love—like what he might feel for a brother or a son. Far from it. For, of course, where such common emotions prevail they are easily expressed smoothly and directly in affectionate ways, poles apart from using roundabout seductions such as those pursued first by the procurer John Cook, and later by Lincoln himself."[24] Smoking guns would be illogical in such a scene, and any demand for them would seem to betray not desire for proof but proof of (heterosexual) desire.

Most famously of all, Tripp scrutinizes the narrative fidelity of the well-worn tale of Lincoln's first encounter with Joshua Speed (in Speed's own words), the occasion that introduced Lincoln to Speed's double bed and commenced "the 'closest' as well as the 'most intimate' relationship of his life."[25] Again, it is not the bed itself that occupies Tripp as it does his many detractors (although he is convinced that Lincoln and Speed made ample use of it), but rather the quotidian discursive entailments of Speed's invitation.[26] Unlike those who pass over this analysis in favor of sleeping arrangements and the salutations in Lincoln's correspondence with Speed, both of which lend themselves to reasonable doubt as erotic "proof," I quote it at length:

> Note that the invitation lacked any of the usual qualifiers such as "for a few days" or "until you get settled." Instead, it was immediately warm, embracing, and open-ended, more geared to desire than to accommodation. Louder still is the fact that while Lincoln did not know Speed at all, Speed had been well aware of Lincoln for months and was filled with admiration for him, ever since having heard the speech he gave the previous summer (July 30, 1836), in which Lincoln had cleverly trounced a rude lawyer and adversary, George Forquer. Why did Speed not mention this, perhaps with a comment about how much he had enjoyed the speech, or his amusement at seeing Forquer get his comeuppance? The probable answer is clear enough. Within moments of Lincoln arriving on that borrowed horse Joshua Speed evidently targeted him as a desirable bed partner, and immediately began choosing his words carefully. Had he said anything about recognizing Lincoln, or expressed admiration for the speech, this would have immediately moved their contact toward a conventional, friendly familiarity—exactly appropriate for, say, the start of either an ordinary friendship or conventional courtship, be it heterosexual or homosex-ual—but enemy territory for any brand of sexual conquest.
>
> Enemy territory? This may sound topsy-turvy, since sexual motives are ordi-narily preceded by many small steps of friendly familiarity, the friendlier the better. True enough. But in plenty of other situations the delays of courtship and a rela-tively slow step-by-step method of winning a partner are cast aside (especially in the absence of onlookers) in favor of a glance or a gesture suddenly indicating not only

attraction but a sexual readiness that can trigger a quick, parallel response in a partner who may or may not have already had the same in mind.[27]

This is a disquisition on the rhetoric of cruising! The implication of Tripp's
insight is that one need not have evidence of homosexual identity, which of
course did not "exist," or sodomy, the humanity of which, given sodomy's
almost exclusive juridical inscription, is virtually lost to history. What we
have instead is evidence of the circumstantial rhetoric that constitutes a
prelude to a (same-sex) kiss.[28] Its value is as much political as historical: in
the presence of such methodological excess, one witnesses what others *make*
of it.

It is precisely those circumstances of evidentiary production, the materialization of "proof," that Tripp reveals in a second mode of analysis. Discussion of the validity of oral testimony, which has been re-embraced by the
Lincoln establishment since the 1980s, still hinges more on the accuracy of
memory than the *motive and context* of memory, with its inextricable
connection to normativity (for both historical witness and historian alike).
Tripp refuses the disjuncture. In the case of Speed, he reconsiders the
narrative bare bones of Speed's spartan and seemingly innocuous account
(published in 1884) regarding his first encounter with Lincoln. Absent doubt
about Speed's recall, most historians have been pleased to let the evidence
speak for itself, but Tripp focuses on the relationship between what is and is
not said as substantively evident.

Yet in later telling the story, he was apparently embarrassed by what
might come through as erotic interest in his moves toward Lincoln and
consequently felt it safer, more innocent sounding, to recast events by
moving back, leaving Lincoln less well attended than he actually was. Thus,
as in so many telltale events, it is not the facts themselves that give the game
away, but precisely such distortions as Speed invented to hide behind. In
short, what he removed from the picture only flags the probable reality and
highlights what he most wanted to obscure.[29]

What is told, on Tripp's reading, cannot be severed from the circumstances of its telling; in evidentiary terms, the indirect is as material as the
direct. Any distinction between the two must be questioned in light of
normativity's sway. Thus, Tripp later concludes that the boon and bane of
William Herndon's method rests with the "unusual nature," the intensity, of
his own heterosexuality. Herndon's "oblivion" skewed his interpretive
faculty—"Not only did he fail to detect any of Lincoln's homosexual trends,
he paid the usual price of completely misinterpreting nearly all of Lincoln's
heterosexual life as well"—so much so that he "did not catch the drift"
regarding the nuances of Lincoln's bed-sharing with Speed, Billy Greene,

and A. Y. Ellis, and could with abandon launch the Ann Rutledge legend. At the same time, Herndon's "innocence" (itself evidence of normativity) functioned as a valuable vehicle in the accumulation of an archive that included the ambiguous fragments of Lincoln's socio-erotic life among men, thwarting the oblivion to which another might have consigned them.[30]

Of course, it is from this vantage on the circumstances of evidentiary production and engagement that Tripp discerns and discloses the sexual politics of contemporary Lincoln historiography: "the rules of revelation" (i.e., silences) regarding David Derickson, the "First Chronicles of Reuben," and Elmer Ellsworth; myopia and literalism regarding the Speed bed and correspondence; and, perhaps especially, the inconsistent application of evidentiary standards concerning Lincoln's heterosexual romance with Ann Rutledge and engagement to Mary Todd, the latter of which Tripp calls "a litmus test for a certain brand of honesty among Lincoln scholars."[31]

Again, I must emphasize that my reading of Tripp's analysis foregoes the question of whether he establishes Lincoln's sexuality, which I believe to be a distraction from the more pressing issue of the process by which the materiality of evidence is constituted and to what ends, and the value of certain bodies of evidence—in this case, Lincoln's vexing corpus—in drawing out the largely invisible desires that motivate their constitution. There is no question that Tripp often errs in moments of unbridled specula-tion, slippery and unreflective application of Alfred Kinsey's (already contested) findings, misogyny, and a neglect of nineteenth-century contexts as an interpretive framework (ahistoricism that I find endemic to the readings of Lincoln's sexuality, most surprisingly by historians themselves!). How-ever, Tripp's case is important precisely because of its boldness and vulner-ability, which affords the occasion and forges the crucible in which material motives and commitments are ferreted out, exhibiting the politics of adduce-ment and inducement. Taking as a point of departure, as many claim, the notion that Tripp's method is driven by his identity, I submit that what is true of the homo-Lincoln paradigm is equally true of the hetero-Lincoln para-digm. More important, I argue that we need a paradigm shift to appreciate the relationship between desire and evidence.

In this regard, I agree in principle with Andrew O'Hehir, who concluded, "This would be a more honest book, and perhaps a more convincing one, if he had simply written: 'Listen, I'm a gay man and a sex researcher, and I'm here to tell you that Abe Lincoln looks, sounds and smells like a homo. I can't prove it, but I know it's true.'" The trouble with O'Hehir's corrective is that, in a contemporary context, most presume that only gays need to be more honest about their desire in constructing the past. O'Hehir understood this inequity:

> I'm not confident that Tripp or Donald [who wrote *"We Are Lincoln Men"*] or any-
> one else can reliably read the signals in a 19th-century same-sex friendship, at least
> not when the evidence is as ambiguous as it is in the Lincoln-Speed case. Tripp es-
> sentially begins by assuming that the only way to explain their four years of bed-
> sharing is that they were lovers. Then he cherry-picks the friendliest details and
> psychologizes, rationalizes and generally massages away any contradictions. Argua-
> bly, of course, Donald or any other heterosexual (myself included) is likely to begin
> with the opposite assumption, and then look for evidence that the sleeping arrange-
> ment was an innocent matter of economics, space and the chilly nights of frontier
> Illinois.

However, he failed to provide an account of the process by which evidence *qua* evidence in the case of Lincoln's sexuality is reified, and therefore miscalculates the implications and promise of a queer Lincoln. "Whatever Abraham Lincoln did in bed, and whomever he did it with, he stands above today's cultural and sexual wars as surely as he dwarfed the factional disputes of his own age. If no man is bigger than history, Lincoln sticks out of it awkwardly as an icon of our unrealized possibilities, the loneliest and strangest man ever to lead this troublesome country."[32]

Lincoln as an "icon of our unrealized possibilities," an indeterminate tex-tual/sexual Lincoln, is what this evidentiary struggle, on both sides, largely seeks to thwart. Ironically, what is clearest from the bewildering traffic of Tripp's reviews by academics and activists alike, which cut a broad swath across the discursive landscape, is that evidence functions less to determine the truth of Lincoln's sexuality than as a measure of evidence's materializa-tion of desire to determine a *particular* truth of Lincoln's sexuality. Gore Vidal's maxim, and its unstated converse, conceptualizes this process in somewhat different terms: "What did researcher Tripp discover over the last decades about Lincoln's lavender streak and those soft May violets? The answer is a great deal of circumstantial detail, of which some is incontro-vertible except perhaps to the eye of faith, which, as we all know, is most selective and ingenious when it comes to ignoring the evidence."[33]

At either end of the spectrum of response to Tripp's Lincoln (and one senses immediately the extent to which Tripp is really a proxy, poster boy, foil, or scapegoat for something else, something more consequential), such investments are easily recognizable. In support of Tripp's case, we find Malcolm Lazin, executive director of the Equality Forum, who proclaimed, "I have read *The Intimate Life of Abraham Lincoln*. As a gay man and an amateur historian, I find the evidence indisputable that the 16th President of the United States, Abraham Lincoln, was a gay man. Anyone not blinded by

homophobia will recognize that the President who preserved our republic
was gay. It is time that U.S. historical figures be emancipated from the
closet."[34] Gay activist and pundit Andrew Sullivan wrote in the *Advocate*,
"Pssst. Abraham Lincoln was most certainly gay. . . . No, we have no strong
evidence that he had sex with men. . . . Yes, any particular piece of evidence
that Tripp presents could be dismissed as hearsay or inconclusive. But the
accumulation of detail left me persuaded that Lincoln was, if not 100% gay,
then at least gay with a touch of bisexuality."[35] Gay historian Charles Kaiser,
in his *Advocate* article "Honest, Abe was Gay," argued,

> Was Lincoln gay? That has been a public question for only a couple of decades,
> even though the proof that his closest emotional attachments were always with men
> has been available to every historian who has written about him during the last cen-
> tury and a half. But in the venerable tradition of making all great men robustly het-
> erosexual, almost every biographer of the great emancipator has ignored,
> suppressed, or distorted the abundant evidence that Lincoln was at the very least
> bisexual in his feelings—and probably his acts. . . . After this book, no future histo-
> rian will be able to ignore those violet streaks again.[36]

Larry Kramer, occupying the same platform at Cooper Union from which
Lincoln launched his presidential ascent, remained unabashed in claiming
that "[y]our family, your brothers and sisters, have been here a very long
time and have an ancient and distinguished lineage. You must learn that
Abraham Lincoln was gay."[37]

Those who discredit Tripp's case are equally fervent in their judgment of
evidence and the biases that render it convincing. R. Albert Mohler Jr.,
president of the Southern Baptist Theological Seminary, argued that in this
"scandalous effort to twist history into service for a political cause," Tripp
and his defenders demonstrated that "the lack of historical evidence should
not deter modern interpreters from arguing for a homosexual Lincoln."[38]
Scott Alarik observed in the *Boston Globe*, "He uses ambiguous evidence,
cherry-picked eyewitness accounts, psychosexual conclusions drawn from
tiny fragments of fact, and ever-changing standards of evaluation."[39] Historian David Greenberg, in surveying the familiar "evidence," revealed that
"[t]o bolster the case for his preferred interpretation, Tripp willfully reads
fact after fact to support his conclusions and to ignore or explain away other
possibilities. . . . Tripp produces not circumstantial evidence but facts that
resemble evidence only if one starts with a closed mind."[40] Greenberg
attributed "charitable" reviews of Tripp's work not to alternative assessments
of the case, but to the forces of political correctness, and, in the wake of
Eleanor Roosevelt and Thomas Jefferson, historical bet-hedging for fear of
being "proven wrong." This is, he concluded, a "shame": "After all, most

historians today are liberal and tolerant enough to happily accept his claims of Lincoln's bisexuality—if only someone were to offer some real evidence to prove it."[41] Greenberg's is an incredible claim, especially given that extant evidence, when marshaled, was deemed by the likes of Michael Bishop, director of the Lincoln Bicentennial Association, as "a mockery of historical method," "overheated speculation," "highly debatable," "extremely selective," "dismissed when put in proper historical context."[42] Or when, without explanation, Lincoln expert and talking head Harold Holzer succinctly rejected Tripp's work as "an embarrassment to serious historical discussion."[43] Despite "tantalizing evidence," Philip Nobile, former collaborator on Tripp's project, went so far as to call the book "a historical hoax."[44]

In light of this brief but representative survey, the impasse should be quite clear. Each side, generously demonstrated by the other, is exposed for its eye of faith, blindness, close-mindedness, willfulness, political agenda, cherry picking, distortion, and suppression. There is at once both a wealth and poverty of evidence: a beautifully rhetorical bind. One response to this bind is simply to generalize from Stansell's critique: "Tripp possesses enough historical training to know that evidence cannot be taken at face value, but he usually takes that principle as license to beat the sources for the confession that he is seeking."[45] The malleability of "real" evidence is evident enough. However, I would extend further to consider the presumption that does, in some sense, resolve the impasse, and the face value (i.e., ethos) that functions to mobilize and stabilize that presumption when the materiality of evidence is at issue.

To reveal the force of heteronormative presumption that weighs against Tripp's constituted evidence in this struggle is to observe the lack of struggle, the shortage of rigorous probing, when the Lincoln establishment itself engages in evidentiary license. With a good-natured smile and legitimating credentials, straight historical experts need little exertion to dismantle queer cases and to obfuscate the rhetorical process by which they themselves materialize Lincoln's sexual corpus. Prominent Lincoln scholar Douglas Wilson makes for a good case in point. While reportedly "very open-minded," Wilson discredited Tripp's book by saying that its evidence was "very, very shabby," that "without concrete proof the information is merely suggestive," and that "the evidence doesn't persuade me."[46] Assured of Wilson's openness and authority (and heterosexuality), one is less likely to question his standard of persuasive proof. If one did, as when Lewis Gannett published a damning exposé of Wilson's evidentiary gymnastics in perpetuating the Ann Rutledge legend, one would discover a beam in the normative eye of the beholder. Gannett concludes,

How did Douglas L. Wilson and other hard-core legend revivalists persuade them-selves that there is "overwhelming evidence" for an Abe-Ann romance? And why did the Lincoln establishment—composed as it largely is of very smart people—so credulously swallow the revival when the evidence behind it can so easily be shown to be far from "overwhelming"? . . . The only explanation that I can think of is that even smart people, when confronted with an argument they want to believe, will sometimes believe the argument despite poor evidence.[47]

That Wilson is as obviously guilty as Tripp in "beat[ing] sources for the confession he is seeking" is less striking than just how muscular Wilson's puny denial of Tripp appears in contrast to the ultimately feeble judgment established by Gannett's able-bodied critique of Wilson. The difference between the two lies in the presumptive silences that govern the process and product of evidentiary materialization.

More significant is David Donald's reading of Lincoln's sexuality, and its response. We may never know whether, as some have suggested, Don-ald's *"We Are Lincoln Men"* was a preemptive strike against Tripp's *Intimate World*.[48] Donald had been confronted with the question of Lincoln's sexuality during the 1995–1996 book tour for his magisterial biography *Lincoln* and amid the storm of controversy surrounding Larry Kramer's outing of Lincoln in 1999. He also was quite familiar with Tripp's project. Whatever the motives, Donald's book sought to definitively address the sexuality question, and to eliminate it. Illuminating are his remarks regarding the Lincoln-Speed relationship (the basis of his case against the homo-Lincoln thesis) in an interview on PBS's *News Hour*:

An extraordinary number of people kept asking on the last book tour, "Was Lincoln gay?" And so I felt it necessary to go into this in some detail. I think, with [*sic*] the gay liberation movement has had [a] need for heroes and heroines, and it would be rather nice to have Abraham Lincoln as your poster boy, wouldn't it? There have been some who tried to do that. There's one in particular [Larry Kramer], a man who's campaigned along this, and I'm amused and rather proud, I must say, that he has denounced me because I don't accept his views. They say, you know, David Donald can't be believed because he is "a dried up old Harvard heterosexual prune." [Laughs]

That's the most wonderful compliment anybody could pay to me. But I have tried to go over it very carefully, not merely what the evidence is, but with psycho-analysts and psychologists, and I think we're just about all agreed that Lincoln and Speed did not have a homosexual relationship. They were obviously fond of each other, they shared a great many things, and they loved each other in the way that Damian and Pytheas [*sic*] and David and Jonathan did. This was, I think, what Aris-totle talked about, the perfect friendship.[49]

Donald framed his research as an obligatory disciplinary response to the gay liberation movement's poster-boy politics (with its discernible circulation among book buyers), one implication of which was to disadvantage counter-normative historical claims while masking motives related to heteronorma-tivity. Why would Donald take jolly pride in Kramer's "compliment" if not for its placement of him, and Lincoln, squarely on the side of sexual nor-malcy? Consensus (a *fait accompli*?) had been achieved, in Donald's judg-ment, "not merely" from the evidence, but in confab with psychoanalysts and psychologists. Is a judgment thus determined more historically "true" than that offered by gay liberationists drawing on sexologists? Can deduction that begins with Aristotle's uninterrogated and uncontextualized definition of "perfect friendship" withstand scrutiny? If one is C. A. Tripp, the answers to the last questions would be "no," as so many of the reviews make plain. But Donald enjoys the affirmative force of presumption, and ethos's privilege of evidentiary license. His case, whatever might be said of its evidentiary flaws, is largely understood as *self-evident,* by which I mean authoritatively normative even when also construed as valid in a positivist sense.

Donald's Lincoln-Speed chapter in *"We Are Lincoln Men"* makes it abundantly clear that his judgment negating a homosexual Lincoln is "not merely" derived from the evidence.[50] In fact, adducing far fewer evidentiary fragments than does Tripp, Donald asserted that Lincoln was unquestionably straight because bed-sharing was common and without sexual implication, for which he offered no proof at all. The "Reuben Chronicles," in Donald's analysis, while being evidence of contemporary knowledge of sex between men, suggests nothing more because sodomy was infrequent and against the law (the former conclusion inferred from the small number of prosecuted sodomy cases). In a distortion of Anthony Rotundo's work, Donald argued that the Lincoln-Speed relationship was not homoerotic because the men were not young, homoeroticism being exclusive to youth (despite Rotundo's inclusion of Lincoln and Speed as an illustration of such "romantic friend-ship").[51] Their correspondence, far from being a smoking gun of homosexu-ality, when compared to "the letters between other enamored males that have been preserved" (undocumented by Donald), was "totally lacking in expres-sions of warm affection." During their cohabitation, Lincoln and Speed were "eagerly trying to get married . . . in love with the idea of being in love . . . interested in any eligible woman . . . so excited by the courtship game" (an effusive claim that, at least in Lincoln's case, is not born out, and perhaps contradicted, by extant evidence). Donald admitted that the evidence is "fragmentary and complex"; thus, he was "strongly influenced" by psycho-analyst/historian Charles Strozier, who concluded that a bisexual Lincoln would have been "torn between worlds, full of shame, confused, and hardly likely to end up in politics" (Strozier's psychoanalytic reading, as an anachronistic projection, is indistinguishable from those using Kinsey or any other contemporary rendering of sexual identity construction).[52] Finally, Donald is ultimately unconvinced of a gay Lincoln because Lincoln casually told the assistant U.S. attorney general in 1864 that he had slept with Speed for four years (another anachronistic inference, or at least an inference without an established provenance of homophobia in the nineteenth century).

Donald's evidence, in short, is shabby, and his method of adducing it is ironically decidedly similar to that of Tripp.[53] However, responses to Donald's book are doubly noteworthy in contrast to Tripp's reception. First, reviews, predominantly celebratory, were descriptive and nearly devoid of commentary regarding Donald's evidence. Especially important is the Speed chapter, Donald's judgment of which is taken on its face by prominent Lincoln historians. William Lee Miller wrote in the *New York Times Book Review*, "It is distressing to read that when Donald was on a publicity tour in 1995–96, the question most frequently asked about the greatest of political leaders was whether he was gay. Donald gamely takes four pages to explain patiently that the relationship between Lincoln and Joshua Speed was not sexual, not homoerotic."[54] Allen Guelzo observed in the *Journal of American History*, "[T]he most remarkable parts of *'We Are Lincoln Men'* are the ones where Donald considers what he is convinced was certainly not true about Lincoln's friendships: Lincoln's possible homoerotic attraction to Joshua Speed (which Donald dismisses sharply)."[55] Appraisals that took Donald's proof against a gay Lincoln as self-evident—and definitive—seem to have had less to do with evidence than the face value of the author and the normative position he was espousing. Harold Holzer revealed much in his review for *Civil War Times Illustrated*: "The great historian David Herbert Donald sheds new light on these questions in a wise, provocative, and scrupulously judicious book. . . . Donald still has a knack for making his conclusions seem the very last words on each subject."[56]

Second, others mobilized Donald's "last word" on Lincoln's sexuality as chief evidence against Tripp's case. Mohler, Alarik, and Ewers grounded Tripp's rejection in Donald's work, and more important, Donald's reputation. Ethos's role in arbitrating and lubricating the materiality of evidence was manifested in Dinita Smith's *New York Times* review, which noted those scholars favorably disposed to Tripp's project but emphasized its authoritative challenge: "Many, including the Harvard professor emeritus David Herbert Donald, who is considered the definitive biographer of Lincoln, disagreed with him. Last year, in his book *'We Are Lincoln Men,'* Mr. Donald mentioned Mr. Tripp's research and disputed his findings."[57] Perhaps this much can be expected in journalistic and overtly partisan coverage. However, historian Michael Burlingame adopted the same mode of refutation. His "dissenting" opinion that the book "does a disservice to history, for the evidence Dr. Tripp adduced fails to support the case" is emphatically shown to be shared by

> David Herbert Donald, author of *Lincoln's Herndon, Lincoln Reconsidered*, and two-time winner of the Pulitzer Prize. (More full disclosure: Professor Donald was my mentor in my undergraduate years at Princeton and in my graduate studies at Johns Hopkins, and though we disagree about Lincoln, I will be eternally grateful for all he did for me throughout the 1960s.) In his 2003 book, *"We Are Lincoln Men": Abraham Lincoln and His Friends*, Professor Donald addresses the two cases . . . that Dr. Tripp dwells on at greatest length and which provide the strongest evidence for his thesis that Lincoln was "primarily homosexual."

Burlingame's scrutiny does not extend to Donald's own assemblage and interpretation of evidence, for he merely restates Donald's case for a heterosexual Lincoln, about which they are in full agreement. Burlingame's leveraging of Donald's bona fides (and his own, for that matter) functions to solidify the materiality of Donald's evidence even as it displaces a direct examination of that evidence: a heteronormative variation on the fallacy of hypostatized proof.[58]

Ultimately, consensus will undoubtedly favor Donald's reading over Tripp's. However, the comparison of their cases, along with other examples of evidentiary usage by the Lincoln establishment, and the survey of responses to *The Intimate World of Abraham Lincoln*, all suggest that hard evidence is not appropriately a name for valid proof assembled in the service of a convincing positivist interpretation. Rather it signifies the rhetorical constitution of evidence's materiality, its cultural force, meaning, and resonance—and in this case, the material force of desire in that rhetorical constitution. By virtue of this illusory evidentiary struggle, we are really no closer to the "truth" of Lincoln's sexual body, and the dynamics of his intimate life, than when we began. Arguably, what we have are two versions of desirous gossip about Lincoln's desire, evidence that "[g]ossip . . . as a form of witnessed knowledge, is often taken by academics as being only as unreliable as the person conveying the information."[59] History and commemoration here are blurred, mutually contaminating, with all interested parties—historians, activists, editorialists, reviewers—functioning as reputational entrepreneurs, those who "attempt to control the memory of historical figures through motivation, narrative facility, and institutional placement."[60]

This judgment would be discouraging lest we differentially configure the stakes and effects of such wrangling over Lincoln's vexing corpus. To do so, we must first dislocate the prevailing understandings of what those stakes are. Perhaps unsurprisingly, those assessing Tripp's Lincoln devoted much space and energy to the question "what does it matter?" Ironically, most presumed to speak on Tripp's behalf, despite his own modest answer to that question:

> In short, the "contributions" of Lincoln's sex life are as yet not specifiable, with many factions expressing profound discomfort at such revelations, and insisting they would rather not hear any such evidence—plus the further risk of damaging a pristine icon—why indeed, not back away from this disagreeable search? One quick answer is that nowhere in science or psychology has it ever proved useful either to hide the truth or to follow a false flag.[61]

Even if one rightly suspects a deeper desire on Tripp's part for what such a revelation might bring, he is unwavering, at least in print, in his conservative commitment to a progressive realism in historiography—a fact-based enlargement of the historical Lincoln.[62]

Answers provided by various commentators to the "so what" question, while in some sense valuable, miss the broader identification and potential of a queer Lincoln. One category of response is historiographical, voiced by Christine Stansell: "Yet the virtue of this little book is to get you wondering. . . . Too insubstantial in themselves to prove anything about Lincoln, they [Tripp's evidentiary and interpretive "oddities"] do add to a larger body of evidence concerning sex before sexuality—that is, bodily life before the advent of the modern notion of an all-encompassing state that lies at the core of identity." Michael Bishop begrudgingly reached a similar conclusion: "Much of Tripp's 'evidence' can be dismissed when put in proper historical context, but not all of it. The author has failed to prove his case, but he has compiled enough suggestive material to ensure that Lincoln's sexuality will remain a matter of debate."[63]

The more prominent implication drawn from Tripp's case, variously articulated, is political. Jonathan Katz observed, "It challenges one of the fundamental prejudices that we continuously communicate: The stage of public life is owned by normative sexuality."[64] Beyond anti-homophobic work, Lincoln's revealed homosexuality portends a reconfiguration of sexuality in relation to national identity and memory, as Richard Schneider Jr. postulated: "It matters because we want America to see that it's quite possible for a great man to have been 'gay.' It matters because, just maybe, his very greatness had something to do with his sexual orientation."[65] Such a reconfiguration fits neatly with David Donald's claim of Lincoln's appropriation as poster boy by gay liberationists, and, more derisively in the judgment of Peter LaBarbera, executive director of the Illinois Family Institute, "[i]t is obviously moved by gays' need for validation."[66] By contrast, Andrew Sullivan pointedly reversed the identity politics in his assessment of the case:

> The truth about Lincoln—his unusual sexuality, his comfort with male-male love and sex—is not a truth today's Republican leaders want to hear. They are well-advised to attack and suppress it. They are more closely related to the forces Lincoln defeated than those he championed; and his candor, honesty and brave forging of a homosocial and homoerotic life in plain sight would appall them. The real Lincoln is their greatest rebuke; which is why they will do all they can to obscure the complicated, fascinating truth about the man whose legacy they are intent on betraying.[67]

Nevertheless, the resonant political investment was understood as gay affirming, not straight negating, eliciting a pseudo-sympathetic cautionary moral. Bret Stephens wrote in the *Wall Street Journal*, "I don't speak for the gay community, but it seems to me there's a risk in using the Gay Lincoln thesis as a political cudgel. . . . But gays are right to insist that Lincoln belongs to them as much as anyone else."[68] Cathy Young of the *Boston Globe* similarly advised, "[T]he desire to find gay heroes in history is understandable, given the vilification of gays that persists. But subordinating history to identity is never a good idea."[69]

The trouble with these stated implications is that they all presumptively depend on a positivist understanding of history, on the illusory promises and perils of evidentiary materiality. Richard Cohen of the *Washington Post* was mostly right when he concluded,

> Even if Lincoln had been gay, even if the book . . . had received mostly respectful reviews instead of general dismissal, it still would not matter. America would be as reluctant to face the prospect that one of its greatest presidents was gay as it once was to acknowledge that Thomas Jefferson fathered a child with one of his slaves, Sally Hemings. It would be dismissed, belittled. . . . Facts do not matter when faith is at stake. Fire the gay linguists.[70]

Instead of issuing a pink slip, I would let the rhetorical critic navigate a pink trajectory out of the morass, following Tom Chatt's call for a Kuhnian "conversion" or cultural paradigm shift toward gay experience—akin, he argues, to coming out—that requires not facts but a "queer eye" for the facts.[71] This will require a particular persuasion, a Lincolnian queer eloquence.

Such a paradigm shift requires, first, recognition that the battle, despite its representation, is not won or lost on the material grounds of historical/sexual "truth" but instead with the material force of desire for that historical/sexual "truth." Michele Orecklin accurately argued in *Time*, "But in assembling his data, Tripp is more persuasive in highlighting the rigidity of modern attitudes toward male friendships than in proving anything about Lincoln's sexuality."[72] More astutely, Christopher Capozzola in his insightful review of the reviews linked those attitudes to a specific motivating power: "But whatever [the affection Lincoln felt and expressed toward men] was, it stands now as a challenge to the orthodoxies of timelessness (whether fostered by the religious right or identity politicians), and as a testament to the power of human desire to shape and reshape our societies, and ourselves."[73]

Lincoln's "challenge to the orthodoxies of timelessness" to succeed must first be openly embodied, however. To become "a testament to the power of human desire," to become, as O'Hehir suggested, "an icon to our unrealized possibilities," Lincoln must be allowed to induce desire—straight desire, gay desire, and otherwise—that openly speaks its name. Rhetoric of evidentiary materiality masks or disavows desire even though desire is at the heart of its animating force, substituting a politics of adducement for a politics of inducement. However, adducement will not deliver the "real" sexual Lincoln; its futility is revealed in Chatt's observation that "[t]here's quite an interesting issue here about how much evidence is required to 'prove' that a historical figure was homosexual. Some of us will read Tripp's work and see a slam-dunk. Others would continue to dismiss it even if shown the stained sheets and the DNA results linking Lincoln and one of his 'longtime companions.' How can it be?"[74] The politics of adducement articulated by the rhetoric of evidentiary materiality only reveals the lovesick suitor and the cocksure cuckold. As this case reveals, on these grounds, Lincoln has eluded both C. A. Tripp and David Herbert Donald, and everyone else.

A queer critical politics of revelatory inducement, by contrast, would disrupt the hegemonic positivist methods and standards for interpreting and adjudicating Lincoln's sexuality. Following Gavin Butt, such a disruption would afford an opportunity to "address head-on the vexing problem of the limits of our knowledge of intimate life, and how the epistemological uncertainties which come to attend the subject of sexuality might come to affect the status of interpretive discourse, of history."[75] This forthright endeavor entails not a rejection of evidence *qua* evidence in constructing the past but a candid and ongoing assessment, what in this context amounts to an outing, of how and why historical fragments of sexual lives function, or are enjoined from functioning, as dispositive proof in the service of and relationship to sexual warrants and claims, past, present, and future.

The question, as Capozzola wisely argues, "should not be whether [Lincoln's sexuality] matters, but how."[76] We need to recognize that a sexual

Lincoln functions best not as a transhistorical/transcendent essentialist ideal, what Barry Schwartz would call a "lamp," nor merely as a "mirror" reflecting back to us our familiar and favorable contingent selves.[77] Rather, Lincoln should function instead as a strobe light, disrupting the seamlessness of our mirrored images, the firmness of our imagined origins, and the blindness with which we attend to them. Thus configured, Lincoln's unsettled and unsettling desire would highlight in flashes of illumination our own desires in motion, the shifting embodiments of our desire for the past. Lincoln's sexual/textual indeterminacy—what we might call his polysemous perversity—already awaits just such a critical politics of revelatory inducement. Lincoln is already queer. The hard evidence of Lincoln's vexing corpus simply needs an issuance of a queer writ of habeas corpus to set our desires free.

Notes

1.   See Charles E. Morris III, "My Old Kentucky Homo: Lincoln and the Politics of Queer Public Memory," in *Framing Public Memory*, ed. Kendall R. Phillips (Tuscaloosa: University of Alabama Press, 2004), 89–114. Jonathan Ned Katz's essay on Lincoln and Joshua Speed, with which he opened his 2001 book *Love Stories*, did not generate the same heat or onslaught of discourse, for reasons that are not entirely clear—perhaps because he did not claim that Lincoln was a homosexual, or due to his scholarship and reputation, or because Kramer and Tripp were more easily stuffed with straw by popular and academic commentators, and especially the Lincoln establishment. Jonathan Ned Katz, *Love Stories: Sex between Men before Homosexuality* (Chicago: University of Chicago Press, 2001).

2.   C. A. Tripp, *The Intimate World of Abraham Lincoln*, ed. Lewis Gannett (New York: Free Press, 2005), xxvii, 20.

3.   Joshua Shenk, based on an interview in June 2003, noted that Kramer has "quietly gone on the record admitting that he invented the documents for a work of fiction." This is the first and only report of Kramer's admission. Joshua Wolf Shenk, *Lincoln's Melancholy: How Depression Challenged a President and Fueled His Greatness* (Boston: Houghton Mifflin, 2005), 34.

4.   Gavin Butt, *Between You and Me: Queer Discourses in the New York Art World, 1948–1963* (Durham, NC: Duke University Press, 2005), 7. See also Stacy Wolf, "Desire in Evidence," *Text and Performance Quarterly* 17 (1997): 343–51; Faedra Chatard Carpenter, "Robert O'Hara's *Insurrection*: 'Que(e)rying' History," *Text and Performance Quarterly* 23 (2003): 186–204.

5.   Tripp, *Intimate World of Abraham*, xxxi; George W. Bush, "Remarks at the Abraham Lincoln Presidential Library and Museum Dedication in Springfield, Illinois" (speech, Sprinfield, IL, April 19, 2005), http://fdsys.gpo.gov/fdsys/pkg/WCPD-2005-04-25/pdf/WCPD-2005-04-25-Pg630.pdf; Stephen Koepp, "Probing the Mysteries of Mr. Lincoln," *Time*, July 4, 2005, 8; Jean Baker, "Introduction," in Tripp, *Intimate World of Abraham*, ix.

6.   Barry Schwartz, *Abraham Lincoln and the Forge of National Memory* (Chicago: University of Chicago Press, 2000), 11–12. For an alternative and instructive discussion

of the relationship between history and memory, see David Lowenthal, *The Past Is a Foreign Country* (Cambridge: Cambridge University Press, 2003), 210–38.

7. Scott Bravmann, *Queer Fictions of the Past: History, Culture, and Difference* (New York: Cambridge University Press, 1997), 25.

8. Joan W. Scott, "The Evidence of Experience," in *Questions of Evidence: Proof, Practice, and Persuasion across the Disciplines*, ed. James Chandler, Arnold I. Davidson, and Harry Harootunian (Chicago: University of Chicago Press, 1994), 366. See also Michel de Certeau, *The Writing of History*, trans. Tom Conley (New York: Columbia University Press, 1988); Alun Lunslow, *Deconstructing History* (London: Routledge, 1997); and Mary Fulbrook, *Historical Theory* (London: Routledge, 2002).

9. Barry Schwartz provides a good functional definition of the Lincoln establishment: "thousands of partisan biographers, historians, antiquarians, organizations, and curators." Of course, I emphasize the rhetorical nature of partisanship as key to this conception, which in part is derived from Carole Blair's discussion of the materiality of rhetoric as symbolic but, *pace* Lyotard and Foucault, at the same time not reducible to its symbolicity in accounting for its political effects. Barry Schwartz, "Lincoln at the Millennium," *Journal of the Abraham Lincoln Association* 24 (2003): 23; Carole Blair, "Contemporary U.S. Memorial Sites as Exemplars of Rhetoric's Materiality," in *Rhetorical Bodies*, ed. Jack Selzer and Sharon Crowley (Madison: University of Wisconsin Press, 1999), 20. For a definition of heteronormativity, see Lauren Berlant and Michael Warner, "Sex in Public," *Critical Inquiry* 24 (1998), 548.

10. Tripp, *Intimate World of Abraham*, xxxiii.

11. Christopher Wills, "Historians Defend Book on Abraham Lincoln," Associated Press, April 18, 2005, http://lexisnexis.com/. It is worth noting that Chesson made this comment on a panel titled "The Intimate Lincoln," part of a scholarly conference included in the dedication events of the ALPLM.

12. I favor Graham Robb's turn on this argument: "The idea that homosexuality is peculiar to certain periods reflects a natural tendency to confuse one's own history with the history of society." His reflection on Foucault is also useful within this context: "The great advantage of this theory was that it allowed sexuality to be studied in the light of history and sociology. Unfortunately, it has popularized the view that gay people have no real heritage before the 1870s. . . . This approach not surprisingly had a wide appeal beyond the scholarly gay community: it meant that that there was no continuous gay culture and that Socrates or Michelangelo could not be seen as 'gay'; it seemed to promise an automatic avoidance of anachronism." Graham Robb, *Strangers: Homosexual Love in the Nineteenth Century* (New York: W. W. Norton, 2003), 3, 11.

13. Katz, *Love Stories*, 10.

14. Christopher Capozzola, "The Gay Lincoln Controversy," *Boston Globe*, January 16, 2005.

15. Emmanuel Hertz, ed., *The Hidden Lincoln: From the Letters and Papers of William H. Herndon* (New York: Blue Ribbon Books, 1940), 208.

16. Katz, *Love Stories*, 11; Christine Stansell, "What Stuff!" *New Republic*, January 17, 2005, 21.

17. Tripp, *Intimate World of Abraham*, 60.

18. Michael Chesson, "Afterword: An Enthusiastic Endorsement," in Tripp, *Intimate World of Abraham*, 239.

19. Richard Brookhiser, "Was Lincoln Gay?" *New York Times*, January 9, 2005; Stansell, "What Stuff!" 25.

20. Baker, "Introduction," xiv.

21. Tripp, *Intimate World of Abraham*, 145.

22. R. W. Emerson, "Biographical Sketch," in *Excursions*, Henry D. Thoreau (Boston: Ticknor and Fields, 1863), 31. I originally discovered this quotation in the OED's listing for "circumstantial evidence." *Oxford English Dictionary Online*, s.v. "circumstantial evidence," http://www.oed.com/.

23. Tripp, *Intimate World of Abraham*, 9.

24. Tripp, *Intimate World of Abraham*, 112–16.

25. Tripp, *Intimate World of Abraham*, 127.

26. In a footnote, one discerns Tripp's sensitivity regarding the bed question: "Yes, 'four years,' as both Speed and Lincoln himself referred to it—and as gay rights advocacy writers repeatedly remind us. Actually, Lincoln and Speed occupied the same room alone for only two years. After that, young Billy Herndon and Charles R. Hurst shared Speed's room, though not his bed." Tripp, *Intimate World of Abraham*, 306n6. It is clear (and within the economy and expanse of his case, expediency seems an unconvincing explanation) that Tripp would not engage in, or be misunderstood as engaging in, any cheap or insubstantial argument regarding the Lincoln-Speed affair. However, he would have been right to ask, as Lewis Gannett and William Percy astutely did, why Lincoln and Speed slept in the same bed when another in the room existed and was most often unoccupied. "When Herndon and Hurst did not stay there—and, according to Donald, they spent their nights elsewhere for much of the four year period—Lincoln and Speed could have slept apart. They preferred to sleep together. For warmth on winter nights? Perhaps, but that still leaves spring, summer, and fall." Lewis Gannett and William A. Percy III, "Lincoln, Sex, and the Scholars," *Gay and Lesbian Review Worldwide* 13 (2006): 21.

27. Tripp, *Intimate World of Abraham*, 127–28.

28. As Tripp points out, the *duration* of Lincoln's residency in Speed's bed beyond the point of economic necessity cannot be accounted for in conventional narratives about same-sex sleeping arrangements, therefore providing another provocative piece of circumstantial evidence. Tripp, *Intimate World of Abraham*, 128.

29. Tripp, *Intimate World of Abraham*, 126.

30. Tripp, *Intimate World of Abraham*, 61–63.

31. Tripp, *Intimate World of Abraham*, xxxii, 39, 42–43, 67–89, 130, 306n10.

32. Andrew O'Hehir, "The Sexual Life of Abraham Lincoln," *Salon*, January 12, 2005, http://archive.salon.com/books/review/2005/01/12/lincoln/index_np.html.

33. Gore Vidal, "Was Lincoln Bisexual?" *Vanity Fair*, January 3, 2005, http://www.vanity fair.com/commentary/content/articles/050103roco02. Vidal's reference to lavender streaks and soft May violets derived from Carl Sandburg's memorable observation: "A streak of lavender ran through him [Speed]; he had spots soft as May violets. . . . Lincoln too had . . . a streak of lavender, and spots soft as May violets. . . . Their births, the loins and tissues of their fathers and mothers, accident, fate, providence, had given these two men streaks of lavender, spots soft as May violets." Carl Sandburg, *Abraham Lincoln: The Prairie Years* (New York: Blue Ribbon Books, 1926), 1:166–67.

34. "Equality Forum: National Celebration to Explore Closeted Gay U.S. Icons," US Newswire, April 11, 2005, http://releases.usnewswire.com/GetRelease.asp?id=45643.

35. Andrew Sullivan, "Abe and the Boys," *Advocate*, March 1, 2005, 72.

36. Charles Kaiser, "Honest, Abe Was Gay," *Advocate*, February 15, 2005, 62.

37. Larry Kramer, *The Tragedy of Today's Gays* (New York: Jeremy P. Tarcher, 2005), 81. In his introduction, Kramer claims that "for the past several years I had worked very hard

indeed—and against repulsive, odious opposition—to help bring to publication *The Intimate World of Abraham Lincoln*, by C. A. Tripp." *Tragedy of Today's Gays*, 19. Tripp makes no mention of Kramer's assistance, but, if his denial of political motive is true, he likely would have disapproved of Kramer's method and motive, as reported by Philip Nobile: "'IF YOU DON'T STOP MAKING A STINK about Tripp's book, I'm going to expose you as an enormous homophobe,' Larry Kramer telephoned me to say last October. 'For the sake of humanity, please, gays need a role model.'" Philip Nobile, "Honest, Abe?" *Weekly Standard*, January 17, 2005, http://www.weeklystandard.com/Content/Public/Articles/000/000/005/107koqzy.asp.

38. R. Albert Mohler Jr., "Was Abraham Lincoln Gay? Homosexuality and History," *Christian Post*, February 22, 2005, http://www.christianpost.com/article/editorial/289/section/was.abraham.lincoln.gay.homosexuality.and.history/1.htm.

39. Scott Alarik, "Questionable Look at President's Intimate Life," *Boston Globe*, January 23, 2005.

40. Scare quotes around the term "evidence" are a familiar feature of the negative reviews, marking Tripp's assemblage as suspect. But suspect on what grounds? One can infer from them a number of critiques questioning the materiality of homosexual proof on grounds of existence, ideology, sufficiency, or inference—but none are specifically designated. Rather, the marks function as a free-floating negation not only of Tripp's evidence, but of queer evidence as such. Although they were not intended to highlight the rhetorical nature of the process by which evidence is constituted as material, on my reading, they offer just such a "tell."

41. David Greenberg, "Why Has a New Book that Claims Lincoln Was Gay Been Treated so Charitably?" History News Network, January 24, 2005, http://hnn.us/articles/9653.html. This posture of benevolent welcome of the queer case, should it materialize, obfuscates the process that ensures such a case will be ever deferred by ambiguous yet authoritative evidentiary standards of the "real." Note, for instance, Lincoln scholar Michael Burlingame's posture regarding the Lincoln-Speed correspondence in an interview with NPR: "Well, I'd be willing to believe it if there were evidence, but I certainly don't see it in those letters." Openness on the subject of queer evidence functions well to obfuscate Burlingame's willful obtuseness and the politics of adducement, especially when coupled with a summary judgment of his "Respectful Dissent" in the afterword of *The Intimate World of Abraham Lincoln*: "Since it is virtually impossible to prove a negative, Dr. Tripp's thesis cannot be rejected outright. But given the paucity of hard evidence adduced by him, and given the abundance of contrary evidence indicating that Lincoln was drawn romantically and sexually to some women, a reasonable conclusion, it seems to me, would be that it is possible but highly unlikely that Abraham Lincoln was 'predominantly homosexual.'" In reading Burlingame's dissent it becomes clear that the force of his position comes not from his own skill in arguing the evidence, but from the heteronormative presumption that underwrites (and obviates the need to explicate and justify) competing measures of paucity and abundance. Scott Simon, "Interview: Exploring Lincoln's Loves," *NPR*, February 12, 2005, http://www.npr.org/templates/story/story.php?storyId =4495619; Michael Burlingame, "A Respectful Dissent," in Tripp, *Intimate World of Abraham*, 238.

42. Michael F. Bishop, "All the President's Men," *Washington Post*, February 13, 2005. For a similar critique, see Matthew Pinsker, review of *The Intimate World of Abraham Lincoln*, by C. A. Tripp, *Journal of American History* 92 (2006): 1442.

43. Quoted in Christopher Capozzola, "'The Lincoln Book: Reviewing the Reviews," *Gay*

and *Lesbian Review Worldwide* 12 (2005): 44. Holzer apparently did not think that pandering on behalf of Lincoln for Discovery Channel's "Greatest American" contest constituted a similar embarrassment to serious historical discussion. More to the point, Holzer's refusal on more than one occasion to seriously engage the case of Lincoln's sexuality seemingly reveals his own ideological investment and the rhetorical gamesmanship that protects it. His response is an equivalent of *U.S. News and World Report*'s cover for Justin Ewer's "special report" on Lincoln: "Gay? Nah, Forget about It." Ewers, "The Real Lincoln," *U.S. News and World Report*, February 21, 2005, 67–73.

44. In an explosive review in the *Weekly Standard*, Philip Nobile, who has become known for exposing prominent authors such as Doris Kearns Goodwin for alleged plagiarism, claimed, "This book is a hoax and a fraud: a historical hoax, because the inaccurate parts are all shaded toward a predetermined conclusion, and a literary fraud, because significant portions of the accurate parts are plagiarized—from me, as it happens." Nobile's article offers provocative and compelling objections regarding Tripp's case, but his use of the word "hoax" is hyperbolic, misleading, and, as defined, would apply to most who have weighed in on Lincoln's sexuality, as my analysis demonstrates. Moreover, Nobile's second charge, that of Tripp's plagiarism of his contributions to the book during their five-year professional partnership, raises serious questions about his motives for such a complete rejection of Tripp's "Gay Lincoln Theory." After all, as Andrew Sullivan correctly pointed out in their heated public exchange, Nobile's 2001 article "Don't Ask, Don't Tell, Don't Publish" discussed his thwarted effort to publish a book on Lincoln's sexuality (bisexuality, he argued) that he planned to title *A Harp of a Thousand Strings: The Queer Lincoln Theory* and that appeared to advance many of the same key examples and evidence utilized by Tripp. Nobile's explanation for this "shift" seems defensive, to say the least, and generally unconvincing. Philip Nobile, "Honest Abe? A Dishonest Book Claims Lincoln as the First Log Cabin Republican," *Weekly Standard*, January 17, 2005, 31–38; Andrew Sullivan, "Philip Nobile Busts Himself," *The Daily Dish*, January 12, 2005, http://www.andrewsullivan.com (article no longer available online); Philip Nobile, "Don't Ask, Don't Tell, Don't Publish: Homophobia in Lincoln Studies?" History News Network, June 10, 2001, http://hnn.us/articles/97.html; Philip Nobile, "Honest Abe? (cont.): The Author Answers Andrew Sullivan," *Daily Standard*, January 13, 2005, http://www.weeklystandard.com/Content/Public/Articles/000/000/005/130schzy.asp.

45. Stansell, "What Stuff!" 24.

46. Wilson quoted in Wills, "Historians Defend Book"; William Bunch, "Was Abe Gay?" Knight Ridder Tribune News Service, May 2, 2005, 1; Joe Crea, "New Book Will Claim Abe Lincoln Was Gay," *Express Gay News*, November 5, 2004, 10.

47. Lewis Gannett, "Scandal Brewing in Lincoln Country," *Gay and Lesbian Review Worldwide* 11 (2004), 17–18. See also Lewis Gannett, "'Overwhelming Evidence' of a Lincoln-Ann Rutledge Romance? Reexamining Rutledge Family Reminiscences," *Journal of the Abraham Lincoln Association* 26 (2005): 28–41. The applications and assessments of the Lincoln-Rutledge relationship by Tripp and his detractors belie Barry Schwartz's claim that "The virtual forgetting of Ann Rutledge manifests the loss of interest in the folk hero, traditional romance, loyalty, and family values. Ann's fading marks the emergence of a new culture, a postmodern culture in which her symbolic presence is not only unneeded but also unwelcome." Barry Schwartz, "Ann Rutledge in American Memory: Social Change and the Erosion of a Romantic Drama," *Journal of the Abraham Lincoln Association* 26 (2005), http://www.historycooperative.org/journals/jala/26.1/schwartz.html.

48. Historian William A. Percy wrote on amazon.com, "When I put C. A. Tripp in contact with David Donald, whom I described to Tripp as the leading Lincoln scholar, I warned him that however much he might learn from David, he could not even hope that David would accept the thesis that Abe had homosexual experiences, and I predicted that David would write a preemptive strike. It duly appeared: 'We Are Lincoln Men: Abraham Lincoln and His Friends.'" William A. Percy, review of *"We are Lincoln Men": Abraham Lincoln and His Friends*, by David Herbert Donald, http://www.amazon.com/gp/cdp/ member-reviews/AUZT24F0U439H/ref=cm_pdp_home_reviews/002-7162442-0898418 ?%5Fencoding=UTF8. The same account is offered in Ganett and Percy, "Lincoln, Sex, and the Scholars," 19.

49. Margaret Warner, "We Are Lincoln Men," *OnlineNewsHour*, November 26, 2003, http://www.pbs.org/newshour/bb/entertainment/july-dec03/donald_11-26.html.

50. David Herbert Donald, *"We Are Lincoln Men": Abraham Lincoln and His Friends* (New York: Simon and Schuster, 2003), 29–64.

51. In reading Rotundo's *American Manhood*, especially chapter 4, one gets a sense of how directly Donald's conceptualization of male friendship must have been oriented by the work. At the same time, it is striking that Donald, in appropriating *American Manhood* for his analysis of the Lincoln-Speed relationship, narrowly construes (to the point of distortion) Rotundo's nuanced discussion of nineteenth-century male friendship, including its sometimes romantic and even erotic dimensions. Despite Donald's claim that Lincoln and Speed should be understood as outside the definition of romantic friendship because of their age, Rotundo in his discussion twice offers their relationship as an example. Ironically, Rotundo's conceptualization of nineteenth-century romantic male friendship would have supported Donald's claim that the Lincoln-Speed relationship was not homosexual in a twentieth-century sense. Note, for instance, Rotundo's commentary on the relationship between Albert Dodd and James Blake, which would apply equally to his understanding of Lincoln and Speed: "Albert Dodd and James Blake shifted easily between their love for men and their love for women. They saw nothing strange in their physical relationships with close male friends, and they felt no sense of tension between their intimate lives and the positions of social respectability which they pursued. Yet, to the twentieth-century eye, the words and deeds of those men do appear strange. How can we grasp their undisguised affection for other males and their lack of anxiety about physical romance with their own sex?" That Donald did not, and perhaps would not, go so far as Rotundo in contextualizing and conceptualizing the Lincoln-Speed romantic friendship is suggestive. I want to note that Tripp's case, too, is impoverished by failing to account for the specificities of nineteenth-century same-sex relationships. E. Anthony Rotundo, *American Manhood: Transformations in Masculinity from the Revolution to the Modern Era* (New York: BasicBooks, 1993), chapter 4, 82, 85, 88. For a more thoughtful engagement of Rotundo's work as it applies to the case of Lincoln's sexuality, see Shenk, *Lincoln's Melancholy*, 34–36. At the same time, Shenk foregoes such careful analysis in his article "The True Lincoln" for *Time*'s special issue on Lincoln, opting instead for a summary rejection of the idea that Lincoln was gay. In the spotlight, one surmises, the heteronormative bandwagon is a comfortable and advantageous location. Joshua Wolf Shenk, "The True Lincoln," *Time*, July 4, 2005, 39, 42.

52. It is interesting to note that Donald emphasized Charles Strozier in this instance instead of Harry Stack Sullivan, whom Donald identifies earlier in the book as a central influence on his conceptualization of male friendship. One could argue that Sullivan's own likely homosexuality and sympathy for homosexuals in his work account for this. Sullivan

wrote, "Since I have set up three classifications of intimacy, four classifications of the interpersonal objective of the integration of lust, and six classifications of genital relationship, this results in seventy-two theoretical patterns of sexual behavior involving two real partners. . . . From this statement, I would like you to realize, if you realize nothing else, how fatuous it is to toss out the adjectives 'heterosexual,' 'homosexual,' or 'narcissistic' to classify a person as to his sexual and friendly integrations with others. Such classifications are not anywhere near refined enough for intelligent thought; they are much too gross to do anything except mislead both the observer and the victim. For example, to talk about homosexuality's being a problem really means about as much as to talk about humanity's being a problem." Strozier, without an iota of proof, dismissed the idea of Lincoln's homosexuality, a much more comfortable and expedient association for Donald. Kathleen Dalton, in one of the few reviews at all critical of Donald's book, observed, "Donald is most sure-footed in the political arena, and he stumbles briefly only when he evokes psychoanalysis to explain Lincoln's sexuality. When it comes time to dismiss the charge made by a few historians that Lincoln and Speed had a homosexual relationship, Donald quotes the psychoanalytically inclined expert, Charles Strozier. . . . Invoking psychoanalysis, which has always suffered from myopia about homosexuality, may not have been the best choice for a biographer." Donald, *"We Are Lincoln Men,"* xv, 9; F. Barton Evans III, *Harry Stack Sullivan: Interpersonal Theory and Psychotherapy* (London: Routledge, 1996), 17–20; Harry Stack Sullivan, *The Interpersonal Theory of Psychiatry* (New York: W. W. Norton, 1953), 194; Kathleen Dalton, "Lincoln's Emotional Life, Ably Rendered," *Boston Globe*, February 29, 2004. See also the trenchant critique of Donald and Strozier in Gannett and Percy, "Lincoln, Sex, and the Scholars."

53. One could, for instance, insert Donald's name in place of Tripp's in Pinsker's *Journal of American History* review, for his criticisms are equally applicable, though no member of the Lincoln Establishment would ever say such things about Donald's scholarship. Pinsker, review of *Intimate World of Abraham*.

54. William Lee Miller, "The Stovepipe League," *New York Times Book Review*, January 18, 2004.

55. Allen C. Guelzo, review of *"We are Lincoln Men": Abraham Lincoln and His Friends*, by David Herbert Donald, *Journal of American History* 91 (2004), 1023. See also Robert S. Eckley, review of *"We are Lincoln Men": Abraham Lincoln and His Friends*, by David Herbert Donald, *Journal of the Abraham Lincoln Association* 25 (2004), 71–81.

56. Harold Holzer, review of *"We are Lincoln Men": Abraham Lincoln and His Friends*, by David Herbert Donald, *Civil War Times Illustrated* 42 (2004), 70.

57. Dinita Smith, "Finding Homosexual Threads in Lincoln's Legend," *New York Times*, December 16, 2004.

58. David Hackett Fischer conceptualizes the fallacy of hypostatized proof: "In historical scholarship, this form of error commonly occurs when a historian reifies a historiographical interpretation and substitutes it for the actual historical event it allegedly represents, and then rejects contradictory interpretations or affirms compatible ones." Hackett, *Historians' Fallacies: Toward a Logic of Historical Thought* (New York: Harper Torchbooks, 1970), 56.

59. Butt, *Between You and Me*, 6–7.

60. Gary Alan Fine, "Reputational Entrepreneurs and the Memory of Incompetence: Melting Supporters, Partisan Workers, and Images of President Harding," *American Journal of Sociology* 101 (1996), 1159. Barry Schwartz's conceptualization is useful in accounting for the present case: "Reputational entrepreneurs sometimes make this connection [be-

tween national identity and national memory] with a view to promoting and protecting their own interests; sometimes, with a view to promoting and protecting the interests of society at large. The consequence differs. An audience manipulated into associating its interests with a particular conception of the past will withdraw its commitment as soon as the manipulation ends; but if entrepreneurs and their audience share the same values, then reputational enterprise will sustain rather than create collective memory." Schwartz, *Abraham Lincoln and the Forge*, 295.

61. Tripp, *Intimate World of Abraham*, xxxi.

62. For an instructive discussion on the progressive realist or just-the-facts perspective, see Richard Handler and Eric Gable, *The New History in an Old Museum: Creating the Past at Colonial Williamsburg* (Durham, NC: Duke University Press, 1997), 78–101.

63. Stansell, "What Stuff!" 21, 25; Bishop, "All the President's Men".

64. Quoted in James Janega, "Book Trying to 'Out' Lincoln Sparks Civil War of Words," *Chicago Tribune*, February 26, 2005.

65. Richard Schneider Jr., "Back to the Future," *Gay and Lesbian Review Worldwide* 12 (2005), 4. Similarly, historian John D'Emilio observed of the recent rise of "craving for disclosing the 'gay lives' of celebrated figures from the past," "[i]t's so American to feel this need to look to past models to legitimize a group's history. It began with women and blacks and now it's taken up by gays and lesbians. The difference with homosexuality is that it is never so clear-cut, so even when the evidence is clear, it's not clear enough." Richard A. Kaye, "Outing Abe," *Village Voice*, June 25–July 1, 2003, http://www .villagevoice.com/news/0326,kaye,45061,1.html.

66. Quoted in Janega, "Book Trying to 'Out' Lincoln."

67. Andrew Sullivan, "True Enough," *The New Republic Online*, January 11, 2005, https:// ssl.tnr.com/p/docsub.mhtml?i=express&s=sullivan011105.

68. Bret Stephens, "Honestly, Abe Is Still One of All of Us," *Wall Street Journal*, January 14, 2005.

69. Cathy Young, "Co-Opting Lincoln's Sexuality," *Boston Globe*, January 31, 2005.

70. Richard Cohen, "Don't Ask, Don't Think," *Washington Post*, January 18, 2005.

71. Tom Chatt, "Gay Abe—A Paradigm Shift," *UpWord*, January 12, 2005, http://upword .blogspot.com/2005/01/gay-abe-paradigm-shift.html.

72. Michele Orecklin, "All the President's Men," *Time*, January 17, 2005, 62.

73. Capozzola, "Lincoln Book," 45.

74. Chatt, "Gay Abe."

75. Butt, *Between You and Me*, 9.

76. Capozzola, "Lincoln Book," 45.

77. To clarify Schwartz's distinction between mirror and lamp as metaphors for the functions of collective memory, take his commentary regarding Lincoln during the Progressive era: "Abraham Lincoln, however, 'stood for' the Progressive era in two senses. He was a model *for* progressivism, shaping and illuminating its values and framing its members' experiences; he was a model *of* progressivism, mirroring progressive ideals that were not altogether his." My critique of the configurations of Lincoln by Tripp and those who responded to *The Intimate World of Abraham Lincoln* suggests that they problematically constituted Lincoln-as-mirror. However, I do not favor Lincoln-as-lamp as an alternative construction because, as I understand Schwartz's conceptualization, I reject an essential-ized, transhistorical or transcendent configuration of Lincoln, even though my under-standing of a queer Lincoln conceives of him as more lamp than mirror. Instead, I opt for the metaphor of Lincoln as strobe light. Schwartz, *Abraham Lincoln and the Forge*, 141,

251–55. Schwartz's conceptualization is derived in part from the work of Abrams and Handelman. See M. H. Abrams, *The Mirror and the Lamp: Romantic Theory and the Critical Tradition* (New York: Oxford University Press, 1953); and Don Handelman, *Models and Mirrors: Towards an Anthropology of Public Events* (Cambridge: Cambridge University Press, 1990).

CHAPTER 8

Encomium of Helen's Body: A Will to Matter

Nathan Stormer, University of Maine

Encomium of Helen's Body

(1) What is becoming to a city is manpower, to a body beauty, to a soul wisdom, to an action virtue, to a speech truth, and the opposites of these are unbecoming. Man and woman and speech and deed and city and object should be honored with praise if praiseworthy and incur blame if unworthy, for it is an equal error and mistake to blame the praisable and to praise the blamable. (2) It is the duty of one and the same man both to speak the needful rightly and to refute the unrightfully spoken. Thus it is right to refute those who rebuke Helen, a woman about whom the testimony of inspired poets has become univocal and unanimous as had the ill omen of her name, which has become a reminder of misfortunes. For my part, by introducing some reasoning into my speech, I wish to free the accused of blame and, having reproved her detractors as prevaricators and proved the truth, to free her from their ignorance.

(3) Now it is not unclear, not even to a few, that in nature and in blood the woman who is the subject of this speech is preeminent among preeminent men and women. For it is clear that her mother was Leda, and her father was in fact a god, Zeus, but allegedly a mortal, Tyndareus, of whom the former was shown to be her father because he was and

(1) What is "becoming" to a discourse is willfulness, to a body matter, to a soul essence, to an action cause, to a sign effect, and their opposites are seen as "unbecoming." Man and woman and sign and deed and discourse and object will remain as "body" if actual and obtain "mind" if virtual, though there is an equal desire and longing to revoke the actual and to invoke the virtual. (2) It fulfills desire and longing for me both to speak of rhetoric uncommonly and to estrange the commonly spoken. Thus it is time to expose that which embodies "Helen," a body about which the testimony of countless theorists has been univocal in eulogizing the fine passivity of her frame, which has become a commonplace for coercion. For my part, by weaving my reasoning into Gorgias's speech, I wish to write her body anew and, having made her a condition for rhetoric to act and shown her strength, to write her body from stillness.

(3) Now it is not unknown, not always to be sure, that in being and in myth the body that is the subject of this text is necessary among necessities of rhetoric. She is born when space opens between substance, and that which inhabits it with power, force, for on a farther shore she stands, Helen's body, a mythic figure for the gap that divides the

the latter was disproved because he was said to be, and the one was the most powerful of men and the other the Lord of all.

(4) Born from such stock, she had god-like beauty, which taking and not mistaking, she kept. In many did she work much desire for her love, and her one body was the cause of bringing together many bodies of men thinking great thoughts for great goals, of whom some had greatness of wealth, some the glory of ancient nobility, some the vigor of personal agility, some command of acquired knowledge. And all came because of a passion which loved to conquer and a love of honor which was unconquered. (5) Who it was and why and how he sailed away, taking Helen as his love, I shall not say. To tell the knowing what they know shows it is right but brings no delight. Having now gone beyond the time once set for my speech, I shall go on to the beginning of my future speech, and I shall set forth the causes through which it is likely that Helen's voyage to Troy should take place.

(6) For either by will of Fate and decision of the gods and vote of necessity did she do what she did, or by force reduced or by words seduced or by love possessed. Now if through the first, it is right for the responsible one to be held responsible; for god's predetermination cannot be hindered by human premeditation. For it is the nature of things, not for the strong to be hindered by the weak, but for the weaker to be ruled and drawn by the stronger, and for the stronger to lead and the weaker to follow. God is a stronger force than man in might and in wit and in other ways. If then one must place blame on Fate and on a god, one must free Helen from disgrace.

(7) But if she was raped by violence and illegally assaulted and unjustly insulted, it is clear that the raper, as the insulter, did the wronging, and the raped, as the insulted, did the suffering. It is right then for the barbarian who undertook a barbaric undertaking in word and law and deed to meet with blame in

world of "what is" from the world that yearns to emerge from "what is said to be," and closing the gap is rhetoric's motive and therein lies a paradox.

(4) Born of this breach, Helen grounds rhetoric, which takes her for and so mistakes, all bodies. In many acts she sparks a great *will to matter*, for her one body is the frame for combining many bodies of rhetoric seeking real flesh for real clout, of which some chase the means of wealth, some the texture of purified ancestry, some the vigor of disciplined biology, some the halls of archived knowledge. And all are moved to seal the rift between worldliness and a will that is always not yet worldly. (5) Who did it and why and how a rift opened, taking Helen so to speak, I shall not say. To tell the knowing no one knows says what is right but brings no delight. Having now gone beyond the theme once set by this speech, I shall steal a myth for the beginning of future theory, and I shall show that to hold will and matter pulled apart by Helen's voyage to Troy lauds Helen.

(6) For either by will of law and decision of the rule and vote of the negative does she ever stand apart, or by pain suffered or by past recalled or by world perceived. Now if through the first, it is clear that the dominant power should be seen as dominant; but the law's predetermination cannot live absent the body's reiteration. It is a riddle of law and things that if the body must take heed of the law, then must the law be already hosted by the body, and so the body may lead and the law may follow. Thus a will to matter confronts a matter enlivened by will. If then one must afford to law the negative, one must let Helen have power.

(7) But if she was raped by violence and illegally assaulted and unjustly insulted, then by these acts the raper, as the subjecter, is embodied, and the raped, as the subjected, is disembodied. Will takes shape then through the violence that energizes such violent enervation in word and law and deed, so

word, exclusion in law, and punishment in deed. And surely it is proper for a woman raped and robbed of her country and deprived of her friends to be pitied rather than pilloried. He did the dread deeds; she suffered them. It is just therefore to pity her but to hate him.

(8) But if it was speech which persuaded her and deceived her heart, not even to this is it difficult to make an answer and to banish blame as follows. Speech is a powerful lord, which by means of the finest and most invisible body effects the divinest works: it can stop fear and banish grief and create joy and nurture pity. I shall show how this is the case, since (9) it is necessary to offer proof to the opinion of my hearers: I both deem and define all poetry as speech with meter. Fearful shuddering and tearful pity and grievous longing come upon its hearers, and at the actions physical sufferings of others in good fortunes and in evil fortunes, through the agency of words, the soul is wont to experience a suffering of its own. But come, I shall turn from one argument to another. (10) Sacred incantations sung with words are bearers of pleasure and banishers of pain, for, merging with opinion in the soul, the power of the incantation is wont to beguile it and persuade it and alter it by witchcraft. There have been discovered two arts of witchcraft and magic: one consists of errors of soul and the other of deceptions of opinion. (11) All who have and do persuade people of things do so by molding a false argument. For if all men on all subjects had both memory of things past and awareness of things present and foreknowledge of the future, speech would not be similarly similar, since as things are now it is not easy for them to recall the past nor to consider the present nor to predict the future. So that on most subjects most men take opinion as counselor to their soul, but since opinion is slippery and insecure it casts those employing it into slippery and insecure successes. (12) What cause then prevents the conclusion that Helen similarly, against her will, might have come under the influence of

made from hate in word, transgression in law, and savagery in deed. And if matter be a victim like Helen raped and robbed of her body and deprived of her strength then will invades as well as incarnates. Hence, bedlam binds them; sex severs them. Riven by brutal union, matter wastes as the will feasts.

(8) But if it was speech that addressed her and compelled her to leave, this only strengthens the necessity to seek a body so to manifest such address. Speech mimics the force of law, which by means of prepossessed and barely visible matter effects great cultural work: it can urge death and define life and create guilds and nurture habits. I shall show memory guides this, since (9) it is necessary to remember the past to address the future: I both deem and define rhetoric as incarnation addressed. Needful invention and fitful habit and canny desire animate its hearers, and for the actions and physical regimens that conserve both good cultures and bad cultures, through the agency of words, the will is thought to extend regimens to new bodies and old. And so I must turn one argument into another. (10) Common invocations wrought from words are bearers of pleasure and begetters of pain, for, merging sensoria with the will, the power of the invocation is wont to compose it and persuade it and fashion it by discourse. I have thus confounded two planes of discourse and address: one consists of ether of will and the other of material media. (11) All who have and do persuade find in things the means needed for molding flesh into discourse. For all persuasions of all people find memory in things past and embedded in things present and prefigured in the future, yet they are not similarly similar, since it is things rather than will that allow us to recall the past and to configure the present and to prefix the future. So then for most desires most people take matter as residue of some will, but matter is resistant and mutable and leaves those deciphering it with resistant and mutable recollections. (12) Does not a breach place the body of Helen similarly, apart from will,

speech, just as if ravished by the force of the mighty? For it was possible to see how the force of persuasion prevails; persuasion has the form of necessity, but it does not have the same power. For speech constrained the soul, persuading it which it persuaded, both to believe the things said and to approve the things done. The persuader, like a constrainer, does the wrong and the persuaded, like the constrained, in speech is wrongly charged. (13) To understand that persuasion, when added to speech, is wont also to impress the soul as it allow wishes, one must study: first, the words of Astronomers who, substituting opinion for opinion, taking away one but creating another, make what is incredible and unclear seem true to the eyes of opinion; then, second, logically necessary debates in which a single speech, written with art but not spoken with truth, bends a great crowd and persuades; and, third, the verbal disputes of philosophers in which the swiftness of thought is also shown making the belief in an opinion subject to easy change. (14) The effect of speech upon the condition of the soul is comparable to the power of drugs over the nature of bodies. For just as different drugs dispel different secretions from the body, and some bring an end to disease and others to life, so also in the case of speeches, some distress, others delight, some cause fear, others make the hearers bold, and some drug and bewitch the soul with a kind of evil persuasion.

(15) It has been explained that if she was persuaded by speech she did not do wrong but was unfortunate. I shall discuss the fourth cause in a fourth passage. For if it was love which did all these things, there will be no difficulty in escaping the charge of the sin which is alleged to have taken place. For the things we see do not have the nature which we wish them to have, but the nature which each actually has. Through sight the soul receives an impression even in its inner features. (16) When belligerents in war buckle on their warlike accouterments of

cleft by the address of discourse that seeks her, yet re-"membering" her through the same force that cleaves? Matter makes possible that which the force of persuasion embodies; persuasion has the form of necessity, but needs memory to have power. Matter constrains the will, persuading it which it persuaded, both to find in things its past and to seek through things its fate. The persuader, like a constrainer, is worldly and the persuaded, as the constrained, is not unworldly either. (13) That for an action to persuade, to be embodied, it must already impress the will with some persuasion, can be seen in: first, the discourse of scientists that, substituting sensation for sensation, suppressing the one but foregrounding another, makes what was once illegible perception now legible dictation; then, second, perfectly ordinary debates as rituals of speech, writing norms through speakers' disciplines, hail a public and persuade; and, third, the verbal reports of talking heads that change in the swiftness of time and only circulate through belief in the senses of subjects that attend them. (14) The effect of matter on the condition of the will is comparable to the power of drugs over the landscape of the mind. For just as different drugs arrange different sensations within the mind, and some bring an end to desires and others to life, so also in the case of bodies, some inspire, others seduce, some can haunt, others satiate cravings, and some flood and besot the will with a kind of evil persuasion.

(15) It has been explained that if she was persuaded by speech she not only was swayed but too was suasive. I shall discuss the fourth cause in a fourth passage. For if the senses are what set her apart, there is another facet to the paradoxical schism and union which I have alleged must take place. For the things we sense do not have a nature which we want them to have, but a nature which has what we want. Through the senses the will is embodied even in its inner yearnings. (16) When belligerents in war battle with their long-range armaments of bombs and bullets,

bronze and steel, some designed for defense, others for offense, if the sight sees this, immediately it is alarmed and it alarms the soul, so that often men flee, panic stricken, from future danger as though it were present. For strong as is the habit of obedience to the law, it is ejected by fear resulting from sight, which coming to a man causes him to be indifferent both to what is judged honorable because of the law and to the advantage to be derived from victory. (17) It has happened that people, after having seen frightening sights, have also lost presence of mind for the present moment; in this way fear extinguishes and excludes thought. And many have fallen victim to useless labor and dread diseases and hardly curable madnesses. In this way the sight engraves upon the mind images of things which have been seen. And many frightening impressions linger, and what lingers is exactly analogous to what is spoken. (18) Moreover, whenever pictures perfectly create a single figure and form from many colors and figures, they delight the sight, while the creation of statues and the production of works of art furnish a pleasant sight to the eyes. Thus it is natural for the sight to grieve for some things and to long for others, and much love and desire for many objects and figures is engraved in many men. (19) If, therefore, the eye of Helen, pleased by the figure of Alexander, presented to her soul eager desire and contest of love, what wonder? If, being a god, love has the divine power of the gods, how could a lesser being reject and refuse it? But if it is a disease of human origin and a fault of the soul, it should not be blamed as a sin, but regarded as an affliction. For she came, as she did come, caught in the net of Fate, not by the plans of the mind, and by the constraints of love, not by the devices of art.

(20) How then can one blame of Helen as unjust, since she is utterly acquitted of all charge, whether she did what she did through falling in love or persuaded by speech or ravished by force or constrained by divine things and constraint?

some destined for soldiers, others for families, if the ear hears this, immediately it is alarmed and it alarms the will, so that often we cry, grief stricken, over future anguish as though it were present. For strong as is the habit of obedience to the law, it is reified in to perceptions of the senses, which coming to people cause them to be contemptuous both of what is judged honorable because of the law and of the advantage to be derived from victory. (17) It has happened that people, after having heard terrible sounds, have lost the safe presence of place for the present moment; in this way sense marks the ends and limits of will. And many have fallen victim to useless pursuits and dread devotions and hardly curable obsessions. In this way perception confines the will with scenes of what was and could be. And many powerful impressions linger, and what lingers is vitally necessary to form rhetoric. (18) Moreover, whenever sculptures perfectly create a single figure and form from many contours and textures, they instruct the touch, while the creation of pictures and the production of artworks furnish an education to the eyes. Thus it is normal for the senses to learn from some and hide from others, and so means and desire to seek out objects and figures are engraved by sensation. (19) If, therefore, with eyes on Helen, as a sexed figure for worldly substance, sight suggests the course to unite desire and Helen's body, what wonder? If, being like law, senses have the marking power of the law, how could the will reject and refuse this course? And if senses are needed to imagine action and to outline the will, matter should not be viewed as blank, but regarded as a repertory. For she stands, as she did stand, as the means to sense, not as the object of sense; and as the constraint on will, not as the canvas of will.

(20) How then can one talk of Helen as docile, since she is utterly essential to action, whether she does what she does by sensing the world or remembering the past or suffering pain or legitimizing the law?

(21) I have by means of speech removed disgrace from a woman; I have observed the procedure which I set up at the beginning of the speech; I have tried to end the injustice of blame and the ignorance of opinion; I wished to write a speech which would be a praise of Helen and a diversion to myself.

(21) I have by mimicry made rhetoric womanly; I have confused the opposition between matter's blunt end and the will's sharp edge; I have tried to ask how rhetoric can act and what sex has got to do with it; I wished to write a speech that would laud Helen's body and be a diversion to myself.

What?

Why would someone do such a thing? Why write such an odd appropriation of a near-sacred text in the history of rhetoric? After spending several years explaining things, I wanted to make something instead. In a way, the materiality of being a scholar can be very confining, what with the specific practices of researching and writing one has to master to produce peer-reviewed articles and monographs. I had the opportunity to try something different and so I did. Armed with a slab of a thesaurus, I took a translation of Gorgias's "Encomium" I had taught many times and, keeping the syllabic and grammatical structure as much as possible, I substituted language to write a meditation on a will to matter.[1] It has been rattling around my head for a long time, "a will to matter." I did not have the usual stack of works to reference. I did not fret over citing concepts that would reveal a clear path out of my briar patch of ideas. I placed stringent, unusual limits on my expression and forced myself to synthesize through play, which I would never have done otherwise. It was annoying but fun.

As I have rewritten them, the four arguments are provocations around this idea of a will to matter, not answers; these are lines, not endpoints. The arguments are an effort to estrange familiar ideas about materiality in rhetoric by estranging a beloved speech that dwells on materiality, yet preserving the allegory at the center of the text. My interest is to create new topoi, neither mutually exclusive nor necessarily dependent, for theorizing materialism and rhetoric. Ultimately, I do not want to talk about what it "actually means," as if there is a didactic lesson I am withholding, but to provoke you.

There is no precise origin for the phrase "a will to matter," no story of its derivation, but it has the ring of several other concepts. Certainly, it calls to mind Nietzsche's "will to power," Nietzsche's (and Foucault's) "will to truth," as well as Butler's play on the word "matter" as meaning both "significant" and "embodied," and these notions have influenced me.[2] However, the process I chose was designed to force a creative synthesis of inspirations rather than compile an itinerary through landmarks, so to speak to the possible significance and relevance of a will to matter, I will now put it in relation to Butler's work, particularly her use of Spinoza's *conatus* as a frame for her philosophy.[3] This exercise is post facto, written two years from the original play on Gorgias.

First, I need to explain Spinoza a little bit. *Conatus* is a Latin word meaning "an effort, endeavor, striving" or "a force, impulse, or tendency simulating human effort." The heart of Spinoza's *Ethics* is a metaphysics of *conatus*: "Each thing, as far as it can by its own power, strives to persevere in its being."[4] It is a concept of life motive that dates back to Stoic philosophy of the fourth century BCE.[5] In its bluntest form, *conatus* is a desire for self-preservation as exemplified by Thomas Hobbes, but Spinoza moves beyond survivalism.[6] Striving to persist in being is not an instinct that threatens to overwhelm reason, it is desire that intertwines the mind and body; for Spinoza, *conatus* depends on a union of mind and body that repudiates Cartesian duality. There are many resonances between Nietzsche's "will to power" and Spinoza's understanding of *conatus*,[7] and Deleuze explains *conatus* as an "effort to augment the power of acting" that directly implicates the relation of mind and body.[8]

For Spinoza, mind and body are not distinct substances existing in binary relation where one determines the other, as in "mind over body" or vice versa. Mind and body are attributes of "one and the same thing," which leads to a rather fantastic formula: the mind is the idea of the body.[9] Genevieve Lloyd explains the relation: "Since 'substance thinking' and 'substance extended' are but one substance under different attributes, there must be a unity of material modes and their corresponding ideas. . . . Knowledge begins as the sensory awareness of body. This awareness is mental and thus radically distinct from body. But it is an expression of the same reality that the body expresses. Its object is not something mental but body itself."[10] If mind and body are one, then self-awareness is not derived from thought generated within itself (as in Descartes' "I think, therefore I am"). The self-awareness of the mind depends on sensory awareness. In other words, if you had no sensations to be aware of, what would you be conscious of? Without body, there is no mind. That is not to say that the mind is a simple imprint of sensory perceptions. That would be like saying your mind is an attic of all the sounds, sights, tastes, and smells you have experienced. For Spinoza, the mind is no museum of embodied memorabilia. To say the mind is the idea of the body is to say that "idea" is awareness, not a facsimile or a representation, of the body. Mind and body are two distinct, interdependent expressions of the same reality, but neither is a copy of the other.

Interdependence extends one body in relation to others as well. For Spinoza, embodiment is not autonomous, but heteronomous or interconnected. To be aware, a body must be affected by other bodies. Was your body never to interact with others again, what would you be aware of? (Here "body" is not limited to human bodies in interaction but material entities writ large.) It is not enough simply to have a body that one can be aware of; one needs connection. Not only must the body have an ability to affect the world it lives in, it requires that it be affected to have awareness. Thus, to persevere in being requires the cultivation of interdependency with other bodies. Spinoza's *conatus* can be restated as "a tendency to maintain and maximize an ability to be affected."[11] This would mean that to know yourself, you would have to cultivate knowledge of other entities through their affects on you. Contrary to a survivalist ethic, under which I might armor myself against interdependence and treat engagement with others as relentless conflict, Spinoza argues that to persist in being is to heighten interdependence with other bodies. If embodiment is shared, then knowledge is shared, too. There is no being that is not interwoven.

Now we can talk about Butler. Butler has quietly centered her theoretical project, if it is fair to call it a singular project, on Spinoza's *Ethics*. For many who read her, this may come as a surprise because in terms of sheer references, total page commitment, Spinoza is something of a drive-by reference in her books, and has only been referenced at all since Butler's *The Psychic Life of Power*.[12] However, as she reveals in *Undoing Gender*, her first exposure to philosophy was to Spinoza's *Ethics*, and it made an indelible mark. In fact, Spinoza shaped her reading of Hegel,[13] which in turn has shaped her theory of how one becomes a subject:

> I did not know at this time that the doctrine of Spinoza would prove essential to my subsequent scholarly work on Hegel, but this is the early modern precedent for Hegel's contention that desire is always the desire for recognition, and that recognition is the condition for a continuing and viable life. Spinoza's insistence that the desire for life can be found nascent in the emotions of despair led to the more dramatic Hegelian claim that "tarrying with the negative" can produce a conversion of the negative into being, that something affirmative can actually come of the experiences of individual and collective devastation even in their indisputable irreversibility.[14]

For Butler, the "subject" is a recognizable self both to oneself and to others. If you look back from *Gender Trouble* to *Giving an Account of Oneself*, you see the continuing theme that how one becomes recognizable involves violation and violence in the process of attaining selfhood.[15] In particular, Butler stresses the violence of exclusion, as in an internalized prohibition on homosexuality, which is involved in incorporating social norms as one learns to recognize oneself. In a heteronormative culture, one is more easily socially identifiable if one incorporates a prohibition on homosexual desire.

Yet one cannot reject exclusive prohibitions entirely. This is most apparent in *Excitable Speech* and *Psychic Life of Power*, wherein Butler stresses
the inherent vulnerability that flows from *conatus*:

> The desire to persist in one's own being requires submitting to a world which is not
> one's own . . . Only by persisting in alterity does one persist in one's "own" being.
> Vulnerable to terms that one never made, one always persists, to some degree,
> through categories, names, terms, and classifications that mark a primary and inau-
> gurative alienation in society. If such terms institute a primary subordination or,
> indeed, a primary violence, then a subject emerges against itself in order, paradoxi-
> cally, to be for itself.[16]

You must surrender part of yourself to be alive as an interconnected being.
Thus, you *have* to be vulnerable in order to become a subject because, as in
Spinoza, you have no awareness if you are not affected by others. For Butler,
conatus means that a founding hurt (self-alienation) grounds entry into
selfhood because you cannot know yourself by yourself; you can only know
yourself by submitting to social norms and discourses. You can read Butler's
recurrent survey of critical philosophy and cultural theory as framed by her
particular reading of Spinoza's *conatus,* filtered through Hegel. What began
as a theory of subjectivity has blossomed into an ethic of essential vulnerability. Given that vulnerability, we must critique how we require each other to
be subjected as a condition of self-awareness. Instead of asking us to accept
the alienations that make up social emergence, Butler argues that we need to
inquire after the conditions that make for a "livable life."[17] One must risk a
part of oneself to be able to give "an account of oneself." Yet despite the fact
that the conditions of self-recognition always remain socially sublimated in
some way we cannot conscience destroying the desire to persist as we seek
recognition.[18]

Butler's appropriation of Spinoza is a point of contrast to help place "a
will to matter" relative to *conatus* and rhetoric. A will to matter is a predicate
for broadly re-thinking what constitutes "rhetorical" action. To persevere in
being requires action of infinitely varied modes, and I consider rhetoric a
perspective on such action, not a unique and separate mode itself. Rhetoric
has consistently been theorized as uniquely human activity that is indeed
about bringing into being the world of social life. Whether it is understood as
a practice of civic engagement, a mode of teaching scripture to compel moral
action, a technique for engineering consent, or the everyday tactics that
sustain and subvert ideologies, rhetoric has been conceived as human
constitutive action. From the action of birthing and maintaining a state, to
fabricating anything expressive, to fashioning the human itself, rhetorical
studies are deeply concerned with the ways in which the will becomes

material. However, the materiality of constitutive action has confounded the assumption of rhetoric's *inherent* humanity. The media that connect one to another, the materiality of objects that signify, the embodiment of perception, the messages interpreted from the rest of nature (from genetic codes to animal behavior)—all of these confound the issue of "what is *rhetorical* action" and beg us subtly but significantly to alter the question to "what is rhetorical *about* action?"

To interact constitutively with other material forms underwrites the ability to persist. As a motive to become, a will to matter is both broader and narrower than Butler's use of Spinoza. It is narrower than her conception of *conatus* in that it is not about an ethic of self-recognition per se. In fact, she considers all desire, via Hegel, from the standpoint of recognition. What is incarnated in the service of *conatus* includes but is not exhausted by subjectivity. Whereas Butler's writing raises questions about the rhetorical nature of becoming human, a will to matter raises questions about the nature of rhetoric. I understand that there must be more than one kind of will to actualize the more general desire to persevere in being; to persist cannot be homogenous because being (or actively doing the persisting) is not homogenous in character. To persevere in being, a thing must regenerate itself through its enjoinment with other things. A will to matter is a desire to continue to be embodied in the world. It speaks to the performative impulse for reiteration in that to persist, a thing must become itself again and it is never the same for the effort. As the body changes, so does the idea of the body.

Hence, a will to knowledge is implicated by *conatus* as well. A will to knowledge is interdependent with a will to matter because, if we stay with Spinoza, knowledge is only the heightened awareness cultivated from the material interactions that are required to persist. Beyond interconnection is the desire to make sense of that connection, as when matter (as physicality) becomes significant (as meaning). The willfulness of a thing to materially reincarnate itself only partially satisfies a general striving to persist because it is only a condition of possibility, not a condition of sufficiency. There must be some cultivation of awareness to approach sufficiency of being. Beyond awareness, there is the desire for recognition, yet another form of will that has been crucial for defining what is "human." As I understand the term and relative to Butler and Spinoza, a will to matter names a part of the desire to persevere in being.

A will to matter is also broader than Butler's use of *conatus*. She is principally concerned with how one acquires subjectivity, which translates "persistence in being" into emerging and then living as a recognizable self through our incorporation of social discourses and norms. It is the struggle to make a livable life. You might ask, what could be broader than that? I don't mean broader on her terms—as an ethical theorist, she works in pretty broad strokes. I mean broader in terms of performativity, or what a will to matter does. A will to matter does not fully actualize the desire to persist (that is the narrower part; it is not an ethic nor does mattering satisfy other forms of will). It does concern incarnation beyond the question of subjectivity, however (that is the broader part; it is not limited to affects on subjectivity). If a will to matter is understood strictly in terms of self-recognition, then what "mattering" does performatively is always reflected back on the creation of the human subject. As it relates to rhetoric, *conatus* need not be exclusively concerned with human subjectivity. Because it is performative, material reiteration is highly variable in form, and so the relations between embodiment, awareness, and selfhood that are part of a "continuation of being" are not limited to mimetic or representational practices of human beings seeking recognition. The four lines of argument in my play on the "Encomium" are but initial explorations into the variability of those relations.

The allegory of Helen poses concrete commonplaces for considering the rhetorical quality and range of performativity involved in material incarnation. How does one bring something into being rhetorically? Or more accurately, how is bringing something into being rhetorical? I use "Helen" both to exemplify and to deconstruct the habit of Western rhetorical theory to displace matter from will as a condition for explaining how the will comes to matter. A key part of that displacement is the age old form/matter dualism of masculine activity and feminine passivity. Helen's story both states and undermines the dualism. I am not re-arguing the existence of the intellectual habit to sex matter as female and will as male, important texts of which Butler synthesizes in the first chapter of *Bodies that Matter*. Rather, I am posing Helen as an allegorical scene for rhetorical theory wherein we can see the dualism done and undone. Instead of re-proving the point that sexual difference shapes materialism in rhetorical theory, we can move on to consider "how rhetoric can act and what sex has got to do with it." If a will to matter has been sexed, how does it impact our understanding of striving to persist in being? What is rhetorical in the materiality of *conatus* if it is sexed?

An unexpected consequence that I will close with is that we should be asking *what* instead of *who* strives to persist. Materiality is the solvent that dilutes the essential "humanity" of rhetorical action. The human quality presumably revealed by rhetorical action is dependent on the very matter that is imagined as exterior to whom or to what is doing the acting. We easily take willfulness as uniquely human and matter as essentially inhuman but borrowed by the will as needed. The soul is what makes us human, not the body. Spinoza did not consider *conatus* exclusively human.[19] If will is part of the same substance as matter, not external to it, then rhetorical performativity is immanent to material interconnection, not a force that enters the world of things as strikes its fancy. That the subject and object of rhetoric are sexed masks the not-so-human materiality of rhetoric. It anthropomorphizes materiality. Tinkering with Butler's wording, it is not about the *human* "materiality of sex, but the sex of materiality."[20] In other words, my play on the "Encomium" does not expose that masculinity and femininity are indistinct in rhetoric so much as it debunks the way that matter is external-ized from rhetoric through its feminization. The responsiveness and vulner-ability of matter to itself is not a human trait, even as being human depends on vulnerability to material influence. To be rhetorical, a thing must be materially vulnerable; to be materially vulnerable is not uniquely human. That is not to say there is no difference between a film and the communica-tion between RNA molecules and proteins. It is to note that they both perform a will to matter. The question then becomes what is rhetorical about material vulnerability without resorting to circular reasoning: to be rhetorical is to be human; to be human is to be capable of rhetoric. A will to matter betrays the inessentially human side of rhetoric by exposing the immanence of rhetoric to material vulnerability. To be human, we need rhetoric and we cultivate it, but the capacity to act rhetorically is not ours *because* we are human. It is because we are material.

Notes

1. From translation, words have been changed but not all; no quotes are remarked. The "Encomium" has been translated variously as "of" or "to" Helen, which is not so much a translation issue as it is a function of how different translators understand what an enco-mium is: is it a praise of someone, or a statement of praise to someone? I have kept Ken-nedy's translation "of" because I wrote an encomium of the materiality that Helen allegorizes and not to her specifically. Gorgias, "Encomium of Helen," in *The Older Sophists*, ed. Rosamond Kent Sprague, trans. George Kennedy (Columbia: University of South Carolina Press, 1972), 50–54.

2. Friedrich Nietzsche, *Beyond Good and Evil: Prelude to a Philosophy of the Future*, trans. Walter Kaufmann (New York: Vintage, 1966), s. 36, s. 259, s. 636; 1967, s. 635, s. 636; Friedrich Nietzsche, *The Will to Power*, trans. Walter Kaufmann (New York: Random House, 1967); Michel Foucault, "The Discourse on Language," in *The Archaeology of Knowledge and the Discourse on Language*, trans. A. M. Sheridan Smith (New York: Pantheon, 1982), 215–38; Judith Butler, *Bodies that Matter: On the Discursive Limits of "Sex"* (New York: Routledge, 1993).

3. Judith Butler, *The Psychic Life of Power: Theories in Subjection* (Stanford, CA: Stanford University Press, 1997), 27–28, 62, 203–4n14; Judith Butler, *Precarious Life: The Pow-*

ers of *Mourning and Violence* (London: Verso, 2004), 140; Judith Butler, *Undoing Gender* (New York: Routledge, 2004), 31–32, 51–52, 193–95, 198–99, 235–38.

4. *The World Book Dictionary*, 2003 ed., s.v. "*conatus*"; Benedictus de Spinoza, *Ethics*, ed. and trans. G. H. R. Parkinson (New York: Oxford University Press, 2000), IIIP6.

5. Susan James, "Spinoza the Stoic," in *Spinoza: Critical Assessments, Vol. I: Context, Sources and the Early Writings*, ed. Genevieve Lloyd (London: Routledge, 2001), 126–48; Paul Oskar Kristeller, "Stoic and Neoplatonic Sources of Spinoza's *Ethics*," in *Spinoza: Critical Assessments, Vol. I: Context, Sources and the Early Writings*, ed. Genevieve Lloyd (London: Routledge, 2001), 111–25.

6. Genevieve Lloyd, *Spinoza and the* Ethics (London: Routledge, 1996), 8–9.

7. Richard Schacht, "The Nietzsche-Spinoza Problem: Spinoza as Precursor?" in *Spinoza: Critical Assessments, Volume IV: The Reception and Influence of Spinoza's Philosophy*, ed. Genevieve Lloyd (London: Routledge, 2001), 257–75.

8. Gilles Deleuze, *Spinoza: Practical Philosophy*, trans. Robert Hurley (San Francisco: City Lights Books, 1988), 101.

9. Spinoza, *Ethics*, IIP7S.

10. Genevieve Lloyd, *Part of Nature: Self-Knowledge in Spinoza's* Ethics (Ithaca, NY: Cornell University Press, 1994), 20. Also see Diana Burns Steinberg, *On Spinoza* (Belmont, CA: Wadsworth, 2000), 31–51; Jonathan Bennett, "Spinoza's Mind-Body Identity Thesis," in *Spinoza: Critical Assessments, Vol. II: The* Ethics, ed. Genevieve Lloyd (London: Routledge, 2001), 114–24; Margaret D. Wilson, "Objects, Ideas, and 'Minds': Comments on Spinoza's Theory of Mind," in *Spinoza: Critical Assessments, Vol. II: The* Ethics, ed. Genevieve Lloyd (London: Routledge, 2001), 97–113.

11. Spinoza, *Ethics*, IVP38; Deleuze, *Spinoza*, 99.

12. Butler, *Psychic Life of Power*, 27–28, 62, 203–4n14.

13. For a critique of Hegel's reading of Spinoza, see Antonio Negri, *The Savage Anomaly: The Power of Spinoza's Metaphysics and Politics*, trans. Michael Hardt (Minneapolis: University of Minnesota Press, 1991), 45–59; and Errol E. Harris, *The Substance of Spinoza* (Atlantic Highlands, NJ: Humanities Press, 1995), 200–14.

14. Butler, *Undoing Gender*, 236.

15. Judith Butler, *Gender Trouble: Feminism and the Subversion of Identity*, 10th anniversary ed. (New York: Routledge, 1999); Judith Butler, *Giving an Account of Oneself* (New York: Fordham University Press, 2005).

16. Butler, *Psychic Life of Power*, 28; also see Judith Butler, *Excitable Speech: A Politics of the Performative* (New York: Routledge, 1997).

17. Butler, *Precarious Life*; Butler, *Undoing Gender*.

18. Butler, *Giving an Account*, 44.

19. Lloyd, *Part of Nature*.

20. Butler, *Bodies that Matter*, 49.

CHAPTER 9

Shades of Derrida: Materiality as the Mediation of Différance

Kenneth Rufo, Independent Scholar

The relationship between rhetoric and materiality has always been one shrouded in mystery, its exposure often more a function of the politics attending criticism than the fruit of some particularly powerful heuristic. Not that this mitigates the value of those exposures in the slightest, since each revelation, each theoretical overture by which materiality and rhetoric are related, reveals much about the political scene and imaginary from which they emerge. These scenes vary widely, of course, something to which the variety of contributions to this volume will testify, but no matter their variance, they will remain united by an essential material reality, one with its own unique politics: their proximity, binding, and incorporation in the book you hold in your hands. This is a collection about a "material turn" in rhetorical studies that, through the simple fact of its compilation, already testifies to what is perchance the most fundamental scene of materiality: the medium itself.

That no communication can take place without some underlying material substrate seems an obvious fact, but in a field of study that prides itself on its appreciation for the subtle nuances of discourse, this fact has often taken a back seat. Content, at least in the history of rhetorical criticism, has often been given an ontological and axiological privilege, while its material form is often relegated to parenthetical asides or addressed as a function of context rather than as part of the text itself. And yet, if thinkers of media like Marshall McLuhan have taught us anything, it is that a greater appreciation for the role of the medium is necessary before we can begin to understand the messages they translate. Media not only determine the possibilities of rhetorical construction, they also change the social frame in which discursive acts are understood and disseminated. Media define what Dilip Gaonkar terms the "technologies of circulation," the mechanisms by which some ideographic themes attain hegemony over others and through which social and psychical networks are thought and mapped. Consequently, I would argue that there can be no substantive thinking of materiality, nor of rhetoric, that does not pay careful attention to the media environments within which the bits and fragments of discourse are constructed and disseminated.

In this chapter, I hope to outline a way of thinking materiality and rhetoric that treats the two as a single ecology in which each makes possible the other, and to contend that the scene of this ecology goes by the name *mediation*.[1] My investigation of this ecology, the so-called "primal scene of communication," will begin by interrogating a strange "haunting" in the work of one who has often been wrongly maligned for his lack of interest in material reality: Jacques Derrida.[2] Haunting is indeed the word for it, for I will be taking as my object those ghosts, spirits, and specters that so often populate Derrida's work. The specter, even spectrality in general, may seem a strange trope to explore when investigating materiality, but it is, I believe, the figure that best makes sense of mediation. In Derrida, this spectrality can be seen in what might appear an alarming intersection: on the one hand, a theme that defines media, that challenges the presence/absence binary by steadfastly refusing to be either, and on the other hand, a phantom that finds its most pernicious and devastating expression in the ghosts that haunt the cinders of Auschwitz.

My goal in this essay is to highlight Derrida as a thinker of materiality *qua* mediation while simultaneously arguing that Derrida's thinking, while valuable, doesn't go far enough, and that a more materialist appreciation for deconstruction can be pursued by "thickening" the context of deconstruction itself, something that can be accomplished by paying attention to the media ecologies that inform its inventional resources.[3] This task of thickening demonstrates, I think, a powerful heuristic for media-sensitive rhetoricians, but it is by no means the only critical path available to them. I hope to show that by taking Derrida's spectrality seriously, by trying to take it even further and making it more explicit than Derrida himself necessarily does, one is forced to confront the materiality of mediation, and to understand that this materiality is inextricably bound to the processes of invention, circulation, and interpretation. This confrontation in turn calls into question inquiries grounded by a logic of representation, an interpretive frame that requires at least the pretense of presence and absence and the possibility of a correspondence between the discourse and some extrinsic referent.[4] By contrast, I argue that a robust appreciation for spectrality sends us in a different direction, one in which criticism plays on a different stage—one that leads to a reassessment and renewal of *mimesis*.

Engaging the Dead

Jacques Derrida died on October 9, 2004, a death brought on by aggressive pancreatic cancer. News reports of his death were not entirely kind, many tossing out words like "infuriating," "abstruse," and "controversial" alongside descriptions of his snappy dressing and snow-white hair. Some, playing with the relativism supposedly inherent in deconstruction, even argued that perhaps Derrida wasn't even dead, or had already been dead. Rod Liddle, writing for the *Spectator*, offered the following:

> [W]e cannot be entirely sure what has happened. We are faced instead with an end-less multiplicity of truths, a string of infinite possibilities. I suppose it is entirely up to the reader to decide. It would be logocentric of us all to assume that Jakki's cor-poreal remains are in a state of decomposition simply because of the unbidden and puzzling presence, in our newspapers, of that signifier "dead" in relation to the name "Jacques Derrida."[5]

Even slavish devotees of Derrida's work should find the excerpt humorous, for a wide variety of reasons, given its obvious (though likely unintentional) mistreatment of undecidability, not to mention the excerpt's publishing venue and the ironic fact that, given the lag time in publishing, the possibilities of translation, and the subsequent drive to archive lectures not already converted into the printed word, Derrida will continue to publish books long after passing away. Despite death, he will in effect live on, even if he does so through the allegedly "dead" media of the book, analog recordings, and, of course, the digital video disc that bears his name, and that famously documents him buttering a piece of toast.

This ghoulish, secondary life is, in these modern times, terribly banal. All thinkers or writers or celebrities, be they prolific enough or recorded sufficiently, live on past their deaths. The survival skills that the written word and the printing press gave to thought—the ability to archive itself so as to pass beyond the life of the author or the witness—the recording technologies of the nineteenth and twentieth centuries have given to life itself. The dead speak, perform, act, emote, live, and they do so every day, through the pictures and video we keep of our own dearly departed and the vast and growing repository of the films and interviews that archive our modern times. But for Derrida, this second life is particularly fitting, for perhaps no other thinker has spent as much time and space writing about the relationship between writing and death.

Still, this moment of death, which is to a certain extent also a moment of survival (as a living beyond), offers us a chance to revisit the recently deceased, to reconsider the nature and extent of the role played by those dead media through which we know or write the name of Derrida. It is a role not without its share of tensions. Engaging with Derrida's work has always been a notoriously difficult task, with its experimental writing styles, dense allusions to figures in the history of philosophy and literature, and the sheer quantity of his writings. He was, without doubt, one of the most prolific writers of the twentieth century, and perhaps not surprisingly, given the sheer volume of his work, his actual influence has often been circumscribed by a kind of "greatest hits" mentality, in which his role in fields of thought not entirely commensurate with his own has often staged itself through the reiteration of themes made popular by his earliest works. Consider the rhetorical scholarship housed in NCA, for example, where terms like "*différance*" and "deconstruction" are common enough now that they appear well worn. This familiarity has brought with it a certain contempt, and one senses that for many, the time of Derrida, of deconstruction, has come and gone, and rightfully so. As a result, Derrida's stock in rhetorical studies has declined notably since the explosion of work he inspired in the 1970s, 1980s, and even the early 1990s.

Sadly, this familiarity obfuscates an underlying refusal, for surprisingly little work has been done in rhetorical studies that engages Derrida's more recent works, and even less has been done to seriously treat this work as itself rhetorical, rather than as "theory" to be used or discarded, whatever the toolbox requires. As rhetoricians begin to pursue areas outside of public address more aggressively, and to move into necessary engagements with film and television and cyberspace, the name "Derrida" has slowly receded into the background. When the name does return, almost ceremonially, it continues to speak through the same terms with which most are comfortably versed—iterability, *différance*, the trace, and so on—and rhetoricians have done admirable, outstanding work thinking through these terms and examining seminal texts like *Of Grammatology* and *Dissemination*. What scholars like Barbara Biesecker, John Durham Peters, and Kevin DeLuca—to name just an obvious few—have shown is that an engagement with Derrida, with his concept of *différance* in particular, is indispensable for rhetorical studies, not to mention advantageous for criticism. Other, more recent texts, however (like *Archive Fever*, *Specters of Marx*, *Echographies of Television*, and *Paper Machine*), despite having a tremendous amount to offer scholars interested in rhetoric and media studies, remain very much on the margins of both rhetorical theory and criticism.

This is unfortunate, for Derrida's recent work offers a supplement to his vocabulary commensurate with his expanded interest in technics, an addition that could prove instructive for rhetoricians interested in the material specificity of mediation. I am alluding here to Derrida's fixation with the figure of the *specter,* and the issues of spectrality and of spirit in their many different guises. In those works in which Derrida explicitly focuses on mediation in general, rather than writing in particular, these are the themes and figures that take center stage. This focus may be due, in part, to the historical fact that, empirically, different media have always been linked to new configurations of ghosts, phantasms, and the paranormal, offering different ways to channel the dead or the paranormal.[6] But the subject of spectrality demands more than simply recognizing various ghost sightings, for mediation is also a fundamental challenge to the logic of presence, and as such, always teases out the sense of reality, altering common perceptions of time and space. Telecommunication is always a play between the there and the not-there, the now and the then, and spectrality names this undeniably "virtual" phenomenon. Hence Friedrich Kittler's succinct declaration: "Media always already provide the appearances of specters."[7]

Perhaps it would be helpful to think of the word "medium" in its more spiritual sense, as a seer of and speaker for the supernatural, a window to the paranormal. This sense certainly fits, for in the act of recording, media technologies capture the present as a past and re-present it as a *this* (the record that is) *was* (whatever is recorded). In effect, these media produce their own sense of history, capturing it as/through a series of artifacts. Transmission media take that same past and send it over distances of space and time, transforming past events and contexts into the reception of live experience. The dead speak to the living and the absent are made present. And while science can explain the mechanics that make recording and transmission possible, they can never banish entirely their funereal comportment.

Writing boasts its share of ghosts as well. The mystique attached to old texts, seen recently as the source of satanic power and mysticism in Roman Polanski's *The Ninth Gate,* can also be seen in the name given to those piles of mail deemed undeliverable: the so-called dead letters, named because of their removal from the more lively process of circulation and the possibly deceased status of their senders and addressees. Even the near-instantaneous exchange of e-mail is phantasmatic, with writing done *here* suddenly manifesting *there,* saved in the inbox until (or after) being read, waiting for one more click of the mouse before initiating a sort of electronic séance. Derrida, we should remember, routinely argues that writing is dedicated to the proposition that the author no longer needs to be for the message to be received, and that the possibility of communicating beyond one's death is necessarily inscribed in every act of writing. Writing, in other words, always entails the possibility of writing a dead letter.

And so, it is no coincidence that Derrida's *Specters of Marx*, which re-
volves around a reading of the ghosts in and of Karl Marx (the great thinker
of materiality), also contains a meditation on the spectrality of contemporary
technics. In it, the specter proves so pivotal that Derrida contends that no
assessment or appreciation of media can be made "without taking into
account so many *spectral* effects, the new speed of *apparition* (we understand this word in its ghostly sense) of the simulacrum, the synthetic or
prosthetic image, and the virtual event, cyberspace and surveillance, the
control appropriations, and speculations that today deploy unheard-of
powers."[8] In other words, the spectral component of media, their ability to
make the dead live again, to proffer a virtual sense of presence, or to simulate
or anticipate an event, are what give new media and their messages their
distinctive character. The specter, we could say, is what produces media as
material phenomena, what shapes the possibilities of response and interpretation in today's evolving media ecology.

Derrida's discussion of spectrality begins with the ghost of Hamlet's father, who appears in the opening act to set in motion the events that will
follow. This is no idle choice. *Hamlet* was an influential text for Marx, to be
sure, but there is more at work here. *Hamlet* is first and foremost a play, a
text to be performed, and as such, points to the quintessentially theatrical
nature of spectral logics. Every act of channeling, be it one of recording or
transmission, is a setting of the stage, a portrayal or presentation of an event,
and will be structured by a set of rules that govern its recognition as such.
Every instance of mediation offers a material and psychical inscription of its
ghosts.[9] As such, an appreciation of spectrality implies that mediation can
never be reduced to or defined by a logic of representation, since media
necessarily unravel the binary between presence and absence, a binary that
simply cannot maintain itself within the structure of telecommunications.

Still, for those wary of Derrida and deconstruction, eyebrows will no
doubt be placed on high alert. How, they might ask, does this idea of spectrality relate to the rest of Derrida's *oeuvre*? Is spectrality as relativist, as
slippery, as his other vocabulary games? Predictably, this answer is not as
clear as Derrida's skeptics might prefer, but I believe this lack of clarity will
offer us a way to take Derrida further as a thinker of materiality and mediation. More on that in a moment. For now, let me offer Derrida's own description, in which spectrality is linked to those characteristics that Derrida has
previously described as the play of *différance* or the movement of deconstruction:

What has . . . constantly haunted me in this logic of the specter is that it regularly exceeds all the oppositions between visible and invisible, sensible and insensible. A specter is both visible and invisible, both phenomenal and nonphenomenal: a trace that marks the present with its absence in advance. The spectral logic is *de facto* a deconstructive logic. It is in the element of haunting that deconstruction finds the place most hospitable to it, at the heart of the living present, in the quickest heartbeat of the philosophical.[10]

This passage, to which I will return later, is remarkable in its assessment. Haunting offers a "place most hospitable" to deconstruction, the specter is likened to the trace, and the specter is said to confront those binaries that have been (in part) the target of Derrida's writing for decades. And yet, there is a stunning ambiguity here, one that centers on the supposed reality or actuality to which the "*de facto*" testifies, for if spectrality is "in fact" deconstruction, where has the specter been hiding itself all this time?

Two questions announce themselves at this point. First, what is the relationship between spectrality and those earlier terms used to describe *différance*, like the "trace," with which rhetoricians are already quite familiar? And second, given its obvious hospitality to deconstruction, given Derrida's long history of writing about *différance* and iterability, and given his allusions to ghosts and simulacra in other texts, including "Plato's Pharmacy," why did spectrality take so long to arrive near the forefront of his thought?

A History of or within *Différance*?

It would be a mistake to begin to answer the second question by thinking that Derrida was, at some earlier point, unconcerned with media and materiality. The materiality of communication has always been a focus of his work, though what I would here name materiality may no doubt seem a very foreign concept to some. In a certain reading—and materiality is always, as I have mentioned, dependent on a certain *reading*—materiality is not the world "out there," to which language points. Materiality need not be a reality accessed through a process of signification, a distal realm appropriated in an intersubjective process. Instead, I want to suggest a thinking of materiality that can be understood as those processes and functions by which something like reading is possible. In this instance, for this essay, it is the eyes, the brain, the printed word, the bound book, the typeface, the placement of the text, the environment of the reader, etc. A politics is already mobilized and established regarding this particular material practice, though it is, if we are to believe the occasionally frightened musings of Sven Birkerts or Neil Postman, a politics that must be militantly defended against the advance of the newer technologies of reading, and therefore, of thinking.

This understanding of materiality resides at the heart of Derrida's notion of *différance*, which can be understood only as a process by which ontological differences and concepts can be deployed, an infinite potential of differential marks that, depending on how they are arranged, produce a series of differences and divisions through which meaning can be construed, and something like structure can be derived. In a general sense, these marks can be anything, productive of any system, and need not necessarily be marks at all. In this sense, *"différance"* is a term that finds its expression in a chain of playful signifiers: the trace, the hymen, the trait, the breach, the spur, etc. Still, no matter how large the sea of potential differences might be, for these differences to be intelligible as such, they must embody some rule or produce a structure. In other words, for *différance* to reduce itself at any point to difference or to the possibility of meaning, to produce any scene or event, *différance* must confront and manifest as a material history—a mediation. In the case of the alphabet, the so-called rules of grammar and syntax, as well as the range of vocabulary or the correctness of spelling are functions of a history of artifacts, which in turn produce norms and govern the production of future artifacts. This is what Derrida means by iteration: absent the agreed-upon norms of exchange, there can be no communication, even though, thanks to those agreed norms, no single act of communication can guarantee the singularity or success of its communique. In a more specific sense, the word *"différance"* marks its own exploration of these differential marks, for its purposeful misspelling (the replacement of an "e" with an "a") shows the disconnect between the written and the spoken, and shows how no set of differential marks can fully capture and contain the play that precedes the ontological, factical realization of a language. Again, the play only makes sense because of a play between two different material instantiations—the aural (spoken) and the visual (written).

In either sense, *différance* works by calling attention to the constant act of assembly that must precede those units through which thinking is structured: the utterance, the concept, the substance, etc. Each of these concepts must be exploded, broken apart to discover the material traces of which they are composed, just as the atom, once thought to be the smallest piece of matter, is exploded by the quantum fields that constitute its innards. In this sense, Derrida's *différance*, with its difference and its deferral, has always been about exposing the components that give us the illusion of a coherent language, a mother tongue. Even at the level of the letter itself, it takes only the slightest alteration in the grapheme, a line that meanders along a curve up and to the left rather than down and to the right, to separate an "a" from an "e." Toss context, syntax, grammar, and colloquialisms into the blender, and each swirling batch produces different possibilities for what we think of as a language, be it ours or someone else's. Speech, of course, is no different. In *Glas*, a book often noted for its emphasis on the "reading effect," the written and the spoken are interwoven in a way that highlights and demarcates the conventions of these possibilities, with Derrida going to great lengths to play with the physiological gestures responsible for speech: the tongue, the throat, the chords, the glottis, the teeth, the lips—all of which work in an intricate conjunction to produce a sound that rings ontologically whole, even if its production reveals that this sense of cohesion is, to say the least, artificial.[11]

Back to our questions. To answer them, it is clear that we must begin with *différance*, for if the potential of *différance* is uniform and infinite in its possibility, if *différance* is somehow beyond history, then the material distinctions between different media remain of lesser consequence than the general structure of iterability through which they posit communication. If this is the case, then the answer to the first question will simply be one of negation: that no substantive difference exists, and we could be content to list spectrality alongside the trace as just another term by which the play of *différance* can be named. But if *différance* does have a history that is not reducible to *différance* itself, if, in other words, the thinking of *différance* is impacted by this history, whether Derrida recognizes it or not, then the recent prominence of spectrality, and the difference between the specter and the trace, may mark this history, and as a consequence tell us something more pronounced about the material force of mediation. For rhetoricians, the stakes of this possibility are profound: if "spectrality" is simply another term for "trace," then it offers little as a heuristic device, and media criticism could then content itself with tracing, as it often does, the logics and strictures that govern the promulgation of their texts. But if "spectrality" is something more, if it names a phantasmal quality both more obvious in modern telecommunications media and more intrinsic to the process of mediation in general, while the trace represents a subset or form of spectrality related specifically to writing, then rhetoricians will do criticism a grave disservice if they approach different media without more discriminant understandings of the rhythms and scenes that comprise their incorporation. Still, we must avoid thinking that spectrality is endemic in a way that transcends its own conditions of emergence. Instead, along with Derrida, we recognize the broad denotative reach of spectrality today precisely because spectrality is with modern telecommunications suddenly abundantly apparent. As Samuel Weber notes, "the new, electronic media have made manifest what was always at work in the 'work' itself: namely, its mediality."[12]

Let me start to determine this history by suggesting that we cannot ignore the conditions of possibility and emergence that inform Derrida's own work.

His writing is not above rhetorical engagement. As rhetoricians are well aware, writing or speaking about a subject requires a particular set of inventional resources, some of which are more apparent than others. These inventional resources, whether addressed specifically within the text or not, should leave "traces" of their passages, traces that cannot be reduced to the economy of the work itself. As Derrida himself notes in a different context, the "circle of invention is only a movement for reappropriating exactly what sets it in motion."[13]

Before attempting to mine Derrida's texts for these traces, I want to note two statements that appear to argue for the privileging of *différance* over the specificity of particular technics, even as they leave the door slightly ajar, open just enough for an alternate possibility. The first comes in *Of Grammatology*: "There cannot be a science of *différance* itself in its operation, as it is impossible to have a science of the origin of presence itself, that is to say of a certain nonorigin. *Différance* is therefore the formation of form. But it is *on the other hand* the being-imprinted of the imprint (*l'empreinte*)."[14] So, *différance* cannot be reduced by way of a science, even if, as seems to be hinted at here, it is itself formed by a material process. The idea of the imprint, which is no doubt meant to be generalizable, nevertheless begs the question, what of different media, media not of impression or inscription, but of instantaneity, simulation, and virtuality? Asked about the specificity of these newer media in *Echographies*, Derrida responds, "These machines have always been there, they are always there, even when we wrote by hand, even during so-called live conversation. And yet, the greatest compatibility, the greatest coordination, the most vivid of possible affinities seems to be asserting itself, *today,* between what appears to be most alive, most *live,* and the *différance* or delay, the time it takes to exploit, broadcast or distribute it."[15] Again, a certain ambivalence is at work here, for his first response is to deny that these newer media can be thought in terms outside of those that first define speech and writing—in a word, *différance*—and yet, they work at such a fantastic pace that they appear increasingly alive, which is to say, increasingly present. But for Derrida, this speed only makes the work of *différance* harder to spot; it does not change fundamentally the character of *différance*; otherwise, he would never commit to the first part of the reply.

These two quotes are representative of a number of agnate passages, and they are notable both for the assuredness with which they support the irreducibility of *différance,* and for their refusal to elevate that assuredness into certainty. They signify the possibility of something unsettled within Derrida, something that perhaps he recognizes hasn't really been thought through in his writing. I want to suggest that this something is his own indebtedness to the media through which and about which he is writing: writing in general and the book in particular, which govern his earlier work, and eventually new media and globalization, which are prominent themes in his later texts. This is not to say that Derrida is unaware of this debt, only that perhaps he does not fully appreciate its magnitude.

Let us recall that *Of Grammatology* begins with an announcement that the more general study of language has given way to a study of writing, and that this progression can be linked to social movements in which Derrida is a participant. The book still occupies a privileged place at the heart of this transition, though its status may be receding or mutating, since the book is undergoing its own crisis brought on by new thinking and new technologies.[16] It is because of this crisis that Derrida can begin to think about the structurality of writing, something he admits explicitly: "The end of linear writing is indeed the end of the book. . . . It is less a question of confiding new writings to the envelope of a book than of finally reading what wrote itself between the lines in the volumes."[17] In other words, Derrida's work on writing is heavily predicated on an explicit relationship to the written (principally printed) word, so much so that in *Dissemination*, a book given over to the philosophical consideration of writing, Derrida notes that "one cannot tamper with [the book] without disturbing everything else."[18] This theme of tampering with the written or printed word and the rules that govern its constitution is a frequent one in Derrida, and explains the motivation behind most of his experimental writing styles.

Given this focus, it should come as no surprise that, when explicating *différance* in the opening chapter of *Of Grammatology*, Derrida will describe it through the language of writing, of "arche-writing," a term that he is quick to confirm is suggestive rather than prescriptive. The word "writing" implies for Derrida not only the common practice in which graphical marks are used to connote meaning but also "all that gives rise to an inscription in general, whether it is literal or not and even if what it distributes in space is alien to the order of the voice: cinematography, choreography, of course, but also pictorial, musical, sculptural writing."[19] Given the more open possibilities of the word "difference," the effort spent circumscribing *différance* with the label of "writing" is curious, especially since that label requires supplemental exposition in order to seem appropriate. Why go to this extra effort? The answer may be that the emphasis on writing, on an arche-writing, helps Derrida to situate rhetorically and therefore explain the cognitive difficulties presented by the notion of *différance*. As an expository device, writing serves as a sort of metonymy, an object with a constitution analogous to *différance*, but much more readily comprehended. This drive, to use writing as a rhetorical aid, explains why Derrida elsewhere repeats the gesture. In an essay dedicated solely to explicating *différance*, for example, Derrida's enunciation again recourses to writing. After speaking of *différance* as temporization and spacing, he asks, "How are they to be joined? Let us start, since we are already there, from the problematic of the sign and of writing."[20] What if this starting point is more than mere convenience, more than a choice? What if this is, in fact, a necessary beginning, emerging from the economy and history of *différance* itself, at least an economy at work during a period of time when Derrida sees his concern as the politics and structurality of writing and its relation to the spoken word?

With all of this writing about writing, with his many texts about textuality, it should come as little surprise that one of the dominant terms through which Derrida describes the play of *différance* during this period is the "trace," a term that carries within it an obvious, graphical resonance. In effect, the "trace" carries within it its own trace, that of the text and of the grapheme. Apart from this resonance, the trace functions much like the specter, or at least the description of the two are, despite being separated by a couple of decades, remarkably similar. The trace is described as a "simulacrum of a presence that dislocates itself,"[21] as that "which opens appearance and signification," and as the "unheard difference between the appearing and the appearance" which is "the condition of all other differences."[22] Given this similarity in function, the differences between the specter and the trace appear at first largely nominal, which may be another way of saying that they are largely contextual, in that the trace has a position of privilege in the earlier writings about writing, and the specter and its ilk (ghosts, phantoms, apparitions) have a similarly elevated status in Derrida's discussions of advanced media technologies. This lack of obvious, "substantial" difference is in part how Derrida can, despite awarding to spectrality a preeminent hospitality to deconstruction, attempt to explain the specter as a trace.[23]

Nevertheless, this is not an entirely satisfactory arrangement, and it remains unclear if even Derrida wants to let the specter and the trace explain each other. After all, even though there can be no science of *différance*, Derrida still argues for an understanding of *différance* as a being-imprinted, which is to say, as a material phenomenon. So even a contextual or nominal difference between the trace and the specter is telling, because it ensures that neither can simply be reduced to the other. The specter manifests as an outgrowth of Derrida's thinking of media in general, particularly new media, while the trace outlines a concern with the written word, the alphabet, and the book. But there is a difference at work here that stretches beyond mere context. In *Echographies*, Derrida routinely avoids arguing for giving to new media a specificity outside of the structure of *différance* as arche-writing,[24] but that he speaks of it most often in terms of spectrality does lend it a quasi-discreet specificity. He has, in fact, previously assigned three functions to the specter, three things that "would decompose in analysis this single thing, spirit, or specter," the first of which is mourning: "It consists always in attempting to ontologize remains, to make them present, in the first place by *identifying* the bodily remains and by *localizing* the dead." The second is the "condition of language—and the voice, in any case of that which *marks* the name or takes its place." And the third is the notion of work: "[W]hether it transforms or transforms itself, poses or decomposes itself: the spirit, the 'spirit of the spirit' is *work*."[25] Much of these might be reconcilable with the functioning of the trace, and as such are not exactly a clear mark of distinction. But the careful specificity is telling, especially when it comes to thinking about mourning. Spectrality, as I have already remarked, matters because of the capacity of the medium to channel the dead and present it as a live event, in the here and now. As such, spectrality is also the process of ontologizing, of defining which ghosts are acceptable and which are not. Derrida accords, "[T]his being-with-specters would also be . . . a *politics* of memory, of inheritance, and of generations."[26]

Something much more obviously political is at work in the specter in a way that it is not at work in the trace, even though the two function in remarkably parallel fashions. This may be, as some have intimated, because of a political "turn" in Derrida, but this psychosocial explanation does rhetorical criticism no credit, not when we have the specificity of the texts before us, and the engrossing details provided by a history of artifacts. It turns out, in fact, that the movement that pushes spectrality to the fore is one that begins with another turn away from the trace, a turn that is most notable in Derrida's writing on the wake of the Holocaust, the cinders of Auschwitz.

A Holocaust of Representation

Although Derrida often broaches the same themes and relationships, he does so each time by following a singular trajectory determined by the texts with which he is engaging. Nevertheless, and at the risk of reducing a great deal of complexity, sometimes the themes that emerge most readily from different textual engagements cluster slightly, crystallizing around particular vocabularies or logics. For example, while Derrida always finds writing and death operating near each other, if not with each other, some of his textual engagements foreground questions of death, while others foreground writing. These clusters should not be read strictly as the result of a chronological progression, which, if it exists at all, exists largely as a secondary effect of the texts and problems he is engaging. Still, these clusters do provide a road map of sorts of different ways of thinking and marking *différance* in Derrida's *oeuvre*. As I have already noted, one relatively early cluster speaks frequently through the language of the trace, while another, decidedly more recent, begins to think of *différance* through the specter. Between these two clusters lies a third (there are others, but there is neither the space nor time here to engage them), one obsessed with flame and fire, and that speaks the language of *différance* as a language of ashes and cinders. Not surprisingly, the flame and fire in question is often a remnant from the crematoria.

For Derrida, there are two holocausts, conjoined but nevertheless distinct, parsed graphically by the play of capitalization. The term "Holocaust," with the formality of capitalization, speaks to that event in which millions of lives were systematically snuffed out, often through gas and flame, under Nazism.[27] To speak of a "holocaust," uncapitalized, is to speak of the susceptibility to burning, the practice of burning, the ending or terminating through flame that takes place in so many different forms and in such a pervasive manner. The word "holocaust," after all, is literally the writing of this concern: that all (*holo-*) is burning (*caust*), or more felicitously, that everything burns.[28] Certain of Derrida's texts are more specific in their consideration of these holocausts, but the emphasis he places on the second, less proper, holocaust shows how fundamental is the threat of consumption in Derrida's approach to thinking language.[29] As Gideon Ofrat notes, "[o]ne way or another, the spirit of the Holocaust or a holocaust hovers over Jacques Derrida's writing."[30]

These holocausts haunt Derrida's work for several reasons, not the least of which is the trauma they induce and the fundamental challenge they pose to the logic of representation as a pretext for meaning. How can a text or an artifact go about representing that which is forever unrepresentable? Any depiction will remain partial, and any testimony will testify only as a fiction that generalizes a singularity that resists its generalization. Representation here is necessarily a fiction (a truth in fiction, to be sure, as there remains, for Derrida, no possibility of truth that is not also the possibility of fiction). But to represent in the more conventional and more classical sense implies the ability to present again, or present anew (a new time or a new audience), a reality now past or disconnected from its happening.

The insight made obvious by the Holocaust, an insight Derrida wants to extend by emphasizing the pervasiveness of holocausts, and therefore of consummation, is the failure of critical schemes invested in either the logic of representation or the investigation of aesthetics, for neither can approach the Holocaust with anything other than a structural derision, a necessary insufficiency. If the alleged paradox of the Holocaust is that it must be remembered so as not to be repeated, neither an appreciation for aesthetics nor a reliance on representation can serve this function. Further, holocausts continue to consume communication in the form of lost lives, lost letters, or lost opportunities. Some of these losses occur through chance, other through design, but both produce a violence that puts representation and meaning to the torch.

It is in this context that Derrida begins to write of ashes and cinders, for cinders ("cinder there is," as Derrida keeps insisting) are what remain after immolation. They are fragile remnants of something that was, but they are not, by any means, re-presentations of what was lost in the fire. Instead, if they signify anything, it is the existence of the fire itself, of consumption. And yet they are a fragile record, easily lost, scattered, or interned. As a metaphor, the cinder is a far more fragile remnant than that implied by the "trace." It is for this reason, perhaps, that Derrida will announce his preference for "ashes as the better paradigm for what I call the trace—something that erases itself totally, radically, while presenting itself."[31] Reading this, one cannot help but see that part of the preference comes from the fact that cinders lack the graphical resonance of the trace—hence the emphasis on their self-erasing property, a property that makes less metaphoric sense in the context of the "trace."

But this dissatisfaction with the trace, and the preference for ashes, is haunted, for it is in this context that the specter is given more frequent purchase, and usually by way of a relation to the ashes of those holocausts that inform his writing. In his discussion of Heidegger and his participation in National Socialism, Derrida explores Heidegger's discussion of spirit as *Geist,* a sense of spirit identified with flame and fire, and its relation to a set of metaphysically differentiated terms (*geistig, geistlich,* even *Gemut*).[32] In the prologue to *Cinders,* Derrida refers to his thinking of ashes, *post hoc,* as a "specter's comings and goings, unforeseen visions of the ghost."[33] In *Shibboleth*, writing that the dating and signature of a poem opens up the space for that poem's "spectral" return, he concludes by noting, "Ash awaits us."[34]

One could then, though with some reservations, think that the question of spirit, of the specter, serves as the witness to a conflagration in Derrida; the specter rises from the fire that consumes the trace, a fire fueled by a growing reservation about the metaphorical tenor of the trace. This is never acknowledged as such by Derrida. But the specter's appearance amid the ashes, the ghost of what no longer exists, that only exists as remains, is its own acknowledgment. For it is this appearance among the dead, which in the obvious analog is the manifestation of the virtual through dead media, that foreshadows the apotheosis of the specter as the preferred, most hospitable way to speak of deconstruction in the context of new media. It should thus come as no surprise that the specter is deployed by Derrida in order to describe the transformation of the written word by the computer, a transformation that follows almost exactly the logic I have outlined previously. From an interview in 1996, Derrida explains, "The figure of the text 'processed' on a computer is like a phantom to the extent that it is less bodily, more 'spiritual,' more ethereal. There is something like a disincarnation of the text in this. But its spectral silhouette remains, and what's more . . . still conforms to the spectral model of the book."[35]

This movement from trace to ash to specter offers insight into the history of *différance*, at least within Derrida's own writing.[36] In effect, the history of *différance* can be understood by exploring the different modalities by which its play is reduced, in other words, by attending to the material incarnation of those discourses in which *différance* is suppressed. Even Derrida's writings are, as he himself would admit, each a site of this reduction, and the original exposition of *différance* through the trace signifies the connection between the act of reduction and the material scene in which that reduction physically takes place. The trace signifies not only a remnant of *différance*, but a remnant of the inventional resources that assist in reducing *différance* for the purposes of exposition and critique. This connection has changed by the time the specter appears at the center of his analysis, for now his concern is no longer principally with the media of the book but with the nature of mediation and the mechanics of new media, and so the trace is no longer particularly appropriate as a means to describe this new horizon for the play of *différance*. The medium is, in this case, very much the parsing of the message.[37]

This does not mean that Derrida needs to be aware of the mediological appropriateness of this history. In all probability, the strange ambivalence I have noted earlier in Derrida's statements shows that he was perhaps never ready to break with his emphasis on *différance* as arche-writing, even if his thinking began to lead his writing in different directions.[38] He predicts as much when, in *Of Grammatology*, he maintains that a theory of writing will likely always come before a more general theory of technics.[39] This elision signifies a failure on Derrida's part, for as much as he is able to think the materiality of the media on which and through which he is writing, he privileges the wrong side of the history.[40] It is not that the specter is a trace, but the other way around: the trace is a specter, one specter, a reduction of *différance* most appropriate to the book and printed word. This is what must be contained within spectrality in order for spectrality to be most hospitable to deconstruction, or to do the work of inheritance. It is why the specter is the frequent witness to the holocaust of representation, for it is a holocaust that becomes more pronounced the greater the gaps of which communication is made.[41] As such, taking Derrida's spectrality seriously means following it, opening one's self to its haunting, rather than exorcising it. Doing so reveals that spectrality cannot be thought as merely one term among many that describe the play of *différance*, but rather a term that designates the potential modality by which each specter might appear in different media environments—in the book a trace, in the fire an ash, in the television a ghost, and so on. These modalities are always, as indicated earlier, theatrical in nature—each mode a setting of the stage.

Conclusion: A Shift in/to *Mimesis*

I have attempted to demonstrate that a need exists for those interested in the productions and seductions of rhetoric and discourse to consider more fully the materiality of the medium of communication, and that this need subsequently testifies as to why a turn, a return, to Derrida is also necessary.[42] The complexities of the primal material scene—that of mediation—require a form and practice of "reading" that negotiates a text's incarnation without letting that reading be overdetermined by the "technologies of circulation" on the one hand and without violently reducing the text to an extracted and idealistic "content" on the other. For the most part, Derrida's work demonstrates the attentiveness required if one is to take seriously that singularity always already situated within *différance*: namely, the textuality of the text that governs its interpretation. But this "work" could go further, could do more and be more explicit in its operations; as I have endeavored to show, a return to Derrida cannot simply take Derrida at his word. One must, in effect, read Derrida against Derrida.

Doing so reveals that even Derrida's most famous term, *différance*, has a history, one both within and outside of his own writings—a history determined by the material specificity of those media about which and through which it is written or thought.[43] It is a history that confirms the primacy of mediation as material and, concomitantly, as a fundamental condition of possibility and invention.

Today, the introduction of spectrality—a thematic that has always been linked to mediation, but that is more explicitly and obviously linked to those media forms produced since the nineteenth century—shows that we must begin to think about these media as unique material practices, each with its own politics and norms that govern the *scene* on which its discourse is played. And "scene" is undoubtedly the correct word to use, as it highlights the crucial dynamic raised by spectrality, that of appearance and manifestation. For Derrida, spectrality is distinguished from spirituality just as ghost is distinguished from *Geist*—the specter appears, it manifests in some way, in a manner that a spirit or essence does not. This is why spectrality accords so well with modern media, media that claim power from their ability to tele-commune, to make present all manner of ghostly apparitions, from canned voices released once more into the world and dead dancers who shill vacuum cleaners, to the tragic footage that permeates our cable bandwidth in the aftermath of disasters like 9/11 and Hurricane Katrina. Radio, television, Internet; the myth of real time, of representation as presence: these are the manifestations of electronic ghosts. Of course, the written word always possessed (or was possessed by) a bit of the specter, but the encoding and decoding were different, and the spectacle of spectrality inherent in writing, its theatricality, is seen more openly, is revealed as more obvious, in the afterglow of the television screen.[44]

So what are we as rhetorical scholars and critics to do? In order to treat the materiality of mediation seriously and with a greater specificity—which is, let me stress one last time, also an understanding that there can be no concept of materiality *sans* the media that disseminate the concept proper—requires a transition from a more conventional logic of representation to a more ecological appreciation of *mimesis* as the scene of communication. It is in this scene, this theater, that meanings are produced, disseminated, and interpreted, and more so, it is this theater that determines, at least in part, the inventional and interpretive possibilities that admit this hermeneutic process. As Sylviane Agacinski explains, "[m]edia spaces, the current locales of democratic visibility, are again a matter of a theatrical structure, even if we are dealing with the screen. This structure organizes the 'production' of power as much as of public opinion. It is theatrical, essentially and not by accident, because for a people, it is a matter of seeing and hearing itself."[45] Contemporary rhetorical practice, then, cannot be understood merely as a question of representation, a question resolvable by a critic's close reading of a text or an artifact in order to understand that X signifies Y; rather, we have before us a question of *mimesis*, in which critics must instead engage the artifact as itself an argument for what qualifies as the appropriate theater for the dissemination of reality, and in so doing, *a posse ad esse*, productive of a symbolic order as effect or affect.

This position induces some tension with other ways of thinking materiality, especially ways that rely fundamentally on a logic of representation. Class relations, for example, are always just that, relational, and thus always the subject of a representational field and an intersubjective assessment of the differences within that field. To speak of anything like an objective relation or an identity requires a prior ontological submission to representation, one that I believe is both dangerous and heuristically impoverished. Discussions of propaganda probably offer the easiest evidence of the problem facing such a critical perspective, and why it is I think a greater appreciation for the theatricality of mediation—of *mimesis*—can enhance critical efforts. Fox News, for example, is without doubt a reality-challenged mouthpiece for the Republican party, but it gains the progressive critic little to expose the obvious lack of factual verisimilitude in its coverage nor does it substantively help the media critic to explain away Fox's rhetorical appeal by asserting that propaganda operates by convincing people that they aren't actually seeing propaganda.[46] For either critical approach to seem remotely coherent, one must believe implicitly in either the sheer stupidity or the overwhelming and inexplicable avarice of Fox's viewing audience, a persona that hardly assists leftists interested in changing the Fox viewer's political imaginary and that hardly bodes well for those who argue for substantive improvements in the production quality of our news media. Such huffing and puffing may have its uses, to be sure, but it ultimately flounders against the walls of those brick houses ostensibly sullying the rhetorical landscape.

A mimetic understanding offers a much more robust insight into the operations of televisual propaganda. News networks do not gain adherents by properly representing the world, as is, or by "tricking" the populace into thinking exactly that, but rather the tele-communing power of the modern news/media networks rests in their ability to sell themselves as *the proper space in which the public can see themselves seeing the world.* This provides at least a reasonable explanation for the inane strategy by which Fox News repeats, *ad nauseum*, that its coverage is "fair and balanced"—it isn't a question of fooling anyone into thinking that Fox News is objective, but rather the act of inviting the conservative portion of the public to view themselves as the ones who are fair and balanced. It is this theatrical staging, this invitational mimicry, that explains the popularity and success of Fox News. Trying to assess and understand its success by analyzing its representational practices misses the mark—and the medium—entirely.

If I am asking that critics call into question a certain representational politics in their work, one that often justifies itself by affirming a political determination of materiality as something outside the text, let me suggest that the renewal and enriching of *mimesis* offers a potentially more productive endeavor. *Mimesis*, like so much of critical vocabulary, is a difficult target to lock down, especially because the meanings assigned to it vary radically through the course of its history and the passing of time.[47] Most conventionally understood as a more technical or originary term for imitation, *"mimesis"* in fact broaches a much broader theme, one that signifies the whole breadth of interactions with and determinations of presentation. This no doubt includes *imitatio*, but it does so because of a certain theatricality at work in its history. In the primary orality of ancient Greece, one learned by imitating the rhythmic patterns embedded in the great epics and poems of the day. Speaking was thus inherently theatrical, since the discourse had to have a hook—much like contemporary pop music—if it was to be memorable. If the rhythmic intonations were easily imitated, through routinized movements of the body, pattern repetition, and the parsing regularities of inflection, then the task of memory was all the easier. Since then, *mimesis* has been dressed in many guises—imitation, repetition, similarity, surreality, even representation—but these guises are bound together by the virtual, theatrical particularities of their modality, the different ways in which the scene is set, in the case of each and every discursive act, through the material substrate that mediates its manifestation.[48] *Mimesis* is, as Gunter Gebauer and Christoph Wulf note, "always concerned with a relational network of more than one person; the mimetic production of a symbolic world refers to other worlds and to their creators and draws other persons into one's own world."[49] It is within its capacity to create these worlds that we can determine the history of *différance* as (in part) a history of the media through which it is invented.

Hamlet's father therefore demarcates not just the ghost that haunts Marx, but also the explicit presentation and acknowledgment of a theatricality, of an ontological tease or reality bleeding that haunts all of us. He is a figure that is simultaneously there and not there, dead and yet living on—like Derrida's survival through text and DVD, like so many who "live beyond" through the archives we keep or the artifacts we broadcast. This living-on, which manifests as the spectral character of all recording and transmission media, is a tease that for rhetoricians means giving up the ghost on the ability to demonstrate rhetorically the facticity of a material world "out there" and instead turns our analytical engines toward the specific, singular materiality by which the word is given the appearance of flesh, by which the word in effect produces the world—in a word, its *mediation*.[50]

Notes

1. I choose the word "ecology" over what may be Derrida's more preferred term—"economy"—precisely to delineate the singular, almost organic imbrication of material form with textual content, something that "economy," with its roots in the norms of the hearth and home, cannot do. One could, of course, speak of the imbrication of materiality and discourse as a single economy, but that phrase would, I dare say, speak of a very

different critical object.

2. Ian Angus, *Primal Scenes of Communication* (Albany: State University of New York Press, 2000).

3. I lift "thickening" from James Jasinski. See "The Status of Theory and Method in Rhetorical Criticism," *Western Journal of Communication* 65 (2001): 249–70.

4. The problem, of course, isn't simply representation, but the politics that so often attend it. To believe that something signifies something else hardly portends some disaster—indeed, to a certain extent representation is inescapable—but to think that this referentiality holds some principal purchase on truth, on progress, or on politics carries with it very real and historically demonstrated risks.

5. Rod Little, "Is Derrida Really Dead?" *Spectator*, October 16, 2004, http://www.lewrock well.com/spectator/spec412.html.

6. See Jeffrey Sconce, *Haunted Media: Electronic Presence from Telegraphy to Television* (Durham, NC: Duke University Press, 2000).

7. Friedrich A. Kittler, *Gramophone, Film, Typewriter* (Stanford, CA: Stanford University Press, 1999), 12.

8. Jacques Derrida, *Specters of Marx* (New York: Routledge, 1994), 54.

9. See Derrida, *Specters of Marx*, 79–80 and 169.

10. Jacques Derrida and Bernard Stiegler, *Echographies of Television* (Oxford: Polity Press, 2002), 117.

11. See Jacques Derrida, *Glas* (Lincoln: University of Nebraska Press, 1986), 22a, 158b, 234b, and 235b.

12. Samuel Weber, *Theatricality as Medium* (New York: Fordham University Press, 2004), 119.

13. Jacques Derrida, *Acts of Literature* (New York: Routledge, 1992), 343.

14. Jacques Derrida, *Of Grammatology* (Baltimore, MD: Johns Hopkins University Press, 1976), 63.

15. Derrida and Stiegler, *Echographies of Television*, 38.

16. Recall that Barthes is, at almost the same time, writing about the "death of the author" and the allure of *ecriture automatique.*

17. Derrida, *Of Grammatology*, 86–7.

18. Jacques Derrida, *Dissemination* (Chicago: University of Chicago Press, 1981), 3.

19. Derrida, *Of Grammatology*, 9.

20. Jacques Derrida, *Margins of Philosophy* (Chicago: University of Chicago Press, 1982), 9.

21. Derrida, *Margins of Philosophy*, 24.

22. Derrida, *Of Grammatology*, 65.

23. Derrida, *Of Grammatology*, 65.

24. In *Echographies*, Stiegler consistently prompts Derrida to emphasize the specificity of newer media, and each time, Derrida defers in a somewhat circular fashion. Most notable is his response on page 39: "One might be tempted to do so." This implies neither affirmation nor outright negation, demonstrating once again a sort of unquiet negotiation of media specificity.

25. Derrida, *Specters of Marx*, 9.

26. Derrida, *Specters of Marx*, xiv.

27. For a brief discussion of the difficulties attending this "proper" name, see "Holocaust as a Common Noun: An Interview with Jacques Derrida," interview by Michal Ben-Naftali, *Eclipse of Humanity* (Jerusalem: Yad Vashem, 2000), CD-ROM, http://www1.yad vashem.org/Odot/prog/index_before_change_table.asp.

28. For more on the difficulty of using this term in relation to the present discussion, see Giorgio Agamben, *Remnants of Auschwitz* (New York: Zone Books, 1999), 26–33.

29. I am thinking of texts like *Cinders, Glas, Of Spirit, Shibboleth, The Gift of Death, The Post Card, Demuere,* etc.

30. Gideon Ofrat, *The Jewish Derrida* (Syracuse, NY: Syracuse University Press, 2001), 152.

31. Jacques Derrida, "On Reading Heidegger: An Outline of Remarks to the Essex Colloquium," *Research in Phenomenology* 17 (1987): 177.

32. Jacques Derrida, *Of Spirit: Heidegger and the Question* (Chicago: University of Chicago Press, 1989).

33. Jacques Derrida, *Cinders* (Lincoln: University of Nebraska Press, 1991), 22.

34. Derrida, *Acts of Literature*, 396.

35. Jacques Derrida, "Word Processor," interview by Béatrice and Louis Seguin, *La Quinzaine Littéraire*, August 1996, repr. In Jacques Derrida, *Paper Machine*, trans. Rachel Bowlby (Stanford, CA: Stanford University Press, 2005), 30.

36. We want to resist any strict periodization, as all the terms under consideration are present, albeit in different and more limited configurations, throughout Derrida's corpus. At the same time, I believe that careful attention to the texts themselves reveals that certain terms are awarded more time and privilege, and that those moments of prominence and privilege correspond to the problematics defined by the media peripherally or directly under Derrida's consideration.

37. I endorse this statement, a minor modification of McLuhan's most famous quip, with some qualifications. As the editors of this volume have noted, I should be cautious about leveling Derrida and McLuhan lest I reduce the genius of both. Nevertheless, there remains what I would like to call a *poietic coincidence,* one that finds the shift in Derrida's terminology roughly corresponding with his own use of inventional media. The privileging of the trace corresponds with a time when Derrida composed by hand, the discussion of ashes and cinders predominates during Derrida's time using mechanical and electrical typewriters, and the specter comes to the foreground after Derrida's shift to his "little Mac" and thus word processing (for a rough timeline, see "Word Processor," in Derrida, *Paper Machine*, 20–21). I want to avoid relying on any psychosocial explanation, as I am suspicious of its ease, but the coincidence is such that it bears mention, and perhaps further consideration. For now, this footnote must suffice.

38. In the interview given in 1996, Derrida is asked if his own use of different writing technologies has changed the content of his writing. His answer: "People often ask me, 'Has your writing changed since you have been writing on the computer?' I'm incapable of replying. . . . There's certainly a change but I'm not sure that it affects what is written, even if it does modify the way of writing." *Paper Machine*, 25. Obviously, I believe that evidence of a change in "what is written" is demonstrable within the writing itself, especially when it comes to the explication of *différance.*

39. Derrida, *Of Grammatology*, 8. He is writing here of arche-writing, of a general theory of writing that would, at least for the earlier Derrida, enable and iterate a theory of technics.

40. As Derrida notes in an interview given in 1997, "I have the impression (the impression!—what a word, already) that I never had any other *subject*: basically, paper, paper, paper." From "Paper or Me, You Know . . ." in *Paper Machine*, 41.

41. John Durham Peters, "The Gaps of Which Communication Is Made," *Critical Studies in Mass Communication* 11 (1994): 117–40.

42. That the study of rhetoric continues to be dominated by interest in public address is true, though it is certainly less true every day. In and of itself, this historical preference sacri-

fices nothing, but this preference does create problems if the methods used in criticism, the means by which critics engage in "reading," continue to be applied to non-oratorical media as if these media were merely oratorical analogs. To write of a famous speech as a speech make perfect sense, at least within an historical context, or if interested in establishing an oratorical canon, or even to explore the artistry of speechwriting. But to write of a speech today as if it was only a speech, and not a complex web of visual imagery and premeditated sound bites governed more by the viral pattern of televisual and Internet dissemination than by the artistry of its composition, makes much less sense if one is interested in current political interventions or understanding how media impact the possibilities of invention. In the same vein, the pedagogical emphasis on particular speakers as exemplars runs afoul of a similar problem, since the structural ADD enabled by the modern deluge of images cuts short the ability for a particular speaker to author and maintain control over a particular meaning. How can an address on terrorism provide the rules for its own interpretation when CNN overlays the voice track with routinized video of terrorists jumping through tires or engaging in target practice? No, to understand these modern media, one must take into account their material practices; one must learn to "read" an image or a camera movement, to learn the language of their particular medium.

43. For more, I recommend Bernard Stiegler, *Technics and Time, 1: The Faults of Epimetheus* (Stanford, CA: Stanford University Press, 1998), 235–37.

44. For a demonstration of this operation, look no further than J. Hillis Miller's *On Literature* (New York: Routledge, 2002), which offers the most enveloping attempt to explain literature/writing as an earlier form of *virtual reality,* an explication that of course only makes sense after the advent of those technics that enable something like the concept of "virtual reality."

45. Sylviane Agacinski, *Time Passing: Modernity and Nostalgia* (New York: Columbia University Press, 2003), 68.

46. A common argument, notably present in Robert Greenwald's *Outfoxed: Rupert Murdoch's War on Journalism*, DVD, directed by Robert Greenwald (Charlotte, NC: Carolina Productions, 2002). Robert McChesney puts it this way in the film: "The first rule of being a great propaganda system, and why our system is vastly superior to anything in the old Soviet Union, is that people [don't] think they're *being* subject[ed] to propaganda. If people don't think that, they aren't looking for that, [so] they're much easier to propagandize." I believe this view to be shortsighted.

47. Gunter Gebauer and Christoph Wulf, *Mimesis: Culture, Art, Society* (Berkeley: University of California Press, 1992).

48. See Phillipe Lacoue-Labarthe, *Typography* (Stanford, CA: Stanford University Press, 1989), 117.

49. Gebauer and Wulf, *Mimesis*, 3.

50. Examples that might be celebrated in this vein include, but are certainly not limited to, Andrea Hyssen, "Of Mice and *Mimesis*," *New German Critique* 81 (2000): 65–82; Trevor Parry-Giles and Shawn J. Parry-Giles, "The West Wing's Prime-Time Presidentiality: Mimesis and Catharsis in a Postmodern Romance," *Quarterly Journal of Speech* 88 (2002): 209–27; Barbara Biesecker, "Remembering World War II: The Rhetoric and Politics of National Commemoration at the Turn of the 21st Century," *Quarterly Journal of Speech* 80 (2002): 393–409; and Christine Harold, "Pranking Rhetoric: 'Culture Jamming' as Media Activism," *Critical Studies in Media Communication* 21 (2004), 189–211.

CHAPTER 10

Disarticulating American Indianness in the National Museum of the American Indian

Daniel F. Schowalter, Rowan University

[We] move decisively from the older image of the museum as a temple with its superior, self-governing priesthood to . . . a forum . . . committed not to the promulgation of received wisdom but to the encouragement of a multi-cultural dialogue.

Robert McCormick Adams

The received tradition of American Indianness is manifest in public culture through a range of common and fairly recognizable cultural practices. In this essay, "American Indianness" refers to the received historical understanding of North American Indians as they have been constituted typically in and through poetry, painting, photography, literature, cinema, statuary, and spectacular outdoor Western shows over the past 125 years. And indeed, it is through these channels that American Indianness continues to resonate with the popular imagination. What is more, Indianness has been made inseparable from "Americanness," making its images intransigent and incorrigible. Henry Wadsworth Longfellow's *Song of Hiawatha*, James Earle Fraser's "End of the Trail," George Catlin's paintings, and Edward Curtis's photographs all helped to constitute American Indianness (especially North American Plains Indianness) as Americanness in the decades surrounding the turn of the twentieth century.[1]

Counter-hegemonic practice, however, requires the attempted undoing of this constituted subjectivity, a disarticulation via experiential and discursive channels.[2] Accordingly, cultural museums have become an important locus for counter-hegemonic practice because today, more than ever, they attract patrons by promising an *experience*.[3] To be sure, traditional anthropological museums offer experiences to patrons, but the experiences are articulated with the received tradition. Furthermore, the new cultural museum makes the experiential its centerpiece, often with interactive technologies. The National

Museum of the American Indian (NMAI) offers an important critique of the received tradition, a counter-hegemonic intervention that works through a process of rhetorical disarticulation that functions to displace the hegemonic sense of American Indianness and to position the museum visitor to engage in an act of rearticulation.

Contemporary cultural museums highlight the potential for disarticulation in a variety of ways. First, we can think of the museum as a text that invites argumentation since, to borrow from Chaïm Perelman and Lucie Olbrechts-Tyteca, "[it] compels us to take into account not only the choice of data but also the way in which they are interpreted, the meaning attributed to them."[4] Similarly, Bruce Ferguson notes that exhibits are always strategic and persuasive, again tying disarticulation to strategy and persuasiveness.[5] Specifically, the strategies of contemporary cultural museums involve calling attention to their own constructedness. Cultural museums also offer an opportunity for disarticulation since their attributions and interpretations of cultures often contrast starkly with the received, ethnographic tradition and thereby emphasize "profound *discontinuity*."[6] In what follows, I argue that the opening of the NMAI on the National Mall in Washington, D.C., offers a unique opportunity to understand the crucial role of rhetorical disarticulation in the reformation of the political imaginary. More specifically, I will show how the museum's exhibits—and, most notably, the interactive technologies used therein—make it possible for patrons to reimagine American Indianness through their experiences of the NMAI's discourses. However, the museum does not accomplish this by imposing its own compelling rearticulation, a common museum practice, but rather by a rhetoric of disarticulation that disrupts American Indianness as fixed and one-dimensional. In other words, the NMAI's counter-hegemonic force is not attributable to a *rewriting of* the received rhetorical tradition that would inadvertently *reinscribe* its materiality, but to a disarticulation of it: to separate American Indianness from its temporal shackles, to rupture and displace familiar articulations through the experience of visitors so that they might rearticulate them. Whereas articulation spatializes "culture and nature by arranging diverse material-semiotic elements into recognizable bodies and languages," disarticulation displaces culture and nature from that familiar spatialization and renders them unrecognizable.[7] Indeed, many of the museum's visitors have and continue to "find the new museological paradigm at work in the exhibitions unfamiliar and confusing."[8]

Specifically, the NMAI disarticulates American Indianness as it fragments voice and invites reflection on the visual. It accomplishes this through the use of new media technologies (particularly digital video technology) that are invested with interruptive force. Rather than posit alternative accounts, the museum's architectural design and its three permanent exhibits offer a model for a rhetoric of disarticulation.

Museums, the Material Paradox of Hegemonic Representation, and Rhetorics of Articulation and Disarticulation

Stuart Hall suggests that ideology is rooted in the disarticulation and rearticulation of discourses.[9] To borrow Hall's phrase, "ideas are not free-floating in people's heads" but instead must be articulated via signifiers and practices, both corporeal and symbolic. Once ideas are *dis*articulated or unlinked, the potential for *re*articulation and, thus, ideological practice, emerges.[10] And because discourse is always dependent on the mutual relationship between what John Fiske calls discursive and nondiscursive realities, articulation always has a material dimension.[11] It follows, therefore, that disarticulation becomes a material pursuit, too, functioning at the intersection of experience and discourse. And since articulation "refers simultaneously to joining together, [and] separating," it is compensatory to disarticulation, and the two essentially are part of the same process.[12] Following this logic, I consider *dis*articulation to be the more useful term since hegemonic articulation, while resisting disarticulation, provides opportunities for counter-hegemonic experiential and discursive practices. Put otherwise, just as articulation is hegemonic, so, too, can disarticulation be counter-hegemonic.

Visual articulations are central to the (re)production of ideological formations, but to the extent that they draw on or affiliate with the conventions of realist representation, they are confronted with the paradox of materiality. Theorists of the photographic and cinematic image have long recognized a material paradox at the heart of realist theories of representation: photographs and films endure as material "traces" of the things they represent long after those referents have dissipated. André Bazin's "mummy complex" and "ontology" at the heart of the photographic image, and Sergei Eisenstein's consideration of the "organicness" of film form, are explorations of this paradox.[13] Specifically, they explain the way in which images gain our adherence as a material version of the real and why they are so difficult to disarticulate.[14] While Walter Benjamin recognized an "aura" in the daguerreotype and later photographic technologies, Alan Trachtenberg suggests that Edward Curtis's "Curt-Tone" Indians were photographically "embalmed."[15] Photographs of "pureblood" Indians were not only of monetary value (as sources of income for their subjects and market value for their merchandisers) but they were valued also for their capacity to articulate a sense of "authenticity" and "originality" to Americanness, ritualistically

grounding it in the traditions of the visual culture, while at the same time
guaranteeing its future by the preservation of these images.[16]

But critical explorations of these imageries too quickly pass over the
specific rhetorical practices by which disarticulation occurs. Experiences are
also rhetorically articulated.[17] "Experiential spaces," like those found in
contemporary cultural museums, highlight rhetorics of experience. Ferguson
links exhibition and speech, claiming that "exhibitions are the material
speech" of political institutions.[18] Indeed, such "material speech" is an
important part of the visitors' experience since exhibitions and visitor
experience directly inform one another.[19] In a similar fashion, disarticulation
is also rooted in the experiential. Since experience has no extra-rhetorical
meaning, it is dependent on the discourses that inform it. As Trachtenberg
notes, while the American Indian "was a figure of literary, religious, political, and scientific imagination more often than of firsthand experience," such
firsthand experience is articulated nevertheless within the received popular
"imagination."[20] Moreover, contemporary American Indianness is often
articulated to traumatic discourses, including high rates of alcoholism,
suicide, and domestic violence.[21] Such hegemonic constructions of American
Indianness have and continue to resist easy disarticulation.

Likewise, traditional museums reproduce and reinforce the paradox of
materiality by articulating the received understanding of American Indianness with the visitor's experience. Traditional museum representations of
American Indianness posit (1) objects of study rather than authorities of that
study and (2) historical subjects rather than contemporary agents. Furthermore, these traditional representations exist within a uniquely visual, yet
voiceless, register. George Catlin's paintings, Edward Curtis's photogravures, and countless Hollywood portrayals have etched American Indian
faces, colors, adornments, skirmishes, and encampments firmly into the
popular imagination. Yet this is a legacy not spoken by native voices.
Alternatively, the American Indian experience is heavily overdetermined by
a "narrative of imperial conquest" (and, later, genocide) that had already
been in place by the 1870s.[22] Rarely has American Indianness spoken with its
own voice, and rarely have its representations in the popular imagination
been of its own making. While this lack of voice and visibility enables a
hegemonic narrative to articulate a certain remembrance of American
Indianness, it also offers the NMAI an opportunity to restore voice and
visibility in order to disarticulate that remembrance. The NMAI offers an
alternative that emphasizes the material experience of the museum visitor as
a site of disarticulation or dissociation that encourages the viewer to reconstruct an understanding of American Indianness. Iwona Irwin-Zarecka

captures the spirit of this opportunity:

> But what appears to matter even more is dislodging the established patterns of think-
> ing and feeling, patterns responsible for the gaps in remembrance. Countering an
> absence with an ever-growing informational base, in other words, provides only for
> the *possibility* of change within collective memory. The harder task is to make draw-
> ing on these new resources both emotionally and cognitively compelling, or to cre-
> ate a shared need to remember what had not been remembered before.[23]

As this suggests, disarticulation is key to counter-hegemonic practice; such is
the imperative of the NMAI. The museum seeks to disarticulate "established
patterns of thinking and feeling" from the received legacy with an "ever-
growing informational base," particularly one constituted by contemporary
technologies. Put otherwise, visitors are offered opportunities to argue with
the stories they have inherited about American Indianness. Perelman suggests that "dissociation" is one of two categories of techniques of argumentation that "[aim] at separating elements which language or a received tradition
have previously tied together."[24] It is, precisely, this separation of received
articulations of American Indianness that the NMAI offers by way of a
critique of visuality itself.

While European subjects in cinema, art, and museology traverse historical eras and contexts, this has not been the case for the American Indian.
Indeed, American Indianness has forever been fixed in time by film, photography, and museology. In the thousands of Hollywood films released since
the early part of the twentieth century, American Indians are always portrayed as "things of the past": "temporally . . . [they] have been consigned to
another dimension entirely."[25] Similarly, Trachtenberg demonstrates that the
greatest legacy of Curtis's photographs "was to make photography itself
seem [the] master trope of the vanishing race."[26] Such is the paradox of
American Indianness: having been visualized while at the same time vanishing. American Indianness has always already been a memory.

The pastness of American Indianness has become familiar not only
through film and photography but also in museums. Anthropological exhibits
constructed as "natural history" have dominated museum displays of American Indians since they became what retired Senator Ben Nighthorse Campbell referred to as "America's first endangered species."[27] Ironically,
however, this close association with anthropology has had the effect of
divorcing American Indianness from the study of history altogether.[28] From
the earliest displays that incorporated paintings, photographs, and silent films
to their most recent reiterations that portray subjects frozen in time, American Indians have remained "a people with a past, but without a history."[29]
Although there can be no doubt that these temporal parameters constrain

American Indianness, they can also become prized points of disarticulation
so that patrons may rearticulate otherwise. In order to begin to disarticulate
American Indianness from the received tradition, then, the NMAI must
subvert its visual legacy.

Disarticulating the Visual

Visitors can track American Indianness in a variety of directions within the
NMAI and its various publications. Many of these images of American
Indianness challenge patrons' common sense and received understandings.
As previously remarked, Perelman notes that one way to "depart from
common sense" is through dissociating ideas from each other.[30] Images are
especially adept at dissociation because they can take on incompatible forms
simultaneously. The cover image of the fall 2004 special commemorative
NMAI issue of the *American Indian* magazine illustrates this capacity
particularly well by highlighting its own impossibility (see figures 1 and 2).
By dissociating American Indianness from its familiar "common" sense
image, it critiques the veracity of the visual image itself. The gatefold cover
depicts Santee Smith (Mohawk) and James Kinistino (Saulteaux) in indexi-
cal, "historical" garb. Smith stands behind Kinistino's right shoulder and
only the right side of his painted face, beaded throat, and chest are included
in the frame. These are historical (North) American Indians as they have
been conventionally remembered; thus, they are comfortable, common
articulations. Once the cover is folded out from the inside, however, the now
double-page spread depicts Kinistino centered, his left side decidedly
contemporary and fashionable, and Smith standing behind his left shoulder,
dressed likewise in contemporary fashion.

Considered individually, these images are free from apparent contradiction yet, when taken together, they are incommensurate with one another in a
manner that disarticulates Indianness from its inherited pastness. Founding
director W. Richard West Jr. elaborates in the "welcome" essay for the issue,
"A Vision Come to Pass," that the NMAI "is a vision that has finally become
tangible."[31] This tangibility is dependent on disarticulatory practices like the
magazine cover image. Only now can the NMAI become a new site of
struggle, an arena wherein patrons can rearticulate a new vision of Indianness. As a disarticulation, the cover image does more than merely erase,
recover, or invent. While "memory projects" often emphasize "the construction of new narratives (and recovery of the ones lost)," it is significant that
the NMAI's project attempts neither.[32] Rather, it boldly rejects such common
rhetorical strategies, imposing instead a rhetoric of disarticulation that
positions patrons to rearticulate an image of Indianness.

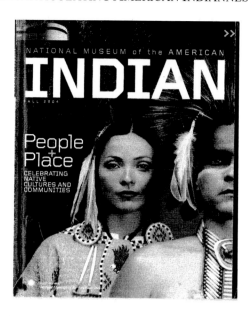

Figure 1: Front page of *American Indian* magazine
Courtesy of the National Museum of the American Indian

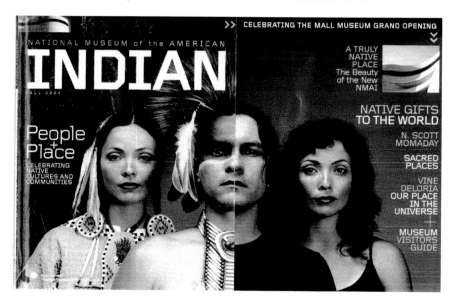

Figure 2: Front page folded out
Courtesy of the National Museum of the American Indian

The cover image ruptures the established and coherent visual discourse of Indianness once it combines three temporally incompatible bodies, portraying them as standing together at the same moment in space and time. While the change from "historical" to contemporary garb makes it appear as if these American Indians have moved through time, the viewer also recognizes that they have maintained their same bodies. Here, bodies become independent of temporality. While they have become visually transformed, we recognize them to be the same bodies but not the same subjects. The two individuals become four, Smith transformed completely and Kinistino divided schizophrenically. A multitude of subject positions exist simultaneously, freed from the past, each alter-identity casting the other into doubt. The image thereby "announces" that the NMAI is a disruptive space, a site of struggle that seeks to "influence the private makings of sense."[33] Here, the magazine cover image evinces a profound splitting of one idea into two.[34] American Indianness is bifurcated between its traditional visual legacy and a more contemporary subjectivity, freeing it from the captivity of pastness.

The NMAI disarticulates American Indianness from pastness in other ways as well. First, even the museum's outward appearance eschews American Indianness as being "timed out" or out of time (see figure 3). Rather than situate itself within clear temporal parameters, it peels them away to emphasize a certain time*lessness*. The NMAI's architectural design rejects temporality and linearity, disrupting the close partnership between the straight line and Western notions of temporality. The structural elements of the museum, like the magazine cover images, utilize the visual as the engine for a critique of pastness.

Disarticulating Architecture

Like most of the structures on the National Mall, the NMAI presents itself as a visual spectacle, both meant to be viewed from the outside and meant to house things to be viewed within. The building's architecture is visually stunning, but it is a visibility that brazenly rejects categorization. The NMAI has mountainous dimensions and no easily identifiable architectural style. Its 250,000-square-foot, five-story bulk is covered by a curved limestone façade and crowned with a hundred-foot-high dome, an architectural spectacle that defies architectural conventions. While the texture and color of the Kasota dolomitic limestone dramatically set it off from the textures and colors of its surrounding geography, the undulations provide a vivid and striking contrast to the other buildings on the Mall and in the area. The NMAI's limestone, glass, and steel are not associated with any discrete historical period. By refusing to speak from a specific architectural era, the NMAI begins to disarticulate pastness from the visual legacy of American Indianness and, like the commemorative magazine cover, confuses temporality.

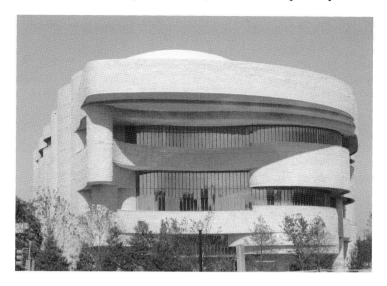

Figure 3: The National Museum of the American Indian, east entrance
Courtesy of the National Museum of the American Indian

Mimicking "a mesa carved by eons of wind and rain," the structure transcends discrete temporalities by referencing the timelessness of nature.[35] This formation cannot be categorized via distinct styles from discrete histories with recognizable architectural habits. Because the rounded contours and cantilevered spaces reject a traceable architectural style that has endured *through* time they suggest instead a moment *in* or *amid* time. Here, the timebound is replaced with the timeless, the linear with the cyclical, a theme that becomes familiar to visitors over the course of their museum experience.

The soaring, rounded exterior of the museum also rejects symmetry, a hallmark of traditional architectural design. There are no two sides or curves that are alike. While the east end reaches toward the U.S. Capitol with its soaring cantilevered roof, the west end is by comparison blunt, relatively flat although still undulated. The window formations are also asymmetrical, their architecture refusing to follow a pattern or predictable configuration. Likewise, there is no symmetry to the undulations of the limestone. Even the trash receptacles surrounding the museum are hidden within irregularly curved stone retaining walls so as not to interrupt the timeless character of the grounds with the familiar industrial form. Finally, the museum's waterfall on its west end cascades from what looks like a rocky outcropping and then snakes its way along the north face of the building, around natural boulders. The stacked granite blocks that form part of the fall's structure have smooth beveled caps that appear natural. Unable to associate the features and characteristics of the museum's architecture and grounds with distinct time periods, American Indianness is further disarticulated from pastness, enabling visitors to rearticulate the relationship between Indianness and temporality.[36] The museum becomes a materialized displacement of pastness.

The museum's exterior appearance most closely resembles an ecological formation that functions as an "identity reference" for American Indianness, recalling typical American Indian spaces such as meadows and croplands, lowland freshwater wetlands, and upland hardwood forest.[37] Internally, however, the museum offers a critique of identity by way of a critique of linear memory itself. While N. Scott Momaday emphasizes the past, claiming that the museum evokes the "ancient spirit of the earth and of life itself in a continuum that is as old as humankind, older than memory," his vision of the past points to the imperative to disarticulate the collective memory of American Indianness from the received legacy.[38] Notably, the museum does not offer a replacement memory, but a critique of linear memory. For Momaday, the museum rejects linear time for a continuum of time and disarticulates memory from its captivity in the past.

The museum's initial interior spaces also reject a linear conceptualization of time. The concentric circles of the soaring, domed entrance, named the "Potomac," which is Algonquian/Powhatan for "where the goods are brought in," reject linearity. Just as there are no straight lines in the Potomac, neither are there relics from the past. The copper wall, a curving, 150-foot, ahistorical architectural sculpture, and the towering vaulted ceiling surround visitors, dwarfing them in an asymmetrical ultra-circularity. The circularity of this space denies visitors directional clues. Like the exterior architecture, this open, rounded, soaring entrance rejects linear direction as well as linear time (i.e., movement *through* time) and serves instead to highlight a moment *amid* time. There are no markers of/from the past in this initial space, just the immediate moment that visitors inhabit. Even the traditional outrigger canoe and kayak found there, although built according to traditional method, are new.

Indeed, the NMAI's design throughout emphasizes the present tense and pushes away deeply entrenched images of the past. This serves to disarticulate Indianness from pastness. Architect Johnpaul Jones explains that there are "four worlds with a voice in the completed Mall Museum . . . the natural world, the animal world, the spirit world, and the human world."[39] While these are familiar themes in American Indianness, the notion of "worlds" is important because it suggests a continual present. The tropes ("worlds") of "nature," "animal," "spirit," and "human," as they are invoked here, transcend past and future as they lack references to either origin or destiny. The voices that speak in these four "worlds with a voice" are present-tense American-Indian voices, as they have been from the museum's inception. From the time when then-congressman Ben Nighthorse Campbell (Northern Cheyenne) envisioned a museum that would be a *living* memorial, to the continual reminders of founding director W. Richard West Jr. (Cheyenne and Arapaho) that the museum refuses to "wallow in the genocide, broken promises and bloody wars of the nineteenth century," the voices of the museum have been Native.[40]

Once visitors enter through the east entrance of the museum, they find themselves inside the Potomac. The copper wall is the first art encountered, and it also serves as a barrier, preventing visitors from proceeding straight to the center of the Potomac. However, far from being a "highly regulated . . . sphere," the NMAI presents few such obstacles.[41] After entering, visitors are not, as is typically the case in museums, required or even encouraged (through roping, pathways, etc.) to take any particular path through the exhibits. Ferguson notes that this results, in part, from the changing expectation museums are faced with today centering around questions of control, agenda, and purpose.[42] Certainly, this claim fits into the rhetoric of disarticulation that we're exploring here. Indeed, Amanda Cobb argues that "the installations do not offer narratives with clear beginnings, middles, and ends at all."[43] This lack of linear structure is a marked departure from more than a century of highly regulated and prescribed representations of American Indianness. Thus, this is in no way a prescribed rewriting of the memory and history of American Indianness, but a rejection of those received memories and histories or, more correctly, lack of history.

Additionally, the museum, and particularly the Potomac, disarticulates "landscape" and "terrain" from the visual legacy of American Indianness, countering the familiar sense that the American Indian belongs "more to the terrain than to history, as if they were features of the landscape."[44] Just as notable as the Potomac's vastness is its emptiness, the absence of landscape features so common in natural history museums. There are no dioramas, bison on the prairie, button-activated rattlesnakes, or tipis illuminated from within. This *lack* of what could have otherwise been represented overtly is what Ferguson muses the "unconscious" of the institution: unspeakable but communicative and understandable.[45] These traditional components of American Indianness simply are not available for viewers and their sense making. All the Potomac offers is vast, flat emptiness, and this emptiness disarticulates more typical landscape and terrain formations from the visual legacy of American Indianness and requires visitors to rearticulate it as they move through the Potomac.

Once visitors pass across the Potomac, they encounter the Chesapeake Museum Store, a high-end outlet filled with beautiful jewelry, prints, artifacts, figurines, dolls, books, pottery, and trinkets. After ascending the stairs (or boarding a discreetly positioned elevator) to the second floor, the visitor confronts another store, the Roanoke Museum Store. Slightly less exclusive but larger than the Chesapeake, this shop contains a greater variety of merchandise. While some critics have bemoaned expensive shops within American Indian museums as ironic, this emphasis on high-end merchandising functions to disarticulate American Indianness from the craft-making Indian peddler, a staple of the traditional narrative.[46] The legacy of American Indian art is one entrenched in cheaply made trinkets, models, and beads, the "Indian art" dealer awash with dream catchers, countless variations of the *End of the Trail* image, carved idols, and moccasins. By presenting high-end goods, the museum disrupts this prominent and deeply entrenched legacy.

The voice of "high" art and merchandise is one heretofore new for visitors to the NMAI, but certainly not the last one to be encountered. Ferguson uses the term "voice" to refer to the "number and kind" of media used in exhibition.[47] On level two, visitors are introduced to an explicitly technological voice should they choose to enter the interactive learning center, a high-tech, brochure-filled resource center overlooking Independence Avenue. The flat-screen monitors and other computer technologies, combined with sleek, boardroom-like interior and corporate-style furniture, define the modern voice of technology. This voice comes into even fuller fruition in the Lelawi theater, a 124-seat circular high-tech spectacle that displays the twelve-minute *Who We Are* multimedia presentation. This spectacle is as much a celebration of digital technology as it is a meditation on American Indian identities. Indeed, the film is emblematic of the other technologies scattered throughout the museum, including countless video exhibits, digital displays, and projected configurations. This is not a space for loin-clothed mannequins and static dioramas. Rather, technologies like these become the engine for the disarticulation of American Indianness from "primitiveness" throughout the museum. Although interactive, pedagogical, and multimediated technologies are often the strategies of choice for new cultural museums, the NMAI's employment of them explicitly confronts the received vision of American Indianness.[48] Put otherwise, the technological displays throughout the museum disarticulate the primitivist visual legacy of American Indianness. Having been articulated via relatively primitive media technologies (paintings, photographs, cinema, literature, etc.), the ultra high-tech atmosphere of many of the museum's exhibits disarticulates those more traditional media, displacing their authority in a celebration of technology. Contemporary technologies like these are used to critique the received articulations of American Indianness throughout the three permanent exhibits specifically through critiques of the image and voice.

Image and Voice within the Three Permanent Exhibits

The permanent exhibits in the NMAI are divided into three frameworks, "Our Universes," "Our Peoples," and "Our Lives." The inclusive pronoun "our" emphasizes a present and dynamic "ownership" throughout the museum's three permanent exhibits. American Indian voices that speak for themselves displace those voices that have otherwise spoken for it. By rejecting the traditionally omniscient voice that speaks about "the" people, universes, and lives of American Indians, the NMAI speaks multivocally. Instead of the familiar voice of history, the NMAI offers an alternative rhetoric consisting of a multitude of voices within intimate, even solitary, technology-rich settings.

Our Universes

This permanent exhibit greets patrons with familiar American Indian themes. The introductory placard for the "Our Universes" exhibit on level four foregrounds Native voices and informs visitors that they'll "discover how Native People understand their place in the universe and order their daily lives," and that ancestors "taught [them] to live in harmony with the animals, plants, spirit world, and the people around [them]." Also, visitors are informed that they will "encounter Native people from the Western hemisphere who continue to express this wisdom in ceremonies, celebrations, languages, arts, religions, and daily life," and finally, they are told that it is the duty of Native people "to pass these teachings onto succeeding generations" in order to ensure that these traditions will be kept alive.[49]

While the articulation of harmony, wisdom, and tradition in this inscription are familiar thematic representations of Indianness, notably, the voices that speak them are less so. The "Our Universes" exhibits are compartmentalized and intimate. Each exhibit corresponds to a different nation and requires that visitors enter into a space that belongs to that nation, usually a typical dwelling (e.g., a Waginogan) or some other setting presented as an important part of that Native experience. Only a few visitors at a time can enter and move about these intimate spaces, vividly marking them as visitors and, in most cases, listeners as well. The voices in these intimate and often confining spaces are not those of the visitor or of history but belong rather to American Indians. Furthermore, the received tradition's "dogmatic narratives" simply have no place within these exhibits.[50] Visitors can move among and between these exhibits to meet the Pueblo of Santa Clara, New Mexico; the Anishnabe; the Lakota; the Qechuan; the Hupa; and so forth, in their own traditional settings. However, these settings, like the Waginogan mentioned, are ironically juxtaposed to multiple technologies. In each intimate exhibit, the mythology of these Native peoples is traced through illustrations, video, audio, and interactive displays that are dramatically set apart from artifacts and dioramas. Here again, received histories are disarticulated from "communities of memory" by hyper-technologized Native voices.[51] As we'll see, the voices that speak the mythology are Native and they disrupt the more familiar European, anthropological voice in their fragmented, videotaped, audiotaped, computerized, and virtual constructions.

Visitors become accustomed to hyper-technologized Native voices. The entire exhibit exists under a "night sky" formed by projected fiber-optic stars and constellations. From the void of the vast Potomac, which highlights absence, to the diverse and spectacular technologies of these Native voices, the monolithic voice of history is dismantled. Visitors are invited to engage and focus closely on a wide array of interactive video displays and projection technologies, including digitally imaged objects and virtual tours, and to study them attentively—or at least to marvel at the technology. Faces from video screens speak to visitors as they pass by. Minute, and often made up of small print and images, the exhibits require the close and sustained attention of visitors. Unlike the more traditional diorama, unmoving and primitive (like the imaginary American Indians themselves), these exhibits emphasize contemporary, interactive technologies. And, as Ferguson reminds us, this is key since it is the medium of the exhibit that determines the ways in which visitors make sense of it.[52] Thus, although the experience of "Our Universes" differs markedly from that of the Potomac, both confront a received vision of American Indianness that is trapped in history.

Our Peoples

While still on level four, visitors encounter the "Our Peoples" permanent exhibit that emphasizes how each hemisphere affected life in the other. Visitors learn from placards that the exhibit "is about how eight communities understand their historical identities" and "how contact between the two hemispheres created the world we know today," transforming "the lives of everyone." The placard emphasizes that "[n]o matter where you are from, the Native history of this hemisphere is part of who you are and how you live" and urges viewers to "think of the exhibition as an excavation site, where evidence that has been buried, ignored, and denied is finally brought to light." The placard concludes, "[T]he evidence suggests that the history of this hemisphere is written in the lives of Native people."[53] The evidence is not locked away in the past, but is here with us today. Over the course of this exhibit, visitors experience eight very different and notably all contemporary Native voices telling their own stories. The placard goes on to invite viewers "to look at the past five centuries from the vantage point of the original Americans," and explains "why so little of this history is familiar." Once past the placard, visitors are presented not with a wall of ancient artifacts or relics, but with the first pieces of evidence for Native life in this hemisphere: brilliant and brightly lit masks, figurines, statues, carvings, and pottery. Likewise, in another area of the exhibit, a wall of gold objects depicts the "tremendous wealth of American cultures before European contact" and "the origin of the first global economy."[54] This global economy, long written out of the received tradition of Native peoples, again positions visitors to re-imagine American Indianness in a new way for themselves.

The term "evidence" takes on great significance here. Perhaps most importantly, on the entrance divider of the "Our Peoples" exhibit, visitors are confronted with the enormously etched word: EVIDENCE. A placard elaborates:

WE ARE THE EVIDENCE OF THIS WESTERN HEMISPHERE
Henry Crow Dog (Lakota), 1974
Native history has long been seen as what happened after Europeans arrived on American shores. Yet for thousands of years, Native people everywhere have told stories and remembered the past. Few people in the world care more passionately or have fought longer and harder to know and understand their histories than we have.

Here, the museum lends "the historical" a slightly different inflection. The placard clearly posits Natives as historical peoples. This is important because the historical is made present *and* embraced in a way that it is not in the Potomac or the "Our Universes" exhibit. The placard offers a straightforward dissociation of Native histories from European histories. But it also serves, more importantly, to disarticulate the Native archetypes of "relic" and "artifact" from the anthropological, received tradition of American Indian-ness with the term "evidence." The term "evidence" invites an active and direct association with something (e.g., a crime) while "relic" and "artifact" have more passive and less clear associations *and* reinscribe the problem of being fixed in time. Furthermore, evidence is commonly defined by those with firsthand experience, whereas relics and artifacts are usually defined by those without it. By pointing to "evidence" of American Indianness, the museum leaves no option to consider "relics" or "artifacts" of American Indianness. Put otherwise, the question "What *were* they?" is displaced by the question "Who *are* they?"

The museum displays virtually no historical photographs in any of its exhibits. This is not surprising given the medium's power to inscribe, embalm, and instantiate American Indianness, as it has now for over a century. A staple of the received image of American Indianness, particularly and most importantly through the published work of Edward S. Curtis, it follows that the museum regards photographic images with some trepidation. Even more and true to form, the NMAI embarks on a critique of the historic photograph via multimedia digital technologies. For example, in one exhibit titled "Making History," visitors are presented with a collection of seventeen George Catlin portrait paintings. Amid the portraits are three thirty-seven-inch vertical plasma screens that present images (mostly photogravures of American Indians) and a narration written by Comanche author Paul Chaat Smith. The narrator, Cree actor Floyd Favel, walks as he claims that "for all our visibility we have been rendered invisible" and that the museum itself is a process of "giving voice." He appears to walk from one plasma screen onto another, a seamless technological display. The fixed, static Catlin portraits are juxtaposed with ephemeral images of photogravures that fade in and out, suggesting that the historical photographs have, in fact, served to make American Indianness less, not more, visible. This technological display questions the role of the photograph in the visual legacy of American Indianness. Here, the digitized photogravures highlight the materiality of the painted portraits just as the portraits highlight the temporary, even fleeting, nature of the digitized photogravures. The digitized images become an analogue to how photographic technologies, like Curtis's, have functioned in history and memory—that is, to make American Indianness disappear. By combining these three technologies—the painted portrait, the (virtual) photogravure, and the digitized plasma screens—the museum disarticulates the visual legacy of American Indianness from one of its primary media, the photograph. It is transformed into nothing more than fading pixels.

As the images cycle past, Favel elaborates at considerable length:

> These pictures that surround you now change the past into stories . . . changes all the time . . . what was gospel then is often in disrepute now . . . yesterday's truth becomes false, or ill informed, or offensive today . . . long accepted histories . . . have been turned upside down . . . we're viewed as . . . barbarians and noble savages . . . the lowest form of humanity . . . rarely are we seen as human beings . . . deeply imbedded . . . hard to dislodge . . . has been fixed in all our minds by histories taught in classrooms generation after generation . . . Hollywood has offered its own image of us . . . a powerful one, forced and reforced by movies seen by countless viewers

. . . repetition over decades has solidified them . . . they were not created by Native Americans . . . not the paintings, not the photos, not the movies . . . and especially not the history . . . this gallery is making history, and like all other makers of history it has a point of view, an agenda . . . other perspectives would have achieved different results . . . our survival . . . the original people . . . is one of the most extraordinary stories in human history . . . here we have done as others have done . . . view what's offered with respect but also with skepticism . . . explore this gallery, encounter it, reflect on it, argue with it.

Arguably the most acute critique of the European voice of history within the museum, Favel's point is clear: pictures tell stories; stories change; neither can be trusted. The narration disarticulates the image from the voicelessness and invisibility of the Native legacy *and* highlights the fluidity of histories. But Favel does more than critique the power of entrenched histories by critiquing the photographic form itself. Indeed, once the image is disarticulated from this history, he must acknowledge that all histories, including those that might be gleaned from the NMAI, are constructed and must be explored, encountered, and, most importantly, argued with.

Our Lives

The only permanent exhibit on level three, "Our Lives," focuses on Native identity in the twenty-first century. Notably, its introductory placard foregrounds the problem of identity as such, claiming that "identity is not a thing, but a lived experience." The exhibit links experience and identity by focusing on eight Native communities and indicates that the NMAI staff members worked closely with these communities in order to be sure that "everything you see, hear, and read reflects their voices, perspectives, and ultimately, their identity as Native people."[55] This exhibit features photographic and video images of hundreds of faces. The central display separates face from embodiment and, ultimately, identity through shifting and fragmented digital images of faces. These exhibits ask what becomes an impossible question to answer: what does it mean to be American Indian?

Figure 4 depicts one of a multitude of segmenting and recombining video images of a face. Ever changing, the exhibit portrays a single face made up of one to sixteen segments of other faces, disarticulating face from American Indian identities. American Indianness speaks through the voice of technology more pointedly here than perhaps anywhere else in the museum. Because the video exhibit is continually changing, it displaces a stagnant pastness with a dynamic present. The face reinvents itself continually in new configurations and therefore inhabits the *now*. Furthermore, like the 2004 commemorative magazine cover, the display topples a stable, totalized American

Indian identity by offering an impossible configuration. Like Santee Smith and James Kinistino, the subjects of the magazine cover image, these subjects are contradictions of themselves and, as such, disrupt Indianness rather than reinscribe it.

Figure 4: Video image of recombining faces
Photograph by Daniel F. Schowalter

In another technological spectacle, visitors pass through a corridor on whose walls life-size contemporary human figures are projected. As they appear to walk past, some are in military uniform, some tradespeople, and others still white-collar workers. All are ostensibly Native peoples. The images suggest that American Indians are, in fact, everywhere among us, even if hardly visible. This digital display visualizes contemporary American Indianness for visitors as they walk through the corridor and become surrounded by the digital specters of diverse Native peoples. Through these and other technologies, the exhibit highlights American Indian voices and images that disrupt received legacies. The experience of the exhibit, the daunting technology and dizzying arrays of nuanced identities, destabilizes the monolithic trope of *the* American Indian.

Trauma

Inevitably, museum visitors will be invited to consider, frankly, the trauma buried within these histories. Although the death of millions at the hands of Europeans is arguably the most visceral facet of the American Indian experience, the museum refuses to be overshadowed by it, much to the chagrin of many critics.[56] While trauma is inseparable from American Indianness, Irwin-Zarecka reminds us that it is the "personal relevance of the traumatic memory, and not personal witness to the trauma" that often defines communities.[57] This is an apt characterization of the museum's treatment of trauma, which highlights the personal relevance of the traumatic history rather than the trauma itself. The NMAI consistently reminds visitors to question what they think they know about American Indianness, and it does not allow this traumatic history to speak for American Indianness. Having urged visitors to "explore this gallery, encounter it, reflect on it, argue with it," the museum enables patrons to approach the rearticulation of the genocide of American Indianness delicately. While it must acknowledge the traumatic but barely visible past of these peoples, we know that the museum refuses to wallow in this genocidal history.[58] Furthermore, the NMAI experience resists its context on the National Mall as a site of memorialization,[59] and instead seeks to portray a "strong and living tradition."[60] While acknowledging the many nations and languages that have been lost to the past forever, the museum's mantra, "survivance," disarticulates the narrative of loss from American Indianness. More than striving for "survival" and "perseverance," a placard in the "Our Lives" exhibit explains that the term raises social and political consciousness with regard to American Indians. Keeping the emphasis on "survivance," the museum frees itself from the debilitating influence of the narrative of genocide.

That being said, two placards in the museum summarize the trauma clearly. One, titled "Infinite Thousands," clearly details that European contact "withered the indigenous people of the Americas" with diseases that claimed "nine lives out of ten" and that "the kingdom of death extended from Chile to New England." "Plagues had emptied entire Indian villages," it intones, while "cold and hungry Pilgrims dug up graves and ransacked abandoned houses in search of buried corn," settling in a deserted Indian village they named Plymouth. The placard concludes unambiguously:

> The epidemics raged for 150 years. The biological catastrophe was unprecedented: an extinction event that spanned continents. Sorrow and heartbreak cloaked a shattered world that in 10,000 years had never faced such disaster.
>
> Paul Chaat Smith, NMAI, 2003

Paul Chaat Smith's words suggest that the devastation seems comprehensible; it seems like a relatively easy part of the story to tell. After all, the narrative of genocide is an all too familiar one. But the ease with which he tells this tale is belied on another placard he penned that reads,

All My Relations
Entire nations perished in the wave of death that swept the Americas. Even their names are lost to us. We cannot tell you where they lived, what they believed, or what they dreamed. Their experiences are buried and unknowable. Like much of Indian history, only fragments are left to us.
This wall names many of the languages spoken by our relatives who are still here, as well as those ancestors who vanished without a trace. The list can never be whole. It will always be incomplete.
Nine of ten Native people perished in the first century of contact between the hemispheres. One in ten survived. They didn't fear change; they embraced it.
Their past lives on in our present. As descendants of the one in ten who survived, we in the 21st century share an inheritance of grief, loss, hope, and immense riches. The achievements of our ancestors make us accountable for how we move in the world today. Their lessons instruct us and make us responsible for remembering everything, especially those things we never knew.
Paul Chaat Smith, NMAI, 2003

This placard is set up next to a large wall on which the names of hundreds of Nations are projected in small, brightly lit print around the much larger print that reads, "We Are the Evidence." Here sentiment displaces knowability altogether. The loss of "entire nations" is so complete that there is no testimony; there are no survivors. Nameless and placeless, like "Indian history" itself, these victims defy knowability altogether. Yet, paradoxically, they materialize as evidence on this swath of wall. Here, first by way of a familiar narrative of genocide, and then through a technological display invoking unimaginable trauma and loss, the museum disarticulates a knowable genocidal history from the legacy of American Indianness. The inherited narrative becomes patently unimaginable.

Dis/Re/Articulation

This reading of the National Museum of the American Indian views it as an arena for a critique of American Indianness that disarticulates many of its components from the received, largely European legacy. The museum fragments voice and face, displaces linearity, and disrupts temporality via often hyper-technologized media. It does not reinscribe familiar tropes and traditions (or even unfamiliar ones), but instead offers new possibilities for American Indianness via these rhetorical disarticulations. Experiences in the museum attempt to displace the very foundations of the received tradition.

Again, ironically, a placard titled "The Americas" reminds visitors that the people living in this hemisphere "aren't 'Indians.' They have never heard of 'America.'"

Despite Hawaii Senator Daniel Inouye's admonition that "in a city of memorials, it is deplorable that there are no memorials to the Native peoples of this country," memorialization is displaced with "survivance."[61] Despite an entrenched pastness that informs American Indianness, the museum displaces historical texts. There are scant few historical photographs, artifacts from antiquity, or dioramas depicting an idealized past. There is nothing overtly historical about the interior or exterior of the museum. In one manner of thinking, the museum turns its back on the past. Hence, the experience of the museum is one that disarticulates what has been learned throughout the twentieth century. The NMAI denies visitors opportunities to recite familiar lessons so that they are prompted to "make new histories using these very same collections [that have written American Indian histories for them up to this point]."[62] The traditional museum preserves, and "preservation, precisely, kills."[63] Traditional museums consign discourses to the past as a way of rendering them knowable and easily consumable by visitors. The NMAI resists this on multiple levels and thus obtains the power to introduce visitors to a living culture. It seeks to *dis*preserve American Indianness. Ferguson claims that exhibits can offer an opportunity for "exorcism."[64] This is a salient metaphor for rhetorical disarticulation at the NMAI. After the "exorcism" via their experiences at the NMAI, visitors can rearticulate understandings of American Indianness as at once immediate, visceral, and *un*knowable. The NMAI offers an experience not of walking in another's footsteps, or of walking down a new and different path, but of coming to recognize how many different paths there are besides that articulated by the conventional anthropological narrative. Faced with such a disarticulation, the museum offers an experience by which American Indianness may be rearticulated anew.

Notes

1. See Alan Trachtenberg, *Shades of Hiawatha: Staging Indians, Making Americans, 1880–1939* (New York: Hill and Wang, 2004).
2. For an excellent summary and discussion of scholarship focused on power and exhibiting, institutional power, colonial spectacles, and the "articulation of pre-existing discourses" within the context of the museum, see Stuart Hall, ed., *Representation: Cultural Representations and Signifying Practices* (Thousand Oaks, CA: Sage, 1997). See also Reesa Greenberg, Bruce W. Ferguson, and Sandy Nairne, eds., *Thinking about Exhibitions* (New York: Routledge, 1996). For a more focused discussion of articulation theory, see Stuart Hall, "On Postmodernism and Articulation: An Interview with Stuart Hall," *Journal of Communication Inquiry* 10 (1986): 45–60. For an exploration of how visitors

make sense of "heritage," "community," and "the people" in experience-centered heritage museums, see Bella Dicks, "Encoding and Decoding the People: Circuits of Communication at a Local Heritage Museum," *European Journal of Communication* 15 (2000): 61–78. Finally, for particular interest in art museums, culture, and historical consciousness, see Stuart Hall, "Museums of Modern Art and the End of History," in *Annotations 6: Stuart Hall and Sarat Maharaj: Modernity and Difference*, ed. Sarah Campbell and Gilane Tawadros (London: Institute of International Visual Arts, 2001), 8–23.

3. Sonya Atalay, "No Sense of Struggle: Creating a Context for Survivance at the NMAI," *American Indian Quarterly* 30 (2006): 612.

4. Chaïm Perelman and Lucie Olbrechts-Tyteca, *The New Rhetoric: A Treatise on Argumentation*, trans. John Wilkinson and Purcell Weaver (Notre Dame, IN: University of Notre Dame Press, 1969), 120–21. Thus, disarticulation in museums stems from argumentation as it is understood here but it is not coterminous with it.

5. Bruce W. Ferguson, "Exhibition Rhetorics: Material Speech and Utter Sense," in *Thinking about Exhibitions*, ed. Reesa Greenberg, Bruce W. Ferguson, and Sandy Nairne (New York: Routledge, 1996), 178.

6. Iwona Irwin-Zarecka, *Frames of Remembrance: The Dynamics of Collective Memory* (New Brunswick, NJ: Tranaction Publishers, 1994), 102.

7. Nathan Stormer, "Articulation: A Working Paper on Rhetoric and *Taxis*," *Quarterly Journal of Speech* 90 (2004): 261.

8. Amanda Cobb, "The National Museum of the American Indian as Cultural Sovereignty," *American Quarterly* 57 (2005): 503.

9. Stuart Hall, "Racist Ideologies in the Mass Media," in *Media Studies*, ed. Paul Marris and Sue Thornham (New York: New York University Press, 1999), 272–73.

10. Hall, "Racist Ideologies," 272.

11. John Fiske, *Media Matters* (Minneapolis: University of Minnesota Press, 1996), 4. For an excellent discussion of articulation, see Stormer, "Articulation."

12. Stormer, "Articulation," 263.

13. See André Bazin, "The Ontology of the Photographic Image," and "The Myth of Total Cinema," in *What Is Cinema?* trans. Jean Renoir (Berkeley: University of California Press, 1967), 9–22; and Sergei Eisenstein, "The Structure of the Film," in *Film Form: Essays in Film Theory*, ed. and trans. Jay Leyda (New York: Harcourt Brace Jovanovich, 1949) 150–78, respectively.

14. Perelman and Olbrechts-Tyteca distinguished between "demonstration" (rule driven, like formal logic, in order to "prove" a claim) and "argumentation" (which aims for "adherence" to a claim). See Perelman and Olbrechts-Tyteca, *New Rhetoric*, 13–17; Chaïm Perelman, *The Realm of Rhetoric*, trans. William Kluback (Notre Dame: University of Notre Dame Press, 1982), 110; and Chaïm Perelman, "The New Rhetoric: A Theory of Practical Reasoning," in *The Great Ideas Today*, trans. E. Griffin and O. Bird (Chicago: Encyclopedia Britannica, 1970), 281.

15. See Walter Benjamin, "A Short History of Photography," in *Classic Essays on Photography*, ed. Alan Trachtenberg (New Haven, CT: Leete's Island Books, 1980), 199–216; and Trachtenberg, *Shades of Hiawatha*, 202, respectively.

16. Trachtenberg, *Shades of Hiawatha*, 203.

17. Michael Calvin McGee, "A Materialist's Conception of Rhetoric," in *Explorations in Rhetoric: Studies in Honor of Douglas Ehninger*, ed. Ray E. McKerrow (Glenview, IL: Scott, Foresman, 1982), 29.

18. Ferguson, "Exhibition Rhetorics," 182.

19. See Maurice Charland, "Constitutive Rhetoric: The Case of the *Peuple Québécois*," *Quarterly Journal of Speech* 73 (1987): 133–51.
20. Trachtenberg, *Shades of Hiawatha*, 16.
21. See Bonnie Duran, Eduardo Duran, and Maria Yellow Horse Brave Heart, "Native Americans and the Trauma of History," in *Studying Native America: Problems and Prospects,* ed. Russell Thornton (Madison: University of Wisconsin Press, 1998).
22. Joy Kasson, *Buffalo Bill's Wild West: Celebrity, Memory, and Popular History* (New York: Hill and Wang, 2000), 71.
23. Irwin-Zarecka, *Frames of Remembrance*, 125–26.
24. Perelman, *Realm of Rhetoric*, 49.
25. Ward Churchill, *Indians Are Us?* (Monroe, MA: Common Courage Press, 1994), 79. Also see Steven Conn, *History's Shadow: Native Americans and Historical Consciousness in the Nineteenth Century* (Chicago: University of Chicago Press, 2004).
26. Trachtenberg, *Shades of Hiawatha*, 182.
27. Bernadine Healy, "The Shame of a Nation," *U.S. News and World Report*, October 4, 2004, 54.
28. Conn, *History's Shadow*, 108.
29. Conn, *History's Shadow*, 21.
30. Chaïm Perelman, "Le réel commun et le réel philosophique," in *Etudes sur l'histoire de la philosophie, en hommage á Martial Gueroult* (Paris: Fischbacher, 1964), 127–38.
31. NMAI, *American Indian*, Fall 2004, 11.
32. Irwin-Zarecka, *Frames of Remembrance*, 135.
33. Irwin-Zarecka, *Frames of Remembrance*, 4.
34. Perelman considers this an important component of reimagining common sense. See *Realm of Rhetoric*, 127.
35. Colleen Popson, "Native Voices," *Archaeology* 57 (2004): 62.
36. See Carole Blair, Marsha S. Jeppeson, and Enrico Pucci Jr., "Public Memorializing in Postmodernity: The Vietnam Veterans Memorial as Prototype," *Quarterly Journal of Speech* 77 (1991): 263–88. These authors examine a similar dynamic in their study of the Vietnam War Memorial.
37. I borrow the term "identity reference" from Irwin-Zarecka, *Frames of Remembrance*, 91.
38. NMAI, *American Indian*, 13.
39. NMAI, *American Indian*, 18.
40. Jacqueline Trescott, "History's New Look; At the Indian Museum, a Past without Pedestals," *Washington Post,* September 13, 2004.
41. Ferguson, "Exhibition Rhetorics," 177.
42. Ferguson, "Exhibition Rhetorics," 177.
43. Cobb, "National Museum," 496.
44. Trachtenberg, *Shades of Hiawatha*, 36.
45. Ferguson, "Exhibition Rhetorics," 182.
46. See Patricia Penn Hilden and Shari M. Huhndorf, "Performing 'Indian' in the National Museum of the American Indian," *Social Identities* 5 (1999): 161–84.
47. Ferguson, "Exhibition Rhetorics," 175–76.
48. Irwin-Zarecka, *Frames of Remembrance*, 102–3.
49. Placard authorship is credited to Emil Her Many Horses, NMAI, 2003.
50. Ferguson, "Exhibition Rhetorics," 178.
51. Irwin-Zarecka, *Frames of Remembrance*, 47.
52. Ferguson, "Exhibition Rhetorics," 180.

53. Placard authorship is credited to Paul Chaat Smith and Ann McMullen, NMAI Curators, and Jolene Rickard, Guest Curator, 2003.

54. Martha Davidson, "A Treasure and a Curse," *American Indian*, Fall 2004, 61.

55. Placard authorship is credited to Jolene Rickard and Gabrielle Tayak, curators, central areas, and Cynthia L. Chavez and Ann McMullen, curators, community galleries.

56. Sonya Atalay is representative of a large number of American Indian scholars who are critical of the NMAI's treatment of trauma, claiming that part of history gets glossed over.

57. Irwin-Zarecka, *Frames of Remembrance*, 49.

58. Trescott, "History's New Look."

59. The Mall in Washington, D.C., has become increasingly a national locus for memorializing. Since the United States Holocaust Memorial Museum opened in 1993, the National World War II Memorial has sprouted to join memorials to the wars in Vietnam and Korea, as well as memorials to two former presidents in the nation's symbolic core.

60. "George W. Bush Delivers Remarks on the Opening of the National Museum of the American Indian," *FDCH Political Transcripts*, September 23, 2004.

61. Richard W. West, "From the Director," *American Indian*, Fall 2004, 17.

62. Quoted from a placard titled "Making History" in the NMAI.

63. Mieke Bal, "The Discourse of the Museum," in *Thinking about Exhibitions*, ed. Reesa Greenberg, Bruce W. Ferguson, and Sandy Nairne (New York: Routledge, 1996), 203.

64. Ferguson, "Exhibition Rhetorics," 179.

CHAPTER 11

Portraits of Rebellion:
Geronimo's Photograph of 1884

Oscar Giner, Arizona State University

The Labyrinth of the Photograph

If it is true, as Baudelaire claimed, that a good portrait is a "dramatized biography," then Geronimo's first photographic portrait is a truly great one.[1] He was sixty years old and living in captivity at the San Carlos agency, headquarters of the White Mountain reservation at the juncture of the Gila and San Carlos rivers in Arizona, when it was taken in the spring of 1884. Barely three months before, he had surrendered his hostile band of twenty-six warriors and seventy women and children to General George Crook—the best Indian fighter of the American West. It was Geronimo's second surrender after three outbreaks from the reservation system imposed on Apache tribes by the U.S. government during the second half of the nineteenth century.

His first recorded words were given to Captain Emmet Crawford on March 21, 1884. One illuminating sentence by Crawford, quoting Geronimo, reveals the spiritual state of the man after his second surrender:

> *He feels now as if he were in a big hole and covered up as far as his chest*, while he is at San Carlos.[2]

Confinement, restriction of movement, a change in the order and composition of the Native personality, and the encasement of the "savage" in a "civilized" framework were all deliberate goals of official U.S. government Indian policy. In the case of Apaches, this resulted in their confinement to reservations beginning in 1872 in elaborate attempts to turn essentially nomadic tribes into communities of farmers precisely because they were obviously better suited for herding livestock, and during Crook's second tenure in Arizona, prohibition of the intoxicant *tiswin* (a fermented beverage made out of mescal or corn) played a part in numerous Apache disturbances. Geronimo himself first came to national attention because of his *raids* on Mexican and American settlers, and became a figure of legend because of his "outbreaks" from the reservation system.

Geronimo's outstanding biographer Angie Debo has advanced convincing evidence for the belief that during the spring of 1884, a unique event in Apache history took place. A series of posed photographs of Apache leaders were taken during a time when all of them lived together in the San Carlos reservation. The photographs have been traditionally attributed to Ben Wittick, the noted Western photographer who won fame and fortune during his lifetime through the sale of Indian prints. Other scholars have attributed the images to other photographers, and have suggested that they were merely copied, captioned, and sold by Wittick.[3] Taken as a whole, this series of portraits forms an invaluable pantheon of Apache leaders during the last years of their armed resistance.

Native American attitudes toward photography varied widely across the Western frontier, and depended largely on familiarity with the medium and degree of trust in the individual photographer. Photography came into the Indian world at a time when tribes had undergone profound changes as a result of encounters with European society. Several Plains Indians tribes believed that photography captured part of their spirit, and gave power to the photographer (whom they called "Shadow Catcher") over them. The Mandans once attacked a photographer who pointed a camera at them: they believed that the camera would spread smallpox, a disease that had ravaged the tribe and that ultimately caused its disappearance.[4] But soon, Indian leaders learned the personal, political, and economic advantages of photography. During a visit to Washington, D.C., for example, the Chiricahua warrior Chato asked to be photographed so his likeness could be sent to his enslaved family in Mexico. In later life, Geronimo would sit for photographs that he would send to Theodore Roosevelt to remind the president of the imprisonment of the Chiricahuas and to appeal for their release. Britton Davis records that his Apache scouts at El Paso once demanded that he buy new clothes for them before they were photographed.[5]

The critical language in modern editions of nineteenth-century Indian photography often reduces the art of posing for a photograph to a submissive event, to an admission of historical and political defeat, to a willing surrender before the harsh reality of economic forces and the unrelenting advances of technology. In an edition of Ben Wittick's Indian photographs, the editor poses a series of rhetorical questions with regards to Wittick's presumed portraits of Apache leaders:

Why were these men willing to cooperate with an Anglo photographer during the very time that they were fighting for the survival of their people? Why did they agree to pose, weapons in hand, wearing part traditional Apache, part European clothing, in front of a background of Indian blankets, cacti and woodland foliage? Were they not already captives of the Anglo-European world? Had they not already accepted their role as living exotic specimens, fierce Apache in a white man's world?[6]

The underlying (unaesthetic) premise of her point of view is that the photographer is in complete control of the photographic event. The person being photographed is reduced to the stature of object that conforms to the visual framework imposed by a subject (the photographer) whose commanding perspective has been granted by a kind of technological manifest destiny. Participants in this interaction are categorized as either dominant or submissive on the basis of a simple capitalist theory of possession: *whoever owns the camera* (or by extension, the gun, or the atomic apparatus) *is dominant*; *whomever the camera is pointed at is submissive.* If we believe this type of cultural dominance to be historically determined and divinely sanctioned, and if we accept the camera as a symbolic agent of the dynamics of conquest, then only one issue remains unresolved with regard to the photographic event: whether the people imposed on are either willing or unwilling participants in the transaction. Are they wise and accept the inevitable (as Loco was praised for doing by whites), or are they foolish, recalcitrant (like Geronimo), and resist destiny up to a thoroughly savage point? In either case, the camera also serves as a recorder of attitudes, and provides an "objective" historical record of "vanished races" and "people at the crossroads." Seen in this light, the Apaches' willingness to pose for photographs in 1884 is interpreted as a permanent sign of complicity.

Anyone still inclined to believe in the absolute power of the photographer and the unquestionable veracity of photographs can be referred to Michelangelo Antonioni's masterpiece *Blow-Up*, and to the story by Julio Cortázar that inspired it. But even if we grant the photographer full credit for the technical operation of the camera, history has shown that the process of photography (which Edgar Allan Poe considered akin to "magical") can be manipulated, even fully dominated, by performers of genius. One has only to observe the great portrait of the young Sarah Bernhardt by Nadar, or the photographic iconography of Marilyn Monroe in our time (whose photographs have bestowed distinction on several modern photographers), or the film careers of Charlie Chaplin and Marlon Brando to sense the impact that a great performer can exert on a photograph. Jacques Daguerre himself saw an opposite balance of power between what is in front and what is behind the camera:

[T]he *daguerreotype* is not merely an instrument which serves to draw Nature; on the contrary, it is a chemical and physical process which gives her the power to reproduce herself.[7]

What Daguerre acknowledges is the reality of Nature as performer when situated as the object of photography. He implies the notion of a limitless power and influence exerted by performance on the final print. Daguerre's humble statement suggests an alternative balance of power in the photographic event: one in which the photographer becomes a human appendage of the camera. In this view, the *camera* is the subject raised to a level of commanding power, and rather than serving as a technological extension of the power of the photographer, it becomes an idol animated by the humanity of the photographer, who subsumes him- or herself to its technology, becoming its devoted servant, or at best, its willing priest. The visual description of the object—especially in posed portraits—is the end result of an agonic struggle for influence between the performer and the camera that is played out in the battlefield of the physical and chemical process of the medium (and at least in the case of early photography) under the glaring sun.

If we are to perceive the photographic event as a struggle for power, then there is little doubt as to who triumphed in the case of the posed portraits of Apache leaders of 1884. No "paper ghost" (to use Susan Sontag's phrase) can ever capture the essence of ancient culture.[8] Nonliterate societies are essentially performative: their culture demands *presence,* song and dance, and a veneration for the fleeting immanence of gesture rather than for its documentation. Performance is both a way of living and thinking and an aesthetic choice that crucially defines cultural identity. A picture will not tell one thousand words—it will speak only one among many absent ones—if the heart and soul of the subject reside outside the unchanging boundaries and visual delineations of photography. The moment in time that the photograph captures will speak more eloquently about what is absent, what was not captured, if the subject's identity is to be found only in movement, in action (vocal and physical) performed in a continuity of time.

Performance was the primary language of Apache culture. Asa Daklugie, Juh's son and Geronimo's relative, has left a vivid description of a ritual celebration in Juh's legendary stronghold in the Sierra Madre (the Blue Mountains) after a successful raid during the outbreak of 1881. Following a celebratory meal, and the ceremonial distribution of the spoils, one of the leaders of the raid (Geronimo) was asked to tell the tribe the story of their attack on a Mexican mining village, and to relate the deeds of the most valiant warriors:

The women refilled the small wicker cups [with *tiswin*] and, when the men had drunk, departed from the circle. Fresh logs were placed on the fire and the space about it was cleared for the victory dance. After the singers and drummers again took their places, my father led, followed by his Nednhi. Then came Nana and the Chihenne; then Chihuahua and the Chokonen; and last Geronimo and the Bedonko-hes . . .

The long line danced about the fire clockwise, in single file. All joined in the singing, but above all I could hear the powerful voice of Juh. The difficulty he sometimes had in speaking did not affect his singing.

The men improvised steps and poses. Some gave pantomimes of their own ideas of fighting, using a rifle to gesticulate. Others knelt momentarily, fired an ar-row or a bullet, or mimicked the thrust of a lance. Each performed as he chose, without effort to duplicate the actions of another.[9]

Many of the Apache leaders photographed in 1884 were medicine men—that is, essentially performers, who could access magical power through song and dance. All of them belonged to a culture in which performance was not, as in ours, a feared and unessential luxury, but rather the basic language of cultural expression. One of them, Naiche (whom Apaches credited with no Power), could have easily become a matinee idol during the silent film era. The images of Loco, Nana, Chihuahua, Mangus, Dos-Teh-Seh, Chato, Naiche, and most especially that of Geronimo (the presumed submissive ones) have survived the anonymity of time, and stand as imperious reminders of the shapes and spirit of a proud and distinctive people. On the other hand, the identity of the Western photographer is not even known. It has vanished into the deep labyrinth of early photographic technology. We cling to the pathetic inscription "Wittick photo" in a few of the surviving prints as faint evidence that once a white man ruled the photographic event, and imposed his descrip-tion in time of the Apache rebel leaders on historical posterity.

The Performative Act

From book plates, cheap posters, and even reproduced by the digital pixels of the Internet, Geronimo's image glares at us from a past moment in time, like an ancient Indian hieroglyph surrounded by mystery. For all its notoriety (see figure 1), the portrait is usually reproduced without documentation notice: without date, without details as to the specific photographic process (wet or dry plate? studio or outside photograph?) used in its creation, without the photographer's name. Patricia Broder attributes Geronimo's portrait to Jack Hillers.[10] She believes an original print was copied into a glass positive by Wittick, who captioned and sold prints developed from it. Debo follows Richard Rudisill in attributing the photograph to A. Frank Randall, who accompanied Crook's expedition into the Sierra Madre, and who was an itinerant photographer in the Southwest between 1881 and 1886, with base of operation in Willcox, Arizona.[11] It is also hardly ever reproduced without modification. Debo, an otherwise impeccable source for Geronimo's life, reproduces a cropped version (the most popular one) of the portrait in her biography.[12] A recent "paired" biography of Geronimo by Peter Aleshire, which parallels his life with that of George Crook, reproduces the portrait with greater integrity: the empty space at the top of the portrait is allowed to remain as part of the print.[13] Notwithstanding, Aleshire assigns the photograph to Wittick (with some reason), but makes a mistake in dating it 1887—a time when Geronimo was out of Arizona and confined to imprisonment in Fort Pickens, Florida.

Figure 1: Geronimo: Rifle photograph
Courtesy of the National Archives

It is a more distant, less threatening image than the one commonly reproduced. The setting of the photograph is fake, and similar to the rest of the 1884 Apache portraits. There is a neutral backdrop common to period photographs, in front of which uprooted desert and forest vegetation is strategically placed around the central image. All outer layers of the photograph—real vegetation in an unnatural arrangement, and backdrop—form what Roland Barthes calls the *studium* of a photograph: a field of vision invested with a recognizable, even familiar landscape of signs for the observer. The *studium* is an intermediary that allows the spectator to partici- pate in photographic images. This participation is cultural, for in this context, culture is defined as a perceptual "contract arrived between creators and consumers." The *studium* reconciles the spectator with the photograph, and allows him or her "to experience the intentions which establish and animate" the practices of the photographer.[14] Barthes also notes, in arresting photo- graphs, the presence of *punctum*: a second, dynamic element "which rises from the scene, shoots out of it like an arrow, and pierces me." *Punctum* is that which disturbs the serenity of the *studium* of a photograph, seizing the observer's attention. "A photograph's *punctum* is that accident which pricks me (but also bruises me, is poignant to me)."[15] Given Barthes's framework of perception, we can affirm simply that the *punctum* of Geronimo's photograph is his own figure.

If we went no further in discussing the portrait, we could accept it as em- blematic of Geronimo's existence in 1884. The play of *punctum* and *studium* reveals a studio arrangement that imprisons the man, his clothes, his rifle, and his fierce demeanor. The portrait can also be taken as a permanent symbol of Indian reservation life, in which an arbitrary environment created by humans is expected to cage the wild wind. Finally, we can advance it also as a signification of the most benign face of U.S. Indian policy: of the attempt to frame, and ultimately erase, the little understood nature of the American Indian by immobilizing it, by transforming a natural pattern of behavior into a new one, a more acceptable and more seemingly orderly one to the Western mind.

There is no doubt that Geronimo posed willingly—as he would do so often throughout his life—for the portrait of 1884. The pose is studied and deliberate (the sign of a great actor), and must have been held for a period of time given the exposure required by the photographic technique of the time. The photograph was one in a series, and the demeanor of individual Apaches in the 1884 photographs makes clear that they each patiently posed and carefully dressed up for the occasion. Why does one pose for a photograph? A vivid definition of photography is offered by the poet Oliver Wendell Holmes in an essay praising the virtues of the stereograph: photography, Holmes contends, *is a mirror with memory*.[16] But a memory of what? The theoretical origins of the medium as objective recorder and the subsequent artistic movement toward pictorial photography imply a passive, static quality in the segment of reality viewed through the lens. Even in cases in which the camera observes movement, this movement is "frozen in time" through its agency, and its stasis is further acted on through the development of the print. We consider this a partial, incomplete account of the photographic event. Daguerre granted Nature the *power* to reproduce itself, presumably through an action that allows it to imprint or influence the photograph in a decisive manner. Walter Benjamin sheds light on this incisive effect of the photographed object by describing the act of posing by models in portraitures with long periods of exposure:

> The procedure itself caused the models to live, not *out* of the instant, but *into it*; during the long exposure *they grew, as it were, into the image.*[17]

We will call this activity described by Benjamin as "growing" into the image *the performative act.* It encompasses a series of conscious and unconscious decisions and deliberate acts on the part of the model, or the performer, that range from the initial decision to pose for a photograph, up to the last action (physical or spiritual, aware or unaware) performed in front of the camera during the moment of exposure. We consider it a specific, nonetheless integral, type of performance, and an essential, however ignored, component of photography. It is most clearly visible in cases of portraits of men and women, but it is no less recognizable in landscape or natural photography (where Nature, or an animated concept of the city, becomes the performer). If we define performance as *action in front of an audience,* then the spectator, or observer of the photograph (the one to whom the performance is aimed), becomes the final party and ultimate receiver of the performative act. In this sense, the camera and its technology can be understood as an intermediary *event,* a type of technological theater that bridges the communication between performer and observer, and which concretizes Jerzy Grotowski's definition of theater: *that which happens between actor and audience.*[18]

Great photography is full of accidents: incidents in which the images are visited by disturbances not always intended by the photographer or attributable to the photographic process (one thinks, for example, of late-nineteenth-century spirit photography). Barthes's conceptual dialectic of *studium* and *punctum* is based on an eruption on the perceptually recognizable plane of the photograph. Benjamin speaks of the "tiny spark of accident, the here and now" that violates the design and preparations of the photographer.[19] These notable, uncharted visitations derive in many cases from the deliberate eye of the photographer and the sensibility of the spectator (audience), but can also originate, with striking efficiency, from the performance of the model.

Having returned awareness and power to the object of photography, we can again pose the question: why does a man or a woman pose for a photograph? To perform an act that will be remembered; to leave a legacy of a moment in time; to send a message to distant observers; to become conscious of one's imprint on life. All these we note in Geronimo's photograph of 1884. It would be wrong to conclude that his participation in this initial (for him) photographic event meant a willing acceptance of his defeated condition, or an agreeable compliance with the intent of the photographer, or the lack of awareness of an audience.

His Face

The portrait is full of contradictions.

Light falls on the figure from the upper left-hand corner—sunlight no doubt, reminding us that early photographs (*heliographs* for Niepce) are truly sun-paintings. The light dissects his face in half, and causes a shadow (from the rifle) to cut across his waist. From the perspective of the viewer, the left side of the face is brightly lit; the right side is dark, and seems to mock at the observer in close proximity to the rifle's barrel. Geronimo was often characterized as a tortured soul, a doubting, ambivalent neurotic who saw both the need and the futility of war, who understood both the necessity and the impossibility of living in reservations. The pain of dichotomy, the dreaded journeys across the abyss of hateful choices, has permanently carved the face in an anxious visage. It is a face that easily conjures the myriad adjectives with which his enemies branded him throughout his life: "cruel," "vicious," "intractable," "treacherous," "bloodthirsty savage," and even in later years, after he had forsaken the warpath, "blatant blackguard." None of the Apache warriors photographed in 1884 smile for the camera, although the faint specter of a smile (the "amused consciousness of the whole photographic ritual," according to Barthes) visits the portraits of Chihuahua and Naiche.[20] Geronimo is never found smiling in the hundreds of portraits made of him. From this we have speculated, with poetic precision, that a war wound turned his face into a grimace and prevented him from smiling. We have also wrongly concluded that this most ironic of individuals had no sense of humor. Painful memories of betrayal, and future ones yet to come, are reflected in his face. The memory of his first massacred family never left him, and the hatred of Mexican soldiers who killed his first wife, his children, and his old mother, never subsided. From a certain angle, it is a face that holds back silent tears, and that can explode in bitter fury.

Curiously, he does not wear the customary long hair of the Apaches, or the distinctive headband of warriors—as if he wanted to expose his face, confront the camera with it unabashedly, aiming anger and fear, tension and suspicion at the observer. There is effort in the construction of the face, exertion of spirit that creates a mask—the deliberate mask of the warrior. His face embodies Crook's description of the Apache warrior: *the tiger of the human race*. In this visage Child of Water, the first warrior of Apache mythology, must have confronted the four-plated monster with his bow and arrow.

His Clothes

He wears elements of the typical attire of the Apache warrior:

> The calico shirt with a muslin breech clout supported by a belt, a headband to keep the long hair from obscuring vision, and one or more cartridge belts constituted the dress of the warrior.[21]

But he is without headband, without cartridge pouch or belt, without a sign of the buckskin medicine bag of sacred *hoddentin* attached to the belt. He wears neither the full trappings of the warrior nor the special attire of the medicine man; he is the straightforward picturization of an attitude, rather than the impersonation of an exotic character. There is nothing extraneous, everything functional about the clothes, as if precisely selected for a studied effect. Only the dandy's kerchief knotted at the throat and the bracelet on the right wrist seem superfluous: subtle statements of his vanity, which would reveal itself more fully in later photographs. The distinctive Apache moccasin is presented in bold fashion, folded below the knee, secured to the foot by a strip of polished leather, as if pronouncing that he belonged to the mountains:

> The footgear was long and could be drawn up for warmth; or it could be folded below the knee for protection against thorns and rock. In those folds we carried our valuable possessions, valuable primarily in the sense of usefulness. Sometimes these included extra cowhide soles, for soles wore out quickly and had to be replaced. We carried the end thorns of a mescal plant with fiber attached for sewing the soles to the uppers. The soles were tanned with the hair left on, and they projected beyond the toes and terminated in a circular flap with a metal button sewed to the center. The piece turned back over the toes for additional protection. Because we frequently had to abandon our horses to scale cliffs, the moccasins was our most important article of dress.[22]

The Posture

He kneels, but not in servility. He kneels in the aggressive posture of the sentinel, alert to danger and ready to shoulder his rifle. He shuns all accessories of period photography—columns, balustrades, chairs or seats covered with blankets that give support to the model throughout the long period of exposure, and chooses a *kinetic* position. Neither sitting nor standing, his is a position in motion, violating the static conventions of period portraiture, but also an in-between position, reflecting ambivalence and doubt. André Bazin's description of baroque art as life in "tortured immobility" describes precisely Geronimo's posture in the portrait. The right elbow (again, from the perspective of the viewer) rests on the right knee, readily grasping the barrel of the rifle with the right hand. The left hand grabs the rifle in front of the trigger guard, caressing the wood with a loving gesture: clearly not the grip of one ready to shoot, but still the grip of one ready to aim. The weight of the body teeters on the hidden leg; the right leg stands firmly on the ground, ready to help the body leap, or help release it to sit back.

The kneeling posture produces an empty space at the top of the portrait where the neutral backdrop is seen, as if created there to hold the holy man's dreams and visions, evanescent and ephemeral, impossible to capture with the emulsion of nineteenth-century photography, but present nonetheless. The spectator's eye is distracted toward it by the arc of the branches against the backdrop. But his eyes never leave yours, shifting from the central point like a warrior changing defensive locations, or like a shaman whose Coyote Power shifts reality to move him unperceived. Apaches demanded the presence of Power in their leaders. It was said that Geronimo had both Coyote and Ghost Power, owning ceremonies—songs and rituals—that pertained to both. Coyote Power gave him the ability to cure, to make himself invisible, and to become hard to see and find. He had the gift of discerning events that occurred at a distance. He could prolong the night and hold back the dawn, whether to cross an open valley without danger, or reach the safety of mountains, or withdraw unseen from the presence of enemies. In later years, one of his followers recounted one of his high magical feats:

> When he was on the warpath, Geronimo fixed it so that morning would not come too soon. He did it by singing. Once we were going to a certain place, and Geronimo didn't want it to become light before he reached it. He saw the enemy while they were in a level place, and didn't want them to spy on us. He wanted morning to break after we had climbed over a mountain, so that the enemy couldn't see us. So Geronimo sang, and the night remained for two or three nights longer. I saw this myself.[23]

When he was young, his Power had revealed to him that no bullets would ever kill him, and this made him superbly courageous and invaluable in battle. As a Bedonkohe Apache, Geronimo never became, as it is casually assumed, chief of the Chiricahua Apaches. He was a war-shaman, and served in the capacity of war-chief, acting in the "relationship of general to commander-in-chief" to Naiche.[24] His generalship was a function as of his Power as a medicine man:

The shaman whose work has to do with war had a strong part in politics and could rise to a position of power. . . . Geronimo got political power from the religious side. He foresaw the results of the fighting, and they used him so much in the campaigns that he came to be depended upon. He went through his ceremony, and he would say, "You should go here; you should not go there." That is how he became a leader.[25]

His Rifle

Most of the Apaches photographed posed with their rifles. Only Geronimo presents his rifle in a hostile manner. The butt of the rifle rests lightly on the ground, but the barrel is in motion, leans toward the lens as if the camera had photographed it in a precipitated state: not passive, but not yet aimed, held in suspension by the fleeting, terrible decision of whether to shoot or not. The angle and position of the rifle is one of both aggression and defense. One further tilt of the rifle and it becomes an instrument of death, but it stands as a barrier, a mystical shield against the onslaught of time, preventing the camera from appropriating, fully absorbing, the warrior's identity.

"Ours was a race of fighting men—war was our occupation," stated James Kaywaykla. "A rifle was our most prized possession."[26] The rifle was made ritually sacred before combat:

In these songs and prayers the parts of the gun are given certain names. The wooden stock is called the earth. The metal barrel is called the moon. The little screws that hold it together are called whirlwind. This is true of all gun ceremonies.[27]

A prayer given to Apaches by Child of Water before his battle with the giant was also used as a "gun ceremony":

Spit on the palm of the left hand. Dip the first finger of the right hand in the saliva and make a cross with it on the left foot, thigh, forearm and cheek. As the crosses are made, call upon the Four Thunders: Black Thunder, Blue Thunder, Yellow Thunder and White Thunder.

Then recite the following prayer, "Black flint is over your body four times. Take your black weapon to the center of the sky. Let his weapons disappear from the earth." This prayer, with only the colors changed, is repeated four times. Then rub the first finger of the right hand horizontally across the lips four times.

Now the bow and arrows (or the gun) are held against the chest, pointing first downward to the left, then upward to the right. At the same time face the east and pray. The weapon is next worked over the right shoulder, across the back, and down to the left hand.[28]

It was said that Geronimo knew a gun ceremony that would cause his enemies' guns to jam, or miss when they shot at him.

His rifle was a particularly envied prize for White Eyes. John Clum arrogantly retained possession of Geronimo's rifle in 1877 [*National Geographic* magazine published a color photograph of it against an Arizona landscape in 1992],[29] and after the last surrender in 1886, General Nelson Miles also took Geronimo's rifle for his collection. He was a legendary marksman. To the boasts of Army guards that he had been captured, in the end, by the U.S. Army, Geronimo would reply: "You never have caught me shooting."[30]

The Hat Photograph

There is another photograph of Geronimo that we believe was also taken as part of the 1884 series (see figure 2). Note the similarities in dress, the same leather straps around the ankles, and the identical shrubbery and neutral backgrounds of the settings. This portrait is closer in spirit to that of other Apache leaders. It is a passive photograph. He sits without hostile rifle, facing the camera in a straightforward manner, eyes drifting beyond the frame of the photograph, wearing a telling curiosity: a store-bought, feminine hat. Once again, there is intent and deliberation in the pose. One can see it in the precise positioning of the discovered left knee (viewer's perspective) and the hidden right leg. The left hand rests in repose on his left thigh; the right hand lies clenched on his right knee in the vague suggestion of a threat. Even in passivity, Geronimo's figure exudes ambiguity. The fierce demeanor, the architecture of the mask of the warrior can still be perceived—but the face is different. This is now Coyote (equivocal and hermaphrodite, the sum of one and all things) winking at the camera, opening a small window into himself, making us realize the presence of the great chameleon of his talent residing in his soul. We understand that the heroic image of the rifle photograph has not been performed by a tragedian, but rather by an infinitely subtle comedian who has assumed the tragic mask (as the great comedians of the *Comedie Francaise* take on the role of Shakespeare's *Richard III*) for a deliberate effect, for an intended meaning to an audience.

In fact, the famous portrait of 1884 is an exception. Most of the Apaches photographed posed with their rifles. Only Geronimo presents his rifle in a hostile gesture, revealing that the aggressive kneeling position is a *chosen* position. Only Geronimo, among the photographed Apaches, makes an attempt to bring life to the fake setting. Other Apaches sit or stand amid the photographic set, paying little attention to the incongruity created by authenticity of their own figures next to the falsehood of the ornaments. In the "rifle" photograph, Geronimo's posture gives plausibility to the vegetation; conceivably, such a man could be found in such a position in a natural setting. He approaches the cacti and other foliage like an actor approaches a theatrical set, with an actor's awareness that only through action and belief in given circumstances will the artificial background that surrounds him live for the spectator. In the "hat" photograph, Geronimo fades into the ornamental shrubbery, suffering its presence like a sage whose mind is focused elsewhere, and who is content to let surrounding reality be as it will. The same actor, by his performance, proposes two different activations of the same setting—like Edwin Booth using the same tattered setting in a Western dance hall to perform both *Hamlet* and *The Merchant of Venice*. The "hat" photograph is the polar opposite of the "rifle" photograph, serving to highlight the studied deliberation, the conscious manipulation of the photographic medium, and the performative act registered in the famous portrait of 1884. The "rifle" photograph raises the art of portraiture to the level of a political statement, of the manifestation of a particular individual sensibility, of a message delivered in time.

Figure 2: Geronimo: Hat photograph
Courtesy of the National Archives

When defeat becomes a certainty, when surrender to superior force is the only remaining option, and imprisonment the only possible consequence, what do the leaders of a rebellious people do? For cultures and individuals with a warrior heart, who are both conversant with the dynamics of song and dance and knowledgeable of the signifying quality of metaphor, rebellion becomes performance. After all Native American tribes were confined to reservations, many of them expressed continued defiance to the European invasion by their magical participation in the Ghost Dance ritual of the 1890s. Sitting Bull, the great medicine man of the Lakotas, left a sublime heritage of political oratory that is one of the great poetical legacies of the nineteenth century. Geronimo—who was not an eloquent man—produced a pictorial legacy in hundreds of photographs that is yet to be understood as the deliberate, performative affirmation of a Native identity, as a myriad sequence of images of defiance. There is no hint in Geronimo's famous portrait of a defeated leader who has come to the reservation to submit and assimilate. Encased in a fake setting, framed by the geographical boundaries of the reservation as well as by the conceptual boundaries of the photograph, he kneels in a profoundly rebellious act, defiant in mind and spirit against confinement, against historical circumstance, even against the passage of time. Among the pantheon of Apache photographs, it is the one photograph whose intrinsic statement of rebellion (created by Geronimo's performance in front of a camera) has lasted until our time.

In our careless modern use of Greek dramatic terminology, we often forget that the dramatic hero is never the victorious individual. Heroism—the stuff of legend, the prime matter of song and dance for ancient cultures—is rather a divine, therefore eternal, quality gained by a noble confrontation with profound loss and inevitable misfortune. In the cramped quarters of a Latin American student living in New England during the early 1970s, I once saw Geronimo's portrait next to the posterized photograph of Ché that was popularized after Guevara's death. It was a sign that Geronimo's legend—in the Greek sense of a palpable, living substance—had triumphed over defeat, over decades of political imprisonment, over death, even over the complicated processes of technology. The image was a living proof of his return, and like a ghost dancer dancing an ambiguous war dance with his rifle, he spoke to a future generation in a fearsome portrait of rebellion.

Geronimo would break out from reservation life a magically significant fourth time in 1886. The outstanding photographic events that took place during his last outbreak would prove conclusively his performative brilliance and his photographic genius.

Notes

1. Maria Morris Hambourg, Francoise Heilbrun, and Philippe Néagu, *Nadar* (New York: Metropolitan Museum of Art, 1995), 247.
2. Captain Emmet Crawford, quoted in Angie Debo, *Geronimo: The Man, His Time, His*

O. GINER

Place (Norman: University of Oklahoma Press, 1976), 204 (emphasis added).

3. See Jeremy Rowe, *Photographers in Arizona 1850–1920* (Nevada City, NV: Carl Mautz Publishing, 1997), 16.

4. Paula Richardson Fleming and Judith Luskey, *The North American Indians in Early Photographs* (New York: Harper and Row Publishers, 1986), 16, 192–95.

5. Britton Davis, *The Truth about Geronimo* (Lincoln: University of Nebraska Press, 1976), 120.

6. Patricia Janis Broder, *Shadows on Glass: The Indian World of Ben Wittick* (Savage, MD: Bowman and Littlefield Publishers, 1990), 106.

7. "Daguerreotype," in *Classic Essays on Photography*, ed. Alan Trachtenberg (New Haven, CT: Leete's Island Books, 1980), 13.

8. Susan Sontag, *On Photography* (New York: Doubleday, Anchor Books, 1977), 48.

9. Eve Ball, *Indeh: An Apache Odyssey* (Norman: University of Oklahoma Press, 1988), 11.

10. Broder, *Shadows on Glass*, 58.

11. Debo, *Geronimo*, 211. See also Richard Rudisill, *Photographs of the New Mexico Territory 1854–1912* (Santa Fe: Museum of New Mexico, 1973), 48–49.

12. Debo, *Geronimo*, vi.

13. Peter Aleshire, *The Fox and the Whirlwind: General George Cook and Geronimo, A Paired Biography* (New York: John Wiley and Sons, 2000), 4.

14. Roland Barthes, *Camera Lucida: Reflections on Photography*, trans. Richard Howard (New York: Hill and Wang, 1999), 28.

15. Barthes, *Camera Lucida*, 26–27.

16. Oliver Wendell Homes, "The Stereoscope and the Stereograph," in Trachtenberg, *Classic Essays on Photography*, 74.

17. Walter Benjamin, "A Short History of Photography," in Trachtenberg, *Classic Essays on Photography*, 204 (emphasis added).

18. Jerzy Grotowski, *Towards a Poor Theatre* (New York: Simon and Schuster, 1968), 34.

19. Benjamin, "Short History of Photography," 202.

20. Barthes, *Camera Lucida*, 11.

21. Eve Ball, *In the Days of Victorio: Recollections of a Warm Springs Apache* (Tucson: University of Arizona Press, 1997), 18.

22. Ball, *In the Days*, 17.

23. Morris Edward Opler, *An Apache Life-Way* (Lincoln: University of Nebraska Press, 1996), 216.

24. Ball, *Indeh*, 11.

25. Opler, *Apache Life-Way*, 200.

26. Ball, *In the Days*, 156.

27. Opler, *Apache Life-Way*, 311.

28. Opler, *Apache Life-Way*, 311–12.

29. *National Geographic Magazine*, October 1992.

30. Debo, *Geronimo*, 107.

CHAPTER 12

The Materialist Dialectic as a Site of Kairos: Theorizing Rhetorical Intervention in Material Social Relations

Dana L. Cloud, University of Texas, Austin

Men make their own history, but they do not make it as they please; they do not make it under self-selected circumstances, but under circumstances existing already, given and transmitted from the past.

Karl Marx, *The Eighteenth Brumaire of Louis Bonaparte*

[A] belief in the necessary interconnection of socialist theory and practice with the working class and the labor movement . . . calls for the development of a practical revolutionary approach seeking to connect, in serious ways, with the various sectors and layers of the working class. . . . This means thoughtfully utilizing various forms of educational and agitational literature, and developing different kinds of speeches and discussions, in order to connect the varieties of working-class experience, and, most important, to help initiate or support various kinds of practical struggles.

Paul Leblanc, "Does Lenin Still Matter?"

This chapter explores how, according to Marxist theory, ordinary people exist in "circumstances transmitted from the past" that shape their consciousness and constrain their action, yet collectively—and in spite of ideological and coercive forces arrayed against them—come to consciousness of their situation, assess the world around them, and plan and enact change in their own interests. Materialist dialectics, as a critical and political method, can describe actual historical change and afford scholars and activists grounds for political and critical judgment.[1] There are two dialectical processes crucial to such judgment. First, class society in general, and capitalist society in particular, is marked by an objective dialectical clash between contending classes and their interests. Second, a materialist perspective emphasizes the idea that class position and the experience of exploitation combine to form an epistemological potential in the dialectical contradiction between the lived experience of exploitation and the mystifications of ideology.

Dialectical clash is the motor of basic economic transformation and shifts of hegemonic power in society, but it cannot operate without human, and specifically rhetorical, intervention. Thus, the class dialectic offers itself as a particular kind of *kairic* opportunity for discursive mediation fostering class consciousness and political motivation. In classical rhetorical theory, the concept of *kairos* mediates the tension between structure and agency by positing a structural context, over which the rhetorical agent has little or no initial control, but which nonetheless comprises a crisis or opportunity for agentive transformation. An understanding of the dialectic as affording *kairic* opportunity is one way to resolve the structure–agency tension integral to Marxist theory, as well as to rhetorical theory broadly considered.

As Marx and Engels explained, and as Marxists since have elaborated, dialectics recognizes capitalism as giving rise to the forces that will under-mine it—namely, the creation of an exploited but powerfully collectivized working class, alongside anarchic economic competition that drives the system to overproduction and crisis. Critics of this model have argued that acknowledging economic determinants of consciousness and culture underes-timates the role of rhetoric in constituting identities and motivating action;[2] that Marxist thought posits economic determination of all things cultural and political; that materialist theory maintains a simple-minded reflection model of truth; that any invocation of the working class assumes a uniform identity among workers; that history has proven revolutionary theory untenable; and finally, that Marxism is, on the whole, insensitive to the complexities of mediation, rhetorical invention, and practice.[3] Michelle Barrett's shift in position from *Women's Oppression Today* to *The Politics of Truth* is em-blematic of this critique, which also characterizes some critical work in rhetoric and cultural studies.[4]

Many of these straw persons arise from a flawed understanding of how Marxists conceptualize class. Contrary to arguments put forward recently by Ernesto Laclau, I regard class position not as a discursively produced nodal point around which a movement antagonism may form, but rather as a real and fundamental *relationship* to the means of producing and distributing goods, *consciousness* of which is neither automatic nor necessary.[5] The materialist dialectic describes the space and motion between experience, relationship, and consciousness, between structure and agency. While antagonisms crafted entirely out of discourses must necessarily limit them-selves to the terms of the prevailing imaginary, a materialist dialectical antagonism opens up space for a potentially revolutionary class agency.

My argument in this chapter is threefold. First, *kairos* is a concept that helps to theorize class-based rhetorical agency through the lens of historical materialism and Marxist dialectics. In particular, the dialectical relationships between contending classes and between experience and consciousness offer significant rhetorical opportunities to the actors of radical social movements. Second, the unfolding objective factors of the mode, means, forces, and relations of production provide the conditions of possibility for what Lenin called the subjective moment of political intervention.[6] Third, the transformation between a class *in itself* and a class *for itself* unfolds out of a dialectical process of interpretation and constitution of working class identity on the basis of an already-existing relationship. A dialectical perspective on *kairos* affords critics and activists a method to understand how shifts in the objective features of capitalist society reach points of crisis or a turning point during which a *kairic* intervention may have a determining influence on the outcome.

In support of this argument, I first define dialectics as a materialist supplement to the Aristotelian principle of *kairos,* which encompasses the role of timing, opportunity, and situation. After a discussion of how dialectics as *kairos* speaks to the rhetorical sensitivity of a Marxism too often disdained as economistic, I explore the productivity of understanding dialectics in this way through an abbreviated case study of labor conflicts during which dissident unionists made rhetorical interventions in a situation of class conflict at the Boeing Company in 1995 (groundbreaking), 2005 (failed), and 2008 (victorious). The contrast of successful and failed outcomes allows us to pinpoint the combination of constraint and possibility. In other words, we must understand both labor's victories and its defeats in dialectical terms if we are to criticize movement discourse productively and think strategically about labor and social movements in general.

I conclude that a dialectical perspective on *kairos* affords critics a theory of the production of class consciousness out of creative and timely combination of basic economic contestation and the intervention of movement discourse. This argument hinges on a definition of materialist dialectics, to which I now turn.

The Marxist Dialectic as Ground for Rhetorical Action

Materialist dialectics is a way of knowing and explaining *relationships* among different aspects of social life that together form a totality. In philosophy, dialectics is most often understood as a form of reasoning toward understanding of the whole on the basis of the discovery of contradictions. This sense of the concept of dialectics has its origin in philosophical idealism, such as that of Plato, whose dialogues enact clash in the rarified realm of ideas, aspiring to what he regarded as ever-higher truths. Observing the self-estrangement produced in unequal relations of power, Hegel described a dialectical process whose solution to estrangement once again involved transcendence of the sensuous, material, political world.[7] Hegel writes,

> The Absolute is Mind (*Geist*)—this is the supreme definition of the Absolute. To find this definition and to grasp its meaning and burden was, we may say, the ultimate purpose of all education and all philosophy: It was the point to which turned the impulse of all religion and science: and it is this impulse that must explain the history of the world.[8]

In this passage, Hegel describes Mind as objective and the sensuous world as subjective and suspect.

In the Hegelian tradition, Theodor Adorno and his Frankfurt School colleagues located oppression in a discursive totality epitomized in mass popular culture, hence Adorno's pessimism regarding the possibility of overcoming cultural alienation in a positive identification between subject and object.[9] Rather than seek a positive or transcendental outcome of "the negation of the negation" (for example, revolutionary transformation as the product of system contradictions), Adorno argues in *Negative Dialectics* for a permanent extension of the critical moment in which the dialectical "negation of the negation" proceeds *ad infinitum*. Even so, Adorno embraces Marx's critique of relativism (as elaborated in Mannheim's "sociology of knowledge"), insisting that there are material objects that condition and are conditioned in turn by the intervention of rhetorical subjects.[10] On the subject of rhetoric, Adorno writes, "Dialectics—language as the organon of thought—would mean to attempt a critical rescue of the rhetorical element, a mutual approximation of thing and expression."[11] Rejecting naïve ontologism, and suspicious of "consequential thinking," Adorno extends Marx's (and Lenin's) concern with the rational mediation of contradictory experience and the critique of ideology.[12] Dialectics is "the subjective moment in the object," Adorno writes.[13]

Although this last idea is useful in materialist dialectics, Marx rejected "thought against thought" as a viable resistance strategy. Even so, he and Engels were drawn to Hegel's dialectics as an alternative either to static views of society or to theories of automatic linear progress. Whereas liberal-democratic, positivist, and utilitarian thinking regard history as the evolution of society according to principles of evidence and reason, materialist dialectics describes the ways in which history unfolds, not as a series of great ideas or scientific reforms, but rather as a product of contending classes, possessing divergent structural interests. This is why Marx and Engels claimed to be "standing Hegel on his head"; theoretical thought is not a transcendence of history, but is itself grounded in the moments of its production.[14] Further,

Marx points out that the clash between noble and alienated concepts cannot challenge the material conditions of labor and privation in which people struggle for less philosophical gains.[15] As Marx puts it in the famous passage from *The German Ideology*,

> [t]his demand to change consciousness amounts to a demand to interpret reality in another way, to recognize it by means of another interpretation. The Young-Hegelian ideologists, in spite of their allegedly "world-shattering" statements, are the staunchest conservatives. The most recent of them have found the correct expression for their activity when they declare they are only fighting against "phrases." They forget, however, that to these phrases they themselves are only opposing other phrases, and that they are in no way combating the real existing world when they are merely combating the phrases of this world.[16]

In Marxism, dialectics is not about the clash of discourses; rather, it is about how discourse mediates objective class relationships in the history of the struggle for hegemony. In the 1873 afterword to the second German edition of *Capital*, volume 1, Marx explains that the dialectic

> is a scandal and abomination to bourgeoisdom and its doctrinaire professors, because it includes in its comprehension and affirmative recognition of the existing state of things, at the same time also, the recognition of the negation of that state, of its inevitable breaking up; because it regards every historically developed social form as in fluid movement, and therefore takes into account its transient nature not less than its momentary existence; because it lets nothing impose upon it, and is in its essence critical and revolutionary.[17]

Marx was writing in response to liberal intellectuals who counseled resignation to capitalist society and denied the revolutionary dynamism of society. Above all, historical materialist dialectics insists that dynamism is neither metaphysical nor directed from above according to invisible laws or principles. Rather, change unfolds out of contradictions in the existing world. Dialectics is thus an explanatory theory of history and social relations, and an epistemological theory that not only describes a state of affairs at any given moment, but also seeks to explain the emergence of that state of affairs out of historical conditions.

Key to this process is the principle of the transformation of quantity into quality. In the natural world, Engels observed how "qualitative changes can only occur by the quantitative addition or subtraction of matter or motion."[18] Engels's understanding of the dialectical process as fundamental to qualitative change has explained how the accrual of localized struggles can become generalized in a systematic political contestation. On the grandest scale, the dialectical process has produced world-historic qualitative shifts in the way society is organized.

So, for example, in the first settled agricultural societies, more and more individuals were able to accumulate a surplus of what was produced. As improved technologies of agriculture and storage enabled the growth of such surpluses, there was a need to justify their holding and control by a minority, as well as the need for an arbiter to negotiate among groups with contending interests in how such surpluses might be appropriated. Over time, the quantity of such incidents and situations produced the conditions for the emergence of a state, with laws, regulations, administrators, and ideologists.[19] In this way, the quantity of accumulation pushed toward a qualitative change in the organization of society, namely, the transition to feudalism from the beginnings of settled agriculture. Subsequent dependence on socialized labor in capitalism and its tendency to overproduction created its own opposition in the formation of an antagonistic working class.

One might extend the idea of the "transformation of quantity into quality" to understand the process by which a number of small changes and experiences can accrue so as to overcome the threshold of stability. "Bread-and-butter" labor actions may multiply into a situation like the one in Russia in February 1917, where a women's strike for bread, land, and peace ignited mass unrest against the tsar. Of course, this strike did not itself overturn the aristocratic regime or start the revolution, the planning of which had been ongoing since 1905. Rather, it was a spark—a *kairic* act that took advantage of the opportunities given in that moment—that galvanized class consciousness of masses of people in the context of political and economic crisis (brought to the fore by World War I) and a revolutionary movement built over a period of decades.[20] The movement from localized class consciousness to a broader political analysis does not happen spontaneously or automatically in most cases, but requires such *kairic* mediation, the naming of the generalized nature of each individual's local situation in the moment of its intelligibility.

Dialectics explains the accrual over time of the conditions of possibility for radical political transformation; when added to a theory of *kairos,* as I illustrate next, it explains how those moments regarded by rhetoricians as opportune for political intervention emerge upon waves of prior moments and prior opportunities. The moment of the transformation of quality into quantity—short-term economic struggles to broader political ones—is the *kairic* moment that is the culmination of one dialectical process and the beginning of the next.

It must be said that, contrary to some post-Marxist allegations, Marxist thought does not regard class struggle as following laws of motion outside of political intervention.[21] In a formulation similar to Marx's distinction between classes "in themselves" and classes "for themselves," Kenneth Burke argued that the rhetorical constitution of identity and antagonism is necessary to human action for social change. Action is "motion with intent." While the capacity for motion (the capacity of a class in itself) must exist before the intention to act, construction of intent (the mobilization of a class for itself) is a rhetorical process.[22] Rhetoric understands human action in terms of the discursive formation of identity and intention; dialectics reminds us that those identities and intentions can have a real basis in the existing antagonisms that move society forward. The question then becomes one of how people come to consciousness of the basic dynamism of society and collectively accrue a sense of shared identity and an intention to act out of and upon the fundamental antagonisms structuring society.

In an explanation of Georg Lukács' rejection of mechanical determination, Ivan Mésáros writes,

> Only if one grasps dialectically the multiplicity of specific mediations can one understand the Marxian notion of economics. For if the latter is the "ultimate determinant," it is also a determined determinant: it does not exist outside the always concrete, historically changing complex of concrete mediations.[23]

Here, Mésáros stresses the mutual inter-determination of economics and the "specific mediations" of a particular rhetorical, cultural, and ideological environment, which shape economic reality even as it is conditioned by economics in turn. This way of looking at dialectics is contrary to a theory positing indeterminate and fundamentally inexplicable social relations; it is also contrary to economic determinism. It is, rather, a theory of the mutual determination of economic and social relations and of the interaction between economic relations and the organized consciousness of society. Dialectics is thus also a way of understanding how ideas, identities, and interventions operate on both economic and symbolic terrain. Dialectical materialism is not only a method of historical explanation but also a guide to political intervention. In its materialist incarnations, it is a theory of a particular kind of rhetorical situation. Economic contradictions motivate antagonism and provide a situation for organized action. A revolutionary rhetoric is one that seizes on dialectical opportunities, and this practice might be captured productively in the Aristotelian concept of *kairos*.

A Materialist *Kairos*

Scholars of classical rhetoric have understood the Aristotelian concept of *kairos* to mean the appropriate situational timing and responsiveness of a rhetorical act to particular situations. Quoting James Kinneavy's earlier work, Kinneavy and Catherine Eskin explain that *kairos* is the "right or opportune time to do something, or right measure in doing something."[24] The concept has depths that are of interest to those theorizing revolutionary political agency. Amélie Benedikt writes, "The concern for *kairos* begins with an effort to recognize opportunity, making one sensitive to the critical character of moments that require decision. The decision concerning the right moment signifies understanding concerning *this* moment as distinct from others, concerning *this* moment as the culmination of a series of events."[25]

An example from the U.S. labor movement clarifies this idea: In December 2008, over 250 workers laid off in violation of federal law occupied the Republic Windows and Doors plant in Chicago to stop their employer from leaving without paying out their vacation and severance. The workers also generated public pressure on Bank of America, which had cut off credit to their employer. Bank of America had received $45 billion in federal bailout cash plus $300 billion in guarantees for "troubled assets." The 250 workers occupying the factory seized on this irony in an action reminiscent of the 1936–1937 sit-down strikes of autoworkers at General Motors.[26] On December 10, the company settled the dispute, granting the workers all their demands.

How should we account for their success? The political confidence engendered in November by the election of Barack Obama (who came out in support of the workers) and the deepening financial crisis constituted a singular opportunity. MSNBC reported that "the bank has been criticized for cutting off the plant's credit while taking federal bailout money."[27] This contradiction was ripe for the picking, and the workers enacted the principle of *kairos*. Their action, like the sit-down strikes of the 1930s, represent laborers' simultaneous commitment to their work and resistance against their employer's decisions. The evocative action garnered widespread sympathy across the United States among labor activists and the progressive left, leading to mass demonstrations in cities across the country.

In highlighting the decision to do the right thing at the right time at the culmination of a longer chronological process, *kairos* entails four features relevant to discussion of Marxism, dialectics, and revolutionary politics. First, *kairos* possesses an ethical-political dimension suggesting that the "right" thing is not only the most effective thing, but also the most just. Second, it marks the definitive, subjective moment or turning point that interrupts objective chronological, quantitative time and requires a qualitative shift or adaptation on the part of a rhetor to address evolving contingencies. Thus, and third, *kairos* is a theory of judgment in both criticism and action. Finally, in modern times as in the ancient, the exhibition of *kairos* requires education in practice enabling its students—scientists, politicians, artists, and so on—to recognize the right time and the right intervention to make in that time so as to animate a decisive turning point in the transformation of society.

These facets of the concept of *kairos* are compellingly similar to what Marx, Lenin, and Gramsci discovered to be the essential capacities of revolutionary judgment. Marx and Engels speak in ways similar to theorists of *kairos* in describing the dialectical process in nature and social life as one in which quantitative changes occurring over linear time reach a threshold or crisis on the cusp of significant qualitative change. Like Engels, for example, John Smith describes the *chronos* of time as "process, the ubiquity of becoming, stretch[ing] over the entire physical and organic world. We are by now well aware that nothing happens at an instant."[28] This characterization of the unfolding of ordinary time resonates with a materialist definition of dialectics. Furthermore, Smith attends to the ways in which *kairos* requires *chronos*. What happened in the past produced the present *kairic* opportunity, an insight that admonishes critics and theorists to overestimate neither the influence of the *kairic* act nor the determination of the past.[29] *Kairos* refers to the moment of opportunity arising from "tension and conflict, a time of crisis implying that the course of events poses a problem that calls for a decision at that time."[30] We could say, in other words, that *kairos* presupposes dialectics.

This idea clearly resonates with Engels's description of the transformation of quantity into quality as the dynamo of major social transformation. The dialectic becomes, then, the situation or site of *kairos,* the point at which agentive intervention into unfolding events completes the qualitative turn. The concept is materialist insofar as it recognizes the paramount position of situational factors, i.e., that people make history but in conditions not of their own making.

Lenin, for his part, stressed that his theory of political intervention was not to be taken as orthodoxy, but rather as a method of discovering the conditions of possibility in a particular historical moment. Benedikt writes similarly of *kairos*:

> Any adequate account of *kairos* must also explain how, and how long, to deliberate when immediate circumstances are changing. This requires understanding as much of the situational context as one can without becoming constrained by too great a respect for the norms of the present. Located in the present time, a sense of *kairos*

leads one to look beyond the factuality of the present to counterfactual worlds that are not, or not yet.[31]

As in Bendikt's example—"A platoon leader scans the horizon and yells, 'Time to go!'"[32]—Lenin scanned the horizon of possibility in October 1917, and called, "All power to the Soviets!"—a declaration that would have been disastrous if made during the July uprising of that same year.[33] Only a keen assessment of the forces arrayed against the Bolsheviks and their allies—which included persecution within the socialist left, military allegiance to the interim government, and a shaky foothold among industrial workers—enabled the decision that a call for wholesale transition of power to workers would not be timely and could, in fact, be tragic. *Kairic* action was contingent and dependent on education in and analysis of prevailing forces and relations of production, in addition to the political and ideological scene.

Antonio Gramsci extended the lessons of historical, theoretical, and social movement education for workers. Like Isocrates, he developed a model of education designed to train intellectuals involved in political struggle to recognize what is possible (and what is not), and when.[34] Gramsci's discussion of the necessity of the ideological war of position (rather than frontal attack on the capitalist system) should not be taken as universal advice generalizable to all contemporary struggles, but as a simple recognition that under conditions of fascism, doing the right thing means hunkering down and preparing oneself through education and consciousness-raising for the future fight. One cannot always storm the palace, which is not to say that one should never do so. That there are times without opportunity (*akairic* situations) is an important aspect of the concept. Like Isocrates, too, Gramsci taught by example before his imprisonment in workers' organizations of various kinds. In each of these ways, *kairos* understood through the lens of historical materialism becomes the situated intelligence of labor and revolutionary actors whose rhetorical interventions might turn the basic relationship of class into self-conscious antagonism.

Materialist *Kairos* and Revolutionary Strategy

Classes in and for Themselves

Marx understood this turning as the transition between a class that exists in itself to one that struggles for itself. In itself, basic class existence poses only an objective situation and opportunity for radical rhetoric. Marxists view class as the objective social relationship of various members of society to its means of production. Confronting oppressions based on the construction of hierarchies of racial, gendered, sexual, national, and religious differences is crucial, but under capitalism, there are fundamentally only two classes: the bourgeoisie, or ruling class, who own the means of production; and the proletariat, whose lack of property and of control over the means of production force them to work as wage laborers. While class position is more complicated and ambiguous for some intellectuals, civil servants, small business owners, the unemployed, and so on (the layers Marx called the "petit bourgeoisie" and the "lumpenproletariat"), it is objectively possible to identify a group's relationship to the means of production.[35] Thus, the working class has objective existence, including those millions who toil so that others might profit and with little or no control over their work and destiny.[36]

Despite sharing fundamental interests, there is no guarantee that workers—of every gender, race, nationality, sexual identity and expression, and creed; in industrial, service, intellectual, white-collar, pink-collar, caretaking, and every other sector—will automatically see their situation as collective or political. On this point, I am in agreement with Laclau and Mouffe's argument that the clash of contending interests is insufficient to make an antagonism; while the former is a given, the latter is essentially political and requires rhetorical articulation across other social divisions and their justifications in racist, sexist, and homophobic ideologies.[37] As Anna Smith explains in her reading of Laclau and Mouffe, we cannot assume that people act automatically on the basis of empirical experience; nor will class automatically be a "meaningful axis of identification." Instead, subjects create a sense of collective social agency based on common interpretations of their subject positions.[38] Yet, to argue that such interpretation and rhetorical articulation of collective subjectivity and purpose are necessary does not necessarily entail embracing the "logic of hegemony" over and above "the logic of capital."[39] My argument here, following Gramsci, is that capital provides the opportunity for the articulation of a counter-hegemonic antagonism; the logic of hegemony depends on the logic of capital, and vice versa—they are dialectically related.

Given, however, that rhetorical articulation is necessary to class struggle, a key question becomes what agent encourages interpretation of lived experience to foster a dialectical transformation. What kind of discourse is needed for a "class in itself" to become a "class for itself"?[40] The difference between these two formulations is the difference between an exploited working class with no sense of its universal character or political agency on the one hand, and the organized proletariat as a particular sociopolitical agent on the other.[41] As Gramsci noted, culture, education, and politics are crucial to class agency; even so, these are based on the recognition of the particular democratic impulse of an objectively real proletariat that can instrumentally challenge capitalist social relations on both economic and cultural terrain.

Objective and Subjective Factors

In Lenin and Trotsky, the relationship between the rhetorical intervention of political agents (such as members of a party) and the given circumstances is theorized in terms of "subjective" and "objective" factors. By attending to the concrete, objective economic situation within which revolutionaries may foster class consciousness, this theory gives the principle of *kairos* a materialist inflection. Objective factors, on this view, consist in not only the economic realities and contradictions facing ordinary people at any given time, but also the balance of political forces pertaining, so that a sober assessment of political opportunity and constraint is possible. The interaction between subjective factors and objective factors is dialectical.

As George Novak explains in a discussion of how Trotsky could have believed at one and the same time that the Russian Revolution was the product of historical circumstance *and* that the role of revolutionaries such as Lenin was indispensable, "Marxist thought generally suggests that no individual, however talented, strong-willed or strategically situated, can alter the main course of historical development, which is shaped by supra-individual circumstances and forces."[42] Lenin's distinction between subjective and objective factors is akin to Aristotle's recognition that there are artistic and inartistic proofs; the revolutionary has constrained strategic influence in any given situation, but the artistry of social movement rhetoric rests on the given proofs of class inequality.

Since class interests exist, just as exploitation is an ongoing fact in capitalist society, these interests can be the real foundation on which an anti-capitalist antagonism can be built. Yet, their mere existence is insufficient to the task. Lukács, among others, rejected the idea that class consciousness is an automatic response to proletarian existence. For this reason, he criticized the Polish revolutionary Rosa Luxemburg for her insistence on the spontaneity of systematic consciousness and revolution.[43] Along these lines, Oskar Negt and Alexander Kluge explain in *Public Sphere and Experience* that interests, grounded in lived experience, are the basis for, but not the realization of, a proletarian public, which is organized in discourse.[44] The right rhetorical intervention in a situation ripe for such a realization constitutes a *kairic* interruption in the ongoing dialectical process of small, quantitative shifts in the balance of forces in capitalism. This interruption in the flow of time-as-usual marks the transformation of quantity into quality. The question remains as to who the agents of this transformation can be. Paul Paolucci observes,

> Marx certainly never argued that the development of capitalism could be reduced to material conditions alone. An internal-relations philosophy of science dictates that analysis take account of the fact that discursive knowledge can lead or cause changes in material conditions rather than simply and/or uniformly trailing them.[45]

And as Negt and Kluge cogently explain,

> [c]lass and consciousness are real categories . . . The Marxist tradition draws them together into a single term so as to outline a program. This program is concerned with the mediation between the coming into being of the proletarian context of living, along with its subjective, "conscious" side.[46]

Now we are in a position to answer the critique advanced by Stuart Hall and others that Marxists were class essentialists. Hall argues that Gramsci rejected the idea of a pre-given class identity, and this is an accurate claim.[47] What Gramsci did argue, however, is that workers share a pre-given, fundamental, and real interest in overcoming their exploitation, which could be the basis for winning them to political organization and class struggle. Thus, in "Working-Class Education and Culture," Gramsci explains that workers are not dupes, though they may require education conducted by and for them to "truly understand the full implications of the notion of 'ruling class.'"[48] For Gramsci, real working class education must debunk "ideologies aimed at reconciling opposing interests" in favor of "the expression of these subaltern classes."[49]

Thus, the Marxist dialectic is rhetorically and argumentatively mediated in this process of education, while lapsing into neither idealism nor spontaneism. What are the media (in the broad sense), then, for class consciousness and class will? For the Bolsheviks, as for Lukács, the medium was the socialist party. Lukács has been charged with vanguardism, or the valorization of a narrow layer of revolutionary leadership who, by virtue of greater experience and knowledge, is in a position to lead workers' movements.[50] Caution about elitist or individualistic leadership of working people's struggle is always appropriate.[51] However, a socialist party or organization is not unlike other types of parties in organizing consciousness and leading political movements. It attempts to win public support and to vie for hegemony in the political realm. It employs rhetorical strategies of identification and attempts to move groups to take particular kinds of action.

Worried about the problem of imposing a political analysis on ordinary people "from the outside" (as Lenin suggested in 1902 but rejected in later, different, circumstances), Gramsci argued for organizations inclusive of organic intellectuals who belong to the working class but whose education and experience may push a struggle forward.[52] In workplaces and in educational settings, organizers and educators can make arguments about the daily experience of work and how those experiences are connected to other workplaces, to experiences of family and consumption, and, eventually, to the requirements of capitalism as a system. Such efforts demonstrate *kairos* when they succeed in organizing audiences and motivating action toward the ends of justice. In a limited way, dissident unionists at Boeing in the 1990s achieved these tasks; in 2005, they failed to do so, but in 2008, in the unlikely situation of a global economic crisis, they were victorious again. The ability to comprehend how and why such interventions articulate or fail to articulate the interests of the class is one advantage of understanding *kairos* dialectically.

Dissident *Kairos* at Boeing

The relationship between the International Association of Machinists and Aerospace Workers (IAMAW) and Boeing historically has been adversarial, marked by major strikes in 1989 and 1995, but by more conciliatory contract negotiations in 1999 and 2002. In the years leading up to 2005, the Boeing Company capitalized (quite literally) on growing passivity and even cooperation with management among union leaders to embark on a number of ruthless corporate reorganizations and layoffs. However, such conciliation was not a foregone conclusion in previous decades.

An indication of the possibility of a revitalized labor movement came in 1995. The national sixty-nine-day strike in that year of the IAMAW at the Boeing Company mobilized more than 40,000 workers in Wichita, Kansas, and Seattle, Washington. During this strike, two dissident union organizations sprang up to rally workers against both the company's incursions on their standard of living and a sluggish union leadership. Unionists for Democratic Change, whose most prominent spokesperson was Keith Thomas, and Machinists for Solidarity, led by David Clay, were small but somewhat influential agitators in this context.[53]

According to Michael Cimini, writing in the *Monthly Labor Review*, the strike in 1995 was motivated by the elimination of nearly 35,000 union jobs, 26,000 of these in the Puget Sound area, in addition to threats to wage increases, safety provisions, and health insurance.[54] The workers went on strike on September 13. Cimini writes,

> On November 19, a tentative agreement was reached between Boeing and the IAMAW. Although the IAMAW bargaining committee unanimously recommended acceptance of the pact, the rank-and-file soundly rejected it. Union members said

that they were dissatisfied with the contract offer because it still called for increases in employee contributions towards health care and contained weak job security language.

It was at the moment of the union endorsement of the second contract that the conditions for challenging a stale bureaucracy were born. It was a *kairic* moment for the shop-floor agitators. In an unprecedented act, the workers of the union slapped down the cautious recommendation of the leaders and voted to remain on strike.

Worker accounts of this event are moving revelations of their sudden recognition of their own power. Keith Thomas's account of the rejection of the contract is worth quoting at length:

> I think the most important event, the portion of that strike that I'll remember for the rest of my life, it has to be the point where we turned down that second proposal. . . . It was just an outstanding event, to think of just your rank and file, and the grassroots out there, had just had enough. They'd been lied to enough, they'd had enough from the company . . . and I think that the best gesture was, they just set that ass down there, they stuck their finger up there and they said I've just had enough. I'm turning it down. . . . [T]he International leadership, the District leadership, some of the Local leadership, the federal mediator, the company, the corporate media of course was selling this and the folks turned it down. And then of course the company was so convinced we were going to take it. I suppose the second happy event was that they sent us letters welcoming us back. . . . People out on the picket lines were waving their welcome back letters to the cameras and to the general public as folks would go by. And just how outstanding that was.[55]

Thomas, who might be considered an organic intellectual, notices in these remarks the *outstanding* sense of fullness of time that marks the opportune response to social crisis, "the most important event," "the outstanding event" that one remembers all one's life as the most fitting and the most agentive. It was a culmination of the work of dissidents combined with the experience of "having had enough" that helped enable ordinary workers at Boeing to see beyond their immediate well-being and financial security to the longer-term collective victory. In theoretical terms, the accrual of injustices and threats against workers led to a turning point at which they "had just had enough."

The dialectical process was ripe at this critical juncture for *kairic* intervention, which was undertaken not only by the dissidents but by the majority of the rank and file. The crafting of collective aims and identities out of particular and local existence is a materialist instance of what Laclau has termed "the synecdoche constitutive of the hegemonic link," in this case between the particular experience and the class as agent of antagonism that led workers to debunk ideological inducements (on the part of the company, the media, and the conservative union leadership) to identify with the company and union leadership.[56] Dissident ideas were broadly shared among the strikers; the dissident agitators were not elite or isolated rhetorical agents. The images of workers Thomas conjures metaphorically (and, in some cases, literally) giving their leaders "the finger" and waving the arrogant welcome back letters from the company on the picket line convey the sense of agency and defiance the rank and file felt at that moment.[57]

Other workers, both members of the opposition caucuses and representatives of established union leadership, also expressed their elation at taking charge of that moment in their history. According to David Clay,

> [t]he shining moment in that strike was when the membership took over the union. The membership realized we're the union. We have a say. We had lunchtime marches out to twin towers, into factory. We disrupted delivery of 777s. We banged on pipes with tools and changed in the plants. We shook the walls. People got the idea that this thing was theirs. We shocked the union leadership.[58]

Clay is describing the protests described by some union members as "Operation Rolling Thunder," in which members marched across lots and through hangars and created havoc in the plants. The "shining" moment when "people got the idea that this thing was theirs" succinctly captures the dialectical and *kairic* formation of class consciousness; out of the accumulation of instances of local power—marches, demonstrations, strike events— unionists achieved a shared awareness of collective power and place. The realization that "we have a say" is elegant shorthand for the dialectical discovery of one's collective rhetorical agency and shared interests in this situation. The "shining" and "outstanding" moments of struggle constitute the moment of opportunity, the crisis point in ordinary time, during which the appropriate action fulfills the promise of the moment.

After 1995, the dissident movement at Boeing (and across a number of unions) entered a period of decline even as Boeing ratcheted up pressure on the workers. But after two concessionary contracts (in 1999 and 2002), members of both dissident groups rallied in 2005 for pensions and job security. However, in 2005, dissident activists and their ideas were isolated. The strike ended after four weeks when workers voted to accept a contract with major concessions; later that year, Boeing sold off its Wichita operation, leaving thousands of workers without jobs and effectively wiping out the unionized workforce.

Beyond the overwhelming objective challenges facing the union, dialectical analysis suggests that the subjective factors of consciousness and confidence are also barriers to victory. If it were simply a matter of economic motivation and the automatic contention of rival classes, strikes would flare without too much effort into class warfare. That they do not do so is evidence that rhetorical intervention is necessary but not always capable of shifting material forces in a progressive direction. The historical dialectical process of workers' struggles does not unfold automatically into generalized class consciousness (as opposed to more basic "trade union consciousness").[59] However, other factors, both material and ideological, foreclose on the *kairic* opportunity so that the outcome of a struggle cannot be determined by the rhetorical posture of organized class-conscious agents.

In sum, materialist dialectics identifies the *kairic* situation as the unfolding combination and inter-influence of economic, ideological, and rhetorical factors—of subjective and objective factors (in Lenin's formulation) that present a shining or outstanding moment of opportunity. Timing and experience become the key rather than ideological correctness or sheer economic clout.[60]

This insight is key to a materialist rhetorical assessment of the successful 2008 strike of the IAMAW at Boeing. The situation for workers in 2008 did not seem on its surface to be particularly opportune. The union had been weakened both numerically and in its confidence over the preceding decade, when Boeing laid off tens of thousands of workers, moved its corporate headquarters to Chicago away from Everett (getting some distance from the workers), sold off its unit in Wichita, and became mired in scandal.[61] Furthermore, the massive economic crisis that began in 2007 threatened workers in all sectors as employers enacted massive layoffs. Yet, the strikers won the strike on several counts. How can we explain the counterintuitive successful outcome of the Boeing strike? What brought the contradictions and injustices at Boeing to the dialectical point of transformation once again? And what role did workers' rhetorical interventions in this situation play in constituting and mobilizing a class for itself?

At Boeing, decades of experience and class-conscious rhetoric, punctuated by sharp, successful labor actions, situated the 2008 negotiation and served as a basis for a confident class consciousness among workers there even after waves of layoffs and the onset of economic crisis. A materialist inflection of the concept of *kairos* helps us understand how class conflict is permanent in capitalist society—but class warfare, presupposing class consciousness, is not. The prior *kairic* and *akairic* turning points become resources and obstacles in the present struggle as salient as the economic and political features of its immediate context. These included a period of optimism and sense of agency among an electorate witnessing Barack Obama's historic victory in the presidential race, which mitigated, to some extent, the potentially negative effects of economic crisis on public morale. Indeed, the gap between a sense of agency and the presence of unfairly meted economic hardship may prompt rather than stay workers' willingness to fight back. At the same time, dissatisfaction with the wars in Iraq and Afghanistan weaken the appeals to loyalty by companies, like Boeing, who sustain themselves through hard times in production for the defense sector.

Most significantly, Boeing has been buffered, at least in the short term, from the deepening economic slump in 2008. The corporate behemoth is fundamental to the industries of warfare and transportation and has never failed to make a profit, even in challenging economic times. Indeed, the company's third-quarter earnings statement for 2008 reveals that, contrary to other firms' troubles, Boeing suffered from *too little* rather than *too much* (over)production. In 2008, its earnings fell slightly, reducing the company's operating margin and denting shareholders' historically high earnings by 4 percent from the preceding year.[62] However, even these small disappointments did not result from Boeing's having more planes than they could sell. Rather, according to the third-quarter report, labor strike and production problems delayed the manufacture and delivery of planes already ordered. The company's net earnings declined 38 percent (to $695 million), but its revenue was higher than in the same quarter of 2007. The report states, "Backlog grew to a record $349 billion [3,400 planes, and an increase of $73 billion during the quarter] as near-term demand remains strong." The Pentagon, NASA, and the nation of Qatar all placed orders during this quarter—meaning that Boeing has record value on the books that could not be realized.[63]

Thus, even as skilled, organized (and therefore expensive) autoworkers take the blame for bankruptcies in that sector and face layoffs, Boeing's similarly skilled and highly paid workers could hurt the company by *not working*.[64] Ironically, although entirely in keeping with Marxist political economy, the stronger the company is economically, the more vulnerable it is to labor action.[65] The moment was extraordinarily opportune, a conjuncture in which even a usually recalcitrant union leadership (which failed workers in 1995, creating an opportunity for the growth of the dissident moment) pushed back company plans to outsource more work and cut back on health care and other benefits.

In a particularly class-conscious moment, District 751 (Puget Sound) president Tom Wroblewski commented, "Your solidarity brought Boeing back to the table and made this company address your issues. Each of you stood up and did your part to win this battle, which was a fight against more than Boeing."[66] Mark Blondin, notorious in the 1995 strike for encouraging workers to ratify a concessionary contract, recognized that the union had made mistakes in 2002 and 2005 in not holding out against outsourcing. In contrast, the fifty-seven-day 2008 strike also won significant wage and pension increases over the four years of the 2008 contract.[67] Beginning in August, experienced union activists, veterans of the 1995, 2002, and 2005 struggles (i.e., the vanguard of organic intellectuals) helped lead weekly, then daily marches and rallies of thousands of workers. The outcome of the machinists' strike discouraged Boeing from a fight with the Society of Professional Engineers in their November negotiations.[68]

The efforts of Don Grinde and other activists like Tom Parsley (both in Everett) attracted and organized a new layer of workers to the dissident movement. Parsley commented, "I think the strike helped the network. There's more communication than there's ever been. Employees' networking together was exceptionally well done." Parsley said that he had learned from this experience to begin to agitate earlier the next time around, perhaps to press the struggle even further.

Of course, the success of such a strategy the next time around will depend not only on what Parsley and others do and say, but also on the objective conditions, opportunities, and constraints that meet them. It is impossible to make a judgment as to a more successful course of action for labor today without the capacity to assess the objective contradictions and situation of the company, the broader economy, the political landscape, the labor movement, its leaders, and its ideas. The present moment in the labor movement is marked by a huge gap between class anger and fear for the future on the one hand, and confidence to stand up against a corporate giant like Boeing on the other.

Conclusion: Change Happens

As Adorno noted, dialectics recognizes "the subjective moment in the object."[69] In this chapter, I have argued that recognizing the possibility of and seizing such subjective moments in a material situation is a marker of *kairos,* a concept that, through the lens of historical materialism and Marxist dialectics, helps to theorize class-based rhetorical agency. The dialectical relationships between contending classes and between experience and consciousness offer radical social movement actors rhetorical opportunities. It simultaneously offers rhetorical scholars a set of criteria for analysis and judgment of radical discourse. The objective factors of class relationship provide the conditions of possibility for what Lenin called the subjective factors of political strategy and tactics. The transformation between a class in itself and a class for itself unfolds out of a dialectical process of interpretation and constitution of working class identity on the basis of an already-existing relationship. As in the case of dissident discourse at the Boeing Company, the dialectical method allows us to see how generalized class consciousness is produced out of the creative and timely combination of basic economic contestation and the intervention of movement discourse.

Dialectical method can also help rhetoricians understand when and how rhetorical intervention might be *kairic,* and also when it is constrained or impossible. Yet communication studies today has embraced a number of critical theories that give up the dialectic between both contending classes and the tensions among interests, experience, and consciousness. A number of cultural studies and poststructuralist theorists have claimed the tradition of materialism while attempting to "go beyond" dialectics, perhaps out of the confusion between dialectics and an indefensible mechanistic economism.[70] But as I have argued elsewhere, such a retreat misunderstands the traditions of historical materialism and Marxist dialectics.[71] Further, "going beyond" the grounding of claims in material reality is the province of idealism and metaphysics, not of any project properly called "materialist."

I believe that the recovery of Marxist dialectics provides an alternative to the post-Marxist nominalism of Laclau and Mouffe and others. Laclau and Mouffe have argued that the kind of social antagonism described by Marx between existing working and ruling classes must become a discursive articulation of forces on the basis of contingent, constructed identities with no fundamental basis in objective social relations.[72] Where they are right, as I have noted earlier in this chapter, is in the recognition that class identity and struggle are not automatic products of economic position. However, it is unnecessary and, in some ways, disabling, to move from the extreme of economism to the equally un-dialectical idea that class and other antagonistic subject positions are wholly products of rhetorical invention.

In their earlier work, Laclau and Mouffe argued that there are no fundamental class interests on which an antagonism faithful to the working class may be built. Rather, there are, on this view, discursive nodal points around which democratic demands may be organized on a contingent basis. In *On Populist Reason*, Laclau extends this argument to suggest that movements should organize themselves according to the universalizing logics of the democratic-liberal imaginary rather than on the basis of class particularity. According to Jared Woodard, settling for the populist agent means rejecting the possibility of a revolutionary agency. Woodard writes, "If every struggle whatsoever—insofar as it depends only on 'contingent power relations'—is in principle put on equal hegemonic footing with all the others . . . then hegemonic struggle obviously can no longer be assumed to be of a class nature, or aimed at anti-capitalist goals. Since hegemonic struggle is no longer operative within the 'purely economic' sphere, the target of antagonist universality must be restated, and this is Laclau's second move: the enemy of emancipatory struggle is now closure or completion as such."[73]

What is at stake in a dialectical as opposed to a discursive view of class agency is the possibility of theorizing revolutionary change. Laclau and Mouffe recognize that they have accepted reforms within "the prevailing liberal imaginary" as the limit of antagonistic struggle, since revolutionary politics is by definition founded on both the actual contestation of rival classes and the recognition of class struggle as the foundation of wholesale social transformation. As histories of broad, qualitative social change in the modern world and recent working class upsurges across Latin America attest, revolution happens.[74] The post-Marxist denial of a fundamental class basis for socialist politics is tied up with an unnecessary refusal of the possibility of founding and evaluating struggle on the basis of actual class antagonisms.

Although Laclau and Mouffe have sustained (to their credit) an emphasis on organized, antagonistic, and collective politics, other poststructuralist theorists have given up this idea in a resort to immanentism, which is profoundly anti-dialectical. Post-dialectical thinking reaches its logical conclusion in the works of Gilles Deleuze and Félix Guattari, and Michael Hardt and Antonio Negri. Deleuze and Guattari's *A Thousand Plateaus* describes social change as an inexplicable shift in the common sense axioms organizing society, across a space imagined as singular and flat, without contrast, depth, or contradiction. In their influential book *Empire* (described by Ellen Wood as "a manifesto for global capitalism"[75]) and its sequel, *Multitude*, Hardt and Negri describe empire as a self-creating form (following Foucault) of everyday governance, or bio-power.[76]

The *multitude* is defined as a vaguely discontented and unpredictable, irreducible resisting multiplicity.[77] As Samir Amin summarizes,

> Hardt and Negri think that we have arrived at this historical turning point, that classes (along with nations or peoples) are no longer the subjects of history. . . . This turning point gives rise to the formation of what they call the "multitude," defined in terms of the "totality of productive and creative subjectivities." Why and how would this turning point occur? Hardt and Negri's texts are quite vague on these questions.[78]

The concept of *kairos* asks *why, how,* and *when* a turning point occurs. Dialectics answers in an analysis of the situation of unfolding events culminating in the opportunity for such a turning point. In what might be read as a critique of immanentist postmodern theory, Adorno writes, "If matter were total, undifferentiated, and flatly singular, there would be no dialectics in it"

(205).[79] In other words, one cannot theorize social change without recognition of the discrete material (i.e., economic) divisions in society as well as the basic distinction between interests and consciousness, and the significance of each.

Understood in a Marxist frame, dialectics affords both critics and activists a perspective on the unfolding of opportunities for judgment and action in capitalist society. Dialectical tensions exist between contending classes and between one's experience as a member of a class and one's consciousness of that position as politically significant. In long-term processes of social transformation, local events and struggles accrue, sometimes until a turning point arises during which appropriate action might effect the transformation of quantity into quality, or from the economic to the political. *Kairos,* or the faculty of recognizing such turning points and exploiting the timely opportunity, is compatible with classical Marxist thought, suggesting that political decision making is grounded in class interests but beyond this fact is radically contingent depending on the array of material and ideological forces at work at any given moment. Here I have demonstrated how this principle is at work in a series of labor struggles at Boeing, whose successes and failures reveal not only the *kairic* conditions of possibility for transformative agentive intervention, but also a way to assess the lack of such opportunity in situations we might describe as *"akairic."*

Thus, a specifically Marxist dialectical approach to *kairos* can tell us how rhetorical intervention is not merely situated in time and place, an insight common to most rhetorical theory and criticism since Lloyd Bitzer's definition of the rhetorical situation.[80] A dialectical perspective suggests that beyond this starting point, all situations of conflict prime for rhetorical intervention involve crisis or contradiction. The question is whether and how critical rhetoricians may productively understand that situation as generated out of real, material class relationships. Ultimately, materialism seeks to understand the actual conflicts of interest against which interventions may be judged ethically and politically and to recognize the instrumental possibilities of collective action on that basis. What is at stake in recovering dialectical materialism for rhetoric is the capacity to recognize the ultimate *kairic* moment in struggles against capitalism for what it is: a revolutionary rhetorical situation.

Notes

1. "Materialist dialectics" as I am using the term is not aligned with Stalin's distorted articulation of "dialectical materialism" or "dia-mat," which in 1938 interpreted Marx and Engels in such a way as to remove the human agent from the process of revolutionary change. See Joseph Stalin, "Dialectical and Historical Materialism," *Marxist Internet*

Archive, http://www.marxists.org/reference/archive/stalin/works/1938/09.htm.

2. See Kenneth Burke, *Rhetoric of Motives* (Berkeley: University of California, 1959); note also Burke's infamous speech to the Communist American Writers' Congress in 1935, where he was booed out of the hall after arguing that the phrase "working class" should be replaced in Party discourse with "the people." Kenneth Burke, "Revolutionary Symbolism in America" (speech to American Writers' Congress, April 26, 1935) in *The Legacy of Kenneth Burke*, ed. Herbert Simons and Trevor Melia (Madison: University of Wisconsin Press, 1989), 267–73. This argument is similar to the one advanced by Ernesto Laclau in *On Populist Reason* (London: Verso, 2005) that a sectarian group achieves hegemony when it articulates its aims and interests in universalizing rather than sectional language.

3. This critique of Marxist thought and the assertion of the relative supremacy of the symbolic and discursive as sites of struggle is emblematic of both what Perry Anderson calls "Western Marxism" and the ideas of post-Marxist thought as represented by Laclau and Mouffe and many others, and in the realm of practical politics, the reaction against Stalinist communism in Eurocommunism, critiqued by Trotskyists and other Marxists for abandoning basic Marxist concepts such as the centrality of the working class and the revolutionary program. Work representing this shift is diverse and includes theory in cultural studies (especially those embracing the "new times" hypothesis that capitalism had been transformed into a system amenable more to cultural and discursive incursion than frontal economic challenge), structuralist and post-structuralist theory, as well as psychoanalysis. The journal *Rethinking Marxism* (London: Taylor and Francis) represents this break, as do the following works: Gilles Deleuze and Félix Guattari, *Anti-Oedipus: Capitalism and Schizophrenia* (Minneapolis: University of Minnesota Press, 1983); Stuart Hall, "Gramsci's Relevance for the Study of Race and Ethnicity," *Journal of Communication Inquiry* 10 (1986): 5–27; Stuart Hall, "The Problem of Ideology—Marxism without Guarantees," *Journal of Communication Inquiry* 10 (1986): 28–44; T. J. Jackson Lears, "The Concept of Cultural Hegemony: Problems and Possibilities," *American Historical Review* 90 (1985): 567–93; Raymond Williams, "Base and Superstructure in Marxist Cultural Theory," in John Higgins, ed., *The Raymond Williams Reader* (London: Blackwell, 2001), 158–78; Michel Foucault, *History of Sexuality, An Introduction* (New York: Vintage, 1980); Paul Rabinow and James Faubion, ed., *Essential Works of Foucault*, trans. Robert Hurley, 3 vols. (New York: New Press, 1998, 2001); Judith Butler, *Bodies that Matter: On the Discursive Limits of "Sex"* (New York: Routledge, 1993); David Morley and Kuan-Hsing Chen, eds., *Stuart Hall: Critical Dialogues in Cultural Studies* (London: Routledge, 1996); Michael Hardt and Antonio Negri, *Empire* (Cambridge, MA: Harvard University Press, 2000); Michael Hardt and Antonio Negri, *Multitude* (New York: Penguin, 2005); Ernesto Laclau and Chantal Mouffe, *Hegemony and Socialist Strategy: Towards a Radical Democratic Politics* (London: Verso, 1985).

    For the Left critique of post-Marxism and Eurocommunism, see Perry Anderson, *Considerations on Western Marxism* (London: Verso, 1979); Perry Anderson, *In the Tracks of Historical Materialism* (Chicago: University of Chicago, 1984); Ernest Mandel, *From Stalinism to Eurocommunism: The Bitter Fruits of "Socialism in One Country"* (London: NLB, 1978); Ellen Meiksins Wood, *Retreat from Class* (London: Verso, 1999); John Clarke, *New Times and Old Enemies: Essays on Cultural Studies and America* (London: Harper Collins Academic, 1991); and the journal *Historical Materialism* (London: Brill, 1999–).

4.   James Arnt Aune, *Rhetoric and Marxism* (Boulder, CO: Westview Press, 1994); Michelle
     Barrett, *The Politics of Truth* (Stanford, CA: Stanford University Press, 1991); Ronald
     Walter Greene, "Rhetoric and Capitalism: Rhetorical Agency as Communicative Labor,"
     Philosophy and Rhetoric 37 (2004): 188–206; Ronald Walter Greene, "Another Material-
     ist Rhetoric," *Critical Studies in Mass Communication* 15 (1998): 21–41; Ronald Walter
     Greene, "The Concept of Global Citizenship in Michael Hardt and Antonio Negri's Em-
     pire: A Challenge to Three Ideas of Rhetorical Mediation," in *Rhetorical Democracy:
     Discursive Practices of Civic Engagement*, ed. Gerard Hauser and Amy Grim (Mahwah,
     NJ: Lawrence-Erlbaum, 2004), 166. For a critique of this turn in rhetorical studies, see
     James Arnt Aune, Dana L. Cloud, and Stephen Macek, "'The Limbo of Ethical Simula-
     cra': A Reply to Ron Greene," *Philosophy and Rhetoric* 39 (2006): 72–84; Dana L.
     Cloud, "*The Matrix* and Critical Theory's Desertion of the Real," *Communication and
     Critical/Cultural Studies* 3 (2006), 329–54.
5.   Laclau, *On Populist Reason*; see also Laclau and Mouffe, *Hegemony and Socialist
     Strategy*.
6.   "Mode of production" refers to the overarching system of producing and distributing the
     necessities of life (for example, capitalism); it comprises the forces, relations, and means
     of production. "Forces of production" refers to the balance of power among contending
     classes (ruling and working); "relations of production" refers to "objective material rela-
     tions that exist in any society independently of human consciousness, formed between all
     people in the process of social production, exchange, and distribution of material wealth,"
     i.e., social structure that organizes the basis of the means of production, or combination
     of natural raw materials, machinery, and plant and infrastructure. See Karl Marx, preface
     to *A Contribution to the Critique of Political Economy*, *Internet Marxist Archive*,
     http://www.marxists.org/archive/marx/works/1859/critique-pol-economy/preface-
     abs.htm.
7.   See any of Plato's dialogues with the Sophists, including *Gorgias* and *Phaedrus*, at *The
     Internet Classics Archive*, http://classics.mit.edu/Plato/. Georg Friedrich Hegel, *Philoso-
     phy of Mind*, trans. A. V. Miller (Oxford: Clarendon, 1971/1894).
8.   Hegel, *Philosophy of Mind*, 18.
9.   Fredric Jameson, "T. W. Adorno," in *The Jameson Reader*, ed. Michael Hardt and Kathy
     Weeks (London: Blackwell, 2000), 73.
10. Theodor Adorno, *Negative Dialectics*, trans. E. B. Ashton (New York: Continuum,
     2007/1966), 197.
11. Adorno, *Negative Dialectics*, 56.
12. Adorno, *Negative Dialectics*, 136, 160, 152.
13. Adorno, *Negative Dialectics*, 170.
14. Frederick Engels, "Old Preface to Anti-Dühring," 1878, first published in 1925 as part of
     Dialectics of Nature, *Marxists Internet Archive*, http://www.Marxists.org/archive/marx/
     works/1878/05/dialectics.htm.
15. Karl Marx, "Critique of Hegel's Philosophy in General," *Economic and Philosophical
     Manuscripts of 1844*, *Marxists Internet Archive*, http://www.marxists.org/archive/marx/
     works/1844/manuscripts/hegel.htm.
16. Karl Marx, *The German Ideology*, *Marxists Internet Archive*, http://www.marxists.org/
     archive/marx/works/1845/german-ideology/index.htm.
17. Karl Marx, *Capital*, vol. 1, *Marxists Internet Archive*, http://www.marxists.org/archive/
     marx/works/1867-c1/p3.htm#3b.
18. Engels, *Dialectics of Nature*.

19. Chris Harmon, *People's History of the World* (London: Bookmarks, 1999), 161–232.

20. Alexander Rabinowitz, *The Bolsheviks Come to Power* (Chicago: Haymarket Books, 2004), xviii.

21. See Laclau and Mouffe, *Hegemony and Socialist Strategy*, 76.

22. Kenneth Burke, "(Nonsymbolic) Motion/(Symbolic) Action," *Critical Inquiry* 4 (1978): 809–38.

23. Ivan Mésáros, *Lukács' Concept of the Dialectic* (London: Merlin Press, 1972), 72.

24. The authors are quoting James L. Kinneavy, "*Kairos*: A Neglected Concept in Classical Rhetoric," in *Rhetoric and Praxis: The Contribution of Classical Rhetoric to Practical Reasoning*, ed. J. D. Moss (Washington, D.C.: Catholic University of America Press, 1986), 80.

25. Amélie Frost Benedikt, "On Doing the Right Thing at the Right Time: Toward an Ethics of *Kairos*," in *Rhetoric and Kairos*, ed. Phillip Sipiora and James S. Baumlin (Albany: State University of New York Press, 2002), 227.

26. See Nelson Lichtenstein and Christopher Phelps, "Chicago Factory Sit-In Fits Nation's Mood," *CNN.com*, December 9, 2008, http://www.cnn.com/2008/POLITICS/12/08/lichtenstein.chicago.labor/index.html.

27. Associated Press, "Workers Who Staged Sit-In at Chicago Plant Win," *MSNBC.com*, December 9, 2008, http://www.msnbc.msn.com/id/28144080/.

28. John E. Smith, "Time and Qualitative Time," in *Rhetoric and Kairos*, ed. Phillip Sippiora and James Baumlin (Albany: State University of New York Press, 2004), 46–57.

29. Smith, "Time and Qualitative Time," 49–50.

30. Smith, "Time and Qualitative Time," 52.

31. Benedikt, "On Doing the Right," 231.

32. Benedikt, "On Doing the Right," 228.

33. Rabinowitz, *Bolsheviks Come to Power*, 10, 60, 75, 168–90. Likewise, socialists actually defended the government during the attempted Kornilov coup but rose up against it in October. Every situation posed a new set of circumstances and consequences of action or inaction. Thus, effective intervention is contingent and must be based on analysis and deliberation.

34. James Kinneavy explains that *kairos* is explicitly connected to civic education. "*Kairos* in Classical and Modern Rhetorical Theory," in *Rhetoric and Kairos*, ed. Phillip Sippiora and James S. Baumlin (Albany: State University of New York Press), 58–76. See also Antonio Gramsci, "Working Class Education and Culture," in *The Antonio Gramsci Reader*, ed. David Forgacs and Eric J. Hobsbawm (New York: New York University Press, 2000), 53–75.

35. See Erik Olin Wright, *Classes* (London: Verso, 1997); contrast J. K. Gibson-Graham, *Re-Presenting Classes: Essays in Postmodern Marxism* (Raleigh-Durham, NC: Duke University Press, 2001).

36. See Sebastiano Timapanaro, *On Materialism* (New York: Humanities Press, 1975), for one caveat to this argument, namely that the "working class" has no ontological being; to label it is an abstraction, an epistemological move that should be based on the ontological status of laboring and of interests.

37. Laclau and Mouffe, *Hegemony and Socialist Strategy*, 123.

38. Anna Smith, *Laclau and Mouffe: The Radical Democratic Imaginary* (New York: Routledge, 1998), 61–62. See also Terry Eagleton, *After Theory* (Cambridge, MA: Basic Books, 2003). It is *not* true, for example, that Marx and Engels argued that a revolutionary outcome class struggle was inevitable in the *Communist Manifesto* or in *The Eight-*

eenth Brumaire; indeed, it would have been nonsensical for them to compose the *Manifesto* if working class revolution required no rhetorical constitution.

39. Laclau and Mouffe, *Hegemony and Socialist Strategy*, 69.
40. Originally articulated by Marx ("Strikes and Combinations of Workers," *Marxists Internet Archive*, http://www.marxists.org/archive/marx/works/1847/poverty-philosophy/ch02e.htm). This distinction was taken up by a succession of Marxists interested in the role of discourse, intellectuals, and political organizations (i.e., parties) in the production of class consciousness and organization.
41. Jared Woodard, "Populists or Proletarians," *Populism Roundup*, http://ghostinthewire.org/2005/12/populism_roundup.php.
42. George Novak, "The Importance of the Individual in History-Making," in *Understanding History* (1956), *Marxists Internet Archive*, http://www.marxists.org/archive/novack/works/history/ch03.htm.
43. Georg Lukács, *History and Class-Consciousness*, trans. Rodney Livingstone (Cambridge: MIT Press, 1972), 168. See also his *A Defence of History and Class-Consciousness*, trans. Esther Leslie (London: Verso, 2000).
44. Oskar Negt and Alexander Kluge, *Public Sphere and Experience*, trans. Peter Labanyi, Jamie Owen Daniel, and Assenka Oksiloff (Minneapolis: University of Minnesota Press, 1993), 250.
45. Paul Paolucci, "The Scientific Method and the Dialectical Method," *Historical Materialism* 11 (2003): 88.
46. Negt and Kluge, *Public Sphere and Experience*, 250.
47. Stuart Hall, "Gramsci's Relevance," 411–40.
48. Antonio Gramsci, "Hegemony, Relations of Force, Historicl Bloc," in *Antonio Gramsci Reader*, 72, 190.
49. Gramsci, "Hegemony, Relations of Force," 197.
50. Aune, *Rhetoric and Marxism*, 68.
51. A number of activists and scholars are critical of a particular kind of vanguard, Leninist "democratic centralism," a phrase describing organization along the principle of the greatest possible freedom of debate, and unity in action. Trotskyist Tony Cliff argues that critiques of democratic centralism confuse this principle with its distortions in the bureaucratic centralism of Stalinist state capitalism. See Cliff's *State Capitalism in Russia* (1955/1974), *Marxists Internet Archive*, http://www.marxists.org/archive/cliff/works/1955/statecap/index.htm.
52. Antonio Gramsci, "The Intellectuals," in *Selections from the Prison Notebooks*, trans. and ed. Q. Hoare and G. N. Smith (New York: International Publishers, 1979), 3–23.
53. For a history of the dissident labor movement in the United States, see Herman Benson, *Rebels, Reformers, and Racketeers* (Brooklyn: Association for Union Democracy, 2005).
54. Michael H. Cimini, "Labor-Management Bargaining in 1995," *Monthly Labor Review* 119 (1996), http://www.bls.gov/opub/mlr/1996/01/contents.htm.
55. R. Keith Thomas, interview by author, April 9, 1998, Park City, KS.
56. Laclau, *On Populist Reason*, 57. However, contrary to Laclau's argument regarding the rhetorical invention of universals, this synecdochal relationship exists on the basis of real interests between the particular individual and the class, not the particular and a fictive universal.
57. The "rank and file" of ordinary union members is distinct from bureaucratic labor organization and its leadership, whose interests often align with management imperatives in industrial conflict.

58. David Clay and Don Grinde, radio interview, September 3, 2005, Seattle, KEXP.
59. V. I. Lenin, "Trade-Unionist Politics and Social-Democratic Politics," in *What Is To Be Done?* (1901), *Marxists Internet Archive*, http://www.marxists.org/archive/lenin/works/1901/witbd/iii.htm.
60. See Ernest Mandel's argument about the folly of ideological purity in "The Leninist Theory of Organisation," *Marxists Internet Archive*, http://www.marxists.org/archive/mandel/196x/leninism/ch10.htm.
61. Dana L. Cloud, "Routine Misconduct: The Employers' Offensive at Boeing, 1989–1999," in *The Debate over Corporate Responsibility*, ed. Steven May, George Cheney, and Juliet Roper (Oxford, UK: Oxford University Press, 2007), 219–31.
62. "Boeing Third-Quarter 2008 report," *The Boeing Company*, http://boeing.com/company offices/financial/; see also "Boeing Strike May Be More Costly than 2005 Work Stoppage," *National Post's Financial Post and FB Investing*, September 11, 2008; Micheline Maynard, "Earnings Drop 38% at Boeing as a Machinist' Strike Wears On," *New York Times*, October 3, 2008; Matt Andrejczak, "Boeing Plane Deliveries Hit Snag amid Worker Strike," *Market Watch*, October 3, 2008; David Robertson, "Strike at Boeing Will Cost Aircraft Maker $11m a Day in Lost Revenues," *Times* (London), September 8, 2008.
63. See Christopher Hinton, "Boeing's Shortfall Grows as Strike Enters Third Week," *MarketWatch*, September 12, 2008.
64. The *Boston Globe* charged the UAW with demanding unsustainable contracts ("Detroit on the Brink," November 15, 2008). The UAW president appeared on MSNBC's *Rachel Maddow Show* (November 25, 2008) to defend autoworkers against the charges against them. Michael Moore told CNN's Larry King that "[t]his is not the workers' fault. Where is their bailout?" (*Larry King Live*, November 19, 2008). See also Lee Sustar, "A Bailout for the Auto Industry?" *Socialist Worker*, November 10, 2008, *Marxists Internet Archive*, http://www.marxists.org/archive/novack/works/history/ch03.htm; Gregg Shotwell, "In Defense of Autoworkers," *Socialist Worker*, December 4, 2008, http://socialistworker.org/2008/12/04/in-defense-of-autoworkers. A number of news writers criticized the Boeing workers for ostensibly intensifying the economic crisis by jeopardizing their suppliers.
65. Workers used the fact that Boeing was flush to justify the strike. See "Boeing's Earnings a Tool in Machinists' Strike," *Morning Edition*, National Public Radio, October 23, 2008.
66. Quoted in Sholnn Freeman, "Boeing, Union Reach Deal," *Washington Post*, October 28, 2008.
67. See Sholnn Freeman, "Boeing Contract Offers Pay Raise, Job Protections," *Washington Post*, October 29, 2008.
68. See Christopher Hinton, "Boeing Reaches Tentative Contract With 21,000 Engineers," *MarketWatch*, November 14, 2008.
69. Adorno, *Negative Dialectics*, 170.
70. Advocates in rhetorical studies of "going beyond" include Greene, this volume; "Rhetoric and Capitalism," 43–65; "Another Materialist Rhetoric." Theories central to this argument include those of Hardt and Negri, *Multitude*; Antonio Negri, *Marx Beyond Marx* (New York: Autonomedia, 1996); Gilles Deleuze and Félix Guattari, *A Thousand Plateaus* (Minneapolis: University of Minnesota Press, 1987).
71. Cloud, "*The Matrix* and Critical."
72. Laclau and Mouffe, *Hegemony and Socialist Strategy*, 113, 120, 122–27, 153–54, 167.
73. Woodard, "Populists or Proletarians."

74. Theda Skocpol, *Social Revolutions in the Modern World* (Cambridge, UK: Cambridge University Press, 1994); Sidney Tarrow, *Power in Movement* (Cambridge, UK: Cambridge University Press, 1998).

75. Ellen Meiksins Wood, "A Manifesto for Global Capitalism?" in *Debating Empire*, ed. Gopal Balakrishnan (London: Verso, 2003), 61.

76. Hardt and Negri, *Empire,* xv; Hardt and Negri, *Multitude.* For a critique, see Alex Callinicos, "Tony Negri in Perspective," in Balakrishnan, *Debating Empire*, 121–43.

77. Hardt and Negri, *Multitude,* 186.

78. Samir Amin, "Empire and Multitude," *Monthly Review*, November 2005, http://www.monthlyreview.org/1105amin.htm#Volume.

79. Adorno, *Negative Dialectics*, 205.

80. Lloyd F. Bitzer, "The Rhetorical Situation," *Philosophy and Rhetoric* 1 (1968): 1–14.

CHAPTER 13

Materiality's Time: Rethinking the Event from the Derridean esprit d'á-propos

William C. Trapani, Florida Atlantic University

> One cannot read Plato's time without Plato; which does not mean that Plato fell from the sky, but rather that one must make use of Plato in order to read his time.
>
> Jacques Derrida, *A Taste for the Secret*

Despite any number of theoretical initiatives that might have prompted a reconsideration of temporality's constitutive role in rhetoric, the lion's share of scholarship in the field of rhetorical studies over the past several decades has continued to advance spatialized analyses that imagine the site, scene, and subjects of symbolic acts as fully present and totalizable.[1] Notably, the single-focused pursuit of this mapping impulse comes at a considerable price: first, of a rich sense of rhetorical invention—its chanciness, its iterative possibility, and the resistances it faces—and, second, of a nuanced understanding of rhetorical effect, its varied forms, and its persistence. These losses are the unwitting opportunity cost of fashioning context in this spatial orientation whereby the analytic frames employed to render a scene legible falsely take on the appearance of metaphysical substance, foreclosing attention to rhetorical alternatives and effects not immediately given to be seen. In short, our thinking about the materiality of rhetoric will continue to *miss the mark* to the degree that it takes the temporality of symbolic action as ancillary, given in advance, or as mere occasion.

Against the tendency to consider the materiality of rhetoric by bracketing out its temporality, I will argue that a more expansive notion of the latter would enable critics to assess invention and rhetorical effect more fruitfully. More specifically, by attending carefully to the complicated relationship between novel, indeed unexpected, rhetorical initiatives and the codes of intelligibility by which those acts make sense (or, put differently, the relay between the singular and the repeated), rhetoric's eventfulness may be made clearer. By conceptualizing temporality not merely as a given occasion but, instead, as a distended force enabling certain rhetorical possibilities (while deferring others), theorists and critics would better understand the ways in which eventfulness, and hence invention and rhetorical effect, are effected. This essay, then, joins those rhetorical, political, and cultural theorists that have recently taken up the task of considering the nature of the event as a way of imagining the character and possibility of discursive rupture—and consequently, of the likelihood for productive social change.[2] As the over-whelming majority of those efforts, on my view, remain inadequate in their consideration of temporality, however, the essay attempts to describe a necessary corrective to the spatialized impulse described. In seeking a supplement capable of equally rigorous attention to the production and force of the temporal, I argue that the Derridean account of the event can move us toward an enriched understanding of rhetoric's materiality as well as the force and possibility of rhetorical invention.

To be sure, a Derridean approach to temporality, materiality, and the event, and therefore to the nature of rhetorical invention and effect, does not promise an easy formulation or formalism. In offering a quite different understanding of temporality's constituted and constituting role than that currently fashionable in rhetorical theory and criticism, however, much may be gained. Specifically, in its consideration of the nonsaturable nature of context, of the double-handed condition of writing that requires consideration of the interdependence of the novel and the archival, of its depiction of eventfulness as that which cannot be measured from the horizon of the given, and of its understanding of materiality as, at once, both less grand and more forceful than we conventionally imagine, the Derridean approach has much to offer. Indeed, in thinking through the disseminating and prosaic resistance of the event, rhetoricians might find themselves moving beyond limiting modes of spatial analysis that concern merely what is taken to be present in the now. Such an endeavor may have much to offer to a discipline derogato-rily branded by scholars outside it as mere rhetoric, just as, internally, it struggles to emerge from limiting accounts of rhetoric's force, which continues to inhibit our understanding of rhetoric's "exorbitant possibili-ties."[3]

Toward advancing these arguments, I first contrast the notion of the rhe-torical situation with the Derridean account of time and the temporal. I next move to an explication of Derrida's account of eventfulness and its relation to materiality. Last, I offer suggestions for what a different conception of temporality might offer to rhetorical analysis by working through key passages of Derrida's *Archive Fever*.

Rethinking the Rhetorical Situation (Again)

Long before the lexicon of a rhetorical situation took hold of rhetorical analysis, a sense of time and temporality were central to rhetoric. "Time," for example, had long been understood to include more than just a specific date or chronology (*chronos*). It also entailed a raft of ideas crucial to early Greek thought including "'symmetry,' 'propriety,' 'occasion,' 'due measure,' 'fitness,' 'tact,' 'decorum,' 'convenience,' 'proportion' . . . [and] 'wise moderation.'"[4] While rhetoricians might often collectivize that varied list under the general rubric of *kairos,* there is a crucial distinction between the opportune (*kairos*), the appropriate (*to prepon*), and the possible—a distinction lost in the general miasma of the rhetorical situation as inaugurated by Lloyd Bitzer, and too often carried over into the work of those that followed.[5] Perhaps the best way to mark this loss is to note that unlike John Poulakos, who understands *kairos, to prepon*, and the possible as distinct but complementary rhetorical considerations, Bitzer's notion of fittingness teeters on the tautological: the timely is appropriate; the appropriate is of the right time. Bitzer's rhetorical remedy draws too strenuously, perhaps, from a return to the first recorded use of the term "*kairos*" as it appears in Homer's *Iliad*, where it designated a "*vital* or *lethal* place in the body, one that is particularly susceptible to injury and therefore necessitates special protection." As such, as Phillip Sipiora notes, though *kairos*, "initially, carries a spatial meaning," over time, and due largely to the work of the Sophists, the notion of *kairos* underwent rhetorical mutation, appearing as the temporal.[6]

Marking this shift, however, tells us little of how we ought to understand temporality's constitutive role in rhetoric. Indeed, one might too readily read the Sophists' *kairotic* commitment to "the novel, the unusual . . . [and] the unprecedented" as simply a call to maximize rhetorical effect by avoiding bland or conservative discourses.[7] Although such an effort would surely qualify as a type of rhetorical invention, any notion of the rhetorical event, occasion, context, or situation that does not work against a sense of time as readily apparent and present unto itself might all too easily slip into a hermeneutics without exit. That is, in taking time as given or natural, and not as itself the product of some discursive labor, the seemingly essential presence of the present would foreclose rhetorical alternatives to that moment.[8] Indeed, this atrophy of the temporal—in which a rich sense of temporality risks being supplanted by a thoroughly spatialized account that imagines the given as the fully rendered range of temporal possibility—cannot but return a too restricted notion of contingency. In turn, theorists and critics would find themselves assessing an artificially reduced range of rhetorical possibility, considering only those rhetorical acts that seemed to fit with the times.[9]

A rich sense of *kairos,* however, need not merely highlight the "mutability of rhetoric," nor need it finish up by noting only the mutability of rhetorical actors themselves.[10] Indeed, since from the vantage of deconstruction rhetorical enterprises are only possible because they are predicated on a certain temporality in which they gain traction, and this temporality is itself an effect-structure, the present is likewise mutable and forever open to the possibility of productive reiteration. Indeed, as Derrida argues in a close reading of Heidegger's effort to scourge the "vulgar concept" of time from the analysis of *Dasein,* we can never approach "pure" time since, strictly speaking, such a thing does not exist.[11] Because presence is an effect of *différance,* the experience of time is nothing more or less than its "now" presence, what Derrida calls "time's accidents."[12]

Différance, then, has long offered rhetorical studies a rich alternative to the rhetorical situation even if the field has responded by favoring the spatial element of the neologism ("to differ") over the temporal ("to defer"). But, as those rhetorical scholars who have embraced deconstruction have argued, precisely because the incessant deferral of alternatives so aids the constitution of the "situation," the refusal to engage robustly rhetoric's temporality comes at a considerable cost. For example, exhorting her colleagues to examine archives not merely for their interested constructions but for the ways in which such newly forged "histories" operate as the platform for inventive discourse, Barbara Biesecker highlights the way in which *différance* illuminates the staging of a certain truth by the deferral of other possibilities. I quote her at some length:

> [S]cholars of persuasive speech have not yet begun robustly to engage the entailments of the archive's irreducible undecidability even though we are uniquely positioned to do so, given that the deconstruction of "fact" or of referential plenitude does not reduce the contents of the archive to "mere" literature or fiction (this is the most common and the silliest of mistakes). Indeed, from the *historicity* of the archive, rhetorics; out of the deconstruction of the material presence of the past and, thus, in relation to what the archive cannot *authenticate* absolutely but can (be made to) *authorize* nonetheless, issues an invitation to write rhetorical histories of archives, which is to say, critical histories of the situated and strategic uses to which archives have been put.[13]

But if the *appearance* of "material proof of the past" gives rise to rhetorical enterprise—that is, if by deferring certain alternative and equally material proofs of a differing past enables the possibility of speaking "in the now"— so, too, do happenings yet to come. As Werner Hamacher put it in his meditation on Derrida's *Spectres of Marx,* if "language is the medium of futurity," it is so not because rhetors entice listeners with the promise of a better tomorrow or the claim that certain initiatives might best fit a given situation.[14] Neither is it because the most skilled of those rhetors can adroitly traipse through varying temporal frames and light upon the discourse of the future as relief from the overburdening weight, perhaps, of an all too promising past and an all too underwhelming present.[15] Nor is it the ability of the rhetor to conjure, or of the critic to characterize, a disposition or sentiment that prods otherwise apathetic audiences into action.[16] Last, it is not even that those discourses of the present begin to contour the future—that the narratives or fictions of this day begin to shape the actuality of our next.[17] Rather, if language has an "amphibious virtuality," a certain dual nature or spectrality, it is because the future is always already imbricated in our "present"—that our now always bears the impression of what is to come.[18]

In the latter stages of his life, Derrida was consumed by an effort to describe the character of varying "arrivants" and of the force of their impression in (constituting) the present. Of these characterizations perhaps the most recurring is that for the future to be, genuinely, a future and not merely an extension of the present, it must be undecidable. So, too, must the arrivant. In either the case of the future or of any particular arrivant (democracy, cosmopolitanism, etc.), it is precisely the lack of foresight or predictability that both ensures the possibility of a future (by definition) and its force in the present. We might say, for example, that democracy "today" turns on what it is to become; we live not just with the burden of democracy's past and our responsibilities and indebtedness to that history but the equally compelling, prosaic, and as I will show in the later parts of this essay, material indeterminancy and impression of (democracy's) futurity on our present. As Hamacher so aptly puts it, "[language's] inherent promising capacity, is the ground—but a ground with no solidity whatsoever—for all present and past experiences, meanings and figures which could communicate themselves in it. Language is a medium insofar as it opens the place of arrival, opens the gate to what is to come, the entrance of an unpredictable and topographically indeterminate other."[19]

Our predominately spatialized readings, however, miss the(se) mark(s). The problem is not so much that a cartographic approach to rhetorical analysis cannot understand the concept of a future; indeed, it can all too readily provide some sense of that future because, in some form, its script (or the permutations that might result in that script) must already be written into the grid.[20] Put differently, given infinite time and resources, the cartographer could describe the arc and content of the future precisely because it is little more than a stage or an already given line of flight in the field of possibility.

And yet, there is nothing radical about a future that can, in advance, predict, program, and prepare for itself.

In his last works, however, and in particular those that tried to theorize rhetoric explicitly as an "event-machine"—as the impossible hybrid of the novel and the archival—Derrida may have lit upon an account of eventfulness that offers a corrective to the field's spatialized accounts of rhetorical invention, resistance, and the materiality of rhetoric.

The Derridean Event-Machine

> The event, the singularity of the event—this is what *différance* is all about.
> Jacques Derrida, *Negotiations: Interventions and Interviews*

Even readers familiar with Derrida could well be forgiven the vertigo they might experience upon encountering the middle sections of "The Typewriter Ribbon: Limited Ink 2." In the midst of a close reading of Paul de Man's account of the confession, Derrida recalls, seemingly *á propos* of nothing, that he had once heard of an archeological dig that had uncovered, encased in amber, the body of an insect trapped over 54 million years ago that was "still visible and intact, the cadaver of someone who was surprised by death at the instant it was sucking the blood of another!"[21] With all the implications this amber arrival might make visible—of memory and desire, perhaps—however, Derrida concludes, "I don't know why I am telling you this."[22] Here he *is* being disingenuous for the anecdote highlights a problematic that animated much of his thinking and to which, he imagined, de Man's work had much to offer, namely the difficulty in thinking the event in relation to the archive. Without rehearsing the entire logic of and argument for *différance,* a neologism that showcases the incongruity between the novel and the norm, suffice it to say that what interests Derrida about the event is that it is a structural impossibility: on the one hand, to be worthy of its title, such an affair would have to be singular, unrepeatable, and unanticipated; on the other hand, in order to register as intelligible, the event must be translatable and, thus, already operate within an ordered economy.[23]

Derrida's most vivid account of the aporetic structure of the event appeared in a much earlier essay, "Freud and the Scene of Writing." Working from Freud's effort to describe the production of the unconscious through the use of the "Mystic Writing Pad," a device that retains imprints of all writing that came before and yet may be made clean for new writing merely by pulling up its top layer of wax, Derrida suggests,

> The machine does not run by itself. It is less a machine than a tool. And it is not held with only one hand. This is the mark of its temporality. Its *maintenance* is not sim-

ple. The ideal virginity of the present (*maintenant*) is constituted by the work of memory. . . . Traces thus produce the space of their inscription only by acceding to the period of their erasure. . . . A two-handed machine, a multiplicity of agencies or origins—is this not the original relation to the other and the original temporality of writing, its "primary" complication: an original spacing, deferring, and erasure of the simple origin, and polemics on the very threshold of what we persist in calling perception.[24]

Here writing is figured as a somewhat mystical affair, even a struggle: writing proceeds as if it is novel and independent of all prior traces, but in order for the writing to be intelligible, a certain amount of memory "work" must operate. In some way, then, for this novel writing to appear, a displacement, deferral, rearrangement, or repression of what came before is necessary. But it equally means that the writing must in some way be open to being recorded, to being archivable. Derrida illustrates the nature of this tension *within* writing in, for example, *Archive Fever: A Freudian Impression*, when he remarks that the introduction of psychoanalysis required a "transformation of the techniques of archivization" but that at the same time the "technical structure" of the archive also determines, in advance, the manner in which content may, or may not, be recorded.[25]

"Typewriter Ribbon" reminds us that we have yet to develop reading practices that account for the radicality of inscription in relation to the archives on which they depend. Indeed, we often name certain moments "events" and yet account for their arrival by seeking their origins in genealogies of the present. However skillful critics may be at their tasks in such an enterprise, and however attuned their various protocols are to the play of historical and rhetorical possibilities, from a Derridean vantage, a solely spatial consideration of rhetoric—that is, one that conceptualizes rhetoric as something to be mapped against a given field—fails to attend to the double-handed and complicated scene of writing just described. Put differently, in imagining a rhetorical situation as present, as totalizable, or as having an "ideal virginity," scholars miss altogether what is deferred from that scene— those forces that, while not present, are nevertheless essential to the given scene's emergence. In short, it is only when we resist the temptation to imagine that an event arises from the horizon of the given that we afford the event its radicality. As Derrida put it in one of his last works,

[i]f I allow myself to play a bit with this sonorous register, it is in order to get closer to this essence of the event, of *what comes to pass* only once, only one time, a single time, a first and last time, in an always singular, unique, exceptional, irreplaceable, unforeseeable, and incalculable fashion, of *what* happens or *who* happens by precisely there where—and this is the end of the horizon, of teleology, the calculable program, foresight, and providence—one no longer *sees it coming,* no longer hori-

zontally: *without prospect or horizon.*[26]

An event, then, is a surprise, something that can neither be anticipated nor understood by appeal to the operative terms and logics of sense making.

To understand more fully the difference between the Derridean account of the event and its traditional counterpart, and hence to illuminate Derrida's argument for the necessity of considering rhetoric through the event-machine, we must return to "Typewriter Ribbon," for it is here, in his analysis of de Man's reading of Rousseau's *Confessions*, that Derrida develops the notion of the event-machine. For his part, de Man is interested in the nature of the excuse. How, he asks, could a confession—of the theft of a ribbon from a young girl no less—appear so threatening, so unsettling? What most interests Derrida about de Man's answer is that it turns on the introduction of the curious figure of a "text-machine," a concept that, for de Man, describes an intricate relay between a narrative (say, of a theft) and the act of writing. Indeed, according to de Man, the act of writing the confession has the paradoxical effect of magnifying the guilt and shame surrounding the act and, yet, de Man argues (identifying the threatening element inherent to the confession) "there can never be enough guilt around to match the text-machine's infinite power to excuse."[27]

Returning to the manner in which temporality might be figured differently in accounts of the rhetorical event, invention, resistance, and materiality, it is notable that what Derrida finds particularly salient in de Man's account of the text-machine is that de Man made it up! He invented the notion of a text-machine, or he invented it by "unveiling the body of what was already there." In either case, Derrida argues, "this invention is an event."[28] To be precise, what is eventful about de Man's reading is not only that he invents the text-machine that operates in Rousseau's excuse. It is also that de Man supplements that invention with another: the insistence that what appears singular to the writing of *Confessions* is, in fact, the condition of all texts: "We call *text* any entity that can be considered from such a double perspective . . . the 'definition' of the text also states the impossibility of its existence."[29] For Derrida, therefore, the event in question is de Man's assertion that the structural singularity of the *Confessions* can only be understood once, retroactively, we understand that its unique character is in fact universal to all writing. By way of positing what is unique about Rousseau's work, then, de Man reordered the very archive by which it might be read.

If de Man's account of the excuse is on point, however, something other than Rousseau's prodigious inventive and rhetorical skill must have enabled his eventual absolution and canonical status. Given the way in which a confession must continually repeat the narrative of the crime, necessarily calling the character of the author into question, it could not have been Rousseau's authorial savvy, his putative sincerity, or the somewhat trivial nature of the purloined object *alone* that could account for the *Confessions'* successful reception. Rather, it was also necessary that the historical confession machine *work,* that it produce the conditions of possibility by which the excuse might, one day, become instituted. As Derrida puts it, "forgiveness and excuse are possible, are called upon to go into effect only where this relative, quasi-machinelike survival of the *oeuvre*—or of the archive as *oeuvre* takes *plac*e . . . taking charge of the forgiveness or the excuse."[30] Here, Derrida redeploys an argument he has used several times before, perhaps the best known of which is in *Limited Inc*, over the course of which he engages J. L. Austin's speech act theory. There, Derrida's point is that the success of any conventional speech act (as in "I apologize") depends on more than the subject's desire, character, or competence, however skilled or inventive. It also depends on the "code" that precedes and exceeds the space of the subject that employs it. For any subject to cite and make use of such code, writing must have the structural condition of iterability since otherwise speech would be so singular, untranslatable, and proper to the instance of its use that it would appear alien and incomprehensible. This event-machine, then, is not merely the pure machinery of a speech act's codes, nor is it simply a linear, additive history of all speech acts that came before. Rather, it describes (1) the structural condition of iterability, by which citation with difference is not only permitted but is writing's very condition of possibility; (2) the tension between the machinic archive and the performances "to come" that would distend, deviate, and disseminate those iterations in unexpected ways; and (3) a certain plasticity of temporality, in which acts open up or close down different futures.

While each of these ways of thinking about the event-machine illuminates its expansive capacity for fashioning alternates to the given, they tell only half of the story. Just as the future may be altered by the work of *l'oeuvre,* so, too, may what is to come impact or impress itself in *l'oeuvre.* That is, the event-machine highlights the more radical temporal possibility that future speech acts might retroactively become grafted into a given archive. In forcing the displacement or recoding of the present, these deferred, unknowable, or impossible acts to come demonstrate that an archive's intelligibility and force depends on its temporal constitution. Just as "Freud" could not have existed without the notion of an archive that psychoanalysis would fundamentally alter, for example, and just as de Man's analysis of Rousseau depends on the condition of writing that his analysis demonstrates to be a necessary impossibility, Derrida performs the logic of these theses by "discovering" in *"Typewriter Ribbon: Limited Ink 2"* something that *Limited Inc* could not have anticipated: the event-machine. This thing, this super-monster, did not "exist" at *Limited Inc*'s "time," and yet, upon its arrival, it retroactively displaces parts of *Limited Inc* (say, its linear account of the speech act) such that speech acts must be rethought from the ground up.

Regardless of the particularities of the writing that might emerge through the event-machine, yet another crucial contribution of "Typewriter Ribbon" is to suggest that it is the persistence of *l'oeuvre* itself that is material. How so? What is it about the *l'oeuvre* that would enable it to persist? What would it mean to call that lingering work "material"? Seeking answers to those questions, Derrida again allies himself with de Man who had argued that "history" is not the accumulation of substance over time but is instead constituted by "traces on the world," the residue and remainder from various events, lingering on well after their own event and exerting force over what is to come.[31] Crucially, de Man suggested, these leftovers are not tied to the physicality of any substance, but rather to their "prosaic resistance." Working from this account, Derrida suggests that it is precisely because these marks on the world are prosaic that they offer "a resistance to every possible reappropriation."[32] Indeed, he emphasizes this point in "Typewriter Ribbon," noting that "materiality becomes a very useful generic name for all that resists appropriation."[33] Underscoring the nature of this materiality, Derrida argues that an *"oeuvre* survives its supposed operation and its supposed operator."[34] Therein lies the materiality of the event-machine: in a "certain irreducibility of the *work*."[35]

In obvious ways, the Derridean conception of *l'oeuvre* stands the tradi-tional understanding of the term on its head. Where *oeuvre* is conventionally used to classify the body of work of a particular author and generally functions as a prelude to great praise thereof, according to Derrida it is precisely the sovereignty of the author that is called into question by the event-machine. On the one hand, for example, *l'oeuvre* exceeds the author in important ways: as part-machine, *l'oeuvre* both predates and persists beyond the author, and even when the author is working through or "using" the machine, he or she is not the sole voice that gives the *l'oeuvre* meaning, explanation, or force. *L'oeuvre,* in short, refuses the author's claims of ownership or control. On the other hand, as Rousseau's *Confessions* demon-strates, *l'oeuvre* functions as a powerful, unavoidable, writing machine, the structure which, even if it cannot return attribution and appropriation to the author per se, still affords that author the possibility of some type of inven-tive writing.

What, then, is the nature of this writing-machine? How does it operate? What engenders its capacity to resist appropriation, to lean toward singularity, and yet to restrict iteration and translation? For clarity, we might note some of the constitutive elements of *l'oeuvre* as it is conceptualized by Derrida. First, *l'oeuvre* operates passively and without form. Although an archive might be just as recalcitrant to and effective in resisting iteration or appropriation, Derrida takes pains to underscore that the graphematic trace-structure of an *oeuvre* implies a different type of structure altogether from that of a genealogical archive. An archive is constituted and ordered by, among other things, tangible, discernible codes and rules of order whose very purpose is to shield its contents from difference or alteration. Through these codes and controls, the archive takes on the appearance of having an essence that can be mapped.

L'oeuvre, by contrast, is "not a thing, it is not *something* sensible or intelligible; it is not even a matter of a body. As it is not something, as it is nothing and yet it works, *cela oeuvre,* this nothing therefore operates, it forces, but as a force of resistance."[36] Taking our cue from the switch to the intransitive verb (*cela oeuvre*: "there is work"), we might say that Derrida is asserting that this resistance does not appear in any (pre)determined place, time, or manner. Indeed, because it is without form, we are not always aware of the "it" that is resisting. Derrida notes,

> Surviving it, being destined to this sur-vival, to this excess over present life, the *oeuvre* as trace implies from the outset the structure of this sur-vival, that is, what *cuts* the *oeuvre* off from the operation. This *cut* assures it a sort of archival independence or autonomy that is quasi-machine-like (not machinelike but *quasi-machinelike*), a power of repetition, repeatability, iterability, serial and prosthetic substitution of self for self. This cut is not so much effected by the machine (even though the machine can in fact cut and repeat the cut in its turn) as it is the condition of production for a machine. The machine is *cut* as well as *cutting* with regard to the living present of life or of the living body.[37]

Second, *l'oeuvre* has force and materiality. To be sure, *l'oeuvre's* formless, passive, and prosaic force may initially appear negligible to those conditioned to think of resistance along traditional models of political or rhetorical action that portray resistance as a stalwart, publicly visible stand. As graphematic trace-structure, however, the event machine is indeterminate but nevertheless determining, a "terrible and tireless writing machine" by which signification occurs.[38] In this way, even a young girl's ribbon "once stolen and passed from hand to hand" might turn out to be "a formidable writing machine, a ribbon of ink along which so many signs transited so irresistibly."[39] At once, then, *l'oeuvre* is "trenchant" and "decisive" in its forcefulness.[40] But because it contains the graft of events that came before and by definition is structurally open to unexpected events, it is also "accidental," "aleatory," and "unforeseeable."[41] Commenting on Derrida's sudden switch to the intransitive verb ("*cela oeuvre*") to describe the event-machine, Peggy Kamuf notes that "[a] certain passive resistance, then, will go on working as resistance, 'infinite or abyssal,' no matter how little respect it is shown."[42] Derrida explains,

> The passivity of resistance resists thought because it is what *does* the most, *makes* the most happen, more than the most, the impossible itself, at the heart of the possible. In fact, one may say of the impossible that it marks a limit of a possible or a power, more precisely, of an "I can" or a "we can." Such passivity remains at work in the work [*à l'oeuvre dans l'oeuvre*]. For one of the enigmas of *l'oeuvre* is that its event does not totally depend on an action carried out by my sovereign initiative.[43]

Third, the Derridean notion of the event-machine reinvigorates a *kairotic* notion of invention. As part-machine, *l'oeuvre* resists innovation, in part because in its passive and "supple" form its contours are never quite clear, are not immediately present as discernible rules or prohibitions.[44] As well, it is the very function of *l'oeuvre* to deny subjects the type of sovereignty they might wish for in order to produce some sort of translation, change, or invention. Indeed, while new inventions and events might be deposited or grafted into the machinery of the work, they nevertheless do so "without any guarantee that is not aleatory, incalculably to some resistant matter."[45] There is, however, another side to the story. Although the *oeuvre*-trace resists appropriation, it also constitutes the condition of possibility for iteration, signification, and, likewise, rhetorical invention. Derrida makes this point most clearly when he comments on, as de Man does not, the striking similarities between Rousseau's *Confessions* and Augustine's *Confessions* a millennium before. Indeed, both men committed their crimes at the age of sixteen, both stole something that they claimed was of little value, and both argued that their public acts of contrition were necessary because their sins, however small, were defining moments in their lives.

But what, Derrida asks coyly, if Rousseau lied in his *Confessions*? What if he was not contrite, but only played at being so? Or what if he hadn't really blamed another for the theft, as he claimed, but merely said he had in order to make his crime seem all the worse and therefore his redemption all the greater? Or, finally, what if he lied about having stolen the ribbon in the first place? He might have done all of these things, Derrida muses, in order to put himself on par with a saint or for reasons that we may never know. In any case, from the perspective of *l'oeuvre,* it simply does not matter. That is, it is not the event-machine's work to discern the truth, but instead to produce the true. As such, the matter of invention becomes less a matter of comporting to the conventions of an archive, of knowing in advance the referents that will count and following them in lockstep. To put it somewhat provocatively, one cannot count on *l'oeuvre*. The event-machine's very structure—if such a word could be used to describe *l'oeuvre*—posits an irreducible indeterminancy that troubles any assurance. Consequently, invention in this sense is more of a chance taking whose possibility is offered by *l'oeuvre,* of writing through the event-machine in ways that—because they cannot be guaranteed in advance—always entail some risk and risk of failure.

Derrida underscores the uncertain status of novel initiatives, indeed of all writing, by emphasizing the role of the *á propos*. Presented with a particular situation, he suggests, a subject forges its invention/intervention by acting in ways other than those thought determined or conventional by that occasion; they take flight, as it were, from the given into unpredictable and therefore incalculable futures. Again, Derrida:

> When one says "a propos," it is because one is at least pretending to leap at the opportunity to speak, metonymically, of something else altogether, to change the subject without changing the subject, or else to underscore that between what is being talked about and what someone wants to talk about there is either a link of organic, internal, and essential necessity or else, inversely, an insignificant and superficial association, a purely mechanical and metonymic association, the arbitrary or fortuitous comparison—"by accident"—of two signifiers. And yet one knows that, at that very moment, one touches on the essential, one at least brushes up against the place of decision. That is when the thing happens, that is where it comes about.[46]

It is, we might imagine, as if Rousseau might have said "*á propos* of wanting to be as important as Augustine, I lie," or perhaps, "*á propos* of having been caught stealing this ribbon I invent (or blame) another." The point, of course, is not that the *á propos* obtains merely in cases of lying but that it marks the subject's capacity to invent in general. Derrida makes the connection between *l'oeuvre,* the *á propos,* and invention directly, arguing that the *á propos* bears a strong resemblance to the rhetorical notion of *kairos*. As he puts it: The *esprit d'á-propos*, in French, is the art, the genius, but also the technique that consists in knowing how to grab an opportunity, to make the best of it, the best economy of contingency, and to make of the *kairos* or the *chaos* a significant, archivable, necessary, or even ineffaceable event.[47] In short, the *á propos* names the irreducibly contingent and chancy character of writing through the event-machine.

From this vantage, rhetorical enterprises are always taken up on a fictionalized premise—"as if" their moves, their inventions, might hold and become grafted into the trace-structure. If, however, contingency is reduced to mere assessments of probability (as in "the disenfranchised have little hope of altering the system"), this more radical sense of the *kairotic* is stunted at the start and the possibility for a much richer understanding of invention is subsequently lost. Following Derrida, we might say that in order to afford the *á propos* its wildly iterative possibilities, the odds of success, so to speak, must always remain incalculable.

Part of what makes the calculation of *l'oeuvre* indeterminate, of course, is that the very question of the future is at stake. Since the future cannot be extrapolated from the now, and because the subjects working through *l'oeuvre* operate from the condition of wanting to become rather than already being, the future can only be provisionally imagined but never assured. We have no better evidence of this than Rousseau's own claim that his *Confessions* would one day find an audience—even if it will only be God "himself"—that will judge him fairly and grant him the grace his writing seeks. As Rousseau puts it, "this is the cause of my confidence. . . . In the end, everything must return to order, and my turn will come sooner or later."[48]

While rhetoric may proceed *as if* the coming of its future is assured, nothing could be less certain. Moreover, should it come to pass, the arrival of that future cannot be thought as the sovereign effect of the speaking subject's will or rhetorical artistry, but because *l'oeuvre* will have done "its work," will have instituted the event by which the future to be will be constituted as such. As Derrida explains,

> [t]his "sooner or later," which signs the last words of the *Second Reverie*, is extraordinary. . . . It promises the survival of the work, but also survival *by* the work as self-justification and faith in redemption. . . . The work will accomplish its work of work, *son oeuvre d'oeuvre*, beyond its signatory and without his living assistance, whatever may be the time required. . . . The time that this will take matters little, time is given, it is on my side, it is taken and has taken sides in advance, thus it no longer exists. Time no longer costs anything. Since it no longer costs anything, it is graciously given in exchange for the labor of the work that operates all by itself, in a quasi-machinelike fashion.[49]

Extending indefinitely into uncertain futures and in unanticipated terrains, *l'oeuvre* offers a strange and chancy ground for rhetoric. Undermining the certitude of the various supports we rely on in our assessment of rhetorical choices and their possible effects—for example, the sovereignty of the speaking subject, the saturation of context, temporal linearity, the stability of the archive and its technologies, the totalization of the given, and, broadly, the relation between contingency and calculation—*l'oeuvre* confounds formalism or patterned predictability. In calling into question those frequent presumptions, Derrida highlights the indeterminancy of invention, the resistance such efforts encounter, and the materiality of that rhetoric in ways that productively challenge our spatialized accounts of agency and the exorbitant possibilities of rhetoric.

How Soon Is Now? Toward a Rhetorical Impression of *L'Oeuvre*

But what would it mean for theorists and critics of rhetoric if, as has been argued, *l'oeuvre* names that contextualized and contextualizing work by which symbolic acts are made possible? In what ways, for example, might it alter the ways we typically account for context given the seemingly contradictory admonishment to "no longer think the general context without taking the event in question into account?"[50] How might the indeterminate and shadowy *oeuvre* confound critical judgment of a rhetor, their intervention in and through the event-machine, and the political and cultural effect such work might have? In short, what would it mean for rhetorical analysis to accommodate the event-machine?

Derrida's account of the "impression" in *Archive Fever* points the way toward answers to these questions. The central problematic of Derrida's *Archive Fever: A Freudian Impression* might be put this way: how can we understand the relationship between the "concept" of an archive and the logic, grammar, and terrain of Freudian psychoanalysis? As suggested previously, one of the things that makes this such an interesting question for Derrida is that neither side of the relation is independent of the other. That is, Freud needed the notion of an archive in order to conceive of and metaphorically describe the various mechanisms of the human psyche. Just as importantly, however, the introduction of psychoanalysis—and with it notions of storage, repression, the death drive, etc.—has fundamentally altered how we think of, and through, archives. But if "archive" and "Freud" are interdependent, perhaps even symbiotic, signifiers, they are also unstable, even today.[51] With regard to archives, for example, we might say that the mechanisms for coding, storing, and protecting data are vastly different in our electronic age than they were in Freud's, that we are undergoing a type of "archival earthquake."[52] "Freud," however, proves no more stable a referent than "archive." For any number of reasons, the Freudian name never quite achieves the status of being self-same.[53]

Despite the indeterminate nature of each term in the relation (archive/Freud), *Archive Fever* identifies something that remains, that is not translatable, that bears an insistent signature, and that maintains a certain consistency even "in the future in a context where reading conditions have changed."[54] That thing that persists, which—following "Typewriter Ribbon"—has materiality because it resists appropriation or translation, is the "impression" of the Freudian *oeuvre*. What type of materiality might this be? How might an "impression" be material? According to Derrida, the Freudian impression has at least three material resonances. First, Freud is responsible for our imagining that archives have substrate, that they have a certain depth or interiority into which substances become deposited. As such, our concepts of writing as well as of storage and memory and the institutional practice of archivization are all structured by this Freudian implication. Second, the entire Freudian corpus cannot rise to the level of a formal concept, but can only attain the status of a notion, an impression. The very notions of repression and suppression that are the "content" of Freudian psychoanalysis are also at work in the Freudian impression; however, those notions cannot achieve the status of a "concept" because such a thing would imply a degree of consistency, formalism, transparency that the impression of an "archive" could not attain. Put differently, the ever-changing depiction of the drives and indeed of the entire psychoanalytic protocol becomes, for Derrida, an implicit demonstration of the archival logic psychoanalysis seeks to utilize: in its perpetual incompleteness, psychoanalysis marks the finitude of knowledge that it is the very function of the structures of repression and suppression to effect. Last, Derrida argues, the Freudian *oeuvre* has left its impression on all those who have encountered it. This would include all academic fields of study as well as anyone who has been influenced, imprinted, by the *oeuvre*. As Derrida notes, "I wish to speak of the *impression left* by Freud, by the event which carries this family name, the nearly unforgettable and incontestable, undeniable impression . . . that Sigmund Freud will have *made* on anyone, after him, who speaks of *him* or speaks to *him,* and who must then, accepting it or not, knowing it or not, be thus marked."[55]

I have described this event-machine at length because Derrida's account of its impression offers insight into how rhetorical analysis informed by a more strident attention to the constitutive, yet supple and ambivalent, nature of temporality might enable theorists and critics to consider the materiality of rhetoric in richer and more expansive ways. Indeed, while Derrida's depiction of the Freudian impression turns on a somewhat alien notion of materiality, in that it is formless and prosaic rather than located in an essential engine of social reproduction or in a putatively material governing apparatus, the reading underscores the advantage of considering materiality's structuring capacity even if the resistance that materiality offers is, strictly speaking, not fully present or given to be mapped in every case where its force it at play.[56] This is, of course, the lesson of *Archive Fever*, where Derrida reads the impression of "Freud" in various contexts where the man and the science, so to speak, are nowhere to be seen yet nevertheless formative. To recall

"Typewriter Ribbon," it is the prosaic, formless, and yet insistent general resistance to appropriation that characterizes materiality's force. This would explain, of course, why Derrida's own *oeuvre*—if it exists and if there is only one—is populated by ghosts, specters, revenants, and signatures without proper names attached. In some way, all of these formless presences without presence impress themselves on various Derridean subjects and structures, altering the ways we understand, with Derrida, the role an absence may play in constituting a "positivity."That their spectral effectivity might "come" at all underscores the ways in which Derrida prompts us to think very differently about context, invention, and resistance. As both open to the coming of the future and in some way always already marked by the condition of being open, *l'oeuvre* renders context porous, nonsaturable, and open at any moment to the possibility of a new maneuver or inventive move.

Finally, then, Derrida's account of the event offers an alternative way of understanding the practice, possibility, and promise of rhetorical invention. Indeed, he accents two specific traits that have all but disappeared in our spatialized readings of invention: the unruly nature of *kairotic* invention captured by the *esprit d'á-propos* (in which discourse gives to itself the capacity to go far afield of any justifying "ground") and the radically chancy nature of that invention. Without assurance of destination or success, rhetoric is best understood as always out of the control of its sender, traveling through indeterminate and uncertain networks, and whose productivity, should it have any, is not tied by any (genetic) design or resemblance to its "origin/originator." It is, in short, the condition of dissemination that enables the possibility of any number of unanticipated *á propos* moments to come.

In recommending the Derridean account of the event as an avenue toward better understanding the constitutive role of temporality and the condition of and resistances to invention, I have tried to highlight distinctions between that approach to considering the materiality of rhetoric and what I fear is a tendency toward overspatialized accounts of subjectivity and power that figure materiality through various forms of presence and visibility. I do not mean to stage this as an absolute either/or: one need not choose between a Derridean conceptualization of the event and a Foucauldian axiomatics of power. There is nothing inherently problematic, for example, about attending to the cartographic arrangement of texts, events, and their effects, and there is certainly a great deal of productive work that comes from such efforts. Unless great care is taken, however, rhetorical analysis written purely under the sign of a spatial inquiry runs the risk of considering its "map" a complete rendering of the rhetorical enterprises at work. Here we might do well to heed Derrida's warning that "one cannot think the trace—and therefore, *différance*—on the basis of the present, or of the presence of the present."[57] Indeed, any notion of the rhetorical event, occasion, context, or situation that does not stridently resist a flattened sense of time as that which is given to be seen, as readily apparent and present unto itself, will likely return unnecessarily limiting conceptions of invention, resistance, and materiality.

L'oeuvre offers a radically different way of understanding context, resistance, materiality, the signature, and the nature of temporality. Supplementing the rhetorical tradition with *l'oeuvre* will be no simple operation, but perhaps nothing underscores the Derridean account of *l'oeuvre* more than that very difficulty. For if the concept takes hold—an uncertain and unpredictable chance at best—what it will mean for it to have done so, and what it will say about how we understand rhetoric and the rhetorical tradition, will have had to involve the kind of sea change in our thinking that, precisely because it cannot be determined in advance, is the very hallmark of the event-machine.

Notes

I wish to thank Brian Lain, Janice Norton, John Lucaites, and especially Barbara Biesecker for their aid and suggestions for this essay. All emphases in quotations are the cited authors'.

1. The point is not merely that these initiatives employ spatial heuristics, nor that they are suffused throughout by a space-centered lexicon but, more important, that rhetorical studies has increasingly adopted approaches that give themselves over to the eminent. Although I cannot catalog all of these initiatives here, some of the more influential theoretical developments that have relied on and spurred along this spatialization include, first and foremost, a Bitzerian sense of rhetorical situation. As I will comment on this more directly later in the essay, here I simply recall Barbara Biesecker's deconstruction of the deadlock between Bitzer and Vatz over whether situations are forged by context or by the speaker herself. The crucial point, Biesecker argues, is that in either case—and therefore in the vast preponderance of ways in which "situation" continues to be used in rhetorical studies—a certain artificial stabilization of the situation (however it is "authored") abets an all too narrowed and *a priori* account of the subjectivity of the audience. See Barbara Biesecker, "Rethinking the Rhetorical Situation from within the Thematic of *Différance*," *Philosophy and Rhetoric* 22 (1989): 110–30.

   A similar problem occurs in much of what constituted the "ideological studies" stage of rhetorical criticism. Grappling with the question of ideology, scholars fashioned various takes on a type of "conversion narrative" in which, given the right circumstances, an audience member would become so enamored of a particular discourse/set of ideas that he or she would fall under its sway indefinitely. So, for example, Edwin Black offered the second persona as a way of assessing the type of audience a discourse sought to create, Michael McGee argued that the presence of certain symbolically loaded terms would invite the audience into a particular political myth, and Maurice Charland claimed that certain discourses moved its auditors into identities that they had not previously imagined claiming. In each of these cases, two things stand out: first, each theory is operated by a constitutive logic of representation in which audience members were always already waiting in the wings (so to speak) for the right words or arguments needed to unlock their (already given) commitment to a cause and, second, that such a reading not only presumed a complete and legible scene but could anticipate, in advance, the type of discourse that would enable the conversion. In short, by overdetermining the situation and its necessary response by audience members, a certain stacking of the rhetorical deck was effected; audiences could hardly refuse their ideological seduction for in the reads offered there were—literally—no alternatives to be had. See Edwin Black, "The Second Persona," *Quarterly Journal of Speech* 56 (1970): 109–19; Michael Calvin McGee, "The Ideograph: A Link Between Rhetoric and Ideology," *Quarterly Journal of Speech* 66 (1980): 1–16; Maurice Charland, "Constitutive Rhetoric: The Case of the *Peuple Québecois*," *Quarterly Journal of Speech* 73 (1987): 133–50.

The debt that public sphere literatures owe to a spatial reading of social arrangements and their production is obvious. Indeed, the very terminology calls to mind the necessary borders, boundaries, and enclosures necessary to make a "sphere" possible in the first place. More interesting, perhaps, than the mere use of the spatial vocabulary is the way in which these spatial arrangements and diagrams have been used to assess the "health" of various political communities. As one might expect, much of this work turns on how one characterizes the ideal "space," distance, and relation to others. See, in part, Jürgen Habermas, *The Structural Transformation of the Public Sphere: An Inquiry into the Category of Bourgeois Society* (Cambridge: MIT Press, 1991); G. Thomas Goodnight, "The Firm, the Park, and the University: Fear and Trembling on the Postmodern Trail," *Quarterly Journal of Speech* 81 (1995): 267–90; and Cindy L. Griffin, "The Essentialist Roots of the Public Sphere: A Feminist Critique," *Western Journal of Communication* 60 (1996): 21–39.

It should hardly be surprising that much of the scholarship on the rhetoric of controversy also trafficked in various spatial metaphors. Goodnight, for example, thought of controversy as a type of "place," perhaps in homage to the salon-like origins of the Habermas's public sphere. Kendall Phillips, alternatively, argued that controversies opened various "spaces" of dissension and contestation. Still others used the term "site"—underscoring the way in which controversies function as arenas of antagonism and investment. For my own purposes, it matters less which is more apt than it does in having shown how the entire debate turned on one's acceptance of some spatial metaphor. See G. Thomas Goodnight, "Controversy," in *Argument in Controversy*, ed. Donn Parson (Annandale, VA: Speech Communication Association, 1991); and G. Thomas Goodnight, "Opening Up the 'Spaces of Public Dissension,'" *Communication Monographs* 64 (1997): 270–75; Kendall Phillips, "The Rhetoric of Controversy," *Western Journal of Communication* 63 (1999): 488–510; Kendall Phillips, "The Spaces of Public Dissension: Reconsidering the Public Sphere," *Communication Monographs* 63 (1996): 231–48; and Ronald Walter Greene and Darrin Hicks, "On Passionate Reason: Controversy and the Making and Revising of Context," in *Argument and the Postmodern Challenge: Proceedings of the Eighth SCA/AFA Conference on Argumentation*, ed. Raymie E. McKerrow (Annandale, VA: National Communication Association, 1993): 176–78. No doubt some of this same impulse to rehabilitate argumentation theory by way of a turn to spatial terminologies animated David Fleming and his work on the "spaces" of argumentation in which he called for a "re-coupling of logos and the polis" and asks whether or not "when rhetoricians, argumentation theorists, and political philosophers talk about public discourse shouldn't they be talking with architects and urban designers as well?"

See David Fleming, "The Space of Argumentation: Urban Design, Civic Discourse, and the Dream of a Good City," *Argumentation* 12 (1998): 151, 152.

The recent emergence and popularity of visual culture studies has helped propel spatial modes of thinking. See, for example, Greg Dickinson, "The *Pleasantville* Effect: Nostalgia and the Visual Framing of (White) Suburbia," *Western Journal of Communication* 70 (2006): 215; Greg Dickinson, Brian L. Ott, and Eric Aoki, "Spaces of Remembering and Forgetting: The Reverent Eye/I at the Plains Indian Museum," *Communication and Critical/Cultural Studies* 3 (2006): 27–47; and Sonja Modesti, "Home Sweet Home: Tattoo Parlors as Postmodern Spaces of Agency," *Western Journal of Communication* 72 (2008): 197–212. Similarly, the body has been predominately analyzed along spatial lines. See, amongst others, Heather Murray, "Monstrous Play in Negative Spaces: Illegible Bodies and the Cultural Construction of Biometric Technology," *Communication Review* 10 (2007): 347–65. Attention to the body has also led many to consider the appropriate role and behavior of such bodies. Theoretical debates over decorum, propriety, and performance have long turned on questions tied to imagining the social as a flattened (or at least horizontal) space by which one could chart one's distance from "normal." See Robert Hariman, "Status, Marginality and Rhetorical Theory," *Quarterly Journal of Speech* 72 (1986): 38–54; and Robert Hariman, "Decorum, Power, and the Courtly Style," *Quarterly Journal of Speech* 78 (1992): 149–72; as well as Melissa Deem, "Decorum: The Flight from the Rhetorical," in *Proceedings from the Alta Conference on Argumentation* (Annandale, VA: National Communication Association, 1995): 226–29, wherein she argues that questions of decorum are always questions of social space in that the policing of the former is always a way of maintaining the integrity and perceived value of the latter.

Finally, work on the materiality of rhetoric itself has been no less susceptible to the cartographic compulsion. McGee's seminal piece on the matter, for example, is a tour de force of theory building written under the influence of the spatial. Michael Calvin McGee, "A Materialist's Conception of Rhetoric," in *Explorations in Rhetoric: Studies in Honor of Douglas Ehninger*, ed. Ray E. McKerrow (Glenville, IL: Scott, Foresman, 1982): 23–48. From its insistence that rhetoric is an "almost mathematical paradigm of terms" (29), to its careful attention to the rhetorical experience at the "microrhetorical," "sociorhetorical," and "macrorhetorical" levels of analysis, and finally its attempt to chart a three-dimensional, "geometrically proportional" molecular model of rhetoric (34), the essay launched a tradition of addressing rhetoric's materiality through spatial terms and tropes. Most notably, perhaps, Ronald Walter Greene has turned to Foucauldian axiomatics—and schematics—of power in order to "map the multidimensional effectivity of rhetoric" and to ensure a "form of cartography that does not reduce the materiality of rhetorical practices to interests of a 'ruling class.'" See Ronald Walter Greene, "Another Materialist Rhetoric," *Critical Studies in Mass Communication* 15 (1998): 39.

2.   I am tempted to suggest that the contemporary interest in "the event" has all the hallmarks of the "return of the repressed." It is, at the very least, curious that just as the cartographic began to take a firm grip on rhetorical analysis, calls to consider the "radicality" of the event became more common. See, for example, Melissa Deem, who has suggested that "it is imperative to theorize new notions of eventfulness and change not recognized by the historical logics and temporalities of the state or modern norms of stranger sociability." Melissa Deem, "Stranger Sociability, Public Hope, and the Limits of Political Transformation," *Quarterly Journal of Speech* 88 (2002): 446.

3.   Biesecker, "Rethinking the Rhetorical Situation," 127.

4. Phillip Sipiora, "The Ancient Concept of *Kairos*," in *Rhetoric and* Kairos*: Essays in History, Theory, and Praxis*, ed. Phillip Sipiora and James S Baumlin (Albany: State University of New York Press, 2002), 1.

5. Lloyd Bitzer, "The Rhetorical Situation," *Philosophy and Rhetoric* 1 (1968): 1–14. See also Richard Vatz, "The Myth of the Rhetorical Situation," *Philosophy and Rhetoric* 6 (1973): 154–61; John Poulakos, "Toward a Sophistic Definition of Rhetoric," *Philosophy and Rhetoric* 16 (1983): 35–48.

6. Sipiora, "Ancient Concept of *Kairos*," 2.

7. Poulakos, "Toward a Sophistic Definition," 44.

8. It is precisely for this reason that late in his life, Derrida increasingly referred to the present as our "artifactuality." In the narrower sense, he was attempting to mark the mediated or teleotechnological nature of the present, but in the larger sense, the term gestured to any force whose work resulted in the production of a seemingly pure present. See Jacques Derrida and Bernard Stiegler, *Echographies of Television*, trans. Jennifer Bajorek (New York: Polity Press, 2002).

9. On this notion of a flattened sense of time being rendered wholly spatial, see Michel de Certeau, *The Practice of Everyday Life*, trans. Steve Rendall (Berkeley: University of California Press, 1988), 35.

10. Sharon Crowley and Debra Hawhee, *Ancient Rhetorics for Contemporary Students*, 3rd ed. (New York: Pearson-Longman, 2004): 36–52. See also Edwin Black, "The Mutability of Rhetoric," in *Rhetoric in Transition*, ed. Eugene E. White (University Park: Pennsylvania State University Press, 1980): 171–86.

11. Martin Heidegger, *Being and Time: A Translation of Sein and Zeit*, trans. Joan Stambaugh (Albany: State University of New York Press, 1996).

12. See also Gayatri Chakravorty Spivak, who suggests, "'Time' is a word to which we give flesh in various ways." Gayatri Chakvravorty Spivak, "Time and Timing: Law and History," in *Chronotypes: The Construction of Time*, ed. John Bender and David E. Welleby (Stanford, CA: Stanford University Press, 1991): 99.

13. Barbara A. Biesecker, "Of Historicity, Rhetoric: The Archive as Scene of Invention," *Rhetoric and Public Affairs* 9 (2006): 130.

14. Werner Hamacher, "Lingua Amissa: The Messianism of Commodity-Language and Derrida's Specters of Marx," in *Ghostly Demarcations: A Symposium on Jacques Derrida's Specters of Marx*, ed. Michael Sprinkler (New York: Verso, 1999), 192. In trying to articulate a(nother) way of understanding the relation between rhetorical production and temporality, in no way should I be read to underestimate the significant contributions that *have* been made in this regard. Indeed, there have been a number of rhetorical scholars and theoretical initiatives that have sought to make a better accounting of time and temporality, and they are all the more notable for running against the near-tidal shift in the field toward vocabularies and methodologies of spatial analysis. While their underdog status provides no necessary guarantor of utility and insight, I take no small measure of hope in those attempts to focus on questions of time and temporality, such as, for example—and one to which I will return at length in a later section of the essay—the attention to timeliness and propriety in debates over the rhetorical situation.

15. On attention to temporality as the study of the rhetor's skillful manipulation of tense, see Michael Leff's examinations of Lincoln's addresses ("Dimensions of Temporality in Lincoln's Second Inaugural," *Communication Reports* 1 [1988]) or Bruce Gronbeck's work on "public communication" ("Rhetorical Timing in Public Communication," *Central States Speech Journal* 25 [1974]: 84–94).

16. Here, see the seminal debate between J. Robert Cox and Robert Hariman over Martin Luther King's rhetoric of gradualism and the ways it was conditioned by King's ability to convey a certain sense of the national moment, of the time of the era. J. Robert Cox, "The Fulfillment of Time: King's 'I Have a Dream' Speech (August 28, 1963)," in *Texts in Context: Critical Dialogues on Significant Episodes in American Political Rhetoric*, ed. Michael C. Leff and Fred J. Kauffeld (Davis, CA: Hermagoras Press, 1989), 181–204; and Robert Hariman, "Time and the Reconstitution of Gradualism in King's Address: A Response to Cox," in *Texts in Context: Critical Dialogues on Significant Episodes in American Political Rhetoric*, ed. Michael C. Leff and Fred J. Kauffeld (Davis, CA: Hermagoras Press, 1989): 205–17. Cox and Hariman's essays are noteworthy in that they are symptomatic of the effort to read time as mood or disposition. In this way, rhetoricians have often used time as a concept-metaphor for "taking the temperature," so to speak, of the community or culture (see also Edwin Black, "Electing Time," *Quarterly Journal of Speech* 59 [1973]: 125–29; and G. Thomas Goodnight, "Public Discourse," *Critical Studies in Mass Communication* 4 [1987]: 428–32) particularly in seasons of discontent or trauma (see Roger Stahl, "A Clockwork War: Rhetorics of Time in a Time of Terror," *Quarterly Journal of Speech* 94 [2008]: 73–99; or Barbara Biesecker, "No Time for Mourning: The Rhetorical Production of the Melancholic Citizen-Subject in the War on Terror," *Philosophy and Rhetoric* 40 [2007]:147–69). Biesecker's essay is particularly interesting in this regard in that while it considers a certain national time as disposition (the melancholia of post-9/11 America) it also interrogates George Bush's dangerous deployment of varying temporal alternate realities ultimately, in Biesecker's view, building a case for the restriction of liberties in America's future to protect a past that never was.

17. See, for example, Paul Ricouer's work on configuration and the hermeneutic circle in which the fiction and narrative drives—or configures—our understanding of the "real" world. Paul Ricouer, *Time and Narrative*, vol. 1 (Chicago: University of Chicago Press, 1990).

18. The term "amphibious virtuality" is Hamacher's, "Lingua Amissa," 192.

19. Hamacher, "Lingua Amissa," 193.

20. Cartographers will no doubt protest that I have both overformulized their practice as well as overstated the degree to which, in advance, a grid of intelligibility preordains all its possible permutations. Such a rejoinder would, however, misunderstand my critique, which is that in the face of these "unknowns," the mapping impulse engages in an infinite regression *into* the grid (in search of the tea leaves of some line of intelligibility or flight) rather than at the limits of or beyond the grid (as in that provided by questions of temporality). If I demonstrate this by pointing to a recent essay by Kendall Phillips, it is only because, in an otherwise elegant essay that attempts to "press the importance" of considering the relationship between Foucault and rhetoric by (once again) multiplying the type of spaces of which we are to keep track (adding spaces of dissension, spaces of freedom, and spaces of thought to an already long list) because the "project of a Foucaultian rhetoric should be taken seriously, seriously enough to keep the peculiarity of this union in the forefront of our minds as we pursue it," Phillips notes a "certain irony in attempting to theorize the 'unseen gaps' within intelligibility," and that "those gaps within the grids of knowing and doing and being will by definition not succumb to our efforts to know or enact or identify them." Kendall R. Phillips, "Spaces of Invention: Dissension, Freedom, and Thought in Foucault," *Philosophy and Rhetoric* 35 (2002): 329, 343.

21. Jacques Derrida, "Typewriter Ribbon: Limited Ink (2)," in *Without Alibi*, trans. and ed.

Peggy Kamuf (Stanford, CA: Stanford University Press, 2002): 130.

22. Derrida, "Typewriter Ribbon," 131.
23. For works more fully detailing the Derridean account of *différance,* in addition to the Biesecker article previously cited, see Jonathan Culler, *On Deconstruction: Theory and Criticism after Structuralism* (Ithaca, NY: Cornell University Press, 1982); Christopher Norris, *Deconstruction: Theory and Practice,* 3rd ed. (London: Routledge, 2002); and Gayatri Chakravorty Spivak, "Translator's Preface," in *Of Grammatology,* corrected ed. (Baltimore, MD: Johns Hopkins University Press, 1998): vii–lxxxvii.
24. Jacques Derrida, "Freud and the Scene of Writing," in *Writing and Difference,* trans. Alan Bass (University of Chicago, 1978): 226. See also *Paper Machines,* one of Derrida's last works, in which he explicitly interrogates the relation between writing and the various technological devices by which it is rendered as well as the ways in which, among others, identity, citizenship, censorship, and resistance are all routed implicitly or explicitly through the machine-works of writing. Jacques Derrida, *Paper Machines,* trans. Rachel Bowlby (Stanford, CA: Stanford University Press, 1995).
25. Jacques Derrida, *Archive Fever: A Freudian Impression,* trans. Eric Prenowitz (Chicago, IL: University of Chicago Press, 1995), 14–15, 17.
26. Jacques Derrida, *Rogues: Two Essays on Reason,* ed. Werner Hamacher, trans. Pascale-Anne Brault (Stanford, CA: Stanford University Press, 2005), 135.
27. Paul de Man, *Allegories of Reading: Figural Language in Rousseau, Nietzsche, Rilke, and Proust* (New Haven, CT: Yale University Press, 1979), 286.
28. Derrida, "Typewriter Ribbon," 104.
29. De Man, *Allegories of Reading,* 270.
30. Derrida, "Typewriter Ribbon," 133.
31. Paul de Man, *Aesthetic Ideology,* ed. Andrzej Warminski (Minneapolis: University of Minneapolis Press, 1996), 132.
32. Derrida, "Typewriter Ribbon," 150.
33. Derrida, "Typewriter Ribbon," 154.
34. Derrida, "Typewriter Ribbon," 133. This removal of the operator, the eventual permanence over the signatory, is one reason why the Derridean *oeuvre* is not the same as the canonical authorial *oeuvre* that Foucault criticizes in *The Archaeology of Knowledge.* Michel Foucault, *The Archaeology of Knowledge,* trans. A. M. Sheridan Smith (New York: Pantheon Books, 1972).
35. Derrida, "Typewriter Ribbon," 75.
36. Derrida, "Typewriter Ribbon," 151.
37. Derrida, "Typewriter Ribbon," 133.
38. Derrida, "Typewriter Ribbon," 123.
39. Derrida, "Typewriter Ribbon," 122.
40. Derrida, "Typewriter Ribbon," 154.
41. Derrida, "Typewriter Ribbon," 158.
42. Peggy Kamuf, "Introduction: Event of Resistance," in *Without Alibi,* trans. and ed. Peggy Kamuf (Stanford, CA: Stanford University Press, 2002), 12.
43. Jacques Derrida, "Provocation: Forewords," in *Without Alibi,* ed. and trans. Peggy Kamuf, (Stanford, CA: Stanford University Press, 2002): xxxiii.
44. Kamuf, "Introduction: Event of Resistance," 20.
45. Derrida, "Typewriter Ribbon," 131.
46. Derrida, "Typewriter Ribbon," 76–77.
47. Derrida, "Typewriter Ribbon," 77.

48. Rousseau, quoted in Derrida, "Typewriter Ribbon," 86.

49. Derrida, "Typewriter Ribbon," 86–87.

50. Jacques Derrida, *A Taste for the Secret*, trans. Giacomo Donis, ed. Giacomo Donis and David Webb (Malden, MA: Polity Press, 2001), 15.

51. As I argue in the body of the essay, this instability or indeterminancy is a function of understanding context as nonsaturable and open to the future. In this manner, no amount of historicizing or theorizing could ever arrest the indeterminancy of these terms. The openness to the future marks its temporality, but it also marks a limit on genealogical methodologies to assess these terms and their force with as much breadth and acuity.

52. A good portion of Derrida's book speculates on how a different archiving technology might have oriented Freud's concepts differently. Although beyond the purposes of this essay, perhaps the best way to illuminate these differences is to compare the ways Derrida discusses the condition of writing in "Freud and the Scene of Writing" with *Archive Fever* or *Paper Machines*. While the former is replete with talk of (im)printing and residues, the latter works gesture toward a very different economy in which technology makes possible the sense that writing (or deletion) completely erases what came before, enabling different ways of thinking about the practices of censorship and control as well as resistance.

53. So, for example, the conflation between the man and the science, the fact that Freud's daughter speaks for him, in his name, etc. Derrida is particularly taken with Yosef Hayim Yerushalmi's work *Freud's Moses: Judaism Terminable and Interminable* and especially its conclusion, where, after a thoroughgoing analysis of Freudian thought, Yerushalmi posts a lengthy open letter to Freud. At one point, Yerushalmi makes it clear that it is impossible to know, now, whether psychoanalysis is a "Jewish" science, for as Yerushalmi puts it, "we shall know, *if it is at all knowable,* only when much future work has been done. Much will depend, of course, on how the very terms *Jewish* and *science* are to be defined." This inevitably open-ended nature of "Jewish" and "science" and of their relation and import to thinking Freud and psychoanalysis is yet another reason why, structurally, "Freud" cannot be a settled term. Yerushalmi quoted in Derrida, *Archive Fever*, 37.

54. Derrida, *Taste for the Secret*, 14.

55. Derrida, *Archive Fever*, 30.

56. This is my concern with a debate in the discipline of rhetorical studies that attempts to assess the relation of a public's emergence to the publicity and circulation networks that might attract them. If I take up the project of gesturing toward the difference between Derridean dissemination and of rhetorical studies' current interest in "circulation" as the latter is primarily figured in the hands of Ronald Walter Greene's essay in a *Quarterly Journal of Speech* forum, it is because, perhaps more than any other scholar today, his work is committed to thinking the problem of rhetoric's materiality and in particular the implications that dissemination might present for rhetorical scholarship. See Ronald Walter Greene, "Rhetorical Pedagogy as a Postal System: Circulating Subjects through Michael Warner's 'Publics and Counterpublics,'" *Quarterly Journal of Speech* 88 (2002); and Greene, "Another Materialist Rhetoric."

    Arguing that it would be fruitful to consider Michael Warner's attention to the "forms and channels of circulation" as a delivery apparatus, Greene appropriates Derrida's notion of a postal system as the apt name for such a system and then immediately argues that "in the hands of Briankle Chang, the delivery apparatus of the postal system reaches the status of a principle." Greene, "Rhetorical Pedagogy," 440. Indeed, Greene informs us, for Chang, the postal service is the "medium," the "universal mediator" that "mediates all events of exchange within a given network" (Greene, "Rhetorical Pedagogy," 440). It is difficult to know how to approach such a description, in part, because of its multihandedness, owing something to Derrida and to Chang and no doubt to Greene himself. In any case, I will simply note that Greene grants the postal service an objective material quality that far exceeds the manner in which Derrida conceptualizes such a function. Perhaps it is here that a significant origin of what I consider to be Greene's conceptual confusion and eventual ambivalence turns: what Derrida calls a function (the necessary condition of texts to circulate beyond their "intended" audience) Greene instead names an "apparatus," even, once Chang's "hands" are involved, a "medium" and a "mediator." As I have already suggested, the Derridean account of the postal system is something altogether different and does not depend on any "material forms." As with *différance,* for Derrida, the postal system is a catechresis, in this case one in which the notion of an actual post office or letter carriers is distended beyond its normal usage. To understand the Derridean postal service as an effect of language rather than as a material "matter," however, makes it all the more significant than if we were to understand it as merely a medium or mediator (even a "universal mediator," whatever that might be).

From my vantage, Greene's account of the postal system not only goes astray from Derrida's, but it does so in ways that undermine Greene's own effort to create a materialist rhetoric. Indeed, by figuring the postal system as a material apparatus, Greene inadvertently smuggles in an unreconstructed notion of communication as mediation and thus risks losing the very prospect of a new "materialist rhetoric" that he and others have worked toward. Were we to follow Greene's impulse to consider circulation in relation to the Derridean concept-metaphor of the postal system but refuse his subsequent reification of that network into a material object, scholars might be better positioned to engage the difficult work of assessing rhetoric's materiality not as the medium through which discourse moves (whether it be a letter, speech, film, monument, or any other discernible "matter") but instead as the effectivity and resistance to reappropriation those "sites" enable.

57. Jacques Derrida, "Différance," in *Margins of Philosophy*, ed. Alan Bass (Chicago: University of Chicago Press, 1985), 21.

CONTRIBUTORS

BARBARA A. BIESECKER is professor in the Department of Speech Communication at the University of Georgia. She teaches and writes at the intersections of rhetorical theory and criticism, feminist theory and criticism, and cultural studies. Her most recent work addresses the rhetoric and politics of WWII remembrance at the end of the twentieth century and the rhetoric and politics of 9/11 and the War on Terror today; as always, she continues to study the relation of rhetoric and social change. She is currently the editor of "The Forum Series" published in *Communication and Critical/Cultural Studies*, serves on the editorial board of several of the field's major journals, and was the 2007 recipient of the Douglas Ehninger Distinguished Rhetorical Scholar Award.

DANA CLOUD is associate professor in the Department of Communication Studies at the University of Texas, Austin. She teaches and conducts research in the areas of Marxist theory, feminist theory, public sphere theory, social movements, rhetorical criticism, and representations of race and gender in popular culture. She is the author of *Rhetorics of Therapy* (Sage, 1998) and co-editor of *Marxism and Communication Studies* (Peter Lang, 2007). She has published in the *Quarterly Journal of Speech*, *Communication and Critical/Cultural Studies*, *Communication and Cultural Critique*, *Western Journal of Communication*, *Rhetoric and Public Affairs,* and *Management Communication Quarterly*, as well as twenty-five invited book chapters. A longtime activist for social justice, she lives in Austin, Texas, with her family.

OSCAR GINER is professor in the Department of Theatre and Film of the Katherine K. Herberger College of the Arts, Arizona State University. His research interests include myth, ritual, performance, and Native American ceremonials. His produced plays include *Nosferatu* and *Stories from the Conquest of the Kingdom of New Mexico*. He has recently completed the manuscript of a forthcoming book titled *Performing Scarface: In Praise of Shakespearean Villains, Cuban Gangsters, and Hip-Hop Myths*.

RONALD WALTER GREENE is associate professor in the Department of Communication Studies at the University of Minnesota. He is also an affiliated faculty member in American Studies and Writing Studies, and an associated faculty member in French Studies. His research focuses on the rhetorical and communicative infrastructure of democracy with an emphasis on the governmental dimensions of political economy. His contributions to rhetorical and argumentation theory have been recognized with awards from the Critical and Cultural Studies Division of the National Communication Association and the American Forensic Association.

BRUCE E. GRONBECK is the A. Craig Baird Distinguished Professor Emeritus of Public Address in the Department of Communication Studies at the University of Iowa. He is director of the UI Center for Media Studies and Political Culture, and has written multiple books, book chapters, and articles on rhetoric, media, and politics. This project was supported by the University of Iowa's Obermann Center for Advanced Studies; he thanks its director, Jay Semel, and academic technologies specialist Karla Tonella for their contributions, as well as the Museum of the City of New York for its help with the Riis materials.

JOHN LOUIS LUCAITES is professor of rhetoric and public culture in the Department of Communication and Culture at Indiana University. His most recent work focuses on the relationship between rhetoric and contemporary visual culture, and in particular on the role that photojournalism plays as a mode of public art that functions to underwrite US liberal-democracy. He is the co-author (with Celeste Michelle Condit) of *Crafting Equality: America's Anglo-African Word* (University of Chicago Press, 1993) and (with Robert Hariman) of *No Caption Needed: Iconic Photographs, Public Culture, and Liberal Democracy* (University of Chicago Press, 2007), as well as several edited collections. He is three-time recipient of the National Communication Association's Golden Anniversary Monograph Award, as well as the Winans-Wichelns Memorial Award for Distinguished Scholarship in Public Address. He is the current editor of the *Quarterly Journal of Speech* (2008–2010) and the senior editor for the University of Alabama's book series

"Rhetoric, Culture, and Social Critique." He also co-hosts a daily blog on rhetoric, politics, and visual culture at http://www.nocaptionneeded.com.

CHRISTIAN LUNDBERG is assistant professor of rhetoric and cultural studies in the Department of Communication Studies at the University of North Carolina, Chapel Hill. He received his PhD from Northwestern University's program in Rhetoric and Public Culture in 2006, and his MDiv from Emory University's Candler School of Theology in 2000. His work has appeared in the *Quarterly Journal of Speech, Rhetoric Society Quarterly, Philosophy and Rhetoric, Communication and Critical/Cultural Studies*, and a number of edited volumes. His current research interests address the intersection of rhetoric and the social, with special attention to the interplay of trope, affect, and the production of social forms.

JOAN FABER MCALISTER is assistant professor of rhetoric and communication studies in the Department for the Study of Culture and Society at Drake University. Her research interests include suburban culture, domestic space, visual rhetorics, aesthetics, Critical Theory, and the politics and performance of class, race, gender, and sexuality in daily life. She was the 2008 recipient of the Gary Gumpert Research Incentive Award from the Urban Communication Foundation and her work has appeared in *Women's Studies in Communication, Liminalities: A Journal of Performance Studies*, and edited volumes in the field of rhetorical studies.

MICHAEL CALVIN MCGEE (1943–2002) was professor of rhetoric in the Department of Communication Studies at the University of Iowa. McGee worked at the conjuncture of rhetorical theory and the critique of liberalism. He was recipient of the National Communication Association's Winans-Wichelns Award for Distinguished Scholarship in Rhetoric and Public Address, as well as the Douglas Ehninger Distinguished Rhetorical Scholar Award.

CHARLES E. MORRIS III is associate professor in the Department of Communication at Boston College. He is the editor of *Queering Public Address: Sexualities in American Historical Discourse* (South Carolina University Press) and the forthcoming *Remembering the AIDS Quilt: Commemoration and Critique of the Epidemic Text* (Michigan State University Press). He is also co-editor of *Readings on the Rhetoric of Social Protest* (Strata). He is a regular contributor to the *Quarterly Journal of Speech*, and has also published in *Rhetoric and Public Affairs, Communication and Critical/Cultural*

Studies, and *Women's Studies in Communication*. For his work on GLBTQ history, he has been the recipient of the Karl Wallace Memorial Award, Golden Anniversary Monograph Award, and Randy Majors Memorial Award from the National Communication Association.

KENNETH RUFO is a stay-at-home father and an independent media scholar living in the wild outskirts of Seattle, where he survives by harvesting books and hunting video game.

DANIEL F. SCHOWALTER is associate professor at Rowan University, where he teaches rhetoric, media theory, and cultural studies. His work in visual studies can be found in *Critical Studies in Media Communication* and *Communication and Critical/Cultural Studies*.

JOHN M. SLOOP is professor of Communication Studies and associate dean of the College of Arts and Science at Vanderbilt University. He is the author and editor of several scholarly essays and books, including *Disciplining Gender: Rhetorics of Sex Identity in Contemporary U.S. Culture*. His work investigates cultural "discussions" about matters of public interest, such as prisoners, immigration issues, and cases of gender transgression. The chapter in this volume represents his current interest involving the intersections of transportation, communication, and public regulation.

NATHAN STORMER is the Bailey Professor of Speech and Theatre at the University of Maine. He researches medical rhetoric about abortion and fetal imaging, as well as theoretical questions of the body, memory, space, order, and aesthetics. His work has appeared in *Critical Studies in Media Communication*, *Signs: A Journal of Women in Culture and Society*, and the *Quarterly Journal of Speech*. His book is *Articulating Life's Memory: U.S. Medical Rhetoric about Abortion*.

WILLIAM TRAPANI is assistant professor in the School of Communication and Multimedia Studies at Florida Atlantic University. His primary areas of interest and influence include rhetorical theory and criticism, critical theory and cultural studies, and visual rhetoric. As part of a larger series of works examining the ways in which American national identity is articulated, his recent research examines the logic of contemporary protest and social movement formation and the conditions of radical, productive, political agency.

INDEX